# RISE OF THE
# WARRIOR COP

# RISE OF THE WARRIOR COP

The Militarization of
America's Police Forces

## RADLEY BALKO

PublicAffairs
New York

Published in the United States by PublicAffairs™, a Member of the Perseus
Books Group

PublicAffairs books are available at special discounts for bulk purchases in
the US by corporations, institutions, and other organizations. For more
information, please contact the Special Markets Department at the Perseus
Books Group, 2300 Chestnut Street, Suite 200, Philadelphia, PA 19103,
all (800) 810-4145, ext. 5000, or e-mail special.markets@perseusbooks.com.

Book design by Linda Mark

Library of Congress Cataloging-in-Publication Data
Balko, Radley.
  Rise of the warrior cop : the militarization of America's police forces /
Radley Balko.
   pages cm
  Includes bibliographical references and index.
  ISBN 978-1-61039-211-2 (hardcover)—ISBN 978-1-61039-212-9 (e-book)
1. Police—Special weapons and tactics units—United States. 2. Police—United
States. I. Title.
HV8080.S64B354 2013
363.20973—dc23
2013009304

First Edition

10 9 8 7 6 5 4 3 2 1

# CONTENTS

*Acknowledgments vii*

*Introduction ix*

CHAPTER ONE:
From Rome to Writs 1

CHAPTER TWO:
Soldiers in the Streets 11

CHAPTER THREE:
A Quick History of Cops in America 27

CHAPTER FOUR:
The 1960s—From Root Causes to Brute Force 43

CHAPTER FIVE:
The 1970s—Pinch and Retreat 81

CHAPTER SIX:
The 1980s—Us and Them 139

CHAPTER SEVEN:
The 1990s—It's All About the Numbers 177

CHAPTER EIGHT:
The 2000s—A Whole New War  239

CHAPTER NINE:
Reform  309


*Conclusion  333*

*Notes  337*

*Index  369*

# ACKNOWLEDGMENTS

I've always felt that I'd never officially feel like a *writer* until I could see a book I'd written sitting on my bookshelf. So I owe a lot of thanks to the people who have helped make that happen.

First, of course, thank you to my family and friends who have supported and encouraged me over the years. Thanks also to my agent, Howard Yoon, and my editor at PublicAffairs, Brandon Proia, for getting this specific book into print. I should also acknowledge Peter Kraska, whose scholarly research on SWAT teams has provided the empirical data to document this trend. Police militarization has largely been fueled by the drug war, so this book also owes a debt to Dan Baum, whose meticulously reported *Smoke and Mirrors* is the be-all, end-all history of the drug war through the 1990s. Thanks also to Samuel Walker, Norm Stamper, Tom Angell, Victoria Dunham, Killian Lapeyre, Jessica Greene, Drew Johnson, and Dan Wang, who contributed to this book with research, comments, referrals, and/or suggestions.

Other thanks go to Robin Wallace and Nick Schulz, the first two editors to publish me regularly. Thanks to P. J. Doland for hosting my blog for ten years—where I first reported many of the incidents you'll read about in this book. Thanks to Ed Crane and David Boaz at the Cato Institute, who published my white paper on SWAT teams, gave me my first full-time job as a writer, and provided a terrific platform from which to write about this issue. Thanks also to current and former Cato folk Susan Chamberlin, Tim Lynch, and Gene Healy. Thanks to Nick Gillespie, who gave me my first journalism job at *Reason* magazine, and to Matt Welch, David Nott, Jesse Walker, and my other former colleagues at *Reason*. Thanks especially to Jacob Sullum, whose editing made me a better writer.

Other media/Internet/journalism people to whom I'm grateful for supporting, promoting, and publishing my work over the years: Glenn Reynolds, Andrew Sullivan, Ryan Grim, Arianna Huffington, Mark Frauenfelder, John Stossel, John Tierney, Ed Brayton, Emily Bazelon, and Dahlia Lithwick.

Finally, a group of people I'd like to personally thank for a variety of different reasons, personal and professional: Bobbie Murphy, Alyona Minkovski, David Pfaff, Jessie Creel, Liliana Segura, Stacie Moats, Courtney Knapp, Marta Rose, Kate Klonick, David Boeyink, and my dad, Terry Balko.

# INTRODUCTION

> There are more instances of the abridgment of the freedom of the people by gradual and silent encroachments of those in power than by violent and sudden usurpations.
>
> —JAMES MADISON

Are cops constitutional?

That may seem like an odd question—perhaps even a little nutty. Police forces have been part of the American criminal justice system since an eight-man department was established in Boston 175 years ago and the first large department was created seven years later in New York City. There has never been a serious constitutional challenge to the general authority of police or to the establishment of police forces, sheriff's departments, or other law enforcement agencies, and it's unlikely there ever would be. Any federal court would undoubtedly have little patience for such a challenge. And any hypothetical world where police were ruled unconstitutional would descend into chaos, probably rather quickly.

But in a 2001 article for the *Seton Hall Constitutional Law Journal*, the legal scholar and civil liberties activist Roger Roots posed just that question.[1] Roots, a fairly radical libertarian, believes that the US Constitution doesn't allow for police as they exist today. At the very least, he argues, police departments, powers, and practices today violate the document's spirit and intent. "Under the criminal justice model known to the Framers, professional police officers were unknown," Roots writes.

> The general public had broad law enforcement powers, and only the executive functions of the law (e.g. the execution of writs, warrants, and orders) were performed by constables or sheriff (who might call upon the community for assistance). Initiation and investigation of criminal cases was nearly the exclusive province of private persons. . . . The advent of modern policing has greatly altered the balance of power between the citizen and the state in a way that would have been seen as constitutionally invalid by the Founders.[2]

Roots's argument may not be practical, but it's certainly provocative. On at least one point, most criminologists agree with him: no one can say for sure whether the Founders would have approved of modern policing, but it's relatively certain that they wouldn't have recognized it. Criminologist and historian Samuel Walker writes in his book *Popular Justice* that in colonial America "most of the modern institutions" of today's criminal justice system, "the uniformed police, prisons, probation, parole . . . did not exist at all." The colonies did have appointed sheriffs and constables, and some also had marshals, but the duties associated with those jobs were largely administrative. Most were not salaried positions; instead, they received fees for tasks like serving subpoenas and collecting taxes. Since there were no fees associated with enforcing the criminal laws, for most sheriffs and constables that task was a low priority. Sheriffs did oversee the jails, but jails were primarily used to hold defendants until trial. Incarceration as punishment was rare.[3]

Law enforcement in the eighteenth century was mostly a private affair. Community mores, social stigma, and shaming were the most important ways of maintaining order. Crime victims could bring their complaints to a grand jury, a panel of private citizens who had the power to indict. But the victim or his proxy was the party to initiate the charges. Professional full-time prosecutors didn't exist.[4]

Under this system, enforcement of the laws was a universal duty. Every male citizen had a civic responsibility to serve on a watch, act as a constable, serve on a grand jury, or join a posse when necessary to apprehend a dangerous criminal. The word *police* wasn't used as a noun. It was a verb, meaning "to watch over or monitor the public health and safety."[5]

This isn't to say that the colonial era's more individualized, private methods of law enforcement would work today. As American towns grew from close-knit communities of people of similar ethnicities, with shared traditions, values, and religion, to cities whose diverse populations of immigrants had none of that in common, centralized police forces emerged to preserve order and enforce a common set of laws. Once neighbors stopped speaking the same language and worshiping in the same buildings, shunning and social stigmatization lost their effectiveness.

Even so, Roots's question is a useful starting point for this book because it shows just how far we have come. The Founders and their contemporaries would probably have seen even the early-nineteenth-century police forces as a standing army, and a particularly odious one at that. Just before the American Revolution, it wasn't the stationing of British troops in the colonies that irked patriots in Boston and Virginia; it was England's decision to use the troops for everyday law enforcement. This wariness of standing armies was born of experience and a study of history—early American statesmen like Madison, Washington, and Adams were well versed in the history of such armies in Europe, especially in ancient Rome.

If even the earliest attempts at centralized police forces would have alarmed the Founders, today's policing would have terrified them. Today in America SWAT teams violently smash into private homes more than one hundred times per day. The vast majority of these raids are to enforce laws against consensual crimes. In many cities, police departments have given up the traditional blue uniforms for "battle dress uniforms" modeled after soldier attire. Police departments across the country now sport armored personnel carriers designed for use on a battlefield. Some have helicopters, tanks, and Humvees. They carry military-grade weapons. Most of this equipment comes from the military itself. Many SWAT teams today are trained by current and former personnel from special forces units like the Navy Seals or Army Rangers. National Guard helicopters now routinely swoop through rural areas in search of pot plants and, when they find something, send gun-toting troops dressed for battle rappelling down to chop and confiscate the contraband. But it isn't just drugs. Aggressive, SWAT-style tactics are now used to raid neighborhood poker games, doctor's offices, bars and restaurants, and head shops, despite the fact that the targets of these raids pose little threat to anyone. This sort of force was once reserved as the last option to defuse a dangerous situation. It's increasingly used as the first option to apprehend people who aren't dangerous at all.

There's now a dominant military culture within modern police agencies. Go to one of the many SWAT conferences and SWAT team competitions held throughout the year and you'll find exhibit halls teeming with military weapons, gear, clothing, and imagery. The vendors at these events know their market. They use war imagery to ply their goods because that's what makes cops and police departments want to buy them. Many sell the same products to both the military and civilian police agencies. In the 1990s and 2000s, the company Heckler and Koch marketed its MP5 semi-automatic weapon with the slogan "From the Gulf War to the Drug War—Battle Proven."[6] Publications like Larry Flynt's *SWAT* magazine feature ads that emphasize knocking heads and kicking ass, and print articles with headlines like "Go for the Throat" and "Warrior Mindset."

There's been nothing secretive about this transformation, but because it's been unfolding over several decades, we don't seem to have noticed. On February 11, 2010, in Columbia, Missouri, the police department's SWAT team served a drug warrant at the home of Jonathan Whitworth, his wife, and their seven-year-old-son. Police claimed that eight days earlier they had received a tip from a confidential informant that Whitworth had a large supply of marijuana in his home. They then conducted a trash pull, which turned up marijuana "residue" in the family's garbage. That was the basis for a violent, nighttime, forced-entry raid on the couple's home. The cops stormed in screaming, swearing, and firing their weapons, and within seconds of breaking down the door they intentionally shot and killed one of the family's dogs, a pit bull. At least one bullet ricocheted and struck the family's pet corgi. The wounded dogs whimpered in agony. Upon learning that the police had killed one of his pets, Whitworth burst into tears.

The Columbia Police Department SWAT team recorded many of its drug raids for training purposes, including this one. After battling with the police over its release, a local newspaper was finally able to get the video through state open records laws and posted it to the Internet. It quickly went viral, climbing to over one million YouTube views within a week. People were outraged. The Columbia Police Department was swamped with phone calls and emails, and its officers were condemned, cursed, and scolded. Some even received death threats.

The video also made national headlines. On Fox News, Bill O'Reilly discussed it with newspaper columnist and pundit Charles Krauthammer, who assured O'Reilly's audience that botched raids like the one in the video were unusual; he warned viewers not to judge the war on drugs based on the images coming out of Columbia. Krauthammer was wrong. This was not a "botched" raid. In fact, the only thing unusual about the raid was that it was recorded. Everything else—from the relatively little evidence to the lack of a corroborating investigation, the killing of the dog, the fact that the raid was for nothing more than pot, the police misfiring, and their unawareness that a child was in the home—was fairly standard. The police raided the house they intended to raid, and they even found some pot. The problem for them was that possession of small amounts of pot in Columbia had been decriminalized. They did charge Whitworth with possession of drug paraphernalia for the pipe they found near the marijuana—a $300 fine.

The reaction to the video was fascinating—and perhaps encouraging—because, again, the raid itself was indistinguishable from the tens of thousands of similar raids conducted each year in America. It was as if the country—or at least the Internet generation—was for the first time seeing firsthand, on-the-ground footage of the way the drug war is fought every day. And they found it terrifying.

Most Americans still believe we live in a free society and revere its core values. These principles are pretty well known: freedom of speech, religion, and the press; the right to a fair trial; representative democracy; equality before the law; and so on. These aren't principles we hold sacred because they're enshrined in the Constitution, or because they were cherished by the Founders. These principles were enshrined in the Constitution and cherished by the Framers *precisely because* they're indispensable to a free society. This book answers the question: *How did we get here?* How did we evolve from a country whose founding statesmen were adamant about the dangers of armed, standing government forces—a country that enshrined the Fourth Amendment in the Bill of Rights and revered and protected the age-old notion that the home is a place of privacy and sanctuary—to a country where it has become acceptable for armed government agents dressed in battle garb to storm private homes in the middle of the night—not to apprehend violent fugitives or thwart terrorist attacks, but to enforce laws against nonviolent, consensual activities? How did a country pushed into a revolution by protest and political speech become one where protests are met with flash grenades, pepper spray, and platoons of riot teams dressed like Robocops? How did we go from a system in which laws were enforced by the citizens, often with noncoercive methods, to one in which order is preserved by armed government agents too often conditioned to see streets and neighborhoods as battlefields and the citizens they serve as the enemy?

Before we begin, a few organizational notes are in order. First, this is not an "anti-cop" book. Although it includes plenty of anecdotes about bad cops, there are plenty of good cops. Some of them are interviewed in this book. The fact is that we need cops, and there are limited situations in which we need SWAT teams. If anything, this is an anti-politician book. Bad cops are the product of bad policy. And policy is ultimately made by politicians. A bad system loaded with bad incentives will unfailingly produce bad cops. The good ones will never enter the field in the first place, or they will become frustrated and leave police work, or they'll simply turn bad. At best, they'll have unrewarding, unfulfilling jobs. This book explores the consequences of having cops who are too angry and too eager to kick down doors and who approach their jobs with entirely the wrong mind-set, but with an eye toward identifying and changing the policies that allow such people to become cops in the first place—and that allow them to flourish in police work.

Second, some of this book is the product of historical research, some of it is original reporting done exclusively for the book, and some of it is original reporting I've done for other publications. Many of the passages taken from reported pieces I've already published are reprinted here verbatim, or nearly verbatim.

Finally, many of the anecdotes mentioned in the book happened years or decades ago. Sometimes there was a flurry of initial coverage of an incident, but then no coverage of the resolution. I've tried to find out how all of these incidents were resolved, but that wasn't always possible. For example, an anecdote may have come from a complaint in a lawsuit against a police department that was resolved with a closed settlement, which means the police account of the incident was never revealed. Or a police department may have refused to disclose information about an internal investigation, leaving only press accounts of an incident. In cases like these, I've indicated the source of the accusations to let you know that they're one-sided narratives.

This story of police militarization in America begins with lessons from ancient Rome, then moves quickly through the Dark and Middle Ages into the origins of modern policing. We examine the foundations of the American experiment laid down during the colonial period and the American Revolution—the right to privacy, the Castle Doctrine, and the demilitarization of free societies—then look at the emergence of the modern, centralized police department in the early nineteenth century. After quickly passing through the Progressive Era, the professionalization movement, and alcohol prohibition, we come to the real beginning of the story of modern police militarization: the social upheaval, civil unrest, and culture wars of the 1960s. At that point the book becomes a more focused narrative. We follow the militarization trend through Nixon's rhetorical wars on crime and drugs in the 1970s, Reagan's all-too-literal drug war of the 1980s, and the massive expansion of SWAT teams, the proliferation of military gear, and the federalization of policing in the 1990s. The final chronological chapter looks at how the war on terrorism has accelerated the militarization of the police, how SWAT teams and the paramilitary approach to policing have moved beyond the wars on drugs and terror, and how frighteningly willing the government has become to use this sort of force to make a political statement. The book ends with a chapter on reforms and recommendations on how to roll back the militarization of policing in America; and whether any meaningful reform is still possible.

# CHAPTER 1

# FROM ROME TO WRITS

Quis custodiet ipsos custodes? (Who will watch the watchers?)

—JUVENAL, FIRST-CENTURY ROMAN POET

G iven that most of the American Founders were students of the Enlightenment and its revival of classical learning, most of them looked fondly on the Roman republic and drew lessons from the rise and fall of the Roman empire. Alexander Hamilton, James Madison, and John Jay, for example, wrote the Federalist Papers under the pen name "Publius" in honor of the first consul of the Roman republic, and one of the revolutionaries who overthrew the monarchy. John Adams in particular was a fan of Cicero, who spent much of his public life warning of the dangers of militarism and dictatorship—and was eventually murdered for it. The American forefathers were keenly aware of the price that Rome paid by permitting the military to gain such power in their society, and they generally sought to avoid its mistakes.

It seems fitting then that the world's first documented, organized police force would have been established in ancient Rome. And the rise of that ancient police force raised many of the same questions about balancing security with liberty that we debate today.

After Julius Caesar was assassinated in 44 BC, Rome fell into chaos as the empire's powerful factions maneuvered to seize power. Anticipating bloodshed, faction leaders began to pull elite troops from their armies to serve as bodyguards. These guard units came to be called *praetorian cohorts,* after the *praetoria cohors* who guarded the tents of Roman generals during war. By the end of the reign of Emperor Augustus, and for the next several centuries, the Praetorian Guard would take on more of the roles we now associate with a conventional police force, including investigating serious crimes, making arrests, providing security during Coliseum games, collecting taxes, spying on suspected revolutionaries, collecting undercover intelligence, and even fighting fires.

During his reign, Augustus established two other policing forces less prestigious than the Praetorians. Around 13 BC he created the *cohortes urbanae,* or urban cohorts, which he charged with quelling riots and keeping order in the streets. And in AD 6 he created an additional order called the *vigiles.* First charged exclusively with fighting fires, the vigiles would also later take on police duties and came to serve as Rome's night watchmen.

Augustus's Praetorian Guard would eventually become one of the most powerful institutions in Rome. In later years the Guard's loyalty often determined who would become the next emperor, and its members may have assassinated as many as a dozen Roman emperors and many more potential heirs.

The interesting thing about Augustus's first police forces is that to implement them he had to navigate some of the same challenges and objections to civic policing that arise today. He had to balance public safety and the maintenance of order by at least appearing to respect civil liberties. More importantly, he had to find ways to assure the Senate and the citizenry that the responsibilities of these bands of order-keeping public servants, all drawn from the Roman army, were distinct from the duties that Romans normally associated with soldiers.

Even in ancient Rome, the public was acutely sensitive to the threat of militarized policing. Prior to Caesar's march on Rome in 49 BC, soldiers were forbidden to enter the capital as soldiers. There had never been a permanent standing army within the city. It was Caesar's crossing of the Rubicon, the city's outer boundary, with his army that triggered the civil war that ended the republic.

After Augustus, the Praetorian Guard became an increasingly powerful force in the upper echelons of Roman power. As conquest and empire became central tenets of Roman society, the day-to-day lives of Romans became infused with militarism. Soldiers and generals began to be held in higher esteem than scholars and statesmen. The Praetorian Guard outgrew its consignment under Augustus to civilian policing and was reconnected with the Roman army. Eventually, the Guard directly interfered with the succession of emperors, sowing further instability. The Praetorian Guard was finally disbanded by Emperor Constantine in AD 312. Its members had made the mistake of backing his opponent. About 1,800 years would pass before the world would see another metropolitan police force as centralized and organized as those that Augustus first established in Rome.

There are also some broader parallels between Rome and the establishment of policing in the modern world. During the Roman republic, disputes were settled between and within families. Criminals were often punished by their own relatives, who faced social pressure to make right by victims and their kin. But under Augustus the state began to take on a much larger role in these traditionally private and provincial affairs. As Rome was transformed from republic to empire, dispute resolution, punishment, and remuneration, which had once been handled privately, fell exclusively to the emperor's executive power. As we will see, Britain and the early United States went through a similar transition centuries later. In the United States, the colonial-era concerns about standing armies gave way to more immediate problems like crime and rioting as the country moved into the industrial age. Cities turned to centralized power—police agencies reporting to the mayor—to impose law and order.[1]

IN THE YEARS THAT FOLLOWED ROME'S FALL, ORGANIZED policing largely disappeared from Europe. One exception were the few cities in Italy that became hubs of trade and culture. As they grew, cities like Florence and Venice had to contend with urban issues of crime, poverty, and disease. To keep order—which kept the trade flowing—leaders established patrols to protect the property of businesses, tradesmen, and manufacturers and to enforce curfews during outbreaks.

By the Middle Ages, a nationalized police force had emerged in France, though more as an effort to protect the monarchy from revolt than to protect the citizens from crime. Maintaining the existing order was the only priority; civil liberties were of little concern.

The English tradition was different. Because of its isolation, England was relatively more stable than continental Europe during the Dark and Middle Ages. It didn't face the constant threat of revolution. Ruling regimes in other parts of Europe had to maintain order by suppressing dissent and keeping the public from posing a threat to them. In Britain, preserving order meant protecting lives, rights, and property from thieves, vandals, and murderers. Consequently, the English benefited from an orientation toward local rather than centralized policing. Before the Norman Conquest of 1066, Britain was organized into *tythings,* groups of about ten families in a given geographical area who were expected to maintain peace and order on their land. If a member of a tything committed a crime, the group was expected to turn the transgressor over to the king, or the tything would be punished as a group. Groups of ten tythings were then grouped into larger units called *shires.* To keep order in the shires, the Crown appointed a representative called a *reeve,* a position usually filled by one of the shire's own residents. The position came to be called the *shire reeve,* the source of our modern word *sheriff.* This mix of incentives for tythings enabled them to maintain order with a balance of liberty and accountability.

The English system also benefited from its adherence to common law rather than Roman law. Because the objective of common law is dispute resolution rather than enforcing the will of the sovereign, it offers more protection of individual rights. English citizens' ability to sue law enforcers who violated their rights was unheard of in countries with centralized policing forces. English trials were also governed by set rules of procedure—again, in stark contrast to the rest of Europe.

Some of that began to change after the Norman Conquest. The Normans used the existing, traditional English structure to impose a more centralized system like those on the Continent. Sheriffs became more beholden to the Crown, and the Normans introduced the position of *constable,* which would come to replace the sheriff as the Crown's preferred local law enforcement officer. Still, while the Normans made some important changes to the way British society kept order, the tradition of common-law rule, trials with set procedures, and individual rights was too ingrained to be overcome.

As with imperial Rome and Italy in the Middle Ages, urbanization in England eventually created the need for a new system. By the fourteenth century, as England grew more populous and industrialized, the tything system grew less useful. Social pressure lost its effectiveness in keeping order as English citizens came to live closer together, next to neighbors they didn't already know. In response, Parliament authorized the position of *urban constable* to keep order. Constables were permitted to draft citizen watchmen to patrol city streets at night and raise the "hue and cry" to call up all men between ages fifteen and sixty in the event of an emergency.

By the early eighteenth century, England—and London in particular—had thoroughly outgrown its antiquated system of preserving order. London at the time held 10 percent of the country's population within its city limits. The streets, overrun with highwaymen, pickpockets, and burglars, were growing more dangerous. The constables and their deputies were overworked and easily corrupted. In more affluent areas magistrates could afford to hire *thief takers*—freelance crime fighters who would capture crooks in exchange for a bounty—but crime persisted, and British officials would soon be forced to look for a better solution.[2]

THE AMERICAN EXPERIENCE WAS SHAPED BY THE LESSONS from the classical period, by Enlightenment ideas about the proper relationship between the people and the state, by English common law, and of course by the colonists' direct experience with British rule. Among the most crucial concepts inherited from these traditions was a term that has since lost a great deal of its original meaning: the *Castle Doctrine*. When used today, the term is most often associated with the gun control debate, but it means a great deal more to the impulses that shaped our national ideas about privacy, liberty, and the proper relationship between the individual and the state. Ironically, America both inherited the Castle Doctrine from British common law and was moved to revolution in part by Britain's refusal to honor the principle in the colonies.

Put simply, the Castle Doctrine holds that "a man's home is his castle." But it springs from an older, much broader sentiment that the home should be protected as a place of refuge, peace, and sanctuary. One of the earliest recorded pronouncements of the idea came from the Roman statesman Cicero: "Quid enim sanctius, quid omni religione munitius, quam domus unusquisque civium?" (What more sacred, what more strongly guarded by every holy feeling, than a man's own home?)[3] Implicit in the sentiment is not only the right to repel criminal intruders but also the idea that the state is permitted to violate the home's sanctity only under limited circumstances, only as a last resort, and only under conditions that protect the threshold from unnecessary violence. Thus, before entering without permission, government agents must knock, announce and identify themselves, state their purpose, and give the occupants the opportunity to let them in peacefully. The Castle Doctrine establishes the home as a sanctum in which a citizen can expect to be let alone, a principle that the US Supreme Court justice Louis Brandeis called "the most comprehensive of rights, and the right most valued by civilized men."[4]

The Castle Doctrine was probably first formally invoked in common law in *Semayne's Case* in 1572; it has been a right recognized and protected by British law ever since.[5] In 1762 the barrister and English legal scholar William Hawkins wrote, "Where one lies under a probable suspicion only, and is not indicted, it seems the better opinion at this day, that no one can justify breaking open doors in order to apprehend him." Even among those commentators on English law who thought the king *could* break into a private home, it was generally accepted that he could do so only after knocking, announcing, and giving the residents time to grant entry and avoid violence. The seventeenth-century English judge and barrister Matthew Hale wrote, "But the breaking of an outer door is, in general, so violent, obnoxious, and dangerous a proceeding, that it should be adopted only in extreme cases, where an immediate arrest is requisite."[6]

The 1757 English trial of Richard Curtis litigated Castle Doctrine principles that would resurface in drug-related cases in the United States two centuries later. Curtis was charged with the murder of a sheriff who had come to his home with an arrest warrant and forced entry without first announcing himself. In his defense, Curtis argued that he had no way of knowing that the man breaking into his home was an officer of the law. The court sided with Curtis, ruling that peace officers could break open a door only "after having demanded admittance and given due notice of their warrant." The subject of the warrant had to be given notice that "the officer cometh not as a mere trespasser, but claiming to act under a proper authority."[7]

The announcement requirement under English law was not a formality, as it has become in police raids carried out today. It was elemental. Its purpose was to give the homeowner the opportunity to avoid violence, distress, and the destruction of his property. A quick knock and announcement in the middle of the night, followed by forced entry ten to fifteen seconds later, before anyone inside can wake, come to the door, and peacefully grant the sheriff entrance, would be only slightly less offensive to the doctrine's spirit than not knocking at all. As we'll see, while the US Supreme Court still recognizes the Castle Doctrine, thanks to the modern drug war the Court has all but abandoned this idea that the doctrine should protect homeowners from unnecessary violence—which has historically been the entire reason for its existence.

Not all English legal traditions were carried on in the United States, of course, but the evidence of the Founders' reverence for the Castle Doctrine is overwhelming. When English authorities began to trample on the principle, the colonists were first moved to protest, then to try to protect themselves through their own courts and legislatures, and finally to openly revolt.

THE REAL CONFRONTATION STARTED IN 1760, WHEN ENGLAND instituted a battery of unpopular taxes and import restrictions on the colonies. Many colonists took to smuggling to avoid paying new taxes on imported goods. The British then responded with heavy-handed laws to move against the smugglers. Then as now, the authorities were required to get warrants before searching private property. But it was the *general warrant* that infuriated the colonists. General warrants lack specificity. They grant broad authority to search broad groups of people, for evidence of any number of crimes, sometimes over long stretches of time.

The variety of general warrant that Britain used to enforce the import and tax laws on the colonists was called the *writ of assistance*. The policy had been authorized by the British Parliament in the 1660s, but it was rarely used in England. Beginning in the 1760s, however, it became an effective way to combat smugglers and tax scofflaws. Writs of assistance gave customs officials the power to enter private homes, search for smuggled or untaxed goods, and command other government officials and even private citizens to assist them.

In some ways, the writs were less intrusive than today's drug warrants. Writs could not be exercised at night, for example, and authorities still had to knock, announce, and allow sufficient time for residents to grant them entrance before breaking down a door. But in other ways writs of assistance granted government officials more sweeping powers than any warrant today. A writ-holder had the power to search any building or residence and confiscate any suspected contraband. And once issued, a writ was essentially permanent—it remained valid until six months after the death of the king in power when it was issued.

The colonists despised the writs, particularly in port cities like Boston, the hub of revolutionary fervor. The Massachusetts legislature banned general warrants in 1756, but that prohibition didn't stop the English from issuing and enforcing them. Aggrieved Bostonians soon found a champion in James Otis Jr., a blustery Boston attorney who had just resigned as advocate general of the Admiralty Court—the court with jurisdiction over the ships importing goods—in protest against the abuses wrought by the writs. When Otis resigned, began advocating against the writs, and offered free legal representation to anyone who wanted to challenge their legality, he attracted attention, in both Boston and London.[8]

In 1761 Otis agreed to represent a group of prominent Boston merchants challenging the writs in *Paxton's Case*. The case was likely to be a loser—British law was fairly settled on the matter—but Otis and the plaintiffs hoped to use the case to stir up opposition. When the trial came, Otis used the court proceedings as his platform to deliver an impassioned, wide-ranging, five-hour polemic against the practice of general warrants. In one passage he called writs of assistance "the worst instrument of arbitrary power, the most destructive of English liberty and the fundamental principles of law, that ever was found in an English law-book."

Otis invoked natural rights, the Magna Carta, and the Castle Doctrine.

> Now, one of the most essential branches of English liberty is the freedom of one's house. A man's house is his castle; and whilst he is quiet, he is as well guarded as a prince in his castle. This writ, if it should be declared legal, would totally annihilate this privilege. Custom-house officers may enter our houses when they please; we are commanded to permit their entry. Their menial servants may enter, may break locks, bars, and everything in their way; and whether they break through malice or revenge, no man, no court can inquire. Bare suspicion without oath is sufficient.

As expected, Otis lost in court. But his speech likely changed the course of history. One member of the courtroom audience that afternoon was John Adams, a twenty-five-year-old lawyer who would become the second president of the United States of America. Later in his life, Adams recalled the impact that Otis's speech had on him. He praised Otis's grasp of history and fiery defense of the rights of man and pointed out that, quite ahead of his time, Otis even declared that black men should be afforded the same rights as white men, including the right to own property. Adams credited Otis and his diatribe against British warrant abuses as the first knocks of the American Revolution. "Every man of an immense crowded audience appeared to me to go away as I did, ready to take arms against writs of assistants," Adams wrote. "Then and there was the first scene of the first act of opposition to the arbitrary claims of Great Britain. Then and there, the child Independence was born."[9]

Writs of assistance and the customs bureaus that carried them out would be among the specific complaints that the signers of the Declaration of Independence laid out against King George III on July 4, 1776: "He has erected a multitude of New Offices, and sent hither swarms of Officers to harass our people and eat out their substance." In 1791 the Castle Doctrine was enshrined in the US Constitution when the Fourth Amendment was ratified with the rest of the Bill of Rights. The Fourth Amendment prohibits general warrants at the federal level (the prohibition would later be extended to the states through the Fourteenth Amendment) by requiring that warrants not be issued without reason and probable cause, that they be sworn with an oath and affirmation, and that they include particular information about the place to be searched and the person and items to be seized.

But the Fourth Amendment was just one part of a larger, ongoing debate about how to police and defend the security of a free society. The country was young, untested, and unstable, and it faced hostile threats, both internal and external. Those threats would test early America's devotion to individual rights and the Enlightenment principles that had animated the fight for independence.

# CHAPTER 2

# SOLDIERS IN THE STREETS

> One of [America's] greatest strengths is that the military is responsive to civilian authority, and that we do not allow the Army, Navy, and the Marines and the Air Force to be a police force. History is replete with countries that allowed that to happen. Disaster is the result.
>
> —MARINE LT. GEN. STEPHEN OLMSTEAD, IN HIS 1987 TESTIMONY BEFORE THE US CONGRESS

The Third Amendment reads, in full:

> No soldier shall, in time of peace be quartered in any house, without the consent of the owner, nor in time of war, but in a manner to be prescribed by law.

You might call it the runt piglet of the Bill of Rights amendments—short, overlooked, sometimes the butt of jokes. The satirical news site *The Onion* once mocked it with an article about a Third Amendment advocacy group and its record 191-year fight to keep the amendment intact. The group's motto: "Keep the fat hands of soldiers out of America's larders!"

The Supreme Court has yet to hear a case that turns on the Third Amendment, and only one such case has reached a federal appeals court.[1] There have been a few periods in American history when the government probably violated the amendment, and on a large scale, but those incursions into quartering didn't produce any significant court challenges. In the War of 1812, for example, federal troops were quartered in private homes by the thousands, and quartering was also widespread during the Civil War. On both occasions, the quartering was neither authorized nor prescribed by Congress. During World War II, US military forces stationed themselves in the homes of Aleutian Islanders in preparation for an anticipated attack by Japan. Though it is likely that the government overstepped its authority in all of these instances, they failed to produce any work for the Supreme Court to hash out the amendment's protections and exceptions. Not surprisingly, then, Third Amendment scholarship is a thin field, comprising just a handful of law review articles, most of which either look at the amendment's history or pontificate on its obsolescence.[2]

Given the apparent irrelevance of the amendment today, we might ask why the Framers found it so important in the first place. After all, citizens were made to sacrifice for national defense in ways far more intrusive. The Constitution allows for conscription, for example, and the Continental Army openly seized property like livestock and food from colonists.[3] Why, then, was quartering so despised?

One answer returns to the Castle Doctrine. If you revere the principle that a man's home is his castle, it hardly seems just to force him to share a portion of it with soldiers—particularly when the country isn't even at war. But the historical context behind the Third Amendment shows that the Framers were worried about something more profound than fat soldier hands stripping the country's larders. The amendment was a placeholder for the broader aversion to an internal standing army.

At the time the Third Amendment was ratified, the images and memories of British troops in Boston and other cities were still fresh, and the clashes with colonists that drew the country into war still evoked strong emotions. What we might call the "Symbolic Third Amendment" wasn't just a prohibition on peacetime quartering, but a more robust expression of the threat that standing armies pose to free societies. It represented a long-standing, deeply ingrained resistance to armies patrolling American streets and policing American communities.

And in that sense, the spirit of the Third Amendment is anything but anachronistic.

AS WITH THE CASTLE DOCTRINE, COLONIAL AMERICA INHERITED its aversion to quartering from England. British opposition to the practice dates back to the decade after the Norman Conquest, when King William first stationed a permanent army in England for national defense. To raise soldiers for an army, subsequent kings would often pardon killers and thieves, conscript them into military service, then billet them in towns and cities. As you might imagine, giving criminals weapons and the authority of soldiers, then billeting them among the population, brought some problems.

Opposition to quartering persisted for centuries, culminating with a ban on the practice in the English Bill of Rights signed by William and Mary in 1689.

Appreciation of the problems associated with putting soldiers among the citizenry ultimately carried over to the New World, just as the Castle Doctrine did. And as with the Castle Doctrine, England wasn't nearly as respectful of the principle in the colonies as it was at home. The first significant escalation of the issue came in the 1750s, when the British sent over thousands of troops to fight the Seven Years' War (known in the United States as the French and Indian War). In the face of increasing complaints from the colonies about the soldiers stationed in their towns, Parliament responded with more provocation. The Quartering Act of 1765 required the colonists to house, feed, and supply British soldiers (albeit in public facilities). Parliament also helpfully provided a funding mechanism with the hated Stamp Act.[4]

Protest erupted throughout the colonies, both in the streets and in the legislatures.[5] Some protests spilled over into violence, most notably the Boston Massacre in 1770. England only further angered the colonists by responding with even more restrictions on trade and imports (the laws that customs officials used general warrants to enforce). Parliament then passed a second Quartering Act, in 1774, this time specifically authorizing British generals to put soldiers in colonists' homes. There were no wars going on at the time. The law was aimed squarely at correcting the colonies' insubordination. England then sent troops to emphasize the point.[6]

It was the deployment of British soldiers to colonial cities strictly for the purpose of enforcing the law that set long-smoldering hostilities aflame. Using general warrants, British soldiers were allowed to enter private homes, confiscate what they found, and often keep the bounty for themselves. The policy was reminiscent of today's civil asset forfeiture laws, which allow police to seize and keep for their departments cash, cars, luxury goods, and even homes, often under only the thinnest allegation of criminality.

Quartering itself—the specific burden of giving up a bed to a soldier, feeding him, and clothing him—was not what edged cities like Boston to the brink of war. The actual quartering of British troops in the private homes of colonists was rare, at least up until the start of the American Revolution.[7] It was the predictable fallout from positioning soldiers trained for warfare on city streets, among the civilian populace, and using them to enforce laws and maintain order that enraged colonists. Contemporary newspaper accounts documented frequent and increasingly bitter altercations between soldiers and citizens.[8] Bostonians were British subjects, but they were being treated like enemies of the state. They began to interpret the stationing of troops in their city as an act of war.

AFTER THE AMERICAN REVOLUTION, THE LEADERS OF THE new American republic had some difficult decisions to make. They debated whether the abuses that British soldiers had visited upon colonial America were attributable to quartering alone or to the general aura of militarism that came with maintaining standing armies in peacetime—and whether restricting, prohibiting, or providing checks on either practice would prevent the abuses they feared.

Antifederalists like George Mason, Patrick Henry, Sam Adams, and Elbridge Gerry opposed any sort of national army. They believed that voluntary, civilian militias should handle issues of national security. To a degree, the federalists were sympathetic to this idea. John Adams, Thomas Jefferson, and James Madison had all written on the threat to liberty posed by a permanent army. Even Alexander Hamilton, the most federalist of the federalists, presciently warned about the temptation to sacrifice liberty at home for security from outside threats:

> The violent destruction of life and property incident to war—the continual effort and alarm attendant on a state of continual danger, will compel nations the most attached to liberty, to resort for repose and security, to institutions, which have a tendency to destroy their civil and political rights. To be more safe they, at length, become willing to run the risk of being less free.[9]

But the federalists still believed that the federal government needed the power to raise an army. Those same liberties faced a greater threat from outside forces, and were likely to be obliterated entirely if the young nation was conquered by a foreign power. In the end, the federalists won the argument. There would be a standing army. But protection from its potential threats would come in an amendment contained in the Bill of Rights that created an individual right against quartering in peacetime. Even during wartime, quartering would need to be approved by the legislature, the branch more answerable to the people than the executive.

Taken together, the Third, Second, and Tenth Amendments indicate the Founders' desire for the power to enforce laws and maintain order to be primarily left with the states. As a whole, the Constitution embodies the rough consensus at the time that there would be occasions when federal force might be necessary to carry out federal law and dispel violence or disorder that threatened the stability of the republic, but that such endeavors were to be undertaken cautiously, and only as a last resort. More importantly, the often volatile debate between the federalists and the antifederalists shows that the Third Amendment itself represented much more than the sum of its words. The amendment was in some ways a compromise, but it reflects the broader sentiment, shared by both sides, about militarism in a free society. Ultimately, the Founders decided that a standing army was a necessary evil, but that the role of soldiers would be only to dispel foreign threats, not to enforce laws against American citizens.[10]

BEFORE THE BILL OF RIGHTS COULD EVEN BE RATIFIED, however, a rebellion led by a bitter veteran tested those principles. Daniel Shays was part of the Massachusetts militia during the Revolutionary War. He fought courageously at Bunker Hill, Lexington, and Saratoga. He was wounded in action and received a decorative sword from the French general Lafayette in recognition of his service. After the war ended, Shays returned to his farm in Massachusetts. It wasn't long before he began receiving court summonses to account for the debts he had accumulated while he was off fighting the British. Shays went broke. He even sold the sword from Lafayette to help pay his debts.

Other veterans were going through the same thing—they were broke, often wounded from battle, and getting little help from the country they'd just fought to create. The debt collectors weren't exactly villains either. Businesses too had taken on debt to support the war. They set about collecting those debts to avoid going under. Shays and other veterans attempted to get relief from the state legislature in the form of debtor protection laws or the printing of more money, but the legislature balked.

In the fall of 1786, Shays assembled a group of eight hundred veterans and supporters to march on Boston. They planned not only to close down the courthouses to prevent them from foreclosing on the veterans' farms but also to forcibly free debtors from prison. The movement subsequently succeeded in shutting down some courtrooms, and some began to fear that it threatened to erupt into a full-scale rebellion.

In January 1787, Massachusetts governor James Bowdoin asked the Continental Congress to raise troops to help put down the rebels, but under the Articles of Confederation the federal government didn't have the power to provide that sort of assistance to the states. So Bowdoin instead assembled a small army of mercenaries paid for by the same creditors who were hounding men like Shays. After a series of skirmishes, the rebellion had been broken by the following summer.

Shays' Rebellion was never a serious threat to overthrow the Massachusetts government, much less that of the United States, and it was put down relatively quickly, without the use of federal troops, and with little loss of life beyond the rebels themselves. But its success in temporarily shutting down courthouses in Boston convinced many political leaders in early America that the country needed a stronger federal government. Inadvertently, Shays spurred momentum for what became the 1787 Constitutional Convention in Philadelphia.

The impact of Shays' Rebellion didn't end, however, at Philadelphia. Memories of the rebellion and fears that something like it could destabilize the new republic blunted memories of the abuses suffered at the hands of British troops and made many in the new government more comfortable with the use of federal force to put down domestic uprisings.[11]

In 1792, just five years after the ratification of the Bill of Rights, Congress passed the Calling Forth Act. The new law gave the president the authority to unilaterally call up and command state militias to repel insurrections, fend off attacks from hostile American Indian tribes, and address other threats that presented themselves while Congress wasn't in session. In addition to the concerns raised by Shays' Rebellion, growing discontent over one of the country's first federal taxes—a tax on whiskey—was also making the law's supporters anxious. The Calling Forth Act allowed the president to federalize and deploy the militia "whenever the laws of the United States shall be opposed or the execution thereof obstructed, in any state, by combinations too powerful to be suppressed by the ordinary course of judicial proceedings, or by the powers vested in the marshals by this act." Two years later, in 1794, President George Washington used the act to call up a militia to put down the Whiskey Rebellion in 1794 in western Pennsylvania.

The Calling Forth Act did expand the power of the executive, and Washington's willingness to invoke it showed that the new government wouldn't hesitate to use an armed force on its own citizens when faced with a violent uprising. But the law still authorized the president to call up such a force only in dire situations, and then only long enough to dispel the threat. That power would be further regulated, in 1807, with the Insurrection Act, which clarified that the president could call up the military to put down a rebellion only if so requested by a state; he could send in the military in spite of a state's wishes only if he determined that the situation was so dire that federal law could no longer be enforced, or if the basic rights of the state's citizens were being violated and the state couldn't or wouldn't do anything about it. The Insurrection Act, which stipulated that the military was to be used only as an absolute last resort, would be used in subsequent decades to put down slave rebellions and prison riots.

So ideas about law and order were already evolving. The young republic had gone from a country of rebels lashing out at the British troops in their midst to a country with a government unafraid to use its troops to put down rebellions. But American presidents had still generally adhered to the Symbolic Third Amendment. For the first half-century or so after ratification of the Constitution, military troops were rarely if ever used for routine law enforcement.

But that would soon change.

—

ON APRIL 8, 1851, CHARLES LORING STOOD UP IN A BOSTON courtroom to deliver his closing argument. He'd represented his client for only a few days, but the man's freedom hung in the balance. Outside the courtroom, federal marshals, militia, and Boston constables and watchmen stood guard. Iron chains blocked all entrances to the building. Four days earlier, Thomas Sims, a seventeen-year-old escaped slave, had been arrested in the free state of Massachusetts.[12] Sims had escaped the Savannah plantation of John Potter, one of the city's wealthiest farmers. Sims then stowed away on a freight ship, which brought him to Boston.[13]

Sims had been arrested under the Fugitive Slave Act, passed the year before as part of the Compromise of 1850, a package of bills aimed at ameliorating the growing tensions between free and slave states. An earlier Fugitive Slave Act, passed in 1793, already prohibited citizens from aiding the escape of slaves and mandated their return to their masters. But as slavery fell out of favor in the North, many cities and towns became places of refuge for freed slaves. State legislatures in the North began passing laws that made it easier for escaped slaves to win their freedom. The 1850 law was passed to plug the holes that had subsequently been poked in the law passed a half-century earlier.

Even for its time, it was an outrageous piece of legislation.[14] Any black person in a free state could be claimed as an escaped slave on little more than the word of a Southerner claiming to own him. The accused would then be arrested and given a hearing (not a jury trial) in front of an appointed federal commissioner (not a judge). Denied habeas corpus, the alleged slave was neither permitted to testify on his own behalf nor allowed to personally challenge the word of the man who claimed him as his property. The commissioner's decision could not be appealed. Anyone aiding a slave's escape—even by merely offering him food or water—was guilty of a federal offense, punishable by a $1,000 fine and six months in prison. Not only were federal marshals paid bounties for capturing escaped slaves, they could be fined $1,000 if they refused to arrest a black person whom any white person claimed was a slave. As if all that weren't enough, the appointed commissioners who decided the fates of the accused were paid $10 if they ruled in favor of the slave owner, but just $5 if they ruled in favor of the alleged slave. The law was so skewed toward slave owners that even blacks who had been free all their lives were at risk of being consigned to slavery by false accusations.

The Sims case attracted national attention among opponents of slavery. When Sims was ordered back to the plantation, prominent abolitionists like Frederick Douglass, Ralph Waldo Emerson, William Lloyd Garrison, and Henry David Thoreau wrote enraged polemics condemning the farcical proceedings, but most of Boston was complacent. The prospect of a civil war was daunting. For the time being, many in the North were willing to tolerate slave-catching as the price for avoiding bloodshed—at least blood shed by people other than slaves.

Three years later, the mood had changed, and Boston was again the site of a fugitive slave hearing. Nineteen-year-old Anthony Burns had escaped to Boston from an estate in Richmond, Virginia.[15] He was working for a clothier when he was apprehended on May 24, 1854, by slave catcher Asa O. Butman, who arrested him under the pretext of a jewelry store robbery.[16] On the morning of Burns's hearing, armed abolitionists calling themselves the Vigilance Committee forced their way into the courtroom with a battering ram. In the ensuing melee, a federal marshal was killed. The rescue was unsuccessful, and the rescuers were arrested, but the event captured Boston's attention—and the country's.

When Burns's hearing resumed the next day, thousands of people came out to protest. Boston mayor J.V.C. Smith called up two companies of the Massachusetts militia to keep order for the remainder of the hearing. Finding those forces inadequate, he then contacted

President Franklin Pierce directly to request that two US Army battalions and fifty Marines be sent to Boston.[17]

During his 1852 campaign, Pierce had vowed more robust enforcement of the Fugitive Slave Act. So when Smith asked for troops, Pierce consented. He also put hundreds more troops on standby just in case Smith needed them.[18] By the end of the week, the hearing still wasn't over. Because Burns would have to be kept in Boston over the weekend, the troops had to stay there too. The protests grew, as did tensions between the troops and the protesters.

On June 2, 1854, slave commissioner Edward G. Loring—a double cousin of the man who had defended Thomas Sims—ordered Anthony Burns returned to Virginia. Some fifty thousand Bostonians poured into the streets and took to rooftops in protest.[19] Some flew American flags upside down, and others shouted "Kidnappers!" at the police and soldiers. One group hoisted a coffin under a banner that read, THE FUNERAL OF LIBERTY.[20] The city was angry, as much at the law as at the amount of force their own state officials had brought to bear to enforce it.

The moment Loring issued his decision, Boston went into lockdown. The troops fired cannons in the air as a warning to the protesters. The mayor declared martial law (probably illegally).[21] Over the next several hours, US soldiers and state militiamen cleared the streets of Boston. On several occasions, the militiamen fired into the crowd. When the troops mistook a crowd surge for an assault, they charged the protesters with bayonets. There were numerous injuries, a few of them serious, but somewhat miraculously, there were no fatalities.[22] Once the streets were cleared, another group of troops marched the prisoner from the courthouse to the steamship waiting for him at the docks. From Boston Harbor, the site of the Boston Tea Party, the ship and the federal troops aboard it took Anthony Burns back to Virginia—from a city nicknamed "the Cradle of Liberty" to the shackles awaiting him in Richmond.

It hadn't yet been one hundred years since the Boston Massacre, in which British soldiers fired first into the air, then directly into a mob of angry protesters, effectively sparking the American Revolution. Yet, on the morning of June 2, 1854, it was US soldiers who lined Boston's streets, who fired shots from a cannon positioned in the town square as a warning to fellow Americans, and who used the threat of military force to silence the speech of American citizens. The reason for the protests—that a man who had escaped the yoke and found refuge in the arms of a free state was being sent back into bondage—only compounded the poignancy of the scene.

The heavy-handed response and the arresting imagery of federal troops imposing martial law on an American city was bad enough. But the Anthony Burns affair also brought about a new and significant breach of the Symbolic Third Amendment. Like Franklin Pierce, who had appointed him, US Attorney General Caleb Cushing was a *doughface,* a Northerner with Southern sympathies. He had been looking for an occasion to strengthen enforcement of the Fugitive Slave Act, as his boss had promised in the campaign. In response to the vigilantism and public backlash in Boston, he issued what became known as the Cushing Doctrine.[23] The policy allowed US marshals to call up the military to help them enforce federal law, without explicit authorization from either the president or the Congress.

Prior to the Cushing Doctrine, when a US marshal needed a posse, he typically drew it from men in his jurisdiction. If he needed backing from the military, he had to get authorization from the president. The difficulty of obtaining that authorization made such requests rare. The Cushing Doctrine made it easier. Calling on federal troops to use force against American citizens had been reserved for insurrection or rebellion, but now there was a new criterion: a single marshal could call up troops merely if he felt that people were preventing him from performing his duties. The opinion would be used to hunt down fugitive slaves in northern states where the fugitive slave law was unpopular, to put down John Brown's antislavery revolt at Harper's Ferry, West Virginia, and to enforce federal law on the relatively lawless western frontier.

A major barrier had come down: the federal military could now be routinely used to enforce federal law. And it happened not by way of a constitutional amendment, or a vote from an elected Congress, or even a Supreme Court decision, but after an opinion issued by a US attorney general.

⌐⌐

THE NEXT CHALLENGE TO THE SYMBOLIC THIRD AMENDMENT came after the Civil War, during Reconstruction. The federal government stationed US troops throughout the southern states to protect ex-slaves from retribution and to enforce the Thirteenth, Fourteenth, and Fifteenth Amendments and the Reconstruction Acts. By most any definition, the troops were an occupying force, performing or closely overseeing nearly all government functions in the former Confederacy.

The mass deployment of troops in the South was made possible by a series of laws called the Force Acts. The first law, passed by Congress in 1870, made it a federal crime to use threats, force, intimidation, or bribery to keep someone from voting based on race or prior status as a slave. It was basically the enforcement mechanism for the Thirteenth Amendment. The second law, passed in 1871, allowed for federal oversight of elections if two or more citizens in any town of more than twenty thousand people requested it. The third law, also passed in 1871, is sometimes called the Ku Klux Klan Act. It gave the federal government sweeping authorization to use the military against any groups suspected of conspiring against federal law. The law also made the terror and intimidation tactics used by white supremacist groups a federal offense and authorized the president to suspend habeas corpus if, in his judgment, other efforts to suppress race-related terror and violence weren't working.

As long as the troops were in place, Reconstruction worked. The federal presence prevented state and local officials in the former Confederate states from denying blacks the right to vote, barring them from holding public office, or consigning ex-slaves to indentured servitude. The troops also helped prevent mob violence and lynching, although both still happened.

But the disputed presidential election of 1876 put an end to all of that. No candidate won a majority of electoral votes, so the election was decided by a backroom deal between Republican and Democratic leaders. Republican Rutherford B. Hayes emerged as the president-elect in a deal that required him to pull federal troops out of the South, effectively ending Reconstruction. The Compromise of 1877 brought in a new era of mob violence, systematic discrimination, segregation, and general second-class status for blacks that endured for the next eighty years—essentially until the civil rights movement started accumulating victories in the midtwentieth century.

A little over a year after Hayes took office, Kentucky representative J. Proctor Knott introduced an amendment to an Army appropriations bill to bar the enlistment of federal troops for law enforcement purposes without authorization from Congress or the president. Knott's aim was modest: he simply wanted to repeal the Cushing Doctrine. The amendment to the law, which became known as the Posse Comitatus Act, reads:

> From and after the passage of this act it shall not be lawful to employ any part of the Army of the United States, as a posse comitatus, or otherwise, for the purpose of executing the laws, except in such cases under such circumstances as such employment of said force may be expressly authorized by the Constitution or by act of Congress.

The law's main effect was exactly what Knott intended. It nullified the Cushing Doctrine. US marshals could no longer call up US troops to help them enforce federal law unless they obtained authorization from the president. Some historians and scholars have claimed that the Posse Comitatus Act was fallout from the Compromise of 1877 and that the true aim of its supporters was to repeal Reconstruction. The suggestion is that the law is tainted by racism and sympathy for the Confederacy. There's some truth to that. The law certainly made it more difficult to enforce Reconstruction.

But Reconstruction was already on the way out. It had lost support in the North. Hayes—a Republican—had even promised to end it during his campaign. And the law actually ended a policy that had been created to catch fugitive slaves. (It's an unfortunate commentary on the plight of freed blacks at the time that they could be made worse off by a new policy, then made worse off still by its repeal.)

Reconstruction was a necessary policy, and it was probably necessary to use troops to enforce it. But it was a once-in-American-history sort of crisis. The deployments were authorized by acts of Congress. The Fourteenth Amendment required the federal government to protect the rights of black Americans in the South, and it seems clear that a few hundred federal marshals weren't sufficient for the job. Reconstruction set a new bar for military involvement in domestic affairs, but there's been nothing like it since. After federal troops were pulled out of the South, the domestic deployment of US troops mostly reverted back to limited situations like large-scale riots and violent insurrections.[24]

The term *posse comitatus* traditionally referred to the population of able-bodied men from which a posse could be drawn. Today both the term and the law have come to represent much more than the text in Knott's amendment indicates. The law itself is now commonly misunderstood to bar the president or Congress from using the military to enforce federal or state law. That isn't quite correct. The law only prevents domestic law enforcement officials from using the military to enforce the law without authority from the president or Congress. It puts no restrictions on the Congress or the president. But more broadly, the term *posse comitatus* has become a signal for the principles behind the Symbolic Third Amendment. It's often used today to indicate our traditional aversion to putting soldiers in the streets. Regardless of the origins of the term, the sentiment behind it has persisted—often in spite of the best efforts of elected officials. More comforting, one institution that has held the principle in especially high regard is the military itself, although here too there have been a few exceptions.

In the nineteenth century, as America was sorting out when and how and under what conditions the military could be deployed domestically, the country was also growing. By the 1830s, US cities were swelling and becoming more diverse. Predatory crime was increasingly a problem. The country needed new ideas and new institutions for maintaining day–to–day order—institutions that could be scaled to accommodate growing urbanization. Once again the country would look to England for inspiration.

# CHAPTER 3

# A QUICK HISTORY OF COPS IN AMERICA

Democratic law tends more and more to be grounded upon the maxim that every citizen is, by nature, a traitor, a libertine, and a scoundrel. In order to dissuade him from his evil-doing the police power is extended until it surpasses anything ever heard of in the oriental monarchies of antiquity.

—H. L. MENCKEN, *NOTES ON DEMOCRACY*

C olonial American towns were usually filled with people who came from the same place, worshiped at the same altar, and shared the same sense of right and wrong. Historian and criminologist Sam Walker writes, "Crime and sin were synonymous; an offense against God was an offense against society, and vice versa."[1] Predatory crimes like murder, rape, and robbery were almost nonexistent. Far more common were punishments for crimes like blasphemy, adultery, or drunkenness. Not surprisingly, law and policing in prerevolutionary America were modeled fairly closely on the English example. Given the rugged conditions of frontier living and the lack of civic structures, trial and punishment were relatively rare.

Mores and shared values were generally sufficient, and when they weren't, shunning and other forms of informal justice usually worked to keep civic order. Not all colonial communities were the same, and laws varied from place to place depending on the prevailing religion and tradition, but there was little need for state agents to enforce the law. Communities tended to handle transgressors on their own. There were Crown-appointed sheriffs and constables, but again, they largely focused on administrative matters.

As the country grew, three distinctive policing traditions began to emerge, coinciding with three regions—the Northeast, the South, and the western frontier.

In the Northeast, as the cities grew larger and more diverse in the early eighteenth century, their residents encountered more crime. Throughout the seventeenth and eighteenth centuries, early American cities first installed *night watch patrols,* first voluntary and then paid. The night watches were fairly successful at rounding up drunks and preventing petty infractions, but the low-paying positions would prove inadequate when cities began to experience riots, mobs, and more serious crimes.

The Southern colonies were more agrarian, less compact, and more homogeneous than the colonies of the Northeast. The primary threat to public safety in the South—at least in the minds of whites— was the possibility of slave revolts. As a result, the first real organized policing systems in America arguably began in the South with *slave patrols.* The patrols were armed and uniformed, and typically had broad powers to arrest, search, and detain slaves. The slave patrols' main responsibilities were to guard against rebellions and to look for escaped slaves. They had the power to enter slave quarters at will, whether or not they had permission from the slaves' owner. They could even enforce some laws against plantation owners, such as laws prohibiting the education of slaves. By the middle of the eighteenth century, every Southern colony had passed laws formalizing slave patrols. It became the primary policing system in the South. In many jurisdictions—most notably Charleston, South Carolina—slave patrols would eventually morph into the official police force.

On the western frontier, early policing was more piecemeal. Northern settlers tended to congregate together and set up systems in the Northern tradition, while pioneers from the South followed the Southern tradition. But the expanse of the frontier didn't always accommodate either system. Often there was just too much ground to cover, and the territory was too sparsely populated. That gap was often filled by *vigilantes* and private police for hire. The vigilante groups came together in response to some threat to public order, then dissolved once the threat had subsided. As the name implies, they tended to operate outside the formal legal system and were naturally more prone to pop up where the legal system either didn't exist or was too weak to maintain order. In some cases, vigilante groups were better than no justice at all. In other cases, they were quite a bit worse.

THE FIRST MODERN POLICE FORCE AS WE KNOW IT TODAY WAS created in 1829 in London by Sir Robert Peel. He and his father had been pushing the idea for decades, but British concerns over the nation's civil liberties tradition had repeatedly killed the idea. Concerned about the worsening conditions in the city, Parliament finally gave its approval in 1829, but only after Peel put in place assurances and checks to retain some local control over the force and ensure that police officers' responsibilities were limited to fighting crime and protecting individual rights—his task was to convince the city that a police force would not be an army enforcing the will of a centralized power.

The British police force began with three thousand officers. They wore uniforms to make themselves recognizable, but Peel made the uniforms blue to distinguish them from the red worn by the British military. Peel was sensitive to concerns about standing armies, but he also believed that a successful police force would need at least some of the structure and discipline of a military influence. Peel appointed a retired colonel as one of his two first supervising justices. Thus, the inaugural police force took on a military-like top-down administrative structure, and even borrowed some military titles. It's a tradition that continues in most police departments in the United States today.

Peel and his justices set out a strict code of conduct. Officers were to avoid confrontation when at all possible. They were to be civil and polite when interacting with citizens. Most of all, Peel hammered home the principle that his police force worked for the people of London, not against them. Nevertheless, it took a while for the public to warm to the idea.

Across the Atlantic in rapidly urbanizing America, larger cities began to adopt the British model, albeit with some Americanized adjustments. The first modern-style police department in the United States was established in New York in 1845. Boston and Philadelphia soon followed. New York began its experiment with eight hundred policemen. Fearing that the London force was already too much like an army, the New York cops began their patrols unarmed, and without uniforms. Early American police departments were also much more democratic than the system in London. Peel and his top aides handpicked the officers to work in London. In the United States, early police officers were nominated by ward leaders and political bosses, then appointed by the mayor. Cops were required to live in the wards they patrolled. All of this tended to make early police departments more like service agencies than law enforcement bodies. Since ward leaders were elected, they found they could pressure local commanders to prioritize police duties in ways that would help get them reelected. In some neighborhoods, police officers ran soup kitchens and homeless people were given shelter in police stations to sleep. This democratic style of policing also gave police (or more accurately, their commanders) discretion to enforce laws in ways that reflected the priorities of the communities they patrolled. Alcohol laws, for example, might be strictly enforced in one part of a city, but rarely if ever enforced in another.

In some ways, this wasn't all that dissimilar to the way laws had been enforced before police departments existed, when transgressions within a community were handled by its members. But there

were some clear drawbacks. The job of police officer had quickly become a patronage position. The only qualification for becoming a
cop was a political connection. Mass firings were common when
power changed hands. The ethnicity of a ward's police force tended
to be exclusively that of the majority of the ward's population. This
could be problematic for, say, an Italian caught in a majority Irish
neighborhood. Training was nonexistent, beatings were common,
and, perhaps most importantly, the system had little effect on
crime—neither preventing it nor helping to bring criminals to justice.

Ironically, the more centralized, less democratic London model
proved to be more protective of individual rights than early American police departments. Centralization allowed Peel to set high,
consistent hiring standards based on merit. Because he was so aware
of the English public's fears about violations of their civil liberties,
Peel knew that the survival of his police department was probably
contingent on his ability to alleviate those fears.

And so by the end of the nineteenth century, London's "bobbies"
(the nickname derived from Peel's name) had managed to win over
the public within a couple of decades, while the reputation of the
American police officer had hit bottom. With no training or standards, and with jobs based on patronage more than merit, the police
in America were best known for corruption, brutality, and incompe-
tence. Wealthy citizens looked instead to private organizations like
the Pinkertons when they needed reliable security or knew of a crime
they wanted solved.

By the early twentieth century, police reform had become a cause
of the progressive movement, whose adherents saw corrupt cops as
just another consequence of cities being run by political machines.
There were two competing voices for reform. Progressive academics
and elites wanted not only to rid police departments of patronage
and corruption but to mandate a more paternalistic role for police.
They wanted cops to enforce good habits and morals among the
urban poor, especially immigrants.

The other voice for reform came from administrators within
the law enforcement community. They too wanted to free police

departments from the political machines, but they focused less on ideology and more on fighting crime. They wanted to give more freedom and autonomy to police chiefs, who were often held responsible for the actions of their officers but had very little power to actually change their behavior.

In the end, the administrators won the long-term debate by embracing the concept of *professionalism*. Through the adoption of best practices, they successfully transformed the job of police officer from a perk of patronage to a formal profession with its own standards, specialized knowledge, and higher personnel standards and entry requirements. To be a police officer was no longer just a job, it was a career. The first thirty or so years of the twentieth century saw the formation of professional societies like the Police Chiefs' Union; the sharing of knowledge and "police sciences" like fingerprinting; and the creation of specialized "squads" to tackle specific problems like alcohol, prostitution, and gambling.

The champion of the professionalism movement was August Vollmer, who served as chief of police in Berkeley, California, from 1905 to 1932. Vollmer pioneered the use of police radios, squad cars, bicycles, lie detector tests, and crime labs. As Walker writes, "The professionalism movement created the modern police organization: a centralized, authoritarian, bureaucracy focusing on crime control."[2]

But the morals-oriented progressives also had some victories, at least in the short term. They succeeded in passing anti-obscenity laws, and in some cities (most notably New York) they were able to put shutting down brothels, adult-book stores, and other sex-related businesses high on the list of police priorities. Their biggest victory was of course the Eighteenth Amendment, which banned the production, sale, and importation of alcohol.

The amendment was enforced by the Volstead Act, passed in 1919. The prohibition of alcohol has some clear parallels with the modern drug war. Homicides spiked during Prohibition, as did public corruption. The federal government had created a lucrative new black market. In legal markets, businesses compete by providing a better product, a less expensive product, or better customer service. In black markets, they compete by warring over turf. Disputes are settled with guns, not in courtrooms. As the bootleggers obtained bigger guns to war with one another, law enforcement agencies felt that they needed bigger guns to go after the criminals. In larger cities, the ensuing arms race produced heavily armed police forces.

Like today's drug prohibition, the Volstead Act was a failure. It almost certainly reduced the amount of alcohol the country consumed, but it came nowhere near stamping out booze entirely. The true believers responded by calling for tougher crackdowns and less coddling of bootleggers and drinkers. In his book *The Spirits of America,* journalist Eric Burns writes that some politicians and civic leaders suggested sending drunks and booze distributors to Siberia or the South Pole. Burns notes that David Blair, the federal commissioner of internal revenue at the time, "recommended that all American bootleggers be lined up in front of a firing squad and shot to death."[3] Foreshadowing the cries the country would hear from drug warriors sixty years later, Henry Ford wanted the military to enforce the laws against illicit substances. Anti-alcohol activist Clarence True Wilson demanded that the Harding administration call up the Marines, "arm them to the teeth and send them to the speakeasies. Give the people inside a few minutes to depart, and if they chose not to, open fire anyhow."[4]

But as hard as the temperance activists tried, they couldn't demonize and dehumanize drinkers the way drug warriors have since succeeded in denigrating drug offenders. One likely reason was that the Volstead Act didn't criminalize the possession or consumption of alcohol, only its production and sale. So the feds could raid speakeasies, but they couldn't raid a home based on a tip that someone had a cupboard full of gin—unless they suspected there was a distillery inside. Since simply ingesting alcohol was not a criminal act, it was more difficult for Prohibition's supporters to cast drinkers as villains. The country was also more federalist in the 1920s. Even after the Eighteenth Amendment passed, some states, cities, and counties simply refused to enforce it.

After the repeal of Prohibition in 1933, the professionalism model returned to police departments.

Although some of the aims of professionalism may have been noble, the story of early American policing is one of overcorrection. While the professionalism reformers were able to end the patronage system, in some cities they managed to insulate police departments from politics altogether, making it difficult for mayors and city councils to hold police officials accountable. At the level of individual cops, the use of squad cars and radios clearly brought a lot of benefits, but could also isolate police officers from the residents of the communities they patrolled. Cops out walking beats could chat with citizens, form relationships, and become a part of the community. Squad cars gave cops a faceless and intimidating presence. They tended not to get out of them except in the event of problems or confrontations. Police and citizens interacted only when police were ticketing or questioning someone, or when a citizen was reporting a crime. In poorer communities, that could bring about an increasingly antagonistic relationship between cops and the citizens on their beats.[5]

Perhaps no police chief better illustrated that double-edged sword of professionalism than William Parker in Los Angeles. Parker took over the LAPD in 1950 and imposed a rigid, hierarchical, militaristic bureaucracy. He took on corruption in the department—successfully—and stressed efficiency and crime fighting above all else. Parker had also worked in public relations for the military for a time, and he used that experience to sell his ideas about policing to the public. He helped create the show *Dragnet,* a virtual commercial for Parker-style police management—or at least an idealized form of it.[6]

But Parker also loathed community policing, the idea that cops should have a stake in the communities they served. He preferred to have a wall between cop and community. That sentiment probably stemmed from the goal of ridding the department of the sort of localized interests that existed in the patronage era. But completely walling off cops from their communities presented its own problems. Making cops indifferent to the areas they patrolled, instilling in them the notion that they were all that stood between order and anarchy—all of this could make police view the citizens in their districts as at best the *other,* and at worst, the enemy. Consequently, while Parker's management rid the LAPD of political patronage and corruption, and instilled some needed structure and standards, he seemed oblivious to growing animosity toward police in the city's black and Latino populations.

Parker's efforts at instilling professionalism provide a good segue into the age of militarization for a couple of reasons. For one, as we'll see, when the racial tension in LA finally blew up in the form of the Watts riots, it went a long way toward scaring middle America about crime, to the point where they were willing to embrace an all-out "war" on crime and drugs to clean up the cities.

But Parker also had a much more direct impact on militarization. Shortly after taking office, the chief made a young LAPD cop barely a year into the job his personal chauffeur, and eventually his protégé. That set the young cop's career on a fast track. By the time of the Watts riots in 1965, Parker's young protégé would take command of the city police department's response. The experience would scar him. The protégé would eventually become LA's police chief himself. And in large part because of his experience in Watts, he did more to bring about today's militarized American police force than any other single person. His name was Daryl Gates.

～

THERE ARE TWO FORMS OF POLICE MILITARIZATION: DIRECT and indirect. *Direct militarization* is the use of the standing military for domestic policing. *Indirect militarization* happens when police agencies and police officers take on more and more characteristics of an army. Most of this book will focus on the latter form of police militarization, which began in the United States in the late 1960s, then accelerated in the 1980s. But the two forms of militarization are related, and they have become increasingly intertwined over the last thirty years. So it's worth looking briefly at direct militarization in the twentieth century as well.

As discussed in the previous chapter, direct militarization has a longer history in the United States but has been more limited in scope. One reason may be that deploying military forces domestically usually requires a formal declaration by the president, which means such deployments have been limited to self-contained events. By the middle of the twentieth century, federal troops had been deployed in response to dozens of domestic disturbances, but the incidents were highly visible, and once the crisis abated the troops left the scene.

One of the more significant policies to move the country toward direct militarization was the Militia Act of 1903—sometimes called the National Guard Act. The antifederalists, remember, advocated that the country rely on state militias for national defense. That didn't work out, but the militias stayed around and were often called up by state governors to dispel less threatening uprisings.

But the militias were also sometimes called into war. In fact, the 1903 law was a response to widespread sentiment that the militias had performed poorly during the Spanish-American War. The new law took what remained of the state militias and converted them into what is today the National Guard. It also established an office in the Pentagon to oversee the Guard and appropriated funds to run the office and train Guard troops. Guard units would still report to their respective states and could still be called up by their governors when needed. But if called up by the president and federalized, they wouldn't be noticeably different from the military. One legacy of the National Guard Act was to make some state governors more likely to request military help from the president and thus more reliant on the use of the military to quell disruptions. Military leaders weren't keen on this trend. They knew from history that sending soldiers to dispel citizens was usually a bad idea, and sowed ill will toward the Army among the public.

The ensuing confrontations between the military and labor protesters and strikers, antiwar activists, and other demonstrators certainly had that effect. Worse, they also sowed a certain contempt for pro-testers among some in the military.[7] That sentiment, along with public anxiety about World War I and the Red Scare fears of communists and anarchists that followed, opened up a brief period in American history when military leaders seemed more willing to intervene in domestic life than ever before.

The most infamous incident came in 1932. In June of that year, forty thousand World War I veterans and their supporters descended on Washington, DC, to demand the bonus payment they had been promised for their service. They set up camps on the Anacostia Flats, a marshy area across the river from the US Capitol, and named their makeshift city "Hooverville" to mock the president. As the Bonus March began on July 28, 1932, there was an altercation in which police shot and killed two marching veterans. President Hoover responded by sending in the US Army. Two regiments and six tanks moved into the nation's capital, under the leadership of Gen. Douglas MacArthur and Maj. George S. Patton. Maj. Dwight Eisenhower went along as an aide to MacArthur. The protesters initially cheered the military, thinking the troops were there to support them. Those cheers quickly turned to screams when the troops charged the protesters with guns and tear gas.

When the protesters retreated back to Hooverville, Hoover ordered MacArthur to stand down. MacArthur defied the order and went after the protesters, razing the Hooverville shacks and chasing veterans, their families, and their supporters out of the makeshift town at the points of bayonets.[8] The sight of veterans being lied to and then bloodied by the same US Army in which they had served didn't sit well with the public. Angry condemnations rang out from newspapers, civil rights organizations, and veterans across the country.[9] The crackdown doomed Hoover's already dim prospects for reelection and turned what had been an ambivalent public firmly in support of the veterans.[10]

Later that year, Patton wrote a remarkable paper recounting the lessons he had learned from the Bonus March. Titled "Federal Troops in Domestic Disturbances," it revealed a startling contempt for free expression—and for civilians in general. The paper first assesses periods of unrest throughout history. Patton ridicules nations and empires that hesitated to use violence against citizen uprisings and praises those that did. "When the foolish and genial Louis XVI lost his head and the Seine ran crimson to the sea, the fault lay not with the people, but with the soldiers," Patton writes. "Yet less than ten years later, Napoleon with a 'whiff of grape shot' destroyed the mob and saved, only to usurp, the directorate." Patton attributes the success of the Bolshevik Revolution to "the hesitating and weak character of the Russian officers," which prevented them from properly slaughtering the Communists while they were merely protesters.

Most alarming are Patton's own suggestions and recommendations on how the military should handle domestic riots and uprisings. He calls the writ of habeas corpus "an item that rises to plague us" and recommends shooting captured rioters instead of turning them over to police to bring before "some misguided judge," who might release the rebellious citizen on a legal technicality. On establishing geographic bearings while breaking up a protest, Patton advises: "It may be desirable to fly over the city to become oriented. If fired upon while in the air, reply at once with small bombs and machine gun fire." Using all-caps for emphasis, he later writes, "When guarding buildings, mark a 'DEAD' line and announce clearly that those who cross it will be killed. Be sure to kill the first one who tries to cross it and to LEAVE HIM THERE to encourage the others."[11] Elsewhere he writes, "If it is necessary to use machine guns, aim at their feet. If you must fire, DO A GOOD JOB. A few casualties become martyrs; a large number becomes an object lesson."[12]

Patton and MacArthur rose through the ranks during the first Red Scare of 1919 to 1921, when the entire country crouched in a panicked fear of radicalism. This was the era of Woodrow Wilson's Sedition Act, the 1919 anarchist bombings, and the responding raids, arrests, and deportations of thousands by Attorney General A. Mitchell Palmer. Every violent labor clash heightened fears that America was on the brink of Bolshevism. Like a number of US political and civic leaders, many military leaders had soured on the notion of affording civil liberties to groups they believed were determined to overthrow the government. At a news conference after the Bonus March fiasco, for example, MacArthur showed no regret. He called the protesters a "mob" that was "animated by the essence of revolution." He said their aim was to take over the government and that "a reign of terror was being started" that, without military intervention, would have caused "insurgency and insurrection."[13]

It was not an uncommon sentiment in the military at the time. When the US Army made its *Basic Field Manual* available to the public for the first time in 1935, it included a section on strategies for handling domestic disturbances.[14] The recommendations were unsettling. The guide suggested firing *into* crowds instead of firing warning shots over their heads, and it included instructions on the use of chemical warfare, artillery, machine guns, mortars, grenades, tanks, and planes against American citizens.[15] Another military manual defined *democracy* as "a government of the masses. . . . Results in mobocracy . . . demagogism, license, agitation, discontent, anarchy." Newspaper editorials and political advocacy groups lashed out, arguing that the US Army had essentially published a how-to guide for waging war on its own people. The military responded, with some justification, that the manuals made no mention of when or under what circumstances these tactics—which were tactics of last resort—should be used in domestic disturbances.[16]

The backlash showed that there was still an ample reserve of public support for the broader principles behind the Third Amendment. The outrage grew loud enough that in early 1936, Army chief of staff general Malin Craig retracted the manual and ordered it removed from circulation. By 1941 much of the offending language had been either removed or replaced with instructions emphasizing the use of nonlethal force.[17] The military had overstepped, and when it was held to account, it retreated: the instructions were revised to strike a more appropriate tone, one more in line with its proper relationship with the American citizenry.

World War II put an end to concerns about Communists and anarchists. Protests died down, and with them the need to send troops to dispel those that got out of hand. But the period wasn't entirely calm. Racial tension mounted in some cities as black servicemen returned from the war to the same segregation, poverty, and limited opportunity they had experienced before they left. In Los Angeles, clashes between stationed Navy and Marine servicemen and the city's Latinos boiled over into the Zoot Suit Riots of 1943. Riots also broke out in Detroit, Chicago, and Harlem, but only the Detroit riots required federal intervention.

The first decade after the war was even quieter, as the economy boomed and veterans settled down with good jobs to start families. But things were about to change. Civil rights victories would inspire revolt in the South, and the counterculture and antiwar protesters were coming.

THE NEW ERA BEGAN IN LITTLE ROCK IN 1957. THE SUPREME Court's 1954 decision in *Brown v. Board of Education* animated civil rights groups and angered segregationists. When nine black students attempted to attend classes at Central High School on September 4, Gov. Orval Faubus sent Arkansas National Guard troops to prevent them from entering the building.

There had been a number of incidents leading up to Little Rock in which efforts to integrate public facilities had also been met with violence. Until Little Rock, President Dwight Eisenhower had opposed sending federal troops to force integration, and he initially resisted sending soldiers to Arkansas as well.[18] Instead, he first held a face-to-face meeting with Faubus, thinking he could convince the governor to stand down. Faubus responded by pulling the tr

oops entirely, allowing an angry mob to force the black students to withdraw from class on September 23.[19] Two days later, Eisenhower ordered troops from the 101st Airborne Division to escort the students to school. The soldiers were soon replaced by troops from the

Arkansas National Guard, which Eisenhower had federalized. Those units stayed until the end of the school year. Beginning the following year, federal courts supervised the Little Rock school system's compliance with *Brown v. Board of Education* until 2007.[20]

Eisenhower's initial reluctance to send troops to Little Rock is often seen as a stain on his record, perhaps justifiably so. But Eisenhower had ridden alongside MacArthur at the Bonus March. In fact, he had advised MacArthur that there was something unseemly about the military's highest-ranking officer leading a charge against a citizen protest. It's possible that Eisenhower was reluctant to send troops south in 1957 because of what he saw in 1932 and the resulting public backlash. Eisenhower eventually did send troops into Little Rock because, he said, federal law was being "flouted with impunity" and he feared that the South could slip into anarchy if something wasn't done. He waited until he felt that sending in troops was his only option. Though an argument could be made that he waited too long, his actions also kept with the protections built into the Insurrection Act.[21]

By the 1960s, the civil rights, counterculture, and antiwar movements would be in full swing, leading the government to call repeatedly on the National Guard and occasionally on US troops to keep order in urban areas. Still, the principle of keeping the US military out of law enforcement remained largely intact. Despite the best efforts of too many politicians, the public still tended to recoil at the idea of putting soldiers on city streets, even for a brief time, much less for day-to-day law enforcement.

That's the good news. The bad news fills most of the rest of this book. While as a nation we have mostly done a good job of keeping the military out of law enforcement, we've done a poor job, to borrow a bit of martial rhetoric, of guarding our flanks. The biggest threat to the Symbolic Third Amendment today comes from indirect militarization. Instead of allowing our soldiers to serve as cops, we're turning our cops into soldiers. It's a threat that the Founders didn't anticipate, that nearly all politicians support, and that much of the public either seems to support or just hasn't given much attention.

No one made a decision to militarize the police in America. The change has come slowly, the result of a generation of politicians and public officials fanning and exploiting public fears by declaring war on abstractions like crime, drug use, and terrorism. The resulting policies have made those war metaphors increasingly real.

# CHAPTER 4

# THE 1960S—FROM ROOT CAUSES TO BRUTE FORCE

Democracy means that if the doorbell rings in the early hours, it is likely to be the milkman.

—ATTRIBUTED TO WINSTON CHURCHILL

Early in the morning of March 25, 1955, narcotics agents in Washington, DC, arrested Clifford Reed on suspicion of distributing narcotics. Reed told a federal agent that he had purchased one hundred capsules of heroin from Arthur Shepherd, who was working for a drug dealer named William Miller. The agents recognized that they might be able to parlay a low-level arrest into a much larger bust.

Reed agreed to cooperate in a controlled drug buy, and at around 3:00 AM he and a federal agent posing as a buyer gave Shepherd $100 in marked bills to buy another one hundred heroin capsules. Shepherd then took a cab to the home of Miller, with the agents following. But the agent tracking Shepherd lost him when he exited the cab and entered Miller's building. Afterward, DC city police stopped the cab that Shepherd was in and found the heroin he had just purchased—but the federal agents had failed to observe the actual drug buy.

In an attempt to salvage the bust, the federal agents returned to Miller's apartment and knocked on the door.

Miller said, "Who's there?"

The agents responded, "Police."

Miller opened the door and asked what the police wanted. But before they answered, he shut the door in front of them. The police then ripped the chain off the door and entered the apartment. They found the $100 in marked bills, along with around one thousand heroin capsules. Miller and Bessie Byrd, who lived with him, were arrested and convicted on narcotics charges.

The police had never obtained a search warrant. Miller appealed his conviction, arguing that the entry into his home was illegal.[1] In 1958 the US Supreme Court agreed with him.

Justice William Brennan's opinion in *Miller v. California* was a spirited defense of the Castle Doctrine. "The requirement of prior notice of authority and purpose before forcing entry into a home is deeply rooted in our heritage," Brennan wrote. "[It] should not be given grudging application."[2]

Regrettably *Miller* was effectively the last stand in defense of the home as a place of sanctuary. In the coming years, the Court would uphold searches far more egregiously violative than the search performed on Miller's apartment.

The first blow came five years later, in *Ker v. California*. A sergeant with the Los Angeles County Sheriff's Department had purchased a pound of marijuana from a man named Terrhagen in the parking lot of a bowling alley. Terrhagen told the sergeant that his "connection" was Roland Murphy, who at that time was out of prison on bail pending charges for distributing marijuana. The police put Murphy under surveillance. The next day, in the parking lot of the same bowling alley, they saw Murphy park behind a new car with a single occupant. From one thousand feet away, at night, they saw Murphy get out of his car and converse with the driver of the new car. The officers couldn't see if anything exchanged hands between the two men. The police tried to follow the new car, but lost it when the driver made a U-turn. They checked the license plate with the state Department of Motor Vehicles and found that it belonged to George Douglas Ker. The police claimed that informants had told them in the past that Ker was known to sell marijuana.

The police then went to Ker's address and found the car in the parking lot of an apartment building. They secured a passkey from the building manager and, without a warrant, simply walked into Ker's apartment with no knock or announcement. Inside, they found a little over two pounds of marijuana. Ker and his wife were arrested.

The *Ker v. California* decision was complex. By an 8–1 vote, the Court concluded that the Fourth Amendment requirement that searches be reasonable applies to the states as well as the federal government, and that evidence obtained in unlawful searches is inadmissible. But the Court also found by a 5–4 split that the search of Ker's apartment was lawful.

Writing for the majority, Justice Tom Clark found that the police had probable cause to arrest Ker, to search his home without a warrant, and to enter his home without first knocking and announcing themselves. Clark wrote that there are common-law exceptions to the knock-and-announce rule known as an "exigent circumstances." One such exception is if police believe that a knock and announcement would result in the suspect destroying evidence. "In addition to the officers' belief that Ker was in possession of narcotics, which could be quickly and easily destroyed, Ker's furtive conduct in eluding them shortly before the arrest was ground for the belief that he might well have been expecting the police," Clark wrote. Clark cited additional exigent circumstances as well. Police need not announce themselves if doing so would jeopardize their safety, if they are in the midst of an emergency, or if knocking would be a futile gesture, such as during the hot pursuit of a fugitive.

Justice Brennan was in the minority in *Ker*, and his dissent bristled with indignation. He began with a thorough history of the Castle Doctrine, even quoting James Otis. He made the point that the writs of assistance that helped inspire the American Revolution were less odious, in at least a couple of ways, than the search of George Ker: such writs could only be served in daylight hours, and they required a knock and announcement before entry.[3] Brennan also questioned Clark's assumption that the common law provided exceptions to the knock-and-announce requirement. "I have found no English decision which clearly recognizes any exception to the requirement that the police first give notice of their authority and purpose before forcibly entering a home," he wrote. The only exception Brennan found that was possibly in contradiction of the Castle Doctrine's intent was one allowing police to enter unannounced if they believe someone inside is in imminent danger of bodily harm.[4]

It is generally accepted today even by critics of forced-entry police raids that officers should be allowed to enter a building or residence unannounced if the suspect is believed to be armed and likely to resist arrest if given the opportunity. After *Ker v. California,* it would soon be accepted by most policymakers that police should also be exempted from the knock-and-announce requirement if they believe that a knock and announcement would allow the suspect to destroy evidence. The courts have since held that police may enter at the scene of a search without announcing even with a regular warrant if they hear or see activity inside the residence that merely suggests someone is destroying evidence.

Brennan thoroughly rebuts all of those assumptions in his dissent. Though the principles he defends are backed by centuries of Anglo-American common law, his *Ker* opinion was one of the last times someone as prominent as a Supreme Court justice would articulate them. His first point is that to allow an exception for the possible destruction of evidence or out of fear for the safety of police officers is to "do obvious violence to the presumption of innocence." In fact, Brennan writes, allowing for those exceptions violates the presumption of innocence twice: first by assuming the suspect is guilty of the crime for which he is suspected, and second by assuming he will attempt to escape, violently confront the police, or attempt to destroy evidence if the police are required to announce themselves.

Second, Brennan points out that to allow police to enter a home because they hear "loud noises" or "running" is to allow them to forcibly enter a home without announcement based on conduct that not only isn't criminal, but is ambiguous. Since the police wouldn't be permitted to prosecute someone for obstruction of justice based only on such sounds, so Brennan objected to the idea that the same sounds could be enough to allow police to enter a home without announcing.

But even accepting an exception that allows the police to enter unannounced if they hear or see activity suggesting that the suspect is destroying evidence, there was no evidence of such activity in the *Ker* trial record. The exception is based only on the officers' testimony that narcotics suspects often attempt to destroy evidence when they realize the police are at the door. This, Brennan notes, was enough to create an exception to the knock-and-announce rule for any narcotics search—indeed, any search related to a crime involving evidence that can be easily and quickly destroyed. "The recognition of exceptions to great principles always creates, of course, the hazard that the exceptions will devour the rule," Brennan writes.

Brennan also touches on a number of practical problems with the repercussions of the ruling. He points out the problem of mistaken identity in criminal investigations, warning that "innocent citizens should not suffer the shock, fright or embarrassment attendant upon an unannounced police intrusion." That was a glimpse of the hundreds of "wrong-door" raids that would go down in the years to come. Brennan also points out the explicit danger that unannounced entries pose to *police,* writing that one common-law reason for the announcement requirement was "to protect the arresting officers from being shot as trespassers." Here too he would be proven correct in the coming decades: dozens of police officers would be shot, maimed, and killed during unannounced raids—often by citizens who could plausibly claim that they thought they were firing at criminal intruders.

Those tragedies transpired because in the coming decades the Court would adopt Clark's reading of the exceptions into statutes that didn't mention them, and eventually into the Fourth Amendment itself. The exceptions would be expanded to the point where, perversely, the Court's interpretation of the Fourth Amendment in regard to the knock-and-announce rule would put more emphasis on preserving evidence and protecting law enforcement than on the Castle Doctrine and protecting the home from violence.

Interestingly, it's far from clear that a majority of the justices in *Ker* actually backed Clark's interpretation of the Castle Doctrine. Although the vote was 5–4 in favor of upholding Ker's conviction, Justice John Harlan II voted with the majority only in the outcome. Harlan didn't agree with incorporating the Fourth Amendment's reasonableness requirement to the states. Instead, he thought the California law under which the Kers were convicted should be evaluated under the Due Process Clause of the Fourteenth Amendment, which he described as "more flexible" than the Fourth Amendment standard applied to federal law enforcement. Harlan didn't expressly write that the *Ker* search violated the Fourth Amendment. If that was indeed what he believed, then a majority of justices believed that, had the *Ker* search been carried out by federal agents, it would have been unconstitutional. And a majority had already indicated that the Fourth Amendment should be incorporated to the states. That would seem to suggest that there's at least a chance that the decision in *Ker*, while bad for the Kers, actually narrowly *upheld* the Castle Doctrine protections in *Miller*.

But that isn't the way the decision was interpreted. When lawmakers, academics, and the media discussed and debated the knock-and-announce rule over the next twenty years, *Ker* would be referenced as accepted law, even by civil liberties advocates.

A year after *Ker*, in 1964, New York governor Nelson Rockefeller pushed two laws that would give police in the state sweeping new powers: the "no-knock" bill and the "stop-and-frisk" bill. (Nine years later he would push through some of the most draconian antidrug laws in the country, collectively known as the Rockefeller Drug Laws.)

The no-knock bill allowed police to get a special search warrant authorizing them to ignore the knock-and-announce requirement, so long as a state judge agreed that one of the exigent circumstances that Justice Clark laid out in *Ker* was present. The stop-and-frisk bill allowed police to stop, detain, and pat down anyone in a public space whom they found suspicious. The no-knock bill passed with overwhelming support from the New York Assembly and State Senate. The stop-and-frisk bill passed by narrower margins.[5]

There was at least some opposition. Civil rights groups like the NAACP and the Congress of Racial Equality (CORE) held rallies in protest of both bills.[6] The Association of the Bar of the City of New York protested the stop-and-frisk bill but supported the no-knock searches. The New York State Bar Association opposed both and argued that the no-knock bill "flies in the face of a long-established policy that 'a man's home is his castle,' and for the state to invade it, it must strictly comply with safeguards which have been found to be important over the years." Rockefeller and other supporters emphasized that officers still had to get a warrant. A judge had to be first "satisfied by proof under oath that notice will endanger the safety of the officer or another person, or that the evidence may be readily destroyed." The bar association answered that "experience has shown that the supposed safeguard of a special oath to the magistrate issuing the warrant would speedily become a boiler-plate routine."[7] That too was a concern that Brennan had expressed in *Ker*. As we'll see, both Brennan and the New York State Bar Association would be proven correct.

In the short term, Rockefeller's no-knock law had surprisingly little impact. The *New York Times* later reported, in 1970, that while the law "score[d] points with the law-abiding public," it had almost no impact on how warrants were served in the state. The paper reported that in a "recent" year since the law had been passed (the precise year wasn't specified), "the New York State Police used the law only 12 times in 1,847 narcotics cases."[8] There were probably more no-knock raids than that. A cop could still decide at the scene that exigent circumstances had materialized after he had obtained a regular search warrant. (It would then be up to a court to decide if that assessment had been correct.)

Nevertheless, there was little indication that the police even wanted the law, and the fact that they used it so little after it was passed suggests that it was more of a political statement than an essential law enforcement tool. Police departments in New York didn't even appear to find this tool *useful*, much less essential. Perhaps they found the tactic unnecessarily invasive and aggressive. Perhaps they feared that barreling into a home unannounced was more likely to invite violent retaliation than prevent it. But the law didn't come with any accompanying public or political cries for New York cops to get more aggressive and confrontational with suspected drug offenders.

Richard Bartlett, one of the bill's sponsors in the legislature, was serving on a state penal law commission at the time. The commission was charged with interviewing law enforcement officials, criminologists, and other experts, then recommending laws to improve the state's criminal justice system. Bartlett says that the no-knock law was not the product of his commission's research. "It was just something one of these groups—I think it was the district attorneys' association—came up with that picked up political momentum. But it wasn't anything we studied on the commission."[9]

If the police seldom used the no-knock law after it passed, that may have been because crime wasn't yet the demagogic issue it would soon be. Rockefeller's push for the laws didn't come with the war imagery and apocalyptic rhetoric that would soon emanate from Nixon and the cadre of crime-fighting Republicans elected to Congress several years later.

The most lasting effect of the Rockefeller's push in 1964 was to legitimize no-knock raids. Prior to the law, police only occasionally raided a residence without an announcement. Sometimes they got away with it, sometimes they didn't. According to the *Oxford English Dictionary*, the first public appearance of the phrase "no-knock raid" came in 1964. That's also the first time the phrase appears in the archive of the *New York Times*. Rockefeller made the no-knock raid a policy, and he gave it a name. No longer merely a decision that cops sometimes make in the heat of the moment, it was now a tactic and an issue. It was something that everyone was either for or against.

~

IN THE SUMMER OF 1965, LOS ANGELES ENDURED A SUFFOCATING heat wave. Few in the city had air conditioning, particularly in the poorer neighborhoods, so the heat collected in homes during the day, sending residents outside in the evenings in search of a breeze.

California Highway Patrol officer Lee Minikus was headed north on Avalon Boulevard in the Watts neighborhood on his motorcycle on an August evening that summer when a motorist pulled up beside him to indicate that the 1955 Buick Special ahead had been weaving, and the driver might be intoxicated. Minikus pulled over the driver, twenty-one-year-old Marquette Frye. After discovering that Frye had no driver's license, Minikus asked him to perform a sobriety test.[10] Frye put on a bit of shtick, and the two men exchanged jokes and banter. Amused passersby stopped and began to accumulate.

Minikus called to have Frye's car impounded, and Frye appeared ready to comply with his imminent arrest. But when Frye's mother, Rena Frye, arrived at the scene, the tenor of the arrest changed. Frye's mother excoriated him in front of the growing crowd. Frye grew embarrassed, then angry. When Minikus tried to put him into the car, he resisted. When another officer who had arrived swung to hit Frye in the arm with his baton, Frye ducked, and it struck him in the eye. Ronald Frye, Marquette Frye's brother, then punched Minikus in the kidney and Rena Frye jumped on his back. More Los Angeles police officers arrived. After more scuffling, all three members of the Frye family were arrested. The crowd turned angry. As the police put the Fryes into the backs of squad cars, a member of the crowd allegedly spit on one of the police officers. She too was arrested. According to the police, she too resisted. That only further angered the crowd. As they drove away, Marquette Frye would later say, a friend of his who had joined the crowd shouted to him, "Don't worry, we're going to burn this mother down."

Watts burned for six days. The riots were different from the unrest that had broken out on the East Coast in the previous year. For one thing, while Watts could be a rough neighborhood and had some poor areas, it wasn't the sort of cramped, crushingly poor ghettos found on the East Coast. Though Watts itself was quite small (about one square mile at the time), the riots spread well beyond its boundaries, eventually covering forty-six square miles. And where previous riots had tended to erupt and then persist in fairly concentrated areas, the Watts rioters were disbursed, random, and disorganized. Once Watts exploded on the night of August 11, 1965, the next five nights were a series of quick flashes and slow burns. Violence would die down in parts of the city, only to flare back up in others. Snipers took positions in elevated windows, then tried to pick off cops, firemen, and pedestrians. Looting and arson were rampant. Yet unlike many previous racial riots, no US military troops were sent to Watts. Instead, on the third night, the state dispatched 13,500 California National Guard troops, who remained under the command of the Los Angeles Police Department (LAPD) for the duration of the rioting.[11]

Frye's arrest was, of course, only the precipitating incident. The riots were the culmination of years of animosity between black Angelenos and the LAPD administration of Chief William Parker. Black rioters took aim mostly at white cops, motorists, and firemen. Looting was directed mostly at white-owned businesses. Parker didn't help the situation when he compared the rioters to "monkeys in a zoo."[12] By the time they finally died down, the Watts riots ranked among the most destructive in American history. The rioters caused $40 million in losses, damaged or destroyed one thousand buildings, and left more than one thousand injured and thirty-four dead. At least four thousand people were arrested.

In a couple of ways, the Watts riots were the first major incident to nudge the United States toward more militaristic policing. First, Watts made middle America begin to fear crime as never before. Much of white, middle-class America spent five nights watching their TVs as black people looted and burned their own neighborhoods. To them, Watts and the riots in Baltimore, Newark, Washington, and Detroit in the following years were signs of a rising criminal class that was increasingly out of control. The political clout of what Nixon would a few years later call "the Silent Majority" would influence a generation of crime policy geared toward giving police more power, more authority, and permission to use more force.

But Watts also had a more direct consequence. The LAPD's point man during the riots was thirty-nine-year-old inspector Daryl Gates, who had been ascending the ranks of the LAPD like a Gemini pilot. The riots left Gates feeling that police training and tactics at the time were inadequate to address the sort of threat posed by the snipers, rioting, and violence he witnessed in Watts. "We had no idea how to deal with this," Gates writes in his autobiography. "We were constantly ducking bottles, rocks, knives, and Molotov cocktails. . . . Guns were pointed out of second-story windows, random shots fired. . . . It was random chaos, in small disparate patches. We did not know how to handle guerrilla warfare. Rather than a single mob, we had people attacking from all directions."[13]

At the time, the US military's foe in Vietnam was using real guerrilla warfare. So Gates thought to ask the military for guidance. There he found not only the tactics and training he thought could help put down the next wave of rioting, but also the inklings of what would become his most enduring legacy.

Gates would create a phenomenon that over the course of his career would reach virtually every city in America. It would change the face, the mind-set, and the culture of US policing from the late 1960s on, through today, and probably into the foreseeable future.

He started America's first SWAT team.

---

IN SEPTEMBER 1953, PRESIDENT DWIGHT EISENHOWER nominated Earl Warren to be chief justice of the Supreme Court. He'd later call it one of his greatest mistakes. Warren was a former district attorney, attorney general, and three-term governor of

California. He was also the federal official who oversaw the internment of Japanese Americans in California during World War II. He seemed an unlikely candidate to build a consensus on the Court to protect the rights of the accused—which probably made his critics all the angrier when he did.

The first major criminal justice decision from the Warren Court was *Mapp v. Ohio* in 1961. Police in Cleveland suspected that Dollree Mapp had some evidence hidden in her house related to a bombing and a gambling ring. When she refused to let them in, they showed a fake warrant, forced their way inside, and searched her home. They didn't find the evidence they were looking for, but they did find some illegal pornography. She was arrested, charged, and convicted. The police never did produce a search warrant. The Court ruled that the Fourth Amendment's protection from unreasonable search and seizures applies to the states through the Fourteenth Amendment. And under the 1914 case *Weeks v. United States,* evidence seized in an illegal search could not be used at trial. Police in every jurisdiction in the country were now obligated to uphold the Fourth Amendment.[14]

The next year the Court found in *Robinson v. California* that incarcerating someone merely for being addicted to drugs is a violation of the Eighth Amendment.[15] Two big cases followed in 1963. In *Gideon v. Wainwright* the Court ruled that states are obligated to pay for an attorney for indigent defendants,[16] and in *Brady v. Maryland* it ruled that prosecutors must turn over exculpatory or mitigating evidence to defendants when the evidence is material to guilt or to the defendant's sentence.[17]

In 1964 the Warren Court ruled that suspects have the right to an attorney, not just at trial, but during police interrogations as well.[18] The famous *Miranda* decision came in 1966, which held that police must notify suspects of their Fifth Amendment rights against self-incrimination, and to be represented by an attorney.[19] The decision was widely derided by conservatives. It wasn't particularly popular with the general public either. It quickly became a rallying cry for the law-and-order crowd, who were appalled at the notion that the police could be required to tell suspects that they weren't obligated to answer their questions.

The Warren Court's final controversial decision, at least from the law-and-order side, was *Katz v. United States* in 1967.[20] In that case, the Court expanded the Fourth Amendment's protections from "unreasonable search and seizure" to the broader standard of "a reasonable expectation of privacy." In practical terms, the Fourth Amendment would no longer be limited to physical intrusions. If law enforcement officials wanted to tap a phone, for example, they would need to get a search warrant.

Critics of the Warren Court blamed its decisions at least in part for the rise in crime that began in the mid-1960s. William F. Buckley called *Miranda* a "venture in abstractionist imperialism" and noted that "already the reports are coming in from the police commissioners who are, not so quietly, despairing."[21] Conservative columnist James Kilpatrick wrote that the Warren Court was "often pleased to turn the Constitution into wax."[22] And it wasn't just conservative intellectuals. The *Philadelphia Inquirer* wrote after *Miranda* that "it would be a pity, at a time of increased lawlessness, if more attention is given to the rights of lawbreakers than the rights of the public to have effective police protection." The Columbia, South Carolina, newspaper *The State* opined that the Court "wrapped its flowing robes around all prisoners so as to virtually immunize them" from police interrogations. The *Richmond Times-Dispatch* was blunter still, calling the Court "an ally of the criminal elements in America."[23]

Ironically, the Warren Court's last controversial criminal justice decision actually expanded police authority. *Terry v. Ohio* was also arguably the decision that would have the most impact on the criminal justice system. In 1968 the Court ruled that police officers can stop, detain, and frisk someone based on no more than "reasonable suspicion" that the person is engaged in criminal activity or about to commit a crime. The vote was 8–1. In the coming years, more conservative Supreme Court lineups would expand the window that the Warren Court created in *Terry*. "Stop and frisk" would become a widely used, highly controversial, often abused police tactic.[24]

The Warren Court's more controversial decisions are still contentiously debated today. In his book *Breaking Rank,* former Seattle police chief Norm Stamper calls the rulings "the ones that most often piss off the cops."[25] Current Supreme Court justices Antonin Scalia and Clarence Thomas continue to express doubts about both *Miranda* and the Exclusionary Rule, which holds that evidence obtained through illegal searches and interrogations can't be used against a defendant at trial. Current chief justice John Roberts argued against both for much of his career, and legal pundits have speculated that the Court may continue to water down or even overturn one or both during his tenure.[26]

But ultimately, Eisenhower's appointment may have served the law-and-order right better than he could have known before his death in 1969. Although the Warren Court's legacy unquestionably granted new protections to criminal suspects, it also gave conservative politicians a villain to rail against—and run against. The Court's controversial decisions spurred a generation-long anticrime backlash that countered its decisions with policies that gave police more power, more discretion, and more authority to use more force.

⌐

EARLY IN THE MORNING OF AUGUST 11, 1966, CHARLES Whitman—an Eagle Scout, an ex-Marine, and a former altar boy—went to his mother's apartment and shot her in the back of the head. He then returned to his own apartment and stabbed his wife to death. He left a note in which he explained that because he loved the two women, he had no choice but to kill them. He wanted to spare them the embarrassment of what was to come.[27]

Whitman had been experiencing changes in his behavior for months. He had seen a university psychiatrist, and during a single two-hour session confessed that he was having violent impulses with increasing frequency, and felt less and less able to suppress them. Dr. Maurice Dean Heatly described in his notes a man who was "oozing with hostility." Whitman relayed a fantasy about "going up on the tower with a deer rifle and start shooting people."

After killing his wife and mother, Whitman did exactly that. He packed a footlocker with sandwiches, gasoline, three rifles, a sawed-off shotgun, two handguns, water, and enough ammunition for a day at the shooting range. At around 11:00 AM, Whitman rolled the footlocker into an elevator in the clock tower building at the University of Texas at Austin. Posing as a maintenance man, he took the elevator to the twenty-seventh floor, just below the clock. There he met fifty-one-year-old receptionist Edna Townsley—and killed her by repeatedly striking her with the butt of a rifle. Whitman hid Townsley's body as two visitors came down from the tower, then barricaded the exit. He killed two more tourists he found ascending the stairs.

Whitman returned to the top of the clock tower and, at about ten minutes before noon, opened fire on the people below. He shot indiscriminately, but with terrifying precision. A practiced and trained sniper, he fired just one bullet at each victim. As the victims fell, bystanders rushed out to help them. Whitman shot at them too. When ambulances began to arrive, Whitman shot at the drivers. As word got out that there was a shooter in the tower, some peered through windows at the scene unfolding, apparently feeling safe within the walls of a building. He shot them too. By the time Whitman was shot himself, he had killed thirteen people and wounded more than thirty, all from a position 230 feet from the ground. One victim, a basketball coach standing in the entrance to a barbershop, was five hundred yards away. Whitman's killing spree lasted more than ninety minutes.

Austin police didn't have guns that could reach the top of the tower. Some went home to get hunting rifles. Remarkably, a number of students and residents came out with rifles too. At least one witness said that the return fire limited Whitman's options and may have prevented more casualties. For more than an hour and a half, Whitman indiscriminately picked off innocent people while the police were helpless to respond. His guns were bigger than theirs. And he'd positioned himself in a spot they couldn't easily access.

Whitman was finally stopped when three police officers and a citizen named Allen Crum worked around his barricade and confronted him on the observation platform. Houston McCoy, a twenty-six-year-old Austin police officer, shot Whitman first, with a Winchester twelve-gauge shotgun. Officer Ramiro Martinez then emptied his revolver into the killer. Whitman was dead.[28] In one of the notes he left behind, Whitman asked that his brain be studied to explain the onset of his violent urges. Doctors found an aggressive brain tumor growing in Whitman's hypothalamus. The tumor was compressing an area of the brain in the hypothalamus known as the amygdala, which regulates primal emotions like fear and anger.[29]

Between Whitman's massacre and the epidemic of urban riots, police leaders across the country started to consider whether they were prepared to respond if such incidents happened in their own cities, towns, and counties. The Austin Police Department clearly wasn't prepared, and the incident there created an appetite for precisely the sort of police unit that Daryl Gates was cooking up in Los Angeles. According to author and twenty-five-year police veteran Robert Snow, after Austin "the country's police chiefs knew they couldn't always depend on luck. They needed a unit that could be called in at a moment's notice and plans that could be carried out immediately."[30] In the magazine *The Tactical Edge*—a publication marketed to SWAT teams—Lt. Sid Heal of the LA County Sheriff's Department writes that the Whitman shootings "marked the birth date of the modern police SWAT concept. Since that day, almost every police department in the United States has formed a special response team to handle similar situations."[31]

The riots in Watts and other urban areas may have instilled in middle America fears of a rising black criminal class, but there was still some sense of safety in the suburbs. Whitman's rampage on a college campus popped that bubble. His victims were college students, administrators, and instructors. The bodies dropping in Austin could have been anyone's kids. Whitman himself was a crew-cut, good-looking ex-Marine. He was married. He played the piano. The shootings made the cover of all the major news magazines. *Life* ran a photo essay that was as heart-wrenching as it was terrifying. And all of this came as the country was still reeling from Richard Speck's trial for torturing, raping, and murdering eight nurses at South Chicago Community Hospital a month earlier. The criminal threat no longer seemed to be limited to the inner cities. The victims were no longer urban toughs fighting among themselves. Both the Associated Press and United Press International called Whitman's mass murder the second biggest story of 1966, behind only the Vietnam War.

Crime had grabbed America by the lapels.

THERE WERE A COUPLE OTHER INCIDENTS THAT CONTRIBUTED to Daryl Gates's SWAT vision. At about the same time as the Watts riots, labor strife was heating up the grape farms in Kern County, California. The first major strike began in September 1965, about a month after Watts, when the county's mostly Filipino farmworkers were joined by labor activist Cesar Chavez and the group that would become the United Farm Workers. Chavez set up shop in Delano, making the small town in the north of Kern County ground zero for the farmworker labor movement.[32]

The Delano Grape Strike lasted five years. The involvement of Chavez and the National Farmworkers Association put the protests in the headlines, sometimes even on state and national television. Given the tumultuous history of labor strikes in the United States, the Delano police department looked for measures to keep the strikes from turning violent. The department turned to specialization. Individual Delano officers were given specific training in specialties like crowd control, sniper skills, specialized weapons, riot response, and surveillance.[33] The strike and picketing in Delano never turned violent, though the reason was more likely Chavez's emphasis on pacifism than the sniping skills of Delano cops. Nevertheless, Delano's strategy and its apparent success caught the attention of senior police officials 150 miles down the road in Los Angeles.

The second incident came about a month after Watts, when LAPD officer Ron Mueller took a late-afternoon call about a domestic incident on Surry Street in northeast Los Angeles. When Mueller ascended a set of steps and knocked on the door, thirty-eight-year-old Jack Ray Hoxsie opened the door and immediately shot him. As Mueller attempted to crawl away, another officer, K. A. Shipp, pulled up. Hoxsie stepped out of the doorway and, with a .30-caliber Winchester, took off part of Shipp's ear. As ambulances arrived, a citizen named Billy Richards attempted to help the medical personnel move Mueller onto a gurney. Hoxsie shot him too. Eventually, more than fifty police officers showed up, and just about all of them were exchanging gunfire with Hoxsie. Gates ordered the house tear-gassed, but as he writes in his autobiography, "by then there were so many holes in the house that the tear gas began spewing out faster than it was going in." Finally, two officers kicked down Hoxsie's front door and entered. The gunman was lying wounded in a rear hallway with a rifle and revolver by his side. Officer R. D. Johnson shot him once in the chest, then arrested him. "The incident alarmed me," Gates writes in his book. "Later, as I analyzed how we had responded, I realized again, as I had during Watts, that we were going to have to devise another method for dealing with snipers or barricaded criminals other than our usual indiscriminate shooting."[34]

After the Surry Street shootout, Gates and a small group of LAPD officials began informally consulting with Marines stationed at the Naval Armory in Chavez Ravine. The group included Jeff Rogers, who would later lead the country's first SWAT team, and Sgt. John Nelson. Often credited along with Gates with inventing the SWAT idea, Nelson became a self-taught expert in guerrilla warfare. The informal project wasn't sanctioned by the LAPD. In fact, when Gates first broached the idea of an elite police team for incidents like Watts and Surry Street, he was rebuffed. The Parker administration had little interest. But Gates, Nelson, and Rogers kept at it. They scoured the department for its best sharpshooters and put them on the shooting range for more training during off hours. They also brought in military personnel to teach strategies for handling snipers.[35]

At an awards banquet held in July 1966, Los Angeles police chief William Parker died of an aneurysm shortly after accepting an honor from a group for military veterans. New chief Thomas Reddin would serve only until May 1969, but his short tenure had a lasting impact on the career of Daryl Gates and the future of SWAT.

Shortly after Reddin took over, the LAPD faced a public crisis after officers clashed with antiwar protesters (and bystanders) in Century City. President Lyndon Johnson had been scheduled to give a public address, so the clashes—in which police were seen clubbing protesters and onlookers, and ramming them with motorcycles—received national attention.[36] In response, Reddin created a new unit called Tactical Operations Planning. The unit's mission was to plan for and respond to big events such as riots, protests, and visits from dignitaries.[37] Reddin put the new unit in the city's Metropolitan Division, an elite, roving unit of officers given broad authority to "suppress criminal activity."[38] The Metro Division's propensity for controversy had earned it the nickname "the Shake, Rattle, & Roll Boys." Their charge from Reddin: "Roust anything strange that moves on the streets." The new unit expanded Metro from 55 to 220 officers.[39] Reddin put Gates in charge.

Gates's first task was to respond to a rash of robberies on the city's buses. Needing personnel, Gates asked other divisions across the city to send him officers. According to Gates's autobiography, "Most of the divisions sent me the least desirable people they had."[40] But the new crew put an end to the bus robberies, earning itself, and Gates, some added credibility with Reddin. Defying the organizational structure used in the rest of the department, Gates explains in his autobiography that he broke his new unit down into sixteen "military-type" squads. He then combined the squads into two "platoons," adding yet more war terminology to the environment around him and the officers he worked with.

Gates was eventually able to get the sixty marksmen he had been working with across the department reassigned to Metro. Now staffed with top-notch, highly skilled cops, Gates mixed the marksmen with his best men from Tactical Operations Planning. He then broke the unit down into five-man teams: a leader, a marksman, an observer, a scout, and a rear guard. Two teams together made up a squad. They were called D-Platoon (somewhat confusingly, since there were only three platoons at the time).[41]

But Gates wasn't fond of "D-Platoon." He had a different name in mind. From his autobiography:

> One day, with a big smile on my face, I popped in to tell my deputy chief, Ed Davis, that I thought up an acronym for my special new unit. He was still, as we all were, glued to the classic concepts of policing, which discourage the formation of military-type units. But he realized some changes would have to be made.
>
> "It's SWAT," I said.
>
> "Oh, that's pretty good. What's it stand for?"
>
> "Special Weapons Attack Teams."
>
> Davis blinked at me. "No."
>
> There was no way, he said dismissively, he would ever use the word "attack." I went out, crestfallen, but a moment later I was back. "Special Weapons and Tactics," I said. "Okay?"
>
> "No problem. That's fine," Davis said. And that was how SWAT was born.[42]

Gates still had some work ahead of him to win over his superiors. "That SWAT operates like a quasi-militaristic operation offended some of the brass," he writes.[43] So D-Platoon trained in secret on some city-owned farmland in the San Fernando Valley. They also began working directly with Marine units at Camp Pendleton in San Diego County, with some help from Universal Studios. The movie company let the abecedarian recruits hone their special forces skills on the replica storefronts, buildings, and houses on its back lot in Burbank.[44] Within a couple of years, Gates's SWAT team would forge its place in history during a televised shootout that made national news. But Gates clearly never got over the lack of support during the project's early years. Of course, that reticence stemmed from a healthy appreciation for the Symbolic Third Amendment that

Gates clearly didn't share—or at least didn't think was threatened by cops who trained with and operated like soldiers.

> Despite [the new unit's] record and reputation, officials balked at police using fully automatic weapons. The standard cry was, "Hey, the LAPD is supposed to be a civil police force. Their job is to *relate* to the community, not put on combat boots and *assault* the community."
>
> For years we tried to assure everyone that, yes, we are a civil police force. The people are the police, and the police are the people. And we hold to that.
>
> Though at times, *assault* is not a dirty word.[45]

For the types of situations Gates had in mind—the Watts riots, the Surry Street barricade, the Texas clock tower massacre—he was right. *Assault* wasn't a dirty word. It was an appropriately swift, forceful response to defuse a violent situation.

As the domestic strife dragged on, other police departments began to see things the way Gates did. In March 1968, the Associated Press conducted a national survey and found that, "in city after city across America, the police are stockpiling armored vehicles, helicopters, and high-powered rifles . . . they are preparing for summer and the riots they hope will not occur." In Gates's Los Angeles, the AP reported, police watched a demonstration in which a twenty-ton armored personnel carrier crushed a barricade of abandoned cars. Tampa police chief James G. Littleton told the news agency that his department had "taken off the kid gloves." He had just purchased 162 shotguns, 150 bayonets, 5 sniper rifles, 25 carbines and M-1 rifles, and 200 gas masks. Florida state attorney Paul Antineri told the AP that he had instructed police officers to "shoot to kill" if they spotted anyone committing or about to commit a felony. A spokesman for the New Jersey State Police told the AP, "We're following through on the military concept in attacking this problem."[46]

This was an understandable response to the growing sense that American cities were spilling over with crime, violence, and rioting. And indeed, starting the month after the AP article was published,

1968 would unfold as one of the most turbulent years of the twentieth century. But when the riots, strife, and unrest finally died down, when the threat of chaos and lawlessness eventually grew remote, the weapons, heavy-duty vehicles, and militaristic culture stuck around. Gates's original intent for the SWAT concept may have been appropriate, but as SWAT teams swelled in number, mission, and frequency of use over the next forty years, Gates not only never spoke out against the trend but took pride in it, and actively encouraged it.

BY THE MID-1960S, THE PIECES WERE FALLING INTO PLACE TO make disorder a national political issue. The crime rate was climbing. High-profile incidents like Whitman's mass shooting had shocked the country. Riots had white America terrified of the cities. All that needed to happen was for a savvy politician to run with the issue.

In an April 1965 Gallup poll, more than half the country cited race relations as their number-one concern, the first time in eight months that a domestic issue topped the poll.[47] Columnists and media outlets on the right were taking shots at the Supreme Court's "criminal-friendly" decisions, as well as President Johnson's failure to address crime with adequately tough measures.[48] Johnson also watched the polls closely (the New York Times wrote in 1966 that "the President appears to retain an almost psychological need for public approval"[49]) and was well aware that his approval ratings had started to sag—a long, slow decline starting in the spring of 1965.[50]

Johnson attempted to co-opt some of his critics' momentum by adopting the crime issue himself. He first turned to a Washington, DC, perennial: the blue ribbon commission. He announced the President's Commission on Law Enforcement and Administration of Justice. His attorney general, Nicholas Katzenbach, would chair it. Its laughably lofty mission: to draw up "the blueprints that we need for effective action to banish crime."[51] The resulting report, The Challenge of Crime in a Free Society, included over two hundred recommendations to fight crime, from establishing a national phone number for emergencies—the precursor to 911—to decriminalizing drug abuse and public drunkenness. But Johnson's critics seized on the more platitudinous and abstract recommendations: the commission asserted that ending poverty would be the single most important crime-fighting initiative and recommended minority outreach bureaus within major police departments, the establishment of multiple crime and justice research institutions, family planning assistance, recommitting to desegregation, funding for drug abuse treatment, and gun control.[52]

To Johnson's critics, this was just more leftist, mealymouthed academese. There was lots of government spending (the commission didn't bother to estimate a price tag for its recommendations), plenty of lofty talk about social uplift, and hand-wringing about the influence on crime of environmental factors—all of which rather conveniently aligned with Johnson's other domestic policies. But there was precious little in the way of taking it hard to the bad guys. For a war on crime, there wasn't nearly enough *fighting*.

Johnson responded by making the federal government more proactive in fighting the drug trade. He created the first major federal agency specifically tasked with enforcing the federal drug laws. The Bureau of Narcotics and Dangerous Drugs (BNDD), which would later become the Drug Enforcement Administration (DEA), combined smaller agencies in the Treasury and the Health, Education, and Welfare Departments into one office that would operate within the Department of Justice. Johnson also expanded the Office of Law Enforcement Assistance into the Law Enforcement Assistance Administration (LEAA),[53] the first federal agency created to stream federal funding, equipment, and technology directly to state and local law enforcement agencies.[54] The United States had long taken a federalist approach to law enforcement. Except for offenses involving the mail, bank robbers, and crossing those state borders, the power to make crime policy had been reserved to the states. Johnson's successors would quickly discover that introducing a funding spigot like LEAA, then threatening to pull it away, was an effective way to persuade local police agencies to adopt their preferred policies.

Johnson's efforts didn't quell his critics. His attorney general, Ramsey Clark, was widely seen on the right as the walking embodiment of the root-causes, soft-on-criminals approach to criminal justice policy. In an interview for this book, Donald Santarelli, a young but influential aide to Nixon's 1968 campaign, said that Nixon would often tell Republican supporters that his administration would "*have* an attorney general," a bit of signaling that to law-and-order conservatives needed no further explanation.[55]

Before the 1968 presidential campaign kicked off, the thirty-one-year-old Santarelli had been the minority counsel on the House Judiciary Committee. In the summer of 1967, he and other House Republicans decided to put together a crime bill that would address (a critic might say *exploit*) public reaction to the rioting and high-profile shootings. "There was an increasing fear of crime," Santarelli says. "And at the same time you had the rise of the civil rights movement, the riots, the Black Panthers, and this increase in drug use. I think the public started to pick up on the idea that these things were linked, because they were all happening simultaneously." The Republicans put together a bill with a host of new anticrime, antidrug measures, including a provision to authorize wiretapping and another that weakened the *Miranda* warning. "Law enforcement is just like any other interest group," Santarelli says. "They're always after greater power. There was a sense that they needed to capitalize on these historic events. And I think there was a real willingness on the part of the public to give them whatever powers they sought."[56]

There were two other controversial provisions in the original 1968 crime bill. The first would have dramatically changed the bail system—by effectively doing away with it completely. The burden would have been shifted to defendants to show that they didn't pose a threat to the public or a flight risk. If they could do so, they'd be released. If they couldn't, they'd be held until trial. Both supporters and detractors dubbed it "preventive detention," a term that served both sides. For conservatives, it sounded like the sort of rigorous, lock-'em-up policy that would play well in the election. For liberals, "preventive detention" was the sort of term used in a police state.

Santarelli stands by the initiative to this day and insists that it was portrayed unfairly. "This was about equity," he insists. "The risk of flight and the seriousness of the crime are factors in who gets held before trial today, but the primary factor is money. If you can't make bail, you stay in jail. That's incredibly unfair. We wanted to take wealth out of the equation."[57]

The other provision was the no-knock raid. Despite the fact that the 1964 Rockefeller law was barely used in New York, other states had since passed similar measures. The law-and-order right had run with the concept as a litmus-test tough-on-crime measure. "The exigent circumstances exceptions to [knock-and-announce] had been pretty well established by that time," Santarelli says. "I didn't intend for [no-knock] to be a political weapon, but it became one."

The Republican crime bill passed relatively easily in the summer of 1968, with little opposition from Democrats. The no-knock raid and preventive detention measures didn't make the bill's final draft, but both ideas would return, and soon.

⌐

AT 6:01 PM ON APRIL 4, 1968, JUST AS MARTIN LUTHER KING JR. stepped out onto a balcony at the Lorraine Motel in Memphis, Tennessee, James Earl Ray fired a single .30-caliber bullet from the Remington rifle he'd perched in the bathroom window of a boardinghouse across the street. King was dead. Within hours, more than one hundred American cities broke out in rioting.

The riots reinforced in white middle-class America the sense that American cities had become zones of lawlessness. And again, it was black people causing all the violence.

In fact, it came at a time when much of that same white, middle-class America began to sense that its values and traditions were under attack from all sides. In his drug war history *Smoke and Mirrors,* journalist Dan Baum points out that black homicide arrests doubled between 1960 and 1967. At the same time, heroin deaths and overdoses were also on the rise. The hippie, antiwar, and counterculture movements were in full swing. All of this also coincided with the rise of the civil rights movement. Nixon's Silent Majority began to see a link between drugs, crime, the counterculture, and race.

The movements had some common elements, but there was little evidence that drug use was causing the spike in violent crime. For example, while it was true that heroin junkies were more likely to commit crimes like burglary and theft to support their habit, it wasn't true that drug use was causing the surge in violent crime. A 1971 study from the Bureau of Narcotics and Dangerous Drugs— the government's antidrug enforcement arm itself—found that illicit drug users were 35 percent *less* likely to be arrested and charged with homicide than non-drug-users, and less than half as likely to be charged with aggravated assault.[58] The rise in pot-smoking among the counterculture was even less threatening, and less of a contributor to the crime rate.

But candidate Nixon and his politically savvy advisers seized on the growing assumption in middle America that all of these things were connected. When Robert Kennedy was assassinated in April 1968, the party used his death to push its crime bill, even though his assassination would prove to have been politically motivated, and Kennedy himself had been opposed to the more controversial parts of the law.[59]

Months later, at the 1968 Democratic National Convention (DNC), police in Chicago would instigate a riot, then indiscriminately beat liberal protesters. Some of the beatings were aired live by the networks covering the convention. Connecticut senator Abraham Ribicoff was nominating George McGovern to be the party's candidate during one clash between police and protesters. Ribicoff strayed from the script in his nominating speech to proclaim, "With George McGovern we wouldn't have Gestapo tactics on the streets of Chicago! With George McGovern, we wouldn't have a National Guard!" Chicago mayor Richard Daley, who had called up more than twenty thousand police and National Guard troops for the convention, didn't do much to distance himself from the Nazi smear. Lip readers later alleged he shouted up from the convention floor,

"Fuck you, you Jew son of a bitch! You lousy motherfucker! Go home!"[60]

Nixon's "ignored Americans" weren't the least bit troubled by what they saw from Daley and the police. According to a Gallup poll taken a few weeks later, 56 percent of the country supported the crackdown, and just 31 percent were opposed.[61] Polls would also show Nixon surging into a comfortable lead over the eventual Democratic nominee, Hubert Humphrey.[62]

In 1969 *Newsweek* commissioned its own Gallup poll for a cover story headlined, "The Troubled American: A Special Report on the White Majority." Its findings: 85 percent of whites thought that black militants were getting off too easily; 65 percent thought that unemployed blacks were more likely to get government aid than unemployed whites; and 66 percent thought that the police needed to be given more power. Nearly half thought that the country had moved backward over the last ten years, and nearly 60 percent thought that things were only going to get worse.[63]

Crime, race, hippies, antiwar protesters—Nixon strategists needed a way to draw all of the concerns of his Silent Majority together. As Baum explains, they found their answer with drugs.

> Nixon looked at "his people" and found them quaking with rage and fear: not at Vietnam, but at the . . . unholy amalgam of stoned hippies, braless women, homicidal Negroes, larcenous junkies, and treasonous priests. Nixon's genius was in hammering these images together into a rhetorical sword. People steal, burn, and use drugs not because of "root causes" . . . but because they are bad people. They should be punished, not coddled. . . .
>
> Another poll taken just weeks before the election showed the power of television: while a majority of Americans feared the country was headed toward "anarchy," just 28 percent felt that crime had gone up in their own communities.[64] Most Americans felt perfectly safe walking in their own neighborhoods, but assumed most of their fellow citizens didn't feel the same way. As he slogged through the

primaries in early 1968, Nixon was well aware of this. People don't have to experience crime firsthand to feel threatened by it, he wrote to his old friend and mentor, Dwight Eisenhower. "I have found great audience response to this [law-and-order] theme in all parts of the country, including areas like New Hampshire where there is virtually no race problem and relatively little crime."[65]

Shortly before the 1968 election, Nixon called illicit drugs "the modern curse of the youth, just like the plagues and epidemics of former years. And they are decimating a generation of Americans."[66] He wouldn't explicitly "declare war" on drugs for another few years. But his rhetoric was already slipping into combat fatigues.

THE LAW-AND-ORDER CAMPAIGN WORKED. NIXON WON THE 1968 election by a comfortable margin in the electoral college. (And when you factor in the votes for George Wallace, Humphrey lost the popular vote by a wide margin.) The Republicans also picked up five seats in the Senate and five in the House. In four years, crime had become the most important issue in the country.

The new administration wasted little time. The White House point man on crime would be Egil Krogh, a twenty-nine-year-old family friend of Nixon aide John Ehrlichman. Though just out of law school, Krogh would make crime policy for the entire country. In December 1968—before Nixon had yet been inaugurated—Krogh and Ehrlichman had a strategy session with Nebraska senator Roman Hruska, the ranking minority member on the Judiciary Committee. Hruska had an idea to assemble a crime bill just for the District of Columbia. Congress had jurisdiction over the city, making it an ideal spot to test out new ideas without worrying about encroaching on the traditional federalist approach to crime. DC at the time wasn't any more dangerous than other large cities. But less than a year had gone by since the riots after the death of Martin Luther King, and there was at least the perception that the city was uniquely dangerous, especially for muggings and robberies. At the top of Hruska's wish list for DC were the preventive detention and no-knock raid provisions that had been cut out of the crime bill passed six months earlier.[67]

Krogh took Hruska's idea to John Mitchell, Nixon's nominee for attorney general. Mitchell had run Nixon's law-and-order-themed campaign, so it was natural for the president-elect to select his good friend to run the Justice Department. A former semipro hockey player, Mitchell had commanded a PT boat during World War II. (Coincidentally, his lieutenant was John F. Kennedy.) After the war he became a successful, self-made municipal bond lawyer. Mitchell was exposed to the power of law-and-order issues while serving as a bond counsel for the Rockefeller administration in New York. He and Nixon became friends when their law firms merged in 1967. John Mitchell would be the public face of Nixon's crime policy.[68]

The new administration held two big strategy sessions on crime, one just before Nixon took office and another shortly after his inauguration. Also attending these meetings, in addition to Krogh, were Santarelli (soon to be an aide to Mitchell), GOP chief house counsel John Dean, Ehrlichman, and future senator Daniel Patrick Moynihan, then a domestic policy adviser. Nixon himself sat in on the initial meeting.[69] The first order of business was to figure out which crimes to target. Mitchell made clear in both meetings that the crimes that seemed to most worry the public—armed robbery and burglary—weren't the purview of the federal government. Moreover, there was no political benefit to tackling those crimes. Even if the administration's policies worked, local law enforcement would get most of the credit.[70]

They decided that the high-profile target of the new administration's promised anticrime effort would be drug control. Drug use, they thought, was the common denominator among the groups— low-income blacks, the counterculture, and the antiwar movement—against whom Nixon had unified "ignored America." Because the drug trade crossed both state and international borders, there were also no federalism issues. So it was decided that the new Nixon administration would push for massive budget increases for agencies like BNDD and LEAA. They would ask for a thousand new police officers for DC—an idea that, oddly enough, came from *Washington Post* publisher Katharine Graham in a personal plea to Ehrlichman. And of course, they'd demand no-knock and preventive detention for federal drug agents, just as they would for police in Washington, DC.[71]

The Nixonites mulled a number of other constitutionally dubious drug war proposals in addition to the preventive detention and no-knock proposals. They wanted to authorize the use of "loose search warrants." These would have allowed police to apply for a warrant for contraband, then search multiple properties to find it. The idea came precipitously close to a writ of assistance, but without the restrictions on nighttime service and knock-and-announce. Combined with the no-knock provision, it would have essentially authorized police to kick down the doors of entire neighborhoods with a single warrant.[72] Loose warrants didn't make the final crime bill, but the idea was really only about ten years ahead of its time. Starting in the 1980s, police would conduct raids of entire city blocks, housing complexes, and neighborhoods. The Nixon administration also wanted to strip away attorney-client privilege, as well as the privilege afforded to conversations with priests and doctors, and to expand wiretapping authority. They even came up with an early precursor to California's eventual "three strikes and you're out" law.[73]

No one had any idea if these policies would work, but in a way it didn't matter. The strategy was as much about symbolism and making the right enemies as it was about effectiveness.[74] There was much discussion over whether the policies sounded harsh enough or sounded too harsh. There was at least some discussion over whether they would actually work. But there was very little internal discussion about whether the policies were constitutional, whether they were susceptible to abuse, whether they would have unintended consequences, or what impact they might have on the communities they'd be enforced against.

On July 14, 1969, Nixon gave his first major address to Congress to outline his antidrug program. He declared drugs a "national threat." He set the tone for a much more aggressive, confrontational federal drug fight. He described the "inhumanity" of drug pushers, laying groundwork for the sort of dehumanizing rhetoric that would be used for years to come to reduce drug users and drug dealers to an enemy to be destroyed. "Society has few judgments too severe, few penalties too harsh for the men who make their livelihood in the narcotics traffic," he said. To that end, he proposed massive budget increases for BNDD and asked for money to hire scores of new federal narcotics officers. He called for the creation of "special forces" within the agency that "will have the capacity to reave quickly into any area in which intelligence indicates major criminal enterprises are engaged in the narcotics traffic." Borrowing more military terminology, he asked that Congress make funding for the units available soon so that they could "fully deploy" by 1971.[75]

Since Nixon had campaigned and staked his reelection hopes on reducing crime, and since crime policy and police procedures were primarily local issues, he had a strong interest in seeing that the states adopted his plan. That was one reason for expanding the LEAA. Local police agencies were likely to be more receptive when they got free stuff in exchange for their cooperation. He also came up with a piece of model legislation based on his federal bills—no-knock, preventive detention, wiretapping, and so on—that state legislatures could pass to show they were allies in the national fight. He told Congress that he had instructed his Justice Department to host a number of drug policy conferences across the country, where federal and local narcotics officers could exchange information and tactics.[76] Nixon also addressed the demand side with a number of rehabilitation and treatment programs. (The next year the administration would even fund a methadone program in Washington, DC, run by addiction specialist Robert DuPont.[77])

In a few areas, Nixon could move immediately, without waiting for money or authorization from Congress. One such area was border enforcement. On September 21, 1969, the Nixon administration launched Operation Intercept, under the direction of

G. Gordon Liddy. Every vehicle crossing into the United States was to be thoroughly searched by US Customs agents. The agents were told to search each car for a *minimum* of three minutes, including trunks, glove compartments, bags, and underneath seats.

For all practical purposes, the operation shut down the border. The resulting lines slowed trade to a crawl. It was an extreme, hostile policy, the sort normally implemented by countries in times of war. It proved so unpopular on both sides of the border that Nixon rolled it back two weeks after it began. But the effort sent a signal to federal, state, and local law enforcement, in Customs and elsewhere, that marijuana was as serious a threat to US interests as spies, revolutionary infiltrators, and enemy combatants—the sorts of threats that would normally move the government to such an extreme crackdown at the border.

ON OCTOBER 3, 1969, SEVEN NARCOTICS AGENTS STORMED apartments B and D at 8031 Comstock Avenue in Whittier, California, in a predawn, no-knock raid. Two officers were from the California State Bureau of Narcotics, four were from the Los Angeles County Sheriff's Department, and the last was Det. Sgt. Frank Sweeney, a police officer from the tiny nearby town of Vernon. In apartment B, fifty-year-old Florence Mehan was asleep with her twelve-year-old daughter Susan.

"I saw three men," Mehan told the *Los Angeles Times*. "One of them grabbed me by the arm. I screamed and I ran out. I thought they were going to attack me." Susan said, "They just grabbed Mommy and said they had a search warrant to look for marijuana."

The officers had raided the wrong apartment. Their search warrant was for apartments B and D at 8033 Comstock Avenue. Those apartments were both on the second floor.

Mehan's other daughter, Linda, who was twenty-three, lived on the second floor—though not in either of the targeted apartments—along with her husband, twenty-two-year-old Heyward Dyer and their twenty-two-month-old son Francis. Heyward Dyer awoke to the screaming and commotion from the mistaken raid in his mother-in-law's apartment, went downstairs to investigate, and was confronted by several police officer guns aimed in his direction.

The narcotics team eventually realized that they had raided the wrong apartment. They immediately left to raid apartments B and D on the second floor. In the meantime, Linda Dyer—seven months pregnant at the time—was also awakened by the noise. She went downstairs with Francis to check on her mother and sister. At some point she handed the baby to her husband.

As the police raided apartment B, Det. Sgt. Sweeney somehow mistakenly fired his .223-caliber rifle into the floor. The bullet ripped through the floor, then through the ceiling of the apartment below, where Heyward Dyer was standing, holding his son. The bullet pierced Dyer's skull, killing him instantly. As his father fell, the infant Francis Dyer went crashing to the floor.

From press accounts, the police never made clear why a police officer from Vernon went along for a raid in Whittier, and why he was carrying a rifle when neither the California Bureau of Narcotics—which directed the raid—nor the Los Angeles County Sheriff's Department allowed it. Police agencies were (and still are) also supposed to notify any agency with overlapping jurisdiction during such raids, in part because local departments—especially in small towns—tend to have local knowledge. One example would have been knowing that this apartment complex had an odd way of assigning addresses. No such notification ever happened. The police did arrest one man in apartment D for possession of "two red capsules" and "two white capsules" believed to be illegal narcotics, along with 150 marijuana seeds.

By 1969, California was one of twenty-five states that had a no-knock law. Of course, Los Angeles County was also where *Ker v. California* had originated, the case in which the US Supreme Court six years earlier had (mostly) given its stamp of approval to the "destroying evidence" exception to the knock-and-announce rule, and

William Brennan had warned of the consequences of such a dangerous precedent.

Though Nixon wouldn't officially "declare war" on drugs until
1972, the modern drug war effectively began with his inauguration
in 1969. It seems likely, then, that Heyward Dyer was the modern
drug war's first innocent fatality. There would be more. Many, many
more.[78]

Five years of unrest and increasingly militarized
police actions culminated with America's very first SWAT raid in
the final months of the 1960s. The December 1969 raid on the Los
Angeles headquarters of the Black Panthers was also about as high-
profile a debut for Daryl Gates's pet project as he could possibly
have imagined. Practically, logistically, and tactically, the raid was
an utter disaster. But in terms of public relations, it was an enormous success.

The Black Panther Party hit its peak in 1969. Started in Oakland
just three years earlier by Huey Newton and Bobby Seale, the activist group's mix of Marxism, militance, and black nationalism
quickly found a following in the counterculture. Panthers often espoused their revolutionary rhetoric and illustrated their "by any
means necessary" motto by toting loaded rifles and handguns during public protests and demonstrations. It wasn't just talk. In a little
over three years, nine police officers and ten Panthers had died in
police-Panther confrontations across the country. By 1969, the
group was ten thousand strong and had become a bright, blinking
flash point on the radar of police in every city in which it had established a presence. FBI director J. Edgar Hoover had made the Black
Panthers a top priority and, naturally, had publicly "declared war"
on them.[79]

There are conflicting accounts of the events that led up to the
Panther SWAT raid. According to Gates's autobiography, sometime
before the final confrontation, LAPD captain Ted Morton received a
complaint from a woman about noise coming from a loudspeaker in

a building occupied by the Panthers. When Morton went in to investigate, he was greeted with several guns and warned to leave immediately. Morton returned to the police station and wrote up a report, and within a few days Gates and the LAPD brass began drawing up plans to raid the building on charges of assaulting a police officer with a deadly weapon.[80]

Based on interviews with several Black Panthers who were in the building the morning of the raid, as well as with LAPD SWAT officer Patrick McKinley, journalist Matthew Fleischer offers a different narrative:

> On November 28, 1969, more than 250 police officers surrounded the Los Angeles [Black Panther] headquarters during a community meeting, sealing the facility off in what Panthers now call the "test run."
>
> On December 4, Fred Hampton, deputy chairman of the Illinois chapter of the Black Panthers, was shot to death at point-blank range while he was sleeping, during a raid by the Chicago Police Department. The incident drew international outrage. Back in LA, there wasn't a Panther alive who didn't think a similar raid by the LAPD was coming their way.
>
> They were right. As it turns out, the night of the test run, police claimed to have seen three Panthers—Paul Redd, "Duck" Smith and Geronimo Pratt—in possession of illegal firearms. The LAPD secured an arrest warrant for the three, as well as a search warrant for the 41st and Central headquarters and two known Panther hideouts.[81]

By all accounts, the raid began at about 5:30 AM on December 6, 1969. The Black Panther building was well armed and well fortified. Gates and his SWAT team had put together blueprints of the building from intelligence they had collected from informants. Unfortunately, the blueprints critically misplaced a massive pile of dirt that the Panthers had built while digging out escape tunnels. The police had the dirt pile off in a corner. It was actually directly behind the back door, the same door through which the assault team was to make its surprise entry.[82]

When they tried to open the back door, the dirt pile prevented them from entering. They'd have to go through the front door. As they did, a helicopter swarmed overhead, and other officers began scaling the sides of the building. By plan, Gates's SWAT team was supposed to have made entry and secured the inside of the building by this point. Instead, a Panther lookout on the roof screamed, "They're here!" to his confederates inside. By the time the SWAT team breached the front door, the Panthers were ready and greeted them with a storm of bullets. Three officers went down.

Even worse, the SWAT team had entered an alcove with no escape except through the door they had just entered. Fortunately, the gunfire had started immediately, which let the officers know their cover had been blown. They dragged out their fallen colleagues and retreated. As Fleischer puts it, "If the Panthers had held their fire for a few moments more, the entire SWAT team would have made it into the alcove—and been shot to pieces."[83]

Over the next three hours, LA police and the Black Panthers exchanged over five thousand rounds in a crowded city setting. The entire neighborhood was evacuated, and the surrounding streets were shut down just before the morning rush hour. Los Angeles police chief Ed Davis was in Mexico at the time, making Gates the acting chief. After a couple hours of gunfire, Gates and his SWAT officers came up with a new idea—they would use a grenade launcher on the building. Gates contacted the Marines at Camp Pendleton. He was told that, at the very least, he'd need permission from the Department of Defense. He'd probably also need it from the president. Gates writes in his book, "I called Mayor Sam Yorty next and asked if he would make the call to Washington. My words seemed unreal. Anytime you even *talk* about using military equipment in a civil action, it's very serious business. You're bridging an enormous gap."[84]

Yorty agreed, and within an hour the Department of Defense gave Gates permission to use a grenade launcher on the Panthers building. It's a remarkable anecdote, not because Gates sought permission to use the weapon, or even because the Pentagon gave it to him. Given the circumstances, it may not even have been all that unreasonable a request. The story is remarkable because of the procedures, the caution, and the trepidation that went into procuring the grenade launcher. About twenty years later, the Pentagon would begin giving away millions of pieces of military equipment to police departments across the country *for everyday use*—including plenty of grenade launchers.

The accounts of the raid again differ about how it ended, but after hours of gunfire the Panthers finally waved a white flag to surrender. In the end, four Black Panthers and four LAPD officers were wounded. Somehow, no one was killed. Six Panthers were arrested, booked, charged, and jailed. If the objective of the SWAT team was to serve the warrants and make the arrests with no fatalities, then the raid was a success. But of course it was far from that. The SWAT officer McKinley summed up the raid to Fleischer. "Oh God, we were lucky. . . . I'm extremely proud of what we did that day. We got our targets and no one died. But oh God, were we lucky."

Gates's surprise tactics had one unexpectedly deleterious effect: they gave the Panthers a plausible argument of self-defense. The Panthers awoke to men with guns breaking down their door and firing bullets into the walls. Paramilitary police tactics were new at the time, and the mixed-race jury apparently found them pretty alarming. All six Panthers were acquitted of the most serious charges, including conspiracy to murder police officers. That again is a stark illustration of how much standards and expectations have changed since then. It's nearly unthinkable that a self-defense claim under similar circumstances would be successful today. Indeed, several subjects of these sorts of raids have made that argument, and they almost always have failed.

Though it was only by sheer luck that the bumbling raid wasn't a bloody disaster, and the tactics themselves ultimately contributed to acquittals of the very dangerous suspects the entire operation was designed to put in prison, the country's maiden high-profile SWAT raid was also a massive, uncompromising show of force against an organization that was widely feared and despised by politicians, law enforcement officials, and most Americans whose politics fell outside the far left. Activists and editorial boards raged, but the Black Panther raid was a public relations triumph. Within five years the Panthers would splinter, fizzle, and for the most part evaporate. SWAT would grow, spread to other cities, and become a pop culture phenomenon.

By the time Gates died in 2010, the institution he started had spread to nearly every city in the country, to most federal agencies, to most medium-sized towns, and even to small and tiny towns. The wisdom of limiting SWAT *assaults* to genuine emergencies was long gone. Across the country, the tactics Gates had conceived to stop snipers and rioters—people already committing violent crimes—had come to be used primarily to serve warrants on people suspected of nonviolent crimes.

## The Numbers

- ○ Percentage of Americans who thought the Supreme Court was too soft on criminals in 1965: 48 percent
  - . . . in 1968: 63 percent
  - . . . in 1969: 75 percent
- ○ Percentage of Americans in 1968 who disapproved of inter-racial marriage: 75 percent
- ○ Percentage of Americans who supported the Chicago police after the 1968 Democratic National Convention riots: 56 percent
  - . . . of Nixon supporters: 63 percent
  - . . . of Wallace supporters: 71 percent
  - . . . of Humphrey supporters: 44 percent
- ○ Percentage of Americans who supported the death penalty in 1966: 42 percent
- ○ Percentage who supported the death penalty in 1969: 51 percent
- ○ Percentage of parents who in 1969 said they would turn in their own kid for using drugs: 42 percent[85]

# CHAPTER 5

# THE 1970S—
# PINCH AND RETREAT

Drug people are the very vermin of humanity. They are dangerous. Occasionally we must adopt their dress and tactics.

—MYLES AMBROSE, HEAD OF NIXON'S OFFICE OF
DRUG ABUSE AND LAW ENFORCEMENT

S am Ervin was an unlikely civil liberties hero. Known for his bushy, high-arching eyebrows, the avuncular senator from Morgantown, North Carolina, was the prototype backwoods bumpkin who passed himself off as "just a simple country lawyer"—right before unleashing the devastating argument that crushed his opponents and won the day. In a thick, jowly drawl, he'd dispense folksy anecdotes, Bible verses, and righteous indignation—and in the next breath drop quotes from Shakespeare, Aristotle, Kipling, or Thomas Wolfe.

Born in 1896, Ervin was a decorated World War I veteran who earned a Silver Star, two Purple Hearts, and a Distinguished Service Cross during his commission as an infantryman in France. When he returned home, the whip-smart veteran quickly ascended the ranks of North Carolina politics. When Democratic senator Clyde Hoey died in 1954, Ervin was sitting on the North Carolina Supreme Court. Gov. William Umstead asked him to fill the vacant seat, and he accepted. Sam Ervin would remain a US senator for twenty years.

What many would come to see as contradictions or surprises in Ervin as a public figure were in fact his way of balancing a collection of values drawn from his faith, his Constitution, his heritage, the mores and traditions of his region, and his scholarship. Though a deeply religious man, for example, Ervin successfully led an effort in the North Carolina legislature to defeat a law that would have prohibited teaching evolution in the state's schools. Ervin found the law embarrassing.[1]

Though Ervin was a Democrat, he and Nixon were often on the same side of the 1960s culture wars. Ervin largely supported Nixon's efforts in Vietnam. He also opposed *Brown v. Board of Education* (though he'd later change his mind) and the 1964 Civil Rights Act. He was a signatory of "The Southern Manifesto," which accused the US Supreme Court of overstepping its authority on integration and breeching state sovereignty. Ervin even reversed course on integration at about the time the Nixon administration made desegregating public schools a Justice Department priority.

Indeed, by the time Nixon ran for president in 1968, Ervin appeared to be precisely the sort of God-and-country, law-and-order Southern Democrat Nixon was hoping to court with his campaign. The two also shared a contempt for the Warren Court. In the 1957 case *Mallory v. United States,* the Court ruled as inadmissible the confession of a subject who had been interrogated for seven hours before he was notified of his rights or given a preliminary hearing.[2] In response, Ervin took to the floor of the US Senate to defend the integrity of law enforcement officers. Ervin complained that the courts had perversely decided that criminals need protection from law enforcement more than society needs protection from criminals.[3] It was a speech that Nixon himself might have given on the campaign trail ten years later.

The Nixonites, then, would be struck dumb when Sam Ervin emerged in the early 1970s not only as Nixon's most formidable Watergate nemesis on Capitol Hill, but also as the angriest, loudest, and most powerful critic of Nixon's crime policy. Even more surprising, he would beat them. Thanks to Ervin, the Castle Doctrine stayed afloat for about another decade before being submerged by the 1980s war on drugs.

ATTORNEY GENERAL JOHN MITCHELL AND HIS SUBORDINATES began their big legislative crime push in the summer of 1969. They found plenty of willing help on Capitol Hill. In both chambers, Nixon administration allies and crime hawks introduced a flurry of bills containing sweeping new provisions. When Stanford law professor and criminologist Herbert Packer asked the Justice Department just how many crime bills there were, one official replied in a letter, "I leave it to you to make the count." In an October 1970 essay for the *New York Review of Books,* he tried. Packer counted twelve bills that came directly from the White House plan and eight more introduced independently that the White House supported. Packer counted at least four Senate and five House committees claiming jurisdiction over some version of a crime bill—and that wasn't counting the appropriations committee in each chamber.[4] And because the two bodies wouldn't pass identical versions of any bill, there would also be a slew of conference committees to sort out all the differences. It seems unlikely that all of this overlapping legislative activity was planned, but it had the benefit of making any organized opposition to the bills rather difficult.

The no-knock raid came up in two bills. The first was the Omnibus Crime Control Act, which authorized no-knock raids, preventive detention, expanded wiretapping, night raids, and other powers in federal investigations. That bill was also split up. The portion including preventive detention hit the House Judiciary Committee in October 1969, while another version headed to the same committee in the Senate, chaired by Ervin.

When the bill hit Ervin's desk, he couldn't believe what he saw. The senator fired an early shot across the president's bow when he called the preventive detention proposals "facile and desperate" and "tyrannical" and added that the very idea of eliminating bail "repudiates our traditional concept of liberty."[5]

The Nixon administration was gobsmacked. Ervin had supported the Republicans' election-year crime package just a year earlier. He was an influential voice in the Senate, especially given his position on the Judiciary Committee. They were counting on his support, and he had just lashed out at the centerpiece of their crime strategy.

The White House regrouped and decided instead to put its initial push behind the crime bill aimed specifically at Washington, DC. No-knock raids were in that bill, as was preventive detention. The bill also eliminated probation and suspended sentences for some crimes, imposed mandatory life sentences for others, and broadly expanded wiretapping authority. The bill allowed police to conduct on-the-spot urinalysis tests during drug raids, allowed them to seize anything they found in a raid (they had been limited to seizing only the items they had listed in the search warrant affidavit), and removed the restriction requiring police to be "certain" that the evidence they were looking for would be found before they could raid a home at night.[6]

Since Nixon and Mitchell were most interested in quickly accumulating legislative victories on the law-and-order issues that had won them election, the major advantage of the DC bill was that, at least early in the process, it could be routed around the unexpected obstacle of Sam Ervin and his Judiciary Committee. Instead, the Washington bill began at the House and Senate committees that oversaw the District of Columbia. In the House, that committee was chaired by Rep. John McMillan, a good-ol'-boy conservative Southern Democrat who had once sent a truckload of watermelons to the black mayor of Washington, DC. He'd be an ally.

In the Senate, the DC oversight committee was chaired by Sen. Joe Tydings, a Democrat from Maryland. Though Tydings was one of the more liberal members of the Senate, he faced a tough reelection in 1970. Maryland was home to a large, white, wealthy batch of DC suburbs, and many of those suburbanites worked in Washington. If they hadn't yet been mugged themselves, they probably knew someone who had; at the very least they had read the press accounts of the city's crime problem. The tougher on crime Joe Tydings could look, the better his prospects for reelection.

Tydings's committee reported out a crime package of more than three hundred pages. It included court reorganization, no-knock raids and preventive detention, allowing raiding cops to administer on-the-spot urine tests, tougher sentencing guidelines, and an absurd proposal to let prosecutors appeal acquittals.

When Ervin learned of those provisions, he demanded they be removed or he'd mount an effort to kill the bill entirely. Most of them were taken out, or at least they were narrowed. Preventive detention was removed entirely and reintroduced as a separate bill. The no-knock provision stayed in but was slightly altered to require police to show a "substantial probability" that evidence would be destroyed if they were to make themselves known before forcing entry. The change was mostly cosmetic, but at least appeared to make the no-knock warrant more difficult to obtain.[7]

In December 1969, the package easily passed the full Senate. Perhaps because the idea still wasn't largely understood outside members of the Nixon administration and a few state legislators and Rockefeller administration officials in New York, there was little objection to the no-knock provision, even from Ervin. But the minor change to the bill's language would later become very important.[8]

On the House side, Representative McMillan was working on a DC bill more in line with what Nixon and Mitchell wanted than what had come out of the Senate. McMillan's hearings on the House bill lasted less than an hour, and only members of the Nixon administration were permitted to testify. When Ervin heard about the House bill, which included everything he'd fought in the Senate bill and worse, he was outraged. He called it "a garbage pail of some of the most repressive, near-sighted, intolerant, unfair, and vindictive" policies he had ever encountered in politics. The bill swept through McMillan's committee and was approved by the full House. It would be up to a conference committee to decide which vision of crime control would be imposed on Washington, DC.

The Senate reconvened after the New Year for a blitz of important votes. In the chaos of the great crime bill orgy of 1970, many senators would vote on bills that took predatory swipes at civil liberties protections dating back centuries—with little knowledge of what was actually in them. Senate majority leader Mike Mansfield—the highest-ranking member of the Senate after the vice president—was typical. Mansfield said at one point that he was so overwhelmed, he'd just given up on trying to figure out if some of the laws he was voting on were constitutional. He said he'd just vote for them all and let the courts sort it out.[9]

The omnibus narcotics bill in particular represented a massive shift of power to the Justice Department. The bill was sponsored by Democratic senator Thomas J. Dodd of Connecticut, father of the future US senator Christopher Dodd. For Nixon, Dodd was a useful confederate. That he was a Democrat from New England helped with building coalitions. He was also a former federal prosecutor who had participated in the Nazi trials at Nuremberg, and he had chaired subcommittee hearings on LSD that led to federal prohibition of the drug. Although Dodd had plenty of anticrime credibility, the senator's personal commitment to law and order was less than impeccable: three years earlier, he had been censured by the Senate for diverting campaign funds to his personal bank account.[10] But that was all the more reason for him to cast his lot with the crime hawks. Also up for reelection in 1970, Dodd needed an issue to make his constituents forget about his personal peccadilloes. He probably thought he'd found it with crime and drugs.

Since the Harrison Narcotics Act of 1913, the federal government's authority to regulate illicit drugs had mostly been limited to the power to tax them. But in 1969 the Supreme Court struck down the Marijuana Tax Act in a case involving the counterculture icon Timothy Leary. Dodd's bill took a new strategy. Instead of trying to prohibit illicit drugs by taxing them, Dodd's bill gave the

Justice Department a wide range of new powers to directly enforce federal drug prohibition under the authority of the Constitution's Commerce Clause.

There was a cruel historical irony at work here. The Commerce Clause gives Congress the power "to regulate Commerce with foreign Nations, and among the several States, and with the Indian Tribes." The Founders intended the power to be used only in a very narrow set of circumstances, such as when one state attempts to favor its own businesses or citizens over those of the other states. Over the years the Supreme Court had forged a much broader interpretation—that the Commerce Clause gives Congress the authority to regulate *any* activity that affects commerce in more than one state. Roosevelt's New Deal–era justices were especially fond of the interpretation, perhaps most famously in the 1942 case *Wickard v. Filburn,* in which the Court ruled that the Commerce Clause gives Congress the authority to impose quotas on the amount of wheat a farmer can grow on his own land, even if he's only growing the wheat for his own use.[11] The Court's rationale was that the wheat the farmer grows for himself is wheat he isn't purchasing on the market, thus affecting interstate commerce. In 1964 Congress drew on that interpretation of the Commerce Clause to pass the Civil Rights Act, which gives the federal government broad powers to target private businesses that engage in racial discrimination. When those powers were challenged, the Warren Court continued to broaden the Commerce Clause in support of the law, ruling, for example, that Congress has the authority to forcibly integrate any businesses along major highways and interstates or any businesses that sells products made in other states.

But the same broad interpretation of the Commerce Clause that allowed the federal government to integrate private businesses in the South also gave Mitchell and Nixon the authority to wage their war on crime and drugs—a war that over the next forty years had some devastating consequences for large swaths of black America. In the omnibus law, Mitchell would claim for his department all authority to oversee the manufacture, distribution, export, import, and sale of addictive drugs. The bill created a classification system for illicit drugs and vested the classification authority with the Justice Department. That met with fierce resistance from researchers and medical organizations, who believed that authority to determine which psychoactive drugs have medical benefits and which cause harm should belong to the Department of Health, Education, and Welfare or to an agency like the FDA instead of an agency whose primary mission was law enforcement. Their pleas were in vain. A version of the Dodd bill would later become the Controlled Substances Act, the law that has authorized the war on drugs ever since.

IT ISN'T CLEAR WHY ERVIN DIDN'T PUT UP MORE OF A FIGHT against the no-knock raid back in December 1969 with the DC crime bill. Perhaps he simply hadn't had time to read it or consider its consequences. By the time the omnibus drug bill came to his committee, he attempted to remove the no-knock provision but failed to muster enough support. But on January 25, 1970, the omnibus bill came to the floor of the full Senate. This time Ervin was ready. He forced the Senate to debate no-knock raids for three days. Ervin was the loudest, most indignant of the policy's opponents. He declared the tactic "incompatible with the essence of liberty," and proclaimed, "I stand on the proposition that every man's home is his castle, and that the Congress should not go on record as allowing Department of Justice officials to break into a home like burglars." Invoking the British common-law cases, he steamed that the tactic was not "using the keys of the king to open all the doors," but instead "using the king's axe to knock down the door and break the window."

For a while, it looked as if Ervin might have had enough support to strip the measure from the larger bill. After the first day of debate, even Senator Dodd, the bill's sponsor, had reservations. Dodd told the *New York Times* that the no-knock raid was "one of the toughest questions I've faced," and that he was now "almost of an open mind" about it.

But Dodd toughened his resolve, and the no-knock supporters fought back. Dodd forebodingly warned his fellow senators that "the hoodlums are watching us, the dope peddlers are watching us. They want to know if we mean what we say." Republican senator Robert Griffin of Michigan argued that the no-knock raid was no big deal because twenty-nine states had already legalized it. In truth, only a handful of state legislatures had explicitly legalized the tactic. In most cases, it was simply that a state appellate court had at some point in the state's history refused to throw out evidence obtained in a raid in which police didn't knock and announce themselves. That was quite different from what the Senate was considering: explicitly authorizing federal agents to use the no-knock raid as a get-tough-on-criminals tactic.

The Senate's two party leaders also lined up against Ervin. Republican minority leader Hugh Scott of Pennsylvania lamented, "We are encountering a certain amount of sob-sisterism from people who tend to weep somewhat excessively about the rights of the drug pusher." Given that the measure's chief opponent was Ervin, a fierce critic of the Warren Court who supported the Republicans' crime bill in 1968, the charge was rubbish. Majority Leader Mansfield, meanwhile, returned to his argument of shifting responsibility: he urged the senators to simply put their trust in the courts to properly oversee no-knock warrants.

Still, Ervin had the momentum, and a growing faction of senators were lining up behind him. By January 27, the *Times* reported, "Senate leaders were predicting that Senator Ervin would win his fight."

But then Senator Griffin pulled off a brilliant bit of legislative maneuvering. He introduced an amendment changing a single word in the no-knock provision. In the original wording, police could enter without knocking if they could show that evidence "*may* be destroyed." Griffin changed the phrase to "*will* be destroyed." Technically, that was supposed to make it more difficult to obtain a no-knock warrant. In practice, it made no difference at all. It was a standard that had no real definition, and in any case, in the event that a police officer did hypothetically exaggerate the threat of a suspect destroying evidence to get a no-knock, the mere fact that it was a no-knock raid meant that it was a standard that could never be verified after the fact.

But it was still a shrewd bit of politicking. Even senators who opposed the no-knock raid in general might vote for an amendment restricting its use, just in case the law itself was passed—and several did. Griffin's amendment passed 44–40. Griffin then revealed his trickery. Once his amendment had passed, he pointed out that the no-knock law in this bill was now identical to the bill the Senate had passed for DC just a month earlier. That one had slipped through without much debate. Any senator voting against this bill would then have to explain why he voted to allow no-knock raids in DC but was now against allowing federal agents to use the tactic in the rest of the country.

On January 28, the no-knock provision passed, 70–15. But there was nothing to fear, Dodd promised. Federal agents would use the new tactic "in the most discriminating manner possible."[12]

THE PURPOSE OF A CONFERENCE COMMITTEE IS TO HASH OUT the differences between the versions of similar bills that emerge from the House and Senate. In theory, these committees are made up of the politicians who shaped the bill in each chamber and are expected to put up a fight for the version of the bill authored by their committee. That didn't happen with the DC crime bill when the House-Senate conference committee began work on it in the spring of 1970. The House version was much tougher than the Senate version, and Senator Tydings completely capitulated on no-knock, preventive detention, and most of the other controversial provisions, sometimes over the objections of four members of his own committee (two of whom were Republicans). In the end, the Senate conferees voted for the House bill and what Ervin called its "garbage pail" of police powers, 5–3. The full compromise bill would return to the full House and Senate one last time before being sent to Nixon for his signature.[13]

Meanwhile, the citizens of DC began to learn about what was in this bill about to be imposed on their city. They wanted no part of it. DC mayor Walter Washington spoke out publicly against the no-knock and preventive detention measures. A city attorney told the *New York Times* that no one in the city's government had been consulted while the bill was being drafted. It was all done by Nixon aides.[14] In late May, a group of black civic and religious leaders, including Democratic National Committee chairman Channing Phillips and future mayor Marion Barry, spoke out against the bill. Incredibly, they told citizens of DC that if they caught police breaking into their homes under the new law they should "resist by appropriate action." What did that mean? One of the community leaders, Julius Hobson, a cofounder of the DC statehood party, suggested greeting the raiding cops with a shotgun. "I would shoot him down in cold blood just like I would swat a fly," he said. Three other black leaders, all clergy, agreed with him.[15] They weren't alone in that sentiment. During the House debate on the bill, Rep. Bertram Podell, a white Democrat from Brooklyn, said that he too would shoot any police officer who tried to enter his home unannounced.[16]

But such objections were up against soaring crime in the city. The figures from 1969 in particular were grim. There were 287 murders that year, up from 195 the previous year and just 82 in 1962. Robberies were up 50 percent from 1968, and rapes—incredibly—jumped more than 300 percent. The media piled on. In March 1970, the *New York Times* ran a long, sensational article about crime in DC. The lead photo showed a woman walking in the dark in front of a notable DC landmark. Embedded in the photo was a drop quote: "You must be out of your mind to be out alone after dark in a neighborhood like this." The caption under the photo read, "The warning quote above was spoken by a passer-by to a woman in Washington. She looked up—and there was the White House." The article also borrowed some of Nixon's war rhetoric. In discussing how some blacks in DC had become distrustful of police, author James Batten (who would later become chairman of Knight-Ridder) wrote, "In the slums of Washington, as in the hamlets of South

Vietnam, if the natives wish to protect fugitives from the authorities, they usually can succeed."[17]

As it turned out, crime in DC peaked before the new crime bills had even passed. By May 1970, crime in the city had fallen for five straight months. At that point, the only Nixon policies that had been implemented in DC were a federally funded methadone program and some funding for additional police officers. The methadone program in particular appeared to be working. But the Nixonites had little interest in taking credit for a treatment program. As Nixon aide Egil Krogh put it to top Nixon adviser John Ehrlichman, "All the liberals need is an argument that if the picture is improving with just the addition of more police and a new narcotics treatment agency, there is no need for the repressive Nixon crime proposals."[18]

That sentiment won the day. The Justice Department withheld the Federal Bureau of Investigation (FBI) data showing improved crime statistics for DC until after Nixon signed the DC crime bill into law. The administration then released the numbers and took credit for them. But the Nixonites also continued to keep the results from the methadone program close to the vest.

But while perception of soaring crime in DC continued to attract support for the crime bill as a whole, the no-knock raid was finally starting to get some attention in the media. *New York Times* columnist Tom Wicker and syndicated columnist Art Buchwald wrote in opposition to it.[19] The *Washington Post* editorialized that the policy treated the city like a penal colony and that it "ought to be opposed by every action appropriate to men who believe in the rule of law."[20] Even conservative prince William F. Buckley Jr. acknowledged the potential for abuse (although he ultimately came down in favor of it).[21] Civil libertarians by then generally agreed that Clark's opinion in *Ker* was accepted law and that Nixon's no-knock proposal didn't go any further than that. So they were left to oppose the bill on policy grounds. "My honest feeling is that it's probably constitutional," ACLU general counsel Norman Dorsen told the *New York Times*. "But there's a grave question about the policy behind it."[22]

Santarelli says the most convincing argument for the law was that it merely brought oversight to something that was already happening. "We found out that many police officers had been conducting no-knock raids anyway. Then they'd get to court and explain why the exigent circumstances at the scene allowed them to break in without an announcement. So we were letting police make the subjective decision on-site about whether exigent circumstances existed. . . . The no-knock law required someone other than police to make the call about exigent circumstances ahead of time. It brought in judicial scrutiny. Or at least it was supposed to."

But police could still make a decision at the scene to enter without announcing. At worst, a judge might later suppress the evidence. And even that was rare, because it was easy to fake exigent circumstances. A DC judge would later cynically call the no-knock law "an anti-perjury bill," explaining that "it excuses the officials from saying they knocked" when they hadn't.[23]

The administration might have had an inkling that the tide was turning. In testimony before a House committee in July—at the same time the Senate was again debating the tactic—Mitchell said that without no-knock authority, drug agents would die and "clever and ruthless drug peddlers" could destroy evidence and go free. But what he did next was far more interesting. Mitchell insisted that the very phrase "no-knock raid" was a "catchword" used by people who coddled criminals. Mitchell blamed "erroneous citizens" and "newsmen" for using such sensationalist language. He then asked the committee to start calling the tactic "quick entry," which he said would be "less misleading and prejudicial."

This was nonsense. Nixonians themselves had been using the term since his campaign kicked into gear in 1967. More to the point, tough-sounding, no-mercy rhetoric had always been part of their anticrime strategy. They had *wanted* the media, civil libertarians, and liberals to characterize Nixon's crime policies in the most draconian terms possible.

The most likely reason Mitchell abandoned that strategy was that the White House sensed that no-knock wasn't playing well with

Nixon's "ignored" Americans. Until then, tough-on-crime, law-and-order rhetoric had been a winner. Most "ignored" Americans didn't think of themselves as criminals, and so could never picture themselves in need of a Miranda warning, an empathetic judge, or the advantages of preparing a defense from outside of a jail cell. But the "ignored" Americans had homes. Many were gun owners. And as a demographic group, they were likely to revere the Castle Doctrine. No polling data on no-knock existed at the time, but it seems at least possible that the increased media coverage of the issue caused even staunch crime fighters to see the possible negative consequences to allowing drug cops to go crashing into homes.

Whatever Mitchell may have wanted to accomplish for no-knock by changing its name, for all practical purposes the political debate over no-knock raids in DC was over. Mitchell and Nixon had won. When Tydings made no effort to cut or water down the provision while the bill was in conference committee, it was irrevocably attached to the DC crime bill. Since the House and Senate had to vote on the conference committee bill as a whole—no changes or amendments are permitted in conference committee bills; otherwise, the legislative process would drag on forever—the only way Ervin and his allies could defeat no-knock was to defeat the entire DC crime bill. Circumstances at the time made that an impossible task. Because Mitchell was sitting on the DC crime figures, there was still the perception that crime was rising in the city. The midterm elections were also just a few months away. Even senators who strongly agreed with Ervin about no-knock or preventive detention weren't ready to sacrifice the entire bill to prevent those policies from passing. Members of the House and Senate who needed to look tough on crime had an incentive to stay and record a vote in favor of the bill. Those who didn't went home to campaign—or just to take a vacation.

The long odds didn't faze Ervin. He'd lost on no-knock the first time because too few of the supporters he'd lined up on the Judiciary Committee bothered to show up to vote against it. He'd lost the second time because of a slick parliamentary maneuver. And he'd lose this time because it wasn't possible to vote against the no-knock measure without also voting against the entire crime bill. But he'd sure as hell put up a fight.

On July 17, 1970, Ervin took the floor and spoke extemporaneously against the bill for four and a half hours. Over the course of an impassioned diatribe on the floor of the Senate, he protested, "Mr. President, the supreme value of civilization is the freedom of the individual, which is simply the right of the individual to be free from government tyranny." He pleaded with his fellow senators not to enact a bill that contained provisions that were so hostile to the traditions that had prevailed in the United States ever since it became a republic. Once gone, he cautioned, the liberties that the bill threatened would be gone forever.[24]

There was some poignant symbolism in Ervin's sustained philippic. This was a man who over the course of his career had signed "The Southern Manifesto," railed against *Brown v. Board of Education,* excoriated the Warren Court, and publicly lamented the criminal-coddling ways of the Johnson administration. Here was a law that at root was part of a mass backlash against the Warren Court, that tapped into public anger over the government being too soft on criminals, and that would primarily and overwhelmingly be utilized against black residents of the District of Columbia. And here was Sam Ervin, standing on the floor of the Senate, passionately orating against it, using notes quickly scribbled on the backs of envelopes to sling obloquy and reproach at the bill's supporters. Liberals like Dodd and Tydings had sold out DC to get reelected. For black folks in the District of Columbia, the biggest, loudest, most potent force keeping the cops from crashing through their doors was Sam Ervin, the country lawyer, folksy Bible-thumper, and only recently reformed segregationist.

But the bill passed easily. Nixon signed the DC crime bill into law on July 29.[25] A few months later, Ervin put up yet another fight when the no-knock raid omnibus drug bill for the entire country came before the Senate in October. He lost that one too, 42–20. More than a third of the Senate didn't stick around to vote. In his autobiography, Ervin writes that he warned his colleagues that the no-knock measures "would be grossly abused by complaisant magistrates and over-zealous officers, and that in consequence, both householders and officers would suffer death, and humble, law-abiding people would be unnecessarily harassed by no-knock raids upon their homes."[26]

The next four years would prove him right. And after a brief period of sanity, so would the next thirty.

$\sim$

"I STARTED TO BECOME MORE AND MORE CONCERNED about potential abuses with the no-knock raid," says Don Santarelli. By 1971, he had been appointed director of the Law Enforcement Assistance Administration, the federal agency that doled out grants and gear to police agencies. But it was more than just the no-knock raids. Some of the police chiefs he worked with, he noticed, had an increasingly gung-ho mentality. Under the 1970 federal crime bill, the annual budget for Santarelli's agency jumped from $75 million to $500 million. It seemed like every police department in the country wanted a piece. That wasn't so unusual. But it was *what* they wanted that Santarelli found concerning. "They didn't value education or training. They valued hardware," he says. The city of Birmingham asked him for an armored personnel carrier (APC). Other chiefs wanted tanks. Los Angeles asked him for a submarine. "Anything the police chiefs could dream up to make themselves look more fearsome, they wanted," Santarelli says.[27]

They were also requesting the gear and military training to start their own tactical teams, like the one quickly becoming famous in Los Angeles. "I was always hesitant about that. There were certain supervised, tightly controlled circumstances where that kind of force was appropriate. But law enforcement has never been good at self-discipline. Once they had that sort of capability, it would be difficult to limit it to those circumstances," Santarelli says.

In Detroit, for example, a new police commissioner took over in 1971 and began implementing a more Nixonian approach to illicit drugs. Chief John Nichols doubled up the personnel on his narcotics unit and started arresting and imprisoning heroin dealers instead of merely chasing them off, as the city had done in the past. The result was an impressive stat sheet on the enforcement side: 1,600 arrests. But cracking down on dealers opened the city up to turf wars. In one ten-day stretch in June, Detroit logged forty murders.[28] It was one of the first examples of the sort of self-perpetuating, self-escalating feedback loop created by the modern drug war. Crackdowns upset the established black markets. That created lucrative new opportunities for rising dealers and those who weren't caught in the crackdowns. They'd then wage war to claim the new markets, with most of the victims being low-level pawns and the occasional bystander. The resulting bloodshed would spur outrage and anger, giving law enforcement and political officials more reason to order more crackdowns and to ask for more authority to use more force. The pattern would repeat itself for decades in US cities, in Latin America, and on a tragically large scale in Mexico in the 2000s.

But in DC, Nixon's model city, events unfolded differently, and the results were intriguing.

WHEN RICHARD NIXON APPOINTED JERRY WILSON TO HEAD the District of Columbia's Metro Police Department (MPD) in 1969, it didn't sit well with the city's black population. Civil rights leaders and black militants wanted a black chief. Wilson was a white Southerner. But Wilson would surprise them and just about everyone else—even himself.

Wilson initially joined the MPD in 1949 after stints in the Marines and the US Navy, where he had enlisted at the age of fifteen. His communication skills got him a job analyzing and reporting on crime statistics in the city, a position he held while getting a bachelor's degree in the administration of justice from American University. His last position before he was appointed chief was field operations commander, a post from which he directed the police response to the 1968 riots after Martin Luther King was assassinated.

That assignment didn't win him much favor from blacks in DC either. But he had been appointed to that position by the Johnson administration, where his intellect and openness to innovative approaches to crime had won him supporters.

Wilson's first priority upon taking office in August 1969 was to improve the department's relationship with the people it served. Already, this was a marked departure from the more aggressive style of his predecessors. "We are working for the people," Wilson explained in a 1971 interview with the *Washington Afro-American*. "We have to have the confidence of the citizens."[29] Previously, the MPD had primarily recruited outside the city—even outside the region. While seven in ten DC residents were black, three out of four DC patrolmen were white. Wilson focused his recruitment efforts on getting blacks who lived in the District to join the department. His first class of recruits was half black. Marion Barry, who just a year earlier had encouraged DC residents to take up arms against any cops who broke into their homes, told the paper that there was "a growing sense among blacks that the police department really is working with the people."[30] After the *New York Times,* just a year earlier, had compared black residents' lack of cooperation with DC police to the relationship between native Vietnamese and American soldiers, the city's leading black advocacy newspaper was now reporting that DC cops were once again getting tips and cooperation from black residents.[31]

Instead of setting up roadblocks, employing stop-and-frisks, and implementing similarly confrontational policies in high-crime areas, Wilson instituted high-profile patrols in those neighborhoods. He adopted what at the time was an innovative use of computer software and radio communication to increase response times to citizen complaints, one of the more proven ways of both deterring crime and improving relations between police and citizens. Police departments in other cities were reluctant to take on college graduates as recruits. Wilson embraced them. He set a goal of putting fifty Ivy League grads on MPD patrols by the end of his first full year on the force.

During the often heated antiwar protests of the early 1970s, Wilson believed that an intimidating police presence didn't prevent confrontation, it invited it. That didn't mean he didn't prepare, but he put his riot control teams in buses, then parked the buses close by, but out of sight of protesters. Appearances were important. In general, instead of the usual brute force and reactionary policing that tended to pit cops against citizens—both criminal and otherwise—Wilson believed that cops were more effective when they were welcomed and respected in the neighborhoods they patrolled. "The use of violence," he told *Time* in 1970, "is not the job of police officers."[32]

At the same time, when it *was* time to use force, Wilson put himself on the front lines. He made a point of being the first cop to confront protesters and, if it was necessary, to lob the first canister of tear gas. This won him respect from rank-and-file DC cops, even if they weren't wild about the close supervision. As *Time* reported, when Wilson publicly criticized his own officers for their aggressive response to protest a couple months after he took office, the police union passed a resolution criticizing Wilson for not backing his men. His response: "I don't stand behind my men, I stand in front of them."[33]

That approach to policing carried over to Wilson's use of no-knock raids—or more accurately, his refusal to use them. As soon as the federal government gave him permission to use the tactic more freely, Wilson concluded that he didn't need it. "I never really bought into the idea that police were getting gunned down while serving warrants," Wilson says. "Drug pushers sold drugs to make money. They might run. But there weren't many drug dealers who were in the business to get into shootouts with narcotics officers." Wilson didn't find the destruction of evidence exception convincing either. "We called that the 'no-flush rule.' Again, I just didn't think that warranted breaking down a door. There were better ways to do it," he says, referring to serving drug warrants. "You couldn't flush much pot down a toilet anyway. Cocaine or heroin, you could flush a good amount. But then it was gone—off the street. They [no-knock proponents] wanted to make sure the evidence was preserved to get a conviction. But a drug conviction just wasn't worth the risk of a no-knock raid."[34] By the one-year anniversary of the DC crime bill, Wilson had removed the no-knock raid from the MPD manual. The department made spare use of the preventive detention measure as well.

Wilson's tenure as MPD chief ran nearly concurrently with Nixon's tenure as president. (Wilson took office five months after Nixon and left a month after Nixon resigned.) Under Jerry Wilson, violent crime in DC dropped 25 percent and property crime dropped 28 percent. Under Nixon, violent crime in the country as a whole went *up* 40 percent and property crime *rose* 24 percent.[35] There are obviously countless variables at work in that sort of comparison. And even under Nixon, crime was still primarily a local issue. But while Nixon may not have had a direct effect on local crime policy, he did set the tone. State legislatures across the country passed get-tough-on-crime bills that gave cops more power, more authority, and more heavy-duty equipment. The country as a whole moved toward Nixon's get-tough policies, and crime continued to soar. Washington, DC, moved away from the aggressive approach over the same period, and its crime rate dropped.

At the time, Wilson credited the DC crime drop to the one thousand additional police officers Nixon had given him funding to hire, the methadone program, and seemingly mundane changes like improved street lighting. Others credited some of the less controversial parts of the DC crime bill pushed by Don Santarelli, like reorganizing the city's courts. But much of the credit undoubtedly belonged to Wilson himself and his less confrontational, community-oriented approach to policing.

Hard-line Nixon officials didn't know quite what to make of the fact that their model city had passed on the two most controversial, high-profile provisions in the DC crime bill, and crime had gone down anyway. So they spun. Mitchell said that Wilson's work in DC was proof that the press had overhyped the dangers of preventive detention and the no-knock raid.

Wilson's reluctance to utilize either law didn't hurt his reputation with the administration in the least. "They didn't really pressure us to use the no-knock raid at all," Wilson says. "We told them we didn't need it, and from what I can remember, they never brought it up again."[36] Nixon and Mitchell were more than happy to tout and take credit for the results in DC. However, they wouldn't go out of their way to publicize just which parts of the crime bill were being used and which ones weren't.[37]

IN 1971 TWO POSITIONS OPENED ON THE US SUPREME COURT with the retirements of Justice Hugo Black and Justice John Harlan. Nixon now had an opportunity to move the Court significantly to the right, especially with respect to how it would handle the law-and-order issues he'd run on. He had already made some progress with his first two nominations, replacing the much-loathed Earl Warren with "strict constructionist" Warren Burger in 1969, and nominating Harry Blackmun after Lyndon Johnson's crony Abe Fortas stepped down. Now he had two more picks—a historic opportunity to remake the Court and, perhaps more importantly in Nixon's world, to "stick it to the left," as White House chief of staff H. R. Haldeman would put it in his diary.[38]

Nixon had run into problems, however, with his last appointment. His first nomination to replace Fortas, Clement Haynsworth, became the first Supreme Court nominee to be rejected by the Senate in nearly forty years. The Senate rejected his next nominee too—G. Harrold Carswell—before finally confirming Blackmun.

This time the White House circulated a preliminary list of names, which met with derision in the media and parts of the Senate. Nixon then had to withdraw the first two nominees he announced after they were deemed unqualified by the American Bar Association. Nixon finally turned to Louis Powell, a Virginia lawyer who had previously served as president of the ABA. Powell was quickly confirmed.

Nixon's nomination for the other position was something of a surprise. William Rehnquist was head of the Justice Department's

Office of Legal Counsel (OLC), where his job was to write legal opinions when the administration requested them. (A critic might argue that the office exists to give the executive branch a legal argument justifying it to do just about anything it wants.) Nixon often mistakenly called him "Renchberg."

From his position in the OLC, Rehnquist signed off on all of the controversial provisions in Nixon's various crime bills, including preventive detention, expansive wiretapping powers, and the no-knock raid.[39] He was as hawkish on crime as anyone in the administration. John Mitchell once said that Rehnquist was the "only lawyer I know who would willingly defend the Sheriff of Nottingham."

Rehnquist had a bumpier road to confirmation than Powell. But after some often contentious hearings and debate—including some aggressive questioning from Sen. Sam Ervin about Rehnquist's time at the OLC—he was confirmed in December 1971 by a vote of 68–26.[40]

The man who had written the legal justifications for Nixon's crime policy now had a seat on the US Supreme Court.

BY THE SUMMER OF 1971, NINETEEN STATES HAD ADOPTED Nixon's model antidrug legislation.[41] His brute force approach to attacking the drug supply had begun to filter down to local police agencies. But Nixon was stewing over the fact that despite their success in making crime an issue and pushing through some of the toughest crime bills the country had ever seen, they'd yet to reap much political benefit from the effort. The evidence lay in the modest results of the 1970 midterms. "We still haven't gotten through the strong position on law and order despite our leadership in this field, all of the public relations devices we use to get it across, and my hitting it hard on the campaign," Nixon wrote in a December 1, 1970, memo to his chief of staff, H. R. Haldeman.[42] An internal poll taken a few months later confirmed his analysis—the public feared crime but was still largely unaware of anything Nixon was doing about it.[43]

The White House needed something tangible to tout to the public. If they couldn't use actual crime data to show their initiatives were working, perhaps they could just create their own impressive statistics by generating lots of arrests and convictions at the federal level. The journalist Edward Jay Epstein writes, "[Nixon] reminded Ehrlichman and Krogh that there was only one area in which the federal police could produce such results on demand—and that was narcotics."[44]

But there remained the question of how to do it. While the federal narcotics enforcement agency, BNDD, had been expanded from four hundred officers in 1969 to two thousand by 1971, Nixon and Mitchell had been persuaded early in the administration to focus the agency's energy on targeting high-level traffickers, at home and overseas. Its mission was to drain the drug supply, which meant long, complicated investigations that in theory would result in high-*quality* arrests, but not in a high quantity of them.[45] Krogh had asked BNDD director John Ingersoll to reverse course and devote resources to making easy, high-profile arrests of low-level offenders that the administration could use for PR purposes. Ingersoll refused, arguing that those sorts of arrests might have made for good politics, but they did little to reduce crime or addiction. The BNDD was just one among several federal bureaucracies that had been pushing back on Nixon's increasingly aggressive antidrug policies. He was also getting frustrated by the lack of cooperation from the Treasury Department and the Department of Health, Education, and Welfare.

So the White House crime team came up with a plan. They would launch an all-out PR offensive to scare the hell out of the public about crime, and to tie crime to heroin. Once voters were good and terrified, they would push for reorganization to consolidate drug policy and enforcement power within the White House. Krogh put together a quick-hitting but multifaceted strategy that included planting media scare stories about heroin, publicly recalling ambassadors to embarrass heroin-producing countries like Thailand and Turkey, and holding high-level (but entirely staged) strategy sessions that they'd invite the media to attend. The plan culminated with a planned speech from Nixon that would forge new frontiers in fearmongering. An aide to Krogh told the journalist Epstein years later, "If we hyped the drug problem into a national crisis, we knew that Congress would give us anything we asked for."[46]

G. Gordon Liddy, who the next month would head up the White House "plumbers" group implicated in the Watergate scandal, motivated his PR team with a series of films to educate and inspire them about the power of government propaganda. According to Epstein, Liddy's movie nights concluded with *Triumph of the Will,* Leni Riefenstahl's infamous (but brilliant and effective) 1934 film glorifying Adolf Hitler and the Nazi Party.[47]

The scare strategy was executed as planned. Nixon's June 17, 1971, speech more than met expectations. He declared drug abuse "public enemy number one" and asked for emergency powers and new funding to "wage a new, all-out offensive."[48] Years later, both this speech and a similar one he gave the following year would alternately be considered the start of the modern "war on drugs." In a poll taken the following month, Americans named drug abuse as the most urgent domestic problem facing the country.[49]

A few weeks after the PR offensive, Liddy began working on a new plan to shift enforcement power to the White House. To work around obstinates like Ingersoll at the BNDD, Liddy ensured that the new elite enforcement agency would operate directly out of the White House. It would consist of narcotics "strike forces" to be dispatched across the country and populated with personnel pulled from other federal law enforcement agencies and local law enforcement. They would fund the program through the LEAA, which would allow them to use grants to persuade local police departments to cooperate. The strike forces would get high-profile, media-friendly arrests, generate empty but impressive-sounding arrest statistics Nixon could tout, and operate directly under Nixon and his top aides. By autumn, Nixon had given it the green light.[50]

The new agency would be called the Office of Drug Abuse Law Enforcement, or ODALE. Nixon appointed forty-four-year-old Myles Ambrose to lead it. Ambrose favored a much more aggressive, rough-'em-up style of drug enforcement. He had been head of Customs during Operation Intercept, and it probably didn't hurt that these clashing philosophies about law enforcement had led to repeated feuds with Ingersoll, the BNDD head who was currently a thorn in Nixon's side. Ingersoll only learned about the new agency while watching a TV news special in late December 1971.[51]

But ODALE was always strictly for show. It would never have more than a few hundred agents. Nixon's executive order creating the agency even included an eighteen-month sunset provision. That wasn't nearly enough time or personnel to fulfill the agency's lofty mission to "stop the proliferating addict population." ODALE existed to show off the Nixon administration's showpiece crime tools—no-knock raids, copious use of wiretaps, preventive detention, and the power to jail witnesses who refused to testify before grand juries. Federal narcotics agent John Finlator would say in a couple years that the office "was strictly a political thing. They were trying to prove the No. 1 problem was drugs, as Nixon said. They were under pressure to produce."[52]

In March 1972, all was set to go. The strike forces began . . . striking. The problem was that they weren't always sure exactly *what* they were striking.[53]

HUMBOLDT COUNTY, CALIFORNIA, LIES ABOUT TWO HUNDRED miles north of San Francisco along the Pacific Coast. It is vast, mountainous, heavily forested, and sparsely populated country, home to a sizable portion of the state's towering redwood trees. Over the last several decades, the county's immensity, forest cover, and terrain have made it ideal for covert marijuana cultivation—and the hippie, agrarian pot culture that goes with it. And that has often put Humboldt County in the crosshairs of the drug warriors. On

April 4, 1972, just a few weeks after the new Office of Drug Abuse Law Enforcement (ODALE) was up and running, Humboldt was also the setting for the violent death of twenty-four-year-old Dirk Dickenson, the first fatality in Nixon's new "all-out war on drugs."[54]

Local Humboldt County law enforcement had already produced one drug war casualty. Deputy Mel Ames, a hard-nosed, fifteen-year cop, had a knack for spotting drug offenders. In the spring of 1971, Ames had sniffed out two four-foot-high marijuana plants growing along the Eel River. After setting up a stakeout nearby, he watched for days in hopes of catching whoever had planted them. When the weekend came, he handed watch duty off to twenty-seven-year-old deputy Larry Lema. On October 4, 1970—a bright Sunday afternoon—Lema spotted twenty-two-year-old Patrick Berti, who was on his way to law school in the fall, and a friend walking along the river. When the two stopped to inspect the plants, Lema realized he'd found his pot cultivators. He emerged from the bushes to apprehend them. Lema and Berti, it would turn out, had known one another all their lives. When Lema confronted Berti, Berti turned, still holding a twig from one of the plants in his hand. Lema mistook it for a gun and shot him.

"Christ, Larry, you shot me," Berti said. Those would be his last words. He died there in the woods. Berti's friend had grown the marijuana. Berti had merely come to see the plants out of curiosity— he'd never seen pot plants that tall. A Humboldt County grand jury ruled Berti's death a justifiable homicide.[55]

The Humboldt County Sheriff's Department had since signed on to Nixon's more warlike federal drug initiative. They welcomed the help. Most local police feared that the county had been overrun by the counterculture. Starting in about 1970, "longhairs" had begun moving into the area and taking up residence in and around the town of Garberville. Probably not coincidentally, there had also been at least a dozen unsolved arsons in that area since 1971. All of the torched buildings had been occupied by the newcomers. If you were to draw a perimeter around the burned residences, somewhere near the middle you'd find the ranch where Dirk

Dickenson lived with his girlfriend. In the fall of 1971, Humboldt County sheriff's deputy Archie Brunkle led a recall campaign against the Garberville justice of the peace for being "too soft on hippies." He ran the campaign out of the Garberville branch of the Sheriff's Department.

Against that backdrop, an informant allegedly told the federal Bureau of Narcotics and Dangerous Drugs (BNDD) office in San Francisco that they'd find a major drug operation on Dirk Dickenson's ranch. Dickenson, the informant said, was running a million-dollar PCP lab. The BNDD office contacted the Humboldt County Sheriff's Department with the tip, and Undersheriff Bob Bollman agreed to investigate. (Bollman, incidentally, had been running the department since Sheriff Gene Cox had taken leave to treat his own addiction—Cox was an alcoholic.) Bollman assigned Deputy Ames to do some reconnaissance. Ames conducted two flyovers of the property. Neither revealed any signs of a drug lab. So Ames then recruited a local dogcatcher to work his way inside the house, under the guise of investigating a complaint about Dickenson's two Saint Bernards. The dogcatcher returned and reported that he'd seen some roaches in a few ashtrays around the house. That and the informant's tip were enough to get a search warrant.

Had they done a bit more research, the Sheriff's Department might have concluded that a million-dollar drug lab on the property was improbable. The tenants—twenty-four-year-old Dickenson and his twenty-two-year-old girlfriend, Judy Arnold—had no electricity or running water. Upon discovering the two were hippies, the local rancher who supplied power and water to the house had turned both utilities off. So the couple piped in their own water. They did without electricity. Dickenson earned money for the two of them from carpentry and woodworking.

Contemporary media accounts of the raid on Dickenson's ranch described it as a BNDD operation. The initial informant's tip to the BNDD office in San Francisco came in February, before ODALE was up and running. But once the raid itself went down in April, ODALE had been operational for a month. It isn't entirely clear that the raid was an official ODALE operation, but it seemed to have all the characteristics of one. ODALE was a transagency endeavor. Ambrose and his staff could detail law enforcement personnel out of several federal agencies to serve on task forces, including BNDD, Customs, the Internal Revenue Service (IRS), and the Bureau of Alcohol, Tobacco, and Firearms (ATF). The nineteen-man assault team assembled to raid Dickenson's home on April 4 included members of both BNDD and the Humboldt County Sheriff's Department, along with two federal chemists and an IRS agent.

On the morning of the raid, the nineteen agents, including the dogcatcher, were split into two teams. Half would arrive at the ranch in a Huey helicopter they had borrowed from the US Army. The others donned military jackets and would arrive by car. The car team would drive to the cabin, sneak onto the property, then hide in the trees. When the helicopter landed, the second team would rush out and storm the house. The car team would then drop down from the trees.

To be sure the operation got maximum exposure, Undersheriff Bollman invited the press to come along and watch. (This was another ODALE strategy.) Bollman told the newspaper reporter and two photographers that there was a good chance they'd be witnessing the biggest drug bust in California history. Later, he'd regret bringing them along. The managing editor of the local newspaper would tell *Rolling Stone* that, were it not for Bollman's ego, the entire raid would probably have been "tidied up" and few outside Humboldt County would ever have known the name Dirk Dickenson.

One of the federal agents on the raid team was twenty-nine-year-old Lloyd Clifton, who had recently been recruited from the Berkeley Police Department to join the federal narcotics office in San Francisco. Four years before the Dickenson raid, Clifton had pulled over a motorist for a traffic violation. Spotting a bottle of gas in the car, Clifton asked the motorist if it was gas. The man said it was. Bizarrely, Clifton then called the man a "murderer," for no apparent reason. (He acknowledged as much in a subsequent lawsuit.) When the motorist smirked at the odd insult, Clifton beat him with his baton.

In another odd incident, a California Highway Patrol officer had arrested a young black man for several outstanding traffic warrants. Inside the Berkeley police station, the man said it was a case of mistaken identity. The car was no longer his, and if they let him make a phone call, he could prove that he didn't own the car when the traffic infractions occurred. They agreed to let him contact the owner. As he was returning from making the call, Clifton—who had nothing to do with the case—confronted the man and asked, "What the fuck are you walking around here for?" He then threw the man into an open elevator and began beating him. Other officers had to pull him off. The man Clifton had beaten was the son of a California Superior Court judge. For that beating, Clifton received a reprimand. In a third incident, he had beaten another black man outside the Berkeley jail, in front of both the man's mother and a bail bondsman. Clifton claimed he was instigated to violence because the man had called him "a motherfucker."

If this new federal initiative against street-level pushers was all about projecting aggression and instilling fear, Clifton was a perfect fit.

On the morning of the day he would die, Dickenson and his girlfriend woke at around 9:00 AM. They went out to inspect the tall, wide tree he planned to fell for wood to build some tables. The couple then walked to the property of the man who owned the tree to inquire about buying it. The man happened to be the dogcatcher who had just given them up to the police. He agreed to sell them the tree, knowing they'd shortly be raided by narcotics agents. The two returned to the ranch, stopping first to purchase a bottle of whiskey to celebrate. The couple also planned to build a bathroom that day. The bathtub they'd already built was sitting out on their porch, and they wanted to create a place to put it. They were cleaning out the tub to bring it inside when they first heard the helicopter.

The agents themselves were undercover narcs. They had long hair, mustaches, and unshorn faces. To Dickenson and Arnold, they looked like peers. So when the couple looked up at the low-flying helicopter, they waved. The agents waved back. Judy Arnold described the scene to *Rolling Stone* reporter Joe Ezsterhas:

> Dirk said—"It looks like it's gonna land." It was over the house and it was really low. We left the back door open and came back inside the cabin. Boogie and Vernon [the Saint Bernards] weren't barking. They were calm. Our front door was open and the copter was starting to land. Dust and dirt were coming into the cabin. Dirk walked over and closed the front door. Most of the door was glass. We stood at the corner of the big redwood table in the kitchen facing out the front door. The copter set down and the men jumped off. . . .
>
> I didn't have anything to be afraid of until I saw the guns . . . shotguns and rifles and everything. I thought it was some kind of ripoff.
>
> I saw a foot come through the door, the foot and then the door was pushed open. It was busted open. And at the time Dirk turned and ran and told me to run. Before I could do anything they had me. Dirk jumped off the back porch and ran. There's a terrace back there and a slope toward the woodline. They told me to freeze. There were at least ten of them inside by now. The one who broke the door down, Clifton, ran through the house after Dirk. . . .
>
> It was terrifying. I was shaking. It was like some terrible storm had crashed down out of the sky at us. They held me. The dogs got excited and they were barking. There was mad confusion in the place.[56]

Local reporter Richard Harris, who rode along, wrote that the raid resembled "an assault on an enemy prison camp in Vietnam."

The area wasn't well suited for a helicopter landing. The gusts generated by the propeller kicked up dirt and rocks and swirled debris. Tree limbs popped as surges of air snapped them from their branches. As Dickenson fled, Clifton called out for him to freeze.

It's likely that Dickenson simply didn't hear the command over the noise of the helicopter. Arnold says she still wasn't aware that the men were police. When Dickenson continued to run, Clifton set the sights of his .38 revolver on the young man's back. He fired one bullet. Dickenson fell to the ground.

Arnold describes what she saw:

> I heard somebody say—"He's been hit!" I didn't hear the shot. The copter was taking off again and making this insane noise and the dogs were really barking. It was chaos. . . .
>
> I heard he was out there and he'd been hit and I asked if I could go out there and see him. They said no. I said—"Well, can I at least go out on the back porch and see how he is?" So they held me and took me to the back porch. I looked off and I could see him. I saw him move his leg. It was spasmodic, like a twitch. . . .
>
> They took me back to the cabin. They still hadn't identified themselves. I finally saw a badge on the inside of this guy's . . . coat, but they still hadn't said who they were. . . .
>
> They wouldn't tell me how he was, wouldn't say anything. . . . They put me in the orange truck and I said again—"Well who are you?" That's the first time they officially told me who they were.[57]

The agents searched Dickenson for a gun. He was unarmed. And he'd been shot in the back.

Bollman made the journalists he had invited along promise to ask questions only of him or Kenny Krusco, the head of the federal team. But once Dickenson went down, photographer Ron Rose was able to freeze his death in one excruciating frame. Taken seconds after the shooting, Rose's photo shows Dickenson lying on his right side, his left arm awkwardly draped over his body, his wrist facing up. His head is tilted back, and Clifton is kneeling next to him. Dickenson appears to be looking directly into his killer's face. A uniformed deputy kneels on the other side of Dickenson, his eyes fixed on the dying man's twitching leg. A rendition of the image would make the cover of *Rolling Stone* the following year.

Again to Arnold:

I kept asking how Dirk was and they wouldn't tell me. The copter was back and they were taking Dirk away and I said—"Can I go with him?" They said, "No, you'd just be in the way." One of the dogs, Boogie, was out there running around Dirk's body. They were carrying Dirk onto the copter and Boogie was crying. . . . The copter took off and Boogie stood underneath it, looking up—the roar wasn't scaring him at all now and he was howling.[58]

The raid team had brought no medical personnel with them. That was odd, given that they had planned a major drug operation and indicated in the search warrant that they anticipated weapons. By the time word got back to the house that Dickenson needed a doctor, the helicopter had already departed for the base. The narcotics agents had to call it back over the radio to return to pick up the wounded man. The same helicopter that had just delivered the men who killed Dirk Dickenson then flew him to a hospital in a bid to save him. He was dead before it landed.

The police searched the house top to bottom. They found a joint, two roaches, several buttons of peyote, two LSD tablets, and a few small baggies of marijuana. No drug lab. They searched the surrounding area for hours. Some agents spent the night and searched more the next day. They didn't find it. Arnold was arrested and jailed for the small quantities of pot, LSD, and peyote. Dickenson's mother found out about her son's death over the radio.

After several hours in the Eureka jail, Arnold said, one of the attendants called her out of her cell.

"He's dead," the attendant said. He then sent her back to her cell.

The Sheriff's Department and federal agents quickly went into ass-covering mode. Undersheriff Bollman told the press, "You can't blame officers for being uptight. They're aware of the situation today. Officers don't go out on duty thinking they're going to shoot someone, but many times they may wonder if they're going to return home that night."

Three days after the raid, agent William Filben claimed he had tripped shortly after exiting the helicopter. The only people who saw him fall were Bollman, the local raid team leader, Krusco, leader of the federal team, and Clifton. The narrative went like this: Clifton thought Filben had been shot by someone in the house. That was why he kicked in the door and entered without knocking or announcing (they did not have a no-knock warrant). When Dickenson fled, Clifton, clad in jeans, boots, and a brown corduroy jacket, assumed he was the one who had shot Filben. When Dickenson then didn't obey his command to stop, Clifton had no choice but to shoot him. As to why Clifton couldn't have shot the fleeing, unarmed man in the leg, federal agent Ed McReedy replied, "The idea of shooting to wound is bush league."

US Attorney James L. Browning promised an investigation. "We are attempting to be as impartial as possible," he said. "We have an open mind." Seconds later, he added, "Nevertheless, on the basis of incomplete reports received by this office, I suspect it will fall into the category of justifiable homicide." He'd keep an open mind, but he had pretty much already made up his mind.

A month after the shooting, Humboldt County district attorney William Ferroggiaro went out to inspect the ranch and to re-create the scene for himself. While walking about two hundred feet from the house, he was stunned to find what looked to be a small drug lab. There was a tent, a platform, two containers of a chemical used to make PCP, a flask, and some broken glass lab equipment. It was far from a million-dollar operation. It was also far from plausible. Dozens of law enforcement officials had scoured the property for hours and found nothing. But now, visiting the site a month later, he easily found the allegedly incriminating evidence pointing to Dickenson's drug operation. To his credit, Ferroggiaro reported the find—then publicly expressed his doubt about how it got there. "There's a certain amount of taint to the discovery," he said. "The possibility must be considered that the materials were planted on the Dickenson property subsequent to the initial search."

A federal judge soon dismissed the charges against Judy Arnold, finding that Clifton violated her Fourth Amendment rights when he entered without announcing. The judge also reprimanded Clifton for his actions. But that would be about as much punishment as Clifton would get. In June, the BNDD came to a "preliminary conclusion" that "Clifton was justified in shooting." At the end of November, nearly eight months after Dickenson's death, US Attorney Browning announced that he too had determined that the shooting was justified and he wouldn't be pressing charges.

That left Humboldt County and District Attorney Ferroggiaro. In recent years, Ferroggiaro had shown a willingness to go after the area's bad cops. But few expected Ferroggiaro to take on the federal government. It was a surprise to nearly everyone when he did. According to Ezsterhas, Ferroggiaro was furious that someone had picked him to be the rube to find the fake PCP lab in the cover-up. The Justice Department had also been uncooperative with his investigation. After hearing about Clifton's abusive track record from an investigator hired by Judy Arnold's attorneys, Ferroggiaro had heard enough. He brought a second-degree murder charge against Clifton. A Humboldt County grand jury indicted the officer in January 1973. It was the first time a federal narcotics agent had ever been indicted for actions he'd taken while on the job.[59] US Attorney Browning quickly pounced on the prosecutor, telling the Eureka newspaper that every other prosecutor he'd talked to said it was a "classical case of justifiable homicide." The paper then reported, amusingly, that "Ferroggiaro's response to Browning's remarks is unprintable."[60]

By now the case had the attention of high-ranking Nixon administration officials, including US Attorney General Richard Kleindienst. Letting this local prosecutor get away with indicting a federal drug cop would set a troubling precedent. They couldn't let this get to trial. Kleindienst's office contacted James McKittrick, a local attorney who was known for defending cops accused of misconduct and who had battled (and beaten) Ferroggiaro in the past. McKittrick was flown to Washington, where Kleindienst then deputized him as a special US attorney. McKittrick wasted little time in needling Ferroggiaro. In February 1973, he wrote a letter to the editor of the *Times-Standard* explaining that people who question the actions of police are usually "radical elements" who want to "bring our country down." Ferroggiaro had a history of questioning police. McKittrick insisted that he'd never suggest Ferroggiaro was *part* of these radical elements. Only that the radicals benefited every time Ferroggiaro brought a cop to trial.[61]

McKittrick moved to get the charges dismissed. In so doing, he made two particularly ridiculous arguments. First, he argued that to allow the prosecution of Clifton to go forward would jeopardize an entire year's worth of drug investigations on which Clifton had worked. This was the same variety of argument that defense attorneys would make at the trials of federal narcotics agents who had conducted mistaken raids in the coming years. But this one was troubling. At this point in the criminal process, no one was adjudicating Clifton's guilt or innocence. Instead, McKittrick, now representing the federal government, was arguing that even if Clifton *did* murder Dirk Dickenson, the charge should be dismissed, because to try him would interfere with the government's efforts to investigate other drug pushers.

McKittrick then unleashed an even more audacious argument. He claimed that allowing Clifton's criminal trial to go forward would be a slap in the face to the *civil rights movement*. By McKittrick's reckoning, a federal investigation had already determined that Clifton had committed no crime. To allow a local prosecutor to bring criminal charges against him now would open the door to racist prosecutors in the South bringing trumped-up charges against federal prosecutors and civil rights investigators. The same administration that had capitalized on white fears about black crime, that had squeezed political capital from white resentment of civil rights protesters, was now arguing that a white federal drug agent should be let off the hook for killing a man . . . to protect the civil rights movement.

McKittrick was eventually able to get the case moved to federal court. A federal district court judge dismissed the charge, finding that Clifton's actions were reasonable under the circumstances of the raid. Nearly five years after Dirk Dickenson's death, the Ninth Circuit US Court of Appeals upheld the ruling.[62]

In the end, a twenty-four-year-old man was chased from his own home by armed men who had just emerged from an Army helicopter. They then shot him dead, from the back, while he was unarmed, and on his own property. The heavy-handed raid was based on false pretenses and didn't turn up the criminal enterprise it was supposed to find. No one would be held accountable for any of it. Dirk Dickenson was collateral damage.

In eleven years, the helicopters would return to Humboldt County.

HERBERT GIGLOTTO MADE GOOD MONEY AS A BOILERMAKER. That made the job's early mornings more tolerable. He and his wife Evelyn went to bed each night at 8:00 PM to be sure he was up by 5:00 AM to get to his job. The couple lived in Collinsville, Illinois, a small suburban town of about twenty thousand people, fifteen minutes outside of St. Louis.

At a little after 9:30 PM on April 23, 1972, the Giglottos woke to a crash. And then another. The couple's inner and outer doors were being ripped from their hinges. Someone was breaking into their home.

"I got out of bed; I took about three steps, looked down the hall and [saw] armed men running up the hall dressed like hippies with pistols, yelling and screeching." Giglotto turned to his wife, who was still in bed, and said, "God, honey, we're dead."

"That's right, you motherfucker!" one of the men screamed. The men—fifteen of them—then stormed the bedroom. One of them threw Giglotto to the bed, bound his hands behind his back, and put a gun to his head.

"Move and you're dead," the man said. He then motioned in the direction of Evelyn Giglotto. "Who is that bitch lying there?"

"That's my wife."

Evelyn Giglotto cried out, "Please don't kill him!"

"Shut up!" the man snapped.

The man with the gun at Herbert's head quickly flashed a badge, though he didn't give Herbert time to read it. *These were cops.* The man then read a list of names and asked Herbert if he knew any of them. He knew none of them.

"You're going to die if you don't tell us where the drugs are."

Giglotto pled with the man, "Please, please, before you shoot us, check my wallet for my identification. Because I know you're at the wrong place."

Seconds later, someone shouted from the stairs. "We've made a mistake!"

The men unbound the Giglottos and began to filter out.

Herbert struggled to put on his pants to chase after them for more information. He shouted, "Why did you do that?"

The man who'd just held a gun to his head answered, "Boy, you shut your mouth."

Evelyn Giglotto was most upset that the police had also thrown the couple's animals—three dogs and a cat—outside. (Given the frequency of dog-shooting during raids in the coming years, the Giglottos' pets got off easy.) "When you don't have children, your pets sort of become your children," she later explained in a newspaper interview. When she asked the police if her pets had been harmed, one of them replied, "Fuck your animals."

And with that they left.

A half-hour later, this time on the north side of Collinsville, Arnold Blass, who had just finished cleaning his pistol and putting it away in the house, was chatting with a friend as the two cleaned the carp they'd just caught. A suspicious car had been circling the neighborhood. The two grew concerned when it pulled into a lot across the street and a group of shabbily dressed men emerged with guns, racing toward the home of Blass's neighbors, Don and Virginia Askew. Blass and his friend walked over to meet the men, only to be brusquely pushed aside as one of them quickly flashed a badge that Blass didn't believe was real. He later told the *New York Times,* "It's a good thing I didn't have my gun."

Inside the Askew home, Charlie, the family dog, began barking at a disturbance outside. Virginia Askew went to the living room to investigate.

"My God, Don," she said to her husband. "There's a man at the window." Every window in fact. The two looked around and saw guns pointed at them from every angle. Outside the front door, three more men stood with shotguns. Virginia Askew reached for the phone to call the police, but one of the men motioned to her from the other side of the window that doing so wouldn't be in her best interest.

Seconds later, one of the men delivered a powerful kick to the door, sending it quickly off its hinges and into the wall. Virginia ran to the bedroom with a shriek, passed out, and smacked her head on a table as she fell. Thinking they were being robbed, the couple's sixteen-year-old son tried to call the police. One of the men put a shotgun in his face. More men poured in from the opposite direction after kicking in a back door. Finally, one of them flashed a badge.

"If I kept a gun by the door, I'd have used it," Don Askew told the *Times,* then added that he'd also likely be dead for doing so.

As the cops ransacked the Askew house, Virginia regained consciousness, then began to hyperventilate. One of the men asked Don, "Do you know John Coleman?" Virginia, still bound, told them she couldn't breathe.

"Take it easy, lady," one of them told her. "We're federal agents, and we've gotten a bum tip."

They started to leave. Don Askew's mood shifted from scared to angry. And he still was not entirely sure the men were who they claimed to be. He followed them outside and asked them to wait until the police arrived.

"We can't," one of them replied. "We've got four more places to go tonight."[63]

The team in Collinsville was one of the thirty-eight strike forces created across the country by Myles Ambrose's ODALE office. It was the new public face of Nixon's drug war: swift, ruthless, overpowering, little tolerance for deviants. Finally Nixon had a team of cops who could utilize the tools he'd fought hard to give them. There would be no more feuding with federal bureaucrats. Namby-pamby local police chiefs and budgetary concerns could no longer get in the way. With LEAA funding, Ambrose was able to target specific state and local police departments that would carry out the drug war the way he wanted. In the five years leading up to the creation of ODALE, the primary federal drug enforcement agency, the Bureau of Narcotics and Dangerous Drugs, had carried out four no-knock search warrants. In its first six months, ODALE carried out over one hundred.

Ambrose even set up a national "heroin hotline" that citizens could call to give tips on heroin dealers. The call center was run out of a Virginia mine shaft that at one time had been a possible destination for high-ranking government officials in the event of a nuclear attack on America. Ambrose was able to get half the staff of the federal Office of Emergency Preparedness transferred to ODALE—to answer phones on the heroin hotline. Promising tips—which could be phoned in anonymously—were forwarded to the closest regional strike force, which in theory would then pounce on the suspected drug dealer.[64]

In an interview with PBS thirty years later, Egil Krogh described the glee in the White House once ODALE was up and running.

> There was a tremendous amount of zeal behind what we were do-ing, too. The people that worked on these programs came to work each day saying, "What can we do today?" It was a very exciting at-mosphere. It was a place where I look back with a fierce affection of what we were able to do that I thought was effective. I regret the mistakes that we made, but we really tried our hardest.[65]

Those mistakes quickly began to add up. The strike force that carried out the Collinsville raids hadn't even bothered to get a search warrant before storming the Giglotto and Askew homes. Ambrose called the mistakes "reprehensible" and attributed them to "stupidity," but quickly added, "Drug people are the very vermin of humanity. They are dangerous. Occasionally we must adopt their dress and tactics." The agents in Collinsville were suspended pending further investigation—with pay.[66]

In what would for the next forty years become a standard line from law enforcement officials, Ambrose also called the Collinsville raids "a very isolated situation."[67] That would become increasingly difficult to believe. Two months later, another victim of the same Collinsville strike force came forward. Twenty-seven-year-old John Meiners of Edwardsville, Illinois, had been raided three days before the raids on the Askews and the Giglottos. He got it even worse. At about 3:00 AM, the armed narcs broke in. He awoke and got out of bed, only to be pinned against the wall with a gun to his head. They then tore his house apart. They smashed up windows even after they had already made their way inside. They "confiscated" his stereo, golf clubs, shotgun, and camera. Meiners himself was arrested, taken to a police station, and held for seventy-seven hours. They wouldn't even let him call his family, much less an attorney. After three days, they let him go with no explanation. And once again, they had no warrant.[68]

By the following August, investigators discovered three additional warrantless raids by the same ODALE strike force at about the same time, bringing the total to six such raids over a five-day span. In the first raid, on April 19, police broke into an East St. Louis home and handcuffed resident Robert Underwood to a chair. One agent then beat him while another held a gun to his head. The next day three agents raided the home of Rev. Karol Rekas. On April 23, the same day as the Askew and Giglotto raids, five agents raided the East St. Louis home of Mr. and Mrs. George Juengel, neither of whom were home at the time.[69]

Three months after those raids, in 1972, the *New York Times* published the results of its own investigation into the use of aggressive drug raids. The paper found that "dozens" of botched raids had occurred across the country since the 1970 federal crime bills and similar bills in the states became law. Agents, "often acting on uncorroborated tips from informants," were "bashing down the doors to a home or apartment and holding the residents at gunpoint while they ransack the house." The paper found that the botched raids were usually on lower-class families and were "tied intimately to the veritable explosion of government drug enforcement activities in recent years," thanks to Nixon's "total war" on drugs. Some victims told the paper that they hadn't come forward because narcotics officers had threatened them. Others had remained silent because "in their hatred for drugs they condoned the tactics but not the specific incidents."[70] Two weeks earlier, the Associated Press published its own investigation, which came to similar conclusions.[71] Little of this seemed to faze Ambrose. Within weeks of the Collinsville raids, he increased the number of strike forces from thirty-eight to forty-one.[72]

Between April 1972 and May 1973, ODALE strike forces conducted 1,439 raids. It's unclear how many were knock-and-announce and how many were no-knock, but even by 1973 the difference between the two kinds of raids had already begun to blur. "You might whisper 'Police! Open up!'" one agent told the *Times*. "Or you could yell it the instant before you hit the door."

Nixon's dehumanization and demonization of drug offenders had been a (literally) smashing success. Tactics like these had rarely been used in the United States, even against hardened criminals. Now they were being used against people suspected of nonviolent crimes, and with such wanton disregard for civil rights and procedure that the occasional wrong door or terrorized family could be dismissed as "an insignificant detail" or as cops "just trying to do their job." Even when acknowledging their mistakes, as Ambrose did, officials could minimize the horror—at least in their own minds—with context. These men were rounding up "the very vermin of humanity," after all. Surely the country understood that some collateral damage would be inflicted in the process.

The tactics could be degrading for the agents too. One ODALE agent told the *Times,* "Your whole lifestyle changes, and perhaps your morals too. Sometimes there's a thin line between the hunted and the hunter." Another agent described what he and his colleagues were thinking just before a raid:

> You have to go in with the idea that [the suspect is] going to fight. He's always being shaken down by other pushers. So you figure you'll be staring down a gun barrel. I've been on 200 or so raids, and the no-knock is the scariest. You ask yourself what would you do if your door came crashing down at 3 am and you had a gun. You'd let go, right? Personally, I think the danger might outweigh the value.[73]

By July, there was some momentum to end the raids and, since Watergate had broken, some momentum against the White House in general. Under the sunset provision, ODALE was about to expire, and Ambrose was planning to leave when it did. He still remained defiant, making no guarantee that the botched raids wouldn't continue. "I can't tell you that in the future there wouldn't be some knuckleheads who might go off half-cocked on their own to conduct raids," he said.[74] He seemed oblivious to— or simply untroubled by—the possibility that as leader of ODALE his own tone and rhetoric might have been part of the reason for the outbreak of knuckleheadery and half-cockedness in the first place.

With the expiration of ODALE, the Nixon administration consolidated all of the federal government's drug enforcement agencies into one, which would be called the Drug Enforcement Administration (DEA). It would remain in the Justice Department, again putting more cops under the same department that oversees federal prosecutors.[75]

The DEA's new director, John Bartels Jr., took a much more conciliatory approach than Ambrose to the problem of botched raids. In July 1973, then as acting DEA administrator, Bartels declared that any future mistakes "would not be tolerated." He issued a new set of guidelines, the most significant of which required that either Bartels himself or his deputy sign off on every no-knock raid carried out by the agency. He also required DEA agents to obtain an arrest warrant "whenever humanly practical" before making a forced entry into a private residence. Previously, they had needed only a search warrant, which could have listed only a residence instead of the name of the resident. The new policy would make it more difficult to wantonly break down doors based on no more than an informant's tip that he had bought or seen drugs in a particular residence.

To clarify the distinction between no-knock and knock-and-announce raids, Bartels added more instruction for the latter: "Before entering any premises, the agent will knock and announce his purpose and authority in an audible and distinctive matter." Agents would then have to pause and wait to be denied admittance before attempting a forcible entry. Bartels would require DEA agents to wear distinctive clothing that identified them as federal law enforcement, and they were explicitly forbidden from firing a weapon "except in self-defense or in the defense of another person." He also created a full-time position whose only responsibility was "to personally ensure that all operations are conducted in a completely legal and professional manner." The first person to fill that position, former BNDD official John Enright, would visit every field office in the country to train drug agents on the new guidelines.[76]

Nixon and Ambrose had wanted to generate publicity for the president's drug war. They certainly accomplished that. But it was increasingly clear that Nixon's tough-on-crime innovations had gone too far, and far too fast. In the fall of 1973, no-knock critics moved ahead with new legislation to halt the raids. Sam Ervin was, of course, at the front of the effort, along with Republican Illinois senator, Charles Percy, who had actively supported the no-knock laws in 1970. The stories of his own constituents getting terrorized apparently changed his mind. Ervin and Percy introduced two bills, both of which were cosponsored by Republican senator Jacob Javits of New York and Democratic senator Gaylord Nelson of Wisconsin. The first, proposed as an amendment to a DEA appropriations bill, repealed the no-knock provision for both Washington, DC, law enforcement and for federal narcotics agents. The second bill made the federal government liable for damages in cases of raids gone awry. Percy took the lead on publicly advocating for the changes, given that he had once supported the no-knock law. "If the past few months have taught us anything, it is that excessive zeal, even in the pursuit of so worthy a purpose as drug law enforcement, cannot be allowed to destroy the fundamental rights of American citizens." No-knock had created an atmosphere, Percy said, "where, on occasion, doors are kicked in, residents are terrorized, property is destroyed, lives are irreparably scarred, and, for the sake of administrative convenience, questions and answers are dealt with later."[77]

In July 1974, the Senate voted 64–31 to repeal the no-knock law, both in DC and for federal agents. Sam Ervin declared the vote a victory for "the privacy of the individual and the sanctity of the home." Senator Hruska, the Nebraska Republican who had been pushing the no-knock provision since 1968, continued to defend the tactic, telling the UPI news service, "There has to be a balancing between law enforcement and personal rights." Percy, having come full circle, called no-knocks "police state tactics."[78] On October 28, 1975, the new president, Gerald Ford, signed the bills into law.[79]

The most notable thing about America's early 1970s experiment with the no-knock raid is that it was repealed. Even in the midst of the era's antidrug fervor, a good number of politicians and public officials who supported the initial law were capable of changing their minds—they could display some shame and remorse for the harm and injury caused by the policy. A major-city police chief like Jerry Wilson could successfully fight crime without feeling compelled to send cops barreling into private residences, even when given the green light to do so—and by no less than the president himself. Embarrassed members of Congress who passed the initial law were not only capable of revoking it, but could pass an additional law holding the government *more* accountable should the abuses continue. The federal government even indicted twelve of its own law enforcement officers for mistakenly raiding the wrong home. (A jury later acquitted them.) The drug war and all its militarizing accoutrements were not yet intractable.

Even Egil Krogh, one of Nixon's fiercer antidrug zealots (who would later go to prison for his role in Watergate), told PBS *Frontline* in 2000, "Some programs that were initiated, in retrospect, got too close to breaching the wall of what is not acceptable under the Fourth Amendment. I know the 'no-knock' authority was one. . . . Those kinds of programs can lead to abuses, and they have."[80]

Don Santarelli—father of the federal no-knock raid—is far more compunctious. When asked to reflect on the legacy of Nixon's drug war in an interview for this book, he says it set in motion an animosity between police officers and the public that may now be beyond repair. "When you speak to a police officer today, you're terrified that you're going to offend him, and that he's going to arrest you and take you off to jail. Sure, a judge will let you out and drop the charges in a few days. But you've spent those days in jail. And now you have an arrest record. There's just no accountability for excessive force." He adds that his old boss's war rhetoric, later taken up by President Ronald Reagan and his successors, is to blame. "There has always been confrontation between the rational, educated way to look at policy and the escalation of language to make a political point. If politicians can get away with calling it a 'war on crime' or a 'war on drugs,' then they will. And yes, that's going to make law enforcement more willing to push the envelope when it comes to the use of force."[81]

After Nixon left office in the fall of 1974, the federal drug war went into a brief period of détente. But the SWAT concept would continue to gain momentum, independent of the break in the drug war. The two institutions would finally merge in the 1980s with Reagan's revival of the Nixonian drug war, applied more literally than even Nixon could have imagined. No-knock raids would return in full force, this time with no room for shame or remorse.

$\smile$

IN NOVEMBER 1973, FOUR YEARS AFTER THE BLACK PANTHER raid, Daryl Gates's SWAT team engaged in another nationally televised shoot-out. This one was with the Symbionese Liberation Army (SLA), a bizarre, cultish, often incoherent, violent band of leftists who borrowed imagery and rhetoric from the Black Panthers, Che Guevera, and Mao Tse-tung, and influence from a variety of religions and mystical traditions.[82] After two of its members were convicted and imprisoned for murdering an Oakland high school principal, the SLA hatched a plan to kidnap newspaper heiress Patty Hearst, then release her in exchange for the release of their imprisoned leaders.

But a couple months after she had been kidnapped, Patty Hearst was seen in a surveillance photo toting a machine gun during an SLA bank robbery in San Francisco. Her conversion and the now-iconic bank robbery photo was an irresistible story. The SLA had the country's attention.

In May 1974, SLA leader "Cinque" (real name: Donald De-Freeze) decided to move the group south to Los Angeles. On May 16, SLA activists William and Emily Harris entered a sporting goods store in Inglewood, California, to purchase some clothes. As they left, a security guard confronted William Harris, who had attempted to steal additional pairs of socks. Harris produced a revolver, which the guard promptly smacked from his hand. Patty Hearst was waiting outside on armed lookout. When she saw the confrontation between Harris and the security guard, she squeezed off fifty rounds from her machine gun. Miraculously, no one was hurt. The SLA fled.

By the afternoon of May 17, the FBI and LAPD had received tips indicating the SLA was hiding out in four houses in the southeastern part of the city. By 5:30 PM, more than two hundred LAPD officers had formed a perimeter around the area. As people emerged from the other suspected houses, the police concluded that the SLA had congregated in one house, located at 1466 East Fifty-Fourth Street. Gates positioned twenty-five SWAT team members around the house, including eight-man teams to the front and rear. Sgt. Ron McCarthy, the squad leader of SWAT Team One, pulled out a bullhorn. "People in the yellow house with the stone porch, address 1466 Fifty-Fourth Street, this is the Los Angeles Police Department speaking," he announced. "Come out with your hands up. Comply immediately and you will not be harmed."

The first to emerge was a terrified eight-year-old boy. A police officer picked him up and escorted him to safety. Moments later, an adult black male came out and walked over to the police line on his own accord. The man told police that the occupants weren't armed. But when the boy calmed down, he told a different story. They were all armed, he said. Well armed, in fact. He'd seen several of them wearing ammunition belts.

The house then went silent. McCarthy made fifteen more announcements, all to no avail. Gates decided to move with the SWAT team.

The SWAT team opted first for tear gas. The SLA responded with gunfire from a Browning automatic rifle. Gates then heard over the radio that the SWAT team was asking for fragmentation grenades. Interestingly, this alarmed him.

> *Jesus,* I thought. We didn't have fragmentation grenades. Used only by the military, they explode into body-piercing shards. . . .
>
> Fragmentation grenades are not funny. They are *meant* to seriously injure people. The SWAT request was made to John McAllister, the field commander. I picked up the microphone in my car and butted in. "You do not have permission to use fragmentation grenades," I said—in effect telling John what *his* decision should be.
>
> Had I been able to see firsthand what was going on, maybe I would have called the military, made the request. But instinctively, *I didn't like a civil police force using a weapon designed for an army.*[83]

Again, it's illuminating just how different attitudes were then than they are today. Here a heavily armed terrorist group had just opened fire in downtown Los Angeles. And we have Gates—the foremost proponent of militarized policing of his era—reflecting back on the incident, remembering that even under those circumstances, he had serious reservations about using military weapons against civilians.

When Gates arrived near the scene of the shoot-out, he saw the same sort of urban battlefield he'd seen during the Watts riots. "Here in the heart of Los Angeles was a war zone, something out of a World War II movie," he writes, "where you're taking the city from the enemy, house by house."

Minutes later, a dazed woman named Christine Johnson emerged from the house. She was one of the tenants before the SLA moved in. A SWAT officer ushered her away from the gunfire.

After about fifty minutes of heavy gunfire between the SLA and SWAT officers, the house caught fire. McCarthy again pulled up his bullhorn and offered to let the occupants surrender. The SLA responded with more gunfire. The fire raged on. There was little anyone could do. Understandably, LA firefighters wanted nothing to do with the blaze. They couldn't get close enough to douse it with water without making themselves vulnerable to gunfire.

Two women did eventually emerge from the rear of the house. Both were shot dead by police. (LAPD officers claimed the women emerged firing guns. Investigators hired by the women's families later claimed they were unarmed.)

The rest of the SLA remained inside as the building burned to the ground. Six more SLA members died, either from being shot, from suicide, or from the fire, including Cinque, the group's leader. Between them, the SLA and LAPD fired more than nine thousand rounds of ammunition.

Patty Hearst wasn't in the building. She'd later be arrested, charged, and convicted for her role in the bank robbery. She claims she had been brainwashed, beaten, and sexually abused by SLA members. The jury apparently didn't find her sympathetic, but her sentence was later commuted by President Jimmy Carter, and President Bill Clinton granted her a pardon in 2001, one of his last acts in office.

Ironically, the most enduring legacy of the SLA—an organization that seemed to see fascism just about everywhere—was to promote, popularize, and facilitate the spread of SWAT teams across America. For Gates, it was the perfect confluence of events. The SLA had attracted national attention when it kidnapped Hearst. The standoff with the LAPD and the FBI was not the result of a quick response to a bank robbery or mass shooting. It came after a full day of news reports that the group was in the city and law enforcement was in the process of tracking them down. That put news teams at the ready, so when it broke that the SLA had been located, they were prepped to send cameras and reporters. Gates, who mostly had an antagonistic relationship with the press, wryly notes in his book that as the gunfire dragged on, "I was briefly amused to notice that the hordes of reporters who had by now materialized were actually keeping their distance—for the only time I can remember."

They may have steered well clear of the flying bullets, but Gates certainly benefited from their presence. Live video of the gunfight was broadcast across the city. The footage then went nationwide. Gates's pet project, now eight years in the making, had finally found a national spotlight.

If the mission of Gates's SWAT teams was to quickly defuse a violent situation with minimal casualties, the confrontation with the SLA was far from an unqualified success. The team's decisions in the field had again led to a protracted exchange of thousands of rounds of gunfire in the middle of a densely populated urban area, not to mention a huge house fire and several deaths. But all of the deaths were SLA members. No police officers and no citizens outside the group suffered any significant injuries. And unlike the Black Panther raid, in which it could be argued that the police provoked a radical group that had some propensity for violence but for whom violence wasn't the primary objective, the SLA radicals had been violent from the start. Violence was the means of the group's activism. It had recently committed violent acts, and gave every indication it would continue to do so in the near future. There was no provocation here. Even if the tactics themselves yielded less than optimal results, there was no question that a police agency charged with protecting the city had no choice but to confront the group once they learned of its location.

After the shoot-out, the LAPD was flooded with letters, as were city newspapers. The letters ran about five-to-one in favor of the police, with praise for the SWAT teams in particular. Chris McNab, a prolific author of books on police and the military, writes that after the SLA shoot-out, "SWAT was now on the public map, most viewers being enthralled by its toughness, others being appalled."[84]

Gates himself writes:

> One thing was certain. That night, SWAT became a household word throughout the world. They were intrepid; they were brilliant in their deployment; their execution was flawless. Soon, other law enforcement agencies began mounting their own SWAT teams. The whole nation had watched the shootout—live, on network TV.

He concludes, "Clearly, SWAT had arrived."[85]

EARLY IN THE MORNING OF FEBRUARY 24, 1975, OFFICER Robert Duran and his partner, Officer Jim Street, were cruising in their squad car. A call came in about a potentially violent domestic disturbance. "Lovely," Duran said. "They're at each other's throats already." He pulled the car up to the intersection of the reported dispute. Nothing to speak of. "Quiet as a tomb," Duran said, forebodingly. "Are you sure we got the right number?" The next day would be Duran's birthday. His pretty wife was pregnant with their third child. All was right with the world. Then a shot rang out. Then several more. The two officers were caught in a deadly triangle of three snipers. Duran went down.

Street held the snipers at bay until the SWAT team could arrive. But by the time SWAT captain Hondo Harrelson and his team could scramble to the scene and ascend to the rooftop where one of the snipers was perched, all three gunmen had already left their positions and met back up on the street. Harrelson could only watch in anger as the assassins hopped into a gold Ford Maverick and sped away.

Sgt. Deacon Kay jooined his colleagues on the rooftop.

"The call was a phony, just like all the others," Kay said to Harrelson. "Ambush. Cold-blooded assassins. But *why?*"

"Because of the color of their skin," Harrelson replied. "Not because they're black or brown or white. But because they're *blue.*"

And so opened the first episode of the ABC drama *S.W.A.T.*, a cheesy, violent (for the time) melodrama from producers Aaron Spelling and Leonard Goldberg. Just eight years earlier, SWAT had been nothing more than a thought bouncing around in Daryl Gates's head. Now, thanks to a series of high-profile raids climaxing with the 1974 rescue of heiress Patty Hearst from the Symbionese Liberation Army, the concept had entered the mass consciousness. Gates's idea was now a prime-time network television show with an audience of millions. The show was set in a large, unnamed California city that vaguely resembled Los Angeles. Former LAPD SWAT officer Richard Kelbaugh was a technical adviser for the show. The first episode followed Hondo Harrelson as he recruited Street, Luca, and others for a second SWAT team to be run out of the "Olympic" division of the police department—all while also hunting down the ambushing cop killers (played by a not-at-all-intimidating trio of middle-aged white guys who delivered lines like, *Man, I just want to ice some pigs!*). Over the course of the first season, Hondo's new SWAT unit took on a suspiciously Manson-like cult leader and mass murderer, mob assassins trying to kill a former associate before he could testify before a Senate committee, a militant leftist group that had taken a professional basketball team hostage, an assassin from India sent to kill a US senator by infecting him with plague, terrorists who took a Nobel Prize–winning scientist hostage in a plant loaded with explosives that could eradicate half the city, and—in his toughest battle yet—a pretty young journalist sent to profile Hondo who didn't really like cops. Cops, she said, are "a necessary evil, but more evil than necessary."

The first season did well, and ABC ordered a second. Milton Bradley soon put out a *S.W.A.T.* board game. Kids could take their sandwiches to school in *S.W.A.T.* lunch boxes. There were *S.W.A.T.* action figures, View-Master sets, jigsaw puzzles, and die-cast miniatures of the S.W.A.T.-mobile. The show's theme song, an up-tempo instrumental by the funk-disco band Rhythm Heritage, was released as a single in 1976. It sold one million copies and briefly hit number one on the Billboard Hot 100. When the second season of S.W.A.T. was set to premiere, Hondo Harrelson made the cover of *TV Guide*.

SWAT had hit the pop culture.

AT THE SAME TIME, REAL SWAT TEAMS WERE SPREADING throughout the country. According to a *New York Times* investigation published in July 1975, by the middle of the 1970s the number of SWAT teams in the United States had grown to around five hundred. Criminologists were concerned. "It is the kind of thing that quickly catches on in police departments because of the pressure to be up to date without any knowledge of what they're actually getting into," said Marvin Wolfgang, director of the Center for Studies of Criminology and Criminal Law at the University of Pennsylvania. Someone the *Times* identified only as "a nationally-known police expert" added, "It reminds me of the nineteen-thirties when some smart salesmen went around the country selling submachine guns to every police department on the theory that they were going to have a shootout with John Dillinger some day."[86]

In its survey of police departments, the paper found that in large cities SWAT teams were usually deployed only in emergency situations and that they tended to perform professionally and skillfully, using their extensive training to deescalate violent situations, often successfully. But smaller towns and suburbs were adopting the SWAT idea too, or at least some version of it. And in many communities SWAT teams and similar units were mostly used to bully protest groups, counterculture enclaves, and minority activists.

Some police officials feared that the SWAT trend, particularly in smaller cities and towns, would succumb to what the philosopher Abraham Kaplan called "the Law of the Instrument": when you're carrying a hammer, everything looks like a nail. "There are some cops who want to solve all society's problems with an M-16," one police chief told the paper. "Some of these men have lost perspective of their role in society and are playing mental games with firearms. . . . And if you set yourself up to use heavy firepower, then the danger exists that you will use it at the first opportunity, and over-reaction—the opposite of what the [SWAT] concept is about—becomes a real danger."[87]

Big-city SWAT teams were getting training in paramilitary tactics and weapons, but that training was balanced by an emphasis on negotiation and deescalation and the use of violence only as the last possible option. In the smaller agencies around the country, not only did the SWAT team not get that sort of training, but the teams were staffed by part-timers, usually cops whose full-time jobs were more conventional police work. The risk was that the entire police department could succumb to a culture of militarism. In some quarters, it was already happening. Within a decade, the SWAT proliferation would accelerate. The emphasis on deescalation would all but disappear. Soon, just about every decent-sized city police department was armed with a hammer. And the drug war would ensure there were always plenty of nails around for pounding.

TO INFILTRATE THE SAN JOSE, CALIFORNIA, CHAPTER OF Hell's Angels, Russ Jones stopped cutting his hair, grew a beard, sported chains and denim, and rode a Harley. He had developed a particular knack for building methamphetamine cases against motorcycle gangs. His undercover getup was so good, in fact, that he'd twice been pulled over and searched, once by the state police and once by one of his colleagues at the San Jose Police Department.

The state cop even roughed him up a little. He never did figure out that Jones was a fellow cop. When Jones had accumulated enough evidence to wind down his 1973 investigation of the Hell's Angels, he cut his hair, trimmed his beard, and then met with a deputy district attorney to sort out what charges to bring against whom.

After several days of planning, Jones held a 4:00 AM briefing the morning of the raids with members of his narcotics team, as well as a few men from the ATF and the FBI. Jones had also specifically asked a lieutenant in the department to send along some uniformed officers to help with the warrants. "We had always sent uniformed officers when we served search warrants, so the suspects clearly and unquestionably knew we were police," Jones says.

When the San Jose backup detail walked in, Jones was startled. "There were all these guys in SWAT gear. Dark overalls, watch caps, all of that. Daryl Gates's SWAT team idea had started to spread across the state, but that was my first interaction with ours, which they called MERGE. They looked like they were about to storm a hostage situation."

Jones approached the lieutenant. "What is this?"

The lieutenant replied, "Our new uniform."

Jones told the lieutenant to have the MERGE team change into regular uniforms, or he'd just pull some beat cops off the street when he neared the Hell's Angels hangout. The tactical getups were inappropriate.

"He was angry as hell," Jones says. Jones had planned to serve the search warrants as he always had—by walking up to the door, knocking, announcing who he was and why he was there, then waiting for someone to answer.

"I've investigated some tough people. A lot of drug dealers, a lot of gangsters. I never had a case where knocking, announcing, and waiting for someone to come to the door created a problem," Jones says. Now retired, Jones's two decades of experience as a drug cop have since turned him into a vocal critic of police militarization and the drug war in general.

"I was already concerned with this militarizing of cops in San Jose. I don't recall ever using a 'no-knock' warrant in my career," Jones says. "But when I got to DEA, I noticed a slow progression in that direction. Guys would say, 'Oh, I heard a toilet flush,' or, 'I heard someone running in the house,' which they'd use as an excuse to break in after knocking instead of waiting for someone to answer. Eventually, the pause between the time they'd knock and the time they'd break down the door was so short that they weren't giving anyone time to get to the door to let them in—even if the suspect wanted to. And most of them did. I guess after I left the task force, they got to the point where they'd sometimes just not bother knocking at all."

The MERGE lieutenant eventually backed down and told his team to change into regular police uniforms. They served the Hell's Angels warrants by knocking, announcing themselves, and then waiting to be let in. They didn't break down a single door. The suspects went peacefully. And the search turned up plenty more evidence of a methamphetamine operation.

Later, Jones's supervisor tracked him down back at the office. The MERGE lieutenant had complained. Jones explained his position. His boss seemed to agree, but added, "You won the argument this morning, but you're going to lose the battle. These guys got new toys. They want to use them."[88]

⌇

BY THE SECOND HALF OF THE 1970s, THE LAW-AND-ORDER hard-liners had temporarily been stalled. President Jimmy Carter took a much less aggressive approach to the drug war than Nixon had. The country took a break from seven years of continual drug war and police power escalation, at least at the federal level.

But Sam Ervin's defeat of the no-knock raid was in many ways merely symbolic. It was never clear that federal agents actually needed the law to conduct such raids in the first place. Indeed, by the early 1980s they were using the tactic again, without any new federal law to officially reauthorize the practice. But Ervin's moral leadership on the issue was important in halting the spread of a dangerous tactic, even if only temporarily. In his autobiography, Ervin writes, "I was convinced that we must not sacrifice the proud boast of our law that every man's home is his castle on the altar of fear."[89]

The lull in the fighting didn't last long. Before Carter left the White House, he'd face allegations that pot-smoking was common among his staff and that two senior-level aides were cocaine users—and that one of them was his drug czar. The Reagan administration would soon come in to staff the drug policy positions with hardened culture warriors.

Ervin's wins were important, but ultimately ephemeral. The drug war and police militarization trends were about to merge. By the time Sam Ervin died in April 1985, the California National Guard was sending helicopters to drop camouflage-clad troops into the backyards of suspected pot growers in Humboldt County; the Justice Department was wiretapping defense attorneys; and Daryl Gates was using a battering ram affixed to a military-issue armored personnel carrier to smash his way into the living rooms of suspected drug offenders.

## The Numbers

○ Value of the property that Nixon claimed in 1972 was stolen each year by heroin addicts: $2 billion
  . . . claimed by Minnesota senator George McGovern: $4.4 billion
  . . . claimed by Nixon administration drug treatment expert Robert DuPont: $6.3 billion
  . . . claimed by Illinois senator Charles Percy: $10 billion–$15 billion
  . . . claimed by a White House briefing book on drug abuse distributed to the press: $18 billion
○ Total value of *all* reported stolen property in the United States in 1972: $1.2 billion

○ Number of burglaries committed by heroin addicts each year, per Nixon administration claims: 365 million

○ Total number of burglaries committed in the United States in 1971: 1.8 million

○ Number of SWAT teams in the United States in 1970: 1

○ Number of SWAT teams in the United States in 1975: approximately 500

○ Total number of federal narcotics agents in 1969: 400

○ Total number of federal narcotics agents in 1979: 1,941

○ Peak year for illicit drug use in America: 1979

○ Total number of no-knock search warrants carried out by the federal government from 1967 to 1971: 4

○ Number of no-knock search warrants carried out by ODALE during its first seven months of existence in 1972: more than 100[90]

# CHAPTER 6

# THE 1980S—US AND THEM

It now appears that . . . victory over the Fourth Amendment is complete.

—WILLIAM BRENNAN

William French set the tone for the Reagan administration early on. In one of the first cabinet meetings, the new attorney general declared, "The Justice Department is not a domestic agency. It is the internal arm of the national defense."

This would be a rough decade for the Symbolic Third Amendment. Reagan's drug warriors were about to take aim at *posse comitatus,* utterly dehumanize drug users, cast the drug fight as a biblical struggle between good and evil, and in the process turn the country's drug cops into holy soldiers.

French surrounded himself with a crew of prosecutors who called themselves the "hard chargers." One was Rudy Giuliani, a rising star brought to Washington by French after he had racked up some impressive federal drug prosecutions in New York. In an interview with the journalist Dan Baum, Lowell Jensen, another of French's advisers, said that the first task French assigned Giuliani was to survey US attorneys, cops, and prosecutors across the country about how the federal government could get more involved in fighting local crime. The overwhelming answer French got back was the same answer John Mitchell got when he posed the same question to his aides in the early days of the Nixon administration: launch a war on drugs.

So they did, with some sweeping new policies. One of the most significant new policies came thanks to a fortuitous bit of timing. Shortly after Reagan took office, the General Accounting Office (GAO) released a report, commissioned by Democratic senator Joe Biden of Delaware a year earlier, on the use of civil asset forfeiture. Civil forfeiture was a concept that had a long tradition in English common law. Under the law of *deodands*—Latin for "given to God"—anytime a piece of property caused a death, the property itself could be deemed guilty of the crime, at which point it or its value had to be forfeited over to the Crown. In colonial times, the concept was extended to allow the state to seize and confiscate ships that had been used to smuggle contraband. The Crown's abuse of the practice is often credited with inspiring the Fifth Amendment's prohibition on the taking of property without due process.[1]

But until the 1970s, the government couldn't take property that wasn't *directly* used in a crime. The government could shut down an illegal brothel, but it couldn't touch a house or car or boat the owner had bought with revenue generated by the brothel. That all changed when a young policy wonk named Robert Blakey, formerly of Robert F. Kennedy's Justice Department, conceived of a way to extend the government's reach. Under Blakey's idea, once the government convicted someone on charges related to organized crime, prosecutors could go after everything the guilty party had bought and earned with the proceeds of the criminal enterprise.

Blakey called the law RICO (Racketeering Influenced and Corrupt Organizations), after Rico Bandello, the fictional gangster in the 1931 movie *Little Caesar*. Originally conceived to target organized crime, by the time the law passed in 1970 it had become so broad that even Nixon's hard-liners were concerned. In opposing the law, Nixon's Justice Department told Congress that its broad reach "would result in a large number of unintended consequences."[2]

Reagan's Justice Department had no such reservations. The 1981 GAO report concluded that the government wasn't using forfeiture nearly enough, and that an excellent opportunity to collect revenue was going to waste. Reagan's people would take care of that.

Reagan also brought in the FBI to help enforce the drug laws. The agency had long resisted joining the drug war, particularly under J. Edgar Hoover. The legendary PR-savvy director knew the issue was a loser and tended to lure law enforcement into corruption. But by 1980 Hoover had been gone for seven years. It was time to bring the FBI into the fold.

The new administration also wanted to do away with the Exclusionary Rule, override *Miranda,* abolish bail and parole, douse pot farms with herbicides, put far more focus on enforcement and far less on treatment, and, perhaps most radically of all, enlist the military in the war on drugs.

The administration would focus most of these efforts on marijuana, on the theory that (1) marijuana is a "gateway" to harder drugs, and (2) people using cocaine and heroin are already too far gone to bother saving. There was also a strategic advantage to going after pot: successfully targeting and demonizing the least harmful illegal drug would push any talk of decriminalizing the others outside the realm of acceptable debate.

But if this was going to be a real war, Reagan would need to secure his role as commander in chief. He couldn't have Congress or rogue bureaucrats going off-message or questioning or holding up his initiatives. Here again, he took a play from Nixon's playbook. Reagan created a new office—a more czar-ish sort of drug czar. The position would report directly to him and would coordinate and oversee all antidrug efforts throughout the executive branch.

At the suggestion of billionaire data-processing mogul and future presidential candidate H. Ross Perot, Reagan chose Carlton Turner to be his new, even czar-ier drug czar. Turner was a native Alabaman who, oddly enough, had spent years running the country's only legal marijuana plot, at the University of Mississippi. That experience with pot gave Turner a convincing air of authority that would become particularly important when he started making patently absurd statements about the drug. Turner had no specialized knowledge of other illicit drugs, but that didn't matter much at the time. Pot was really all that was important.

By the time Reagan publicly announced the appointment in June 1982, Turner was already a favorite among the increasingly dogmatic anti-pot parent organizations proliferating in the suburbs. His appointment was also an early indication that the federal government's new drug war would no longer pay much attention to treating addicts. In previous administrations, the "drug czar" had been a treatment-oriented position. Under Turner, it became an enforcement office.

Underlying all of this focus on pot was a surge of cultural conservatism into positions of power in the new administration. The late 1960s and early 1970s had seen the emergence of a movement of conservative intellectuals. Periodicals like *Commentary, The Public Interest,* and occasionally *National Review* were featuring think pieces from people like Robert Bork, Ernest van den Haag, James Q. Wilson, and James Burnham. Where someone like George Wallace openly appealed to base prejudices, and the Moral Majority might openly cite the Bible as an authority when discussing public policy, the right's emerging tweed caucus intellectualized the culture wars. They made essentially the same points that Nixon political strategists had made among themselves in memos and behind closed doors, only with more erudition, and more for public consumption. Their general message was that some people are simply "born bad" and there's just no helping them. Talk about root causes, social intervention, or curing or rehabilitating deviancy was a futile attempt to debate away evil. Rioters, drug pushers, drug addicts, career criminals—these people were beyond redemption. The only proper response to evil was force—and then only to keep the evil from harming the good. These ideas found a home in the Reagan administration, where many of the people who had been advancing them found high-ranking appointments.

Nixon had figured out that drugs were the common element among all of his culture war enemies. Reagan's people took that idea and ran with it. Carlton Turner's focus on pot was a way to rekindle the culture war. In a revealing early interview with *Government Executive* magazine, Turner lumped pot with rock music, open and abundant sex, and ripped jeans. Drug use, Turner warned, was "a behavioral pattern that has sort of tagged along during the present young-adult generation's involvement in anti-military, anti–nuclear power, anti–big business, anti-authority demonstrations." People engaged in this behavior, he explained, "form a myriad of different racial, religious or otherwise persuasions demanding 'rights' or 'entitlements' politically," while scoffing at civil responsibility. At a 1981 meeting with his staff, Turner laid out his office's mission: "We have to create a generation of drug-free Americans to purge society."

There would be little tolerance for dissent. Turner was especially determined to purge psychiatrists from federal drug agencies. "They're trained to treat," he said, "and treatment isn't what we do." Methadone was out, so Turner blocked advocates of the treatment who were still in the federal government from speaking about it publicly. He took on the public health crowd at the National Institute on Drug Abuse (NIDA), working to rid the agency of officials and researchers who advocated a treatment-oriented federal drug policy. In 1982 a Turner ally at the agency sent a letter to libraries across the country urging them to pull and destroy sixty-four prior NIDA publications he'd found that included information that was inconsistent with the new narrative about drugs. In one particularly brilliant piece of propaganda, drug warriors argued that one of the symptoms of marijuana addiction was "refusal to believe the hard medical evidence that marijuana is physically and psychologically harmful." Questioning the drug war was *in and of itself* a sign of addiction.

Reagan himself delivered the stridently moral message better than anyone. In a 1982 speech to a convention of police chiefs in

New Orleans—his first major crime speech after inauguration—Reagan claimed that a recent study had found that just 250 criminals were responsible for half a million crimes over the course of eleven years. That boiled down to a crime every two days. That may have been possible if all the criminals in the study were drug users and the researchers counted drug use as a crime. But the statistic was given in the context of the harm that criminals do to society. It doesn't appear that Reagan ever sourced the study, but the notion that a team of researchers just happened to find 250 criminals with that sort of dedication seems unlikely.

In the same speech, Reagan called for expanding the list of crimes for which judges could deny bail, revoking *Miranda* and the Exclusionary Rule, a major new role for the military in fighting the drug war, an overhaul of the federal criminal code to include dozens of new laws, and in general a massive expansion of the powers and authority afforded to police and prosecutors. Without missing a beat, he then explained that America's crime problem was not only a moral problem, but a problem inextricably linked to . . . the expansion of government.

> A tendency to downplay the permanent moral values has helped make crime the enormous problem that it is today, one that this administration has, as I've told you, made one of its top domestic priorities. But it has occurred to me that the root causes of our other major domestic problem, the growth of government and the decay of the economy, can be traced to many of the same sources of the crime problem. This is because the same utopian presumptions about human nature that hinder the swift administration of justice have also helped fuel the expansion of government.[3]

Conservatives had always held the somewhat contradictory position that government can't be trusted in any area of society *except* when it comes to the power to arrest, detain, imprison, and execute people. But Reagan didn't dance around the contradiction, he embraced it. He blamed crime on big government—and in the same breath demanded that the government be given significantly more power to fight it. In words dripping with rectitude, he appealed to morality and defined the greatest challenge of the era as the struggle between good and evil. "For all our science and sophistication, for all of our justified pride in intellectual accomplishment, we must never forget the jungle is always there waiting to take us over," Reagan said. "Only our deep moral values and our strong social institutions can hold back that jungle and restrain the darker impulses of human nature."[4]

THE VERY FIRST CHANGE IN PUBLIC POLICY THAT REAGAN pushed through the Congress was the 1981 Military Cooperation with Law Enforcement Act, a proposed amendment to the Posse Comitatus Act that would carve out a much larger role for the military in the drug war. The White House was particularly eager to use military radar systems to actively search for drug smugglers. Since Nixon's anticrime push in the early 1970s, the courts had interpreted the Posse Comitatus Act as to allow the military to provide "indirect" assistance to federal law enforcement. Generally, that meant allowing the Navy to tip off the Coast Guard when it spotted vessels that fit the profile of those used by drug smugglers. The amended law encouraged the Pentagon to go further and give local, state, and federal police access to military intelligence and research. It also encouraged the opening up of access to military bases and equipment, and explicitly authorized the military to train civilian police in the use of military equipment. The law essentially permitted the military to work with drug cops on all aspects of drug interdiction short of making arrests and conducting searches.

The next year Reagan pushed for more. He wanted the Posse Comitatus Act amended yet again, this time to allow soldiers to both arrest and conduct searches of US citizens. He also made official his desire to repeal the Exclusionary Rule, which would essentially free police to violate the Fourth Amendment at will. Republican senator Strom Thurmond of South Carolina introduced a bill to accomplish both of those goals, in addition to other items on the White House wish list, such as expanded wiretapping powers. Reagan also wanted to expand asset forfeiture power to make it even easier for the government to take property away from people who had never been charged with a crime. The 1978 law had exempted real estate from the types of property that could be seized. Reagan wanted that distinction removed. He also wanted the standard of proof for confiscation lowered to a mere "suspicion" that the property had been used in a drug crime, and to permit the government to take property before even issuing an indictment. The aggressive legal minds at DOJ also invented a new type of forfeiture called *substitute assets*. This would allow prosecutors to estimate the amount of money a suspect had made in the drug trade, then confiscate a portion of his property equal in value to their estimate, even if they couldn't meet the already low standard for showing that the specific property they were eyeing was connected to any crime.

Unfortunately for the Americans who would later be victimized by these new crime-fighting techniques, there were no Sam Ervins left in Congress to protect them. The Democrats were eager to eliminate the perception that they were softer on crime than the Republicans. Senators Joe Biden and Hubert Humphrey preempted the White House–sponsored bill with a bill of their own. The Biden-Humphrey bill gave Reagan everything he wanted.[5]

On September 30, 1982, the crime bill loaded up with most of the provisions Reagan wanted passed the Senate 95–1.

Two weeks later, Reagan gave another speech at the Department of Justice with new proposals—most of which he could enact without authorization from Congress. The speech began and ended with Reagan's now-familiar invocations of good and evil, then made the connection between drug trafficking and the mob. He praised America's great crime fighters, politicians, and journalists who'd had the courage to take on the mafia over the years—including, notably, Eliot Ness, the federal agent who enforced alcohol prohibition in the 1920s. He laid out an eight-point plan to fight drug trafficking and organized crime.

One of the proposals was to set up antidrug task forces all along the border. In fact, one of Reagan's first initiatives was to establish an initial task force in southern Florida. He asked Vice President George Bush to oversee it. The concept was almost identical to Nixon's ODALE strike forces. The mission was to put money, drugs, and guns on the table—to generate photo-op busts to show that the government was hard at work fighting drug dealers. The task force didn't do much to stem the south Florida drug trade, but it was enormously successful at producing headlines. So Reagan created twelve new task forces just like it.

Like Nixon, Reagan planned to enlist governors and state legislatures to pass laws that mirrored the laws and policies of the federal government. So he promised to create new commissions, training programs, and intelligence-sharing infrastructure to merge federal, state, and local law enforcement into a single drug-fighting army. Finally, he explained that America's jails and prisons would soon need "millions of dollars" to prepare for the inevitable surge of new inmates that would follow.[6]

SINCE THE RAID THAT ENDED THE LIFE OF DIRK DICKENSON, marijuana had become a lucrative cash crop in Humboldt County. It wasn't just biker gangs and seasoned drug traffickers anymore. By the 1980s, some in the county's green and granola community were also getting rich. That attracted the attention of the pot warriors and hippie haters in the Reagan administration. And so drug-fighting helicopters would again take flight in Humboldt County. But not just one. This time there would be dozens.

The project was called the Campaign Against Marijuana Production, or CAMP. It was a joint operation dreamed up by Carlton Turner and California attorney general John Van de Kamp. The plan: bring in the National Guard to search for, find, and eradicate the marijuana fields popping up all over northern California. The program began in the summer of 1983, when the federal government sent U-2 spy planes to glide over the area in search of pot.

That's worth repeating. The government *sent U-2 spy planes* to the state of California to search for marijuana. Then they sent the helicopters. In all, thirteen California counties were invaded by choppers, some of them blaring Wagner's "Ride of the Valkyries" as they dropped Guardsmen and law enforcement officers armed with automatic weapons, sandviks, and machetes into the fields of California.

William Ruzzamenti, the DEA official in charge of the operation, explained to reporter and drug law reformer Arnold Trebach in 1984 why the helicopters were important. "The helicopters have provided us with a sense of superiority that has in fact established a paranoia in the growers' minds. . . . When you come in with a helicopter there's no way they're going to stop and fight; by and large they head for the hills."[7] It's probably worth emphasizing again that Ruzzamenti wasn't talking here about the Viet Cong or the Sandinistas. He was talking about American citizens.

In CAMP's first year, the program conducted 524 raids, arrested 128 people, and seized about 65,000 marijuana plants. Operating costs ran at a little over $1.5 million. The next year, 24 more sheriffs signed up for the program, for a total of 37. CAMP conducted 398 raids, seized nearly 160,000 plants, and made 218 arrests at a cost to taxpayers of $2.3 million. The area's larger growers had been put out of business (or, probably more accurately, had set up shop somewhere else), so by the start of the second campaign in 1984, CAMP officials were already targeting increasingly smaller growers. By the end of that 1984 campaign, the helicopters had to fly at lower and lower altitudes to spot smaller batches of plants. The noise, wind, and vibration from the choppers could knock out windows, kick up dust clouds, and scare livestock. The officials running the operation made no bones about the paramilitary tactics they were using. They considered the areas they were raiding to be war zones. In the interest of "officer safety," they gave themselves permission to search any structures relatively close to a marijuana supply, without a warrant. Anyone coming anywhere near a raid operation was subject to detainment, usually at gunpoint.

Describing the 1984 operation, the journalist Dan Baum writes, "For a solid month, the clatter of helicopters was never absent from Humboldt County. CAMP roadblocks started hauling whole families out of cars and holding them at gunpoint while searching their vehicles without warrants. CAMP troops . . . went house to house kicking in doors and ransacking homes, again without warrants."

In his book *The Great Drug War,* Arnold Trebach writes that in 1983 and 1984 Ruzzamenti claimed that the entire town of Denny, California, was so hostile to the drug warriors that he'd need "to virtually occupy the area with a small army." Denny residents Eric Massett and his wife Rebecca Sue told Trebach that when they pulled out of their driveway during a CAMP raid in 1983, there were six men in camouflage pointing rifles at them. They fled into town, where CAMP officials then put up roadblocks to keep everyone in town while they conducted their eradication campaign. When CAMP left, a military convoy drove out of the small village, guns trained on the townspeople. The couple told Trebach that one of them was waving a .45 as the others chanted, "War on drugs! War on drugs!"[8]

But CAMP was just the marijuana eradication program in California. The Reagan administration had begun similar federal-state programs all over the country. In 1984 the federal-state marijuana eradication efforts conducted twenty thousand raids nationally, resulting in the destruction of 13 million plants (many of them wild) and around five thousand arrests. The following year, newly appointed attorney general Ed Meese put his own stamp on the program by ordering the largest armed law enforcement operation in American history. On the morning of August 5, 1985, Meese flew to Harrison, Arkansas, to kick off Operation Delta-9, code for the scientific name (delta-9 tetrahydrocannabinol) of the psychoactive chemical in marijuana, more commonly known as THC. The plan was for Meese to take part in the raid of a pot grower in the Ozark National Forrest. Unfortunately, the fifty-four-year-old politician's plan to cast himself as a heroic drug cop fell short when bad weather got in the way. Heavy rain, fog, and flash flooding reduced Meese's role to photo-ops of him observing hillside pot growth from a heli-copter and, during a press conference, inspecting the catch that other agents had brought back. Operation Delta-9 sent 2,200 drug cops on simultaneous eradication raids in all fifty states over two days. It was mostly for show, of course. Even the most feverish of drug warriors had to know that at best the massive effort would register as little more than a blip in the market for pot.[9]

~~

THE SUPREME COURT ALSO DID ITS PART IN THE 1980s TO dismantle civil liberties for the cause of saving the country from drugs. In 1983 the Court heard oral arguments in *Illinois v. Gates*.[10] At issue was whether information gleaned from an anonymous letter sent to police was enough to establish probable cause for a search. Under the existing law and the Exclusionary Rule, the case should have been open and shut. Since a 1969 Court decision, police had had to meet a two-pronged test to determine if information provided by an informant was reliable enough to establish probable cause for a search warrant. They first had to demonstrate to a judge that the informant was credible. Second, they also had to show that there was a factual basis for the informant's allegations. In *Gates,* the police had no way of knowing whether the informant was credible. They only had the letter that the informant had sent to the police department.

The Court's conservative wing initially saw the case as an opportunity to carve out a "good-faith exception" to the Exclusionary Rule. The facts of *Gates* didn't allow for that, but the Court did dismiss the two-pronged test for an easier-to-meet "totality of the circumstances" test. The next year, in *US v. Leon,* the conservatives got their good-faith exception.[11] After *Leon,* if a police officer inadvertently violated a suspect's Fourth Amendment rights during a search, but was acting in good faith, the Exclusionary Rule no longer applied. Moreover, the Court wouldn't second-guess the officer's intentions. A defendant would have to prove bad faith, generally an impossible task. The ruling was essentially an instruction manual for police to use to get around the Fourth Amendment.

Subsequent rulings further narrowed the Fourth Amendment. In *Massachusetts v. Sheppard,* the majority again declined to apply the Exclusionary Rule, this time after police *knowingly* provided a defective warrant to a magistrate.[12] When the magistrate returned the warrant, the police didn't bother to read it before conducting the search to see if the mistake making the warrant defective had been removed. The Court said that was fine. In *Segura v. United States,* the Court ruled that police who broke into a residence without a warrant, then hung out inside for nineteen hours until they were able to get one, didn't violate the defendant's Fourth Amendment rights because they didn't actually begin searching the place until they had obtained the warrant.[13] The Court also declined to sanction the officers, because the majority didn't believe the ruling would make illegal breaking and entering by police a regular problem. In *Nix v. William,* the Court introduced the doctrine of "inevitable discovery," which states that if the police find evidence during an illegal search that they would likely have found if they had conducted the search legally, the Exclusionary Rule doesn't apply.[14]

Prior to these rulings, as previously noted, there were still plenty of forced-entry raids into private residences in the name of the drug war. There had already been a number of wrong-door raids and a handful of resulting fatalities. But there were still some checks in place to prevent violent raids from becoming an everyday occurrence and to induce drug cops to work carefully and avoid shortcuts. The Exclusionary Rule was the biggest and most important of these checks. If police didn't follow the proper procedures before breaking into a house, they risked losing any evidence they might find and wasting the time and effort they'd spent conducting the investigation. It was a significant disincentive—and the Court's 1983 and 1984 decisions cleaved much of it away.

⌒

BECAUSE 1984 WAS AN ELECTION YEAR, IT WOULD NEED TO have an omnibus crime bill of its own. Polls showed that crime was the most pressing domestic issue with the public, so everyone running for reelection needed something to tout on the campaign trail. At this point, there wasn't any real debate about crime policy. It was really only about which party could come up with the most creative ways to empower cops and prosecutors, strip suspects of their rights, and show they were more committed to the battle than their opponents were. The most significant provision in the newest crime bill again dealt with asset forfeiture. The new proposal was to let law enforcement agencies involved with federal drug investigations share in any asset forfeiture proceeds that the case might produce. Previously, forfeiture revenues went toward general operations. Under the new law, the Justice Department would set up a fund with the cash and auction proceeds from its investigations. After the lead federal agency took its cut, any state or local police agencies that had helped out would also get a share.

The measure was considered uncontroversial at the time, but it is difficult to overstate the effect it would have on drug policing over the next thirty years. With drug investigations now a potential source of revenue for police departments, everything would change.

The law's impact was immediate. After it passed, for example, the CAMP raids and those like them in other parts of the country were no longer just about putting on a good show and terrorizing the counterculture. Now the raids could generate revenue for all of the police agencies involved. The DEA's Ruzzamenti was rather frank about it in an interview with Ray Raphael for his 1985 book on the CAMP program, *Cash Crop*. "The biggest focus of what we're doing is going to be on land seizures," Ruzzamenti said. "Anybody who is growing marijuana on their land, we're going to take their land. It's as simple as that. It's done civilly through the federal system. Basically, people have to prove that they weren't involved and didn't know about it. Just the act of having marijuana grown on your land is enough to tie it up; then you have to turn around and prove you're innocent. It reverses the burden of proof."[15]

Some people in northern California owned thousands of acres of land, much of it densely forested. Growers were also known to set up operations on someone else's land, without the owner's permission. If the feds started a forfeiture process, the owner was then in the difficult position of having to prove his innocence. Even then, federal prosecutors could argue that he should have been more vigilant about policing his property for pot plants. Some landowners faced the loss of hundreds of acres of property over a few dozen marijuana plants grown in an area the size of a backyard garden. Because it was much easier to win land through civil forfeiture than to win a conviction in criminal court, federal prosecutors often offered to drop the criminal charges if the landowners agreed to hand their property over to the federal government.

Those sorts of offers exposed just how fraudulent the government's justification for its terror tactics really were. Allegedly, these pot growers were the dregs of humanity, greedily poisoning America's children with their sinister harvest. They were dangerous enough that the government had to send virtual armies to occupy entire towns, buzz homes and chase children with helicopters, set up roadblocks to search cars at gunpoint, and strip suspects and innocents alike of their Fourth Amendment rights. These growers were *that* dangerous. However, if they were willing to hand over their land, the government was more than happy to let them go free.

Because of the new forfeiture law, police agencies now had a strong incentive to "find" a connection between valuable property and drug activity, even if there was none. They now had an incentive to conduct drug busts inside homes when the suspects could just as easily—and more safely—have been apprehended outside the house. They now had a strong financial incentive to make drug policing a higher priority and to devote more personnel to drug investigations than to investigating other crimes. Closing a rape or murder case didn't come with a potential kickback to the police department. Knocking off a mid- or low-level drug dealer did. Most perversely of all, the promise of a financial reward actually provided drug cops with an incentive to wait until drugs had already been sold to move in with searches and arrests. A suspect flush with pot or cocaine didn't offer much forfeiture potential. If they waited to bust him until he'd sold most or all of his supply, the police department got to keep the cash. Subsequent media and academic investigations would bear this out, finding examples of police waiting to bust stash houses until most of their supply had been sold, or of being far more likely to pull over suspected drug-running vehicles in the lanes leading *out* from large metropolitan areas (when they were likely to be full of cash) than the lanes leading in (when they were more likely to be filled with drugs).

Over the next twenty years, many states would attempt to correct these incentive problems by requiring that any money earned from drug forfeitures be given to a general fund or to a schools fund instead of going back to the police. But under a provision in the federal law called *equitable sharing* (also known as *adoption*), all that a state or local police agency looking at a potentially lucrative forfeiture case needed to do was call up the DEA to assist in their investigation. Even cursory involvement from a federal agency made the investigation federal, and subject to federal law. Whatever laws the state legislature tried to pass to curb abuses no longer applied. The federal government then took its cut and gave the rest of the proceeds (sometimes as much as 80 percent) back to the local police agency.

These forfeiture policies would soon help fund the explosion of SWAT teams across the country—forging yet another tie between the escalating drug war and hypermilitarized policing.

IT WAS AN UNUSUALLY COLD FEBRUARY NIGHT IN LOS ANGELES, and Daryl Gates was riding shotgun in his newest toy, a modified armored personnel carrier. Gates had been asking the city for armored vehicles for years, and he had always been denied. Though Los Angeles officials had fully embraced the city's SWAT teams by the mid-1980s, they were still squeamish about letting city police use military equipment. But in preparing security for the 1984 Olympics, Gates was able to obtain a couple of old APCs from the Department of Energy. In a former life, they had been used to guard nuclear power plants. After the Olympics, Gates had the vehicles painted blue, emblazoned with a city seal, and—cleverly—identified on the outside with the words RESCUE VEHICLE. It worked. The police commission let him keep them.

Of course, Gates had no intention of using APCs for rescue. He was growing frustrated with the problems his SWAT teams encountered when breaking into fortified crack houses. They had tried ripping doors off their hinges by attaching them to tow trucks. That took too long, giving suspects too much time to destroy evidence. They had tried blasting locks open with specialized explosives called shape chargers. But those could throw off shrapnel and debris, making them dangerous for the raiding cops. Then one of Gates's subordinates came to him with a new idea: they could attach a battering ram to the front of one of the armored personnel carriers. So Gates had one of the vehicles outfitted with a battering ram and found some abandoned houses slated for demolition that the SWAT team could use for practice.

On this particular night in February 1985, Gates planned to unveil the new weapon on a suspected crack house in a relatively nice Pacoima neighborhood. Gates even invited along a couple of photographers to document his latest innovation for the archives.

After stopping a few blocks away to attach the ram, the APC and the SWAT team approached the targeted house, this time with no less than the city's police chief riding along. The SWAT team took position. The APC revved up some momentum, hopped the driveway, and punched a hole in the side of the house. It then moved in and out of the hole several times to widen it. (Yes, the symbolism is inescapable.) Once the hole was large enough, the vehicle pulled out, and the SWAT team pounced. Inside, they found two women and three children eating ice cream. No drugs, though police later claimed to have found "traces" of cocaine and items they said were drug paraphernalia. Meanwhile, as the APC withdrew from the house, it hit a patch of ice. The driver lost control, which sent the driver, Gates, and the chief's new toy careening into the side of a Cadillac parked in the driveway. "It was not our shining hour," Gates would later write.[16]

Gates insisted that they had the correct house—he writes in his autobiography that the drug dealer had merely run out of crack and had gone to get more. But it sure didn't seem like a crack house. Crack houses were usually filthy, heavily fortified, and furnished with the sorts of things necessary to make and sell crack. (Nancy Reagan once famously visited an alleged crack house and remarked, "Where is the furniture?") Gates had raided a home. It had furniture, a fireplace, a den. More problematic for Gates, it also contained two women and three children. Eating ice cream.

The media and civil liberties advocates piled on. That only made Gates more defiant. He vowed to take his new battering ram to "every single fortified rock house in this town!" In his autobiography, Gates argues that the ram had a deterrent effect, that "it frightened even the hard-core pushers to imagine that at any moment a device was going to put a big hole in their place of business, and in would march SWAT, scattering flash-bangs and scaring the hell out of everyone."[17]

The ACLU took Gates to court over the ram. While LAPD officials insisted at the time that they weren't backing down, the department discontinued its use during litigation. By the time the California Supreme Court resolved the case in 1987, the ram had basically been retired—at least for the time being. The court found the ram to be so excessive as to violate the Fourth Amendment requirement that searches be reasonable, and it ruled that prior to each raid the LAPD would need to get special permission from a judge before using a battering ram. (In the same case, the court also ruled that city police did *not* need a judge's permission to use flash-bang grenades.)

Gates's antics aside, the battering ram at least showed that as of 1985 we were still capable of finding that some drug war tactics went too far. It wasn't just the California Supreme Court. Public opinion polls also showed strong opposition to the ram. The ram was only used four times before community outrage compelled the department to stop. Gates had been forced to "demilitarize" his APCs by painting them blue and calling them "rescue vehicles" in order to get the city's police commission to approve them. City officials were still wary about using battle gear on the streets of Los Angeles. A state supreme court was still capable of finding at least some militaristic police tactics unreasonable under the Fourth Amendment. We still had some limits.

~~

UNFORTUNATELY, THAT WOULDN'T LAST. AT THE NATIONAL level, the once-separate trends of militarization and the war on drugs continued to converge. On April 8, 1986, President Reagan signed National Security Decision Directive 221, which designated illicit drugs a threat to US national security. In addition to adding to the drug interdiction responsibilities of agencies like the CIA and the State Department, the directive also instructed the US military "to support counter-narcotics efforts more actively," including providing assistance to law enforcement agencies "in the planning and execution of large counter-narcotics operations," "participat[ing] in coordinated interdiction programs," engaging in combined exercises with civilian law enforcement agencies, and training and helping foreign militaries conduct antidrug operations. The declaration put pot, cocaine, and heroin at nearly the same class of enemy as any nation against whom the United States had fought a conventional war.

There were a few other policies enacted toward the end of the Reagan years that were little noticed at the time but further cleared the way for mass militarization of civilian police agencies. One of the most destructive was a massive influx of federal money to local police departments solely for the purpose of drug policing. The money could be used to start, fund, and maintain SWAT teams, to expand narcotics units, or to pay cops overtime for doing extra drug investigations. Taken with the potential bounty available in asset forfeiture, police departments across the country were now heavily incentivized to devote more time, personnel, and aggression to drug policing and less to investigating murders, rapes, and robberies. There was no money in investigating crimes with actual victims. Drug investigations could pay for themselves—and often brought in additional revenue.

Another new policy was buried in the National Defense Appropriation Act for Fiscal Year 1987. It instructed the National Guard to provide full cooperation with local and federal law enforcement agencies in drug investigations. The law gave the Guard its first budget for counterdrug operations. In 1989 Congress expanded the budget to $60 million. In some places, Guard troops were now even conducting searches and making arrests. But in the short term, the main effect of the new law was to give local law enforcement agencies access to National Guard aircraft.

The other major new policy came in 1987, when Congress ordered the secretary of Defense and the US attorney general to notify local law enforcement agencies each year about the availability of surplus military equipment they could obtain for their departments. The pre-election GOP crime bill of 1968 had already authorized the military to share equipment with local police agencies. But the 1987 law was more proactive. It established an office in the Pentagon specifically to facilitate transfers of war gear to civilian law enforcement. Congress even set up an 800 number that sheriffs and police chiefs could call to see what was available, and it ordered the General Services Administration to work with the Pentagon to produce a catalog from which police agencies could make their wish lists.

It had not been that long since Darryl Gates had been compelled to hide from his own police commission the fact that he had obtained a military-issue armored personnel carrier, or since he had had to have his mayor call the US secretary of Defense to get permission to use a grenade launcher. Congress had now authorized—encouraged, really—the transfer of vehicles, armor, and weapons (along with more mundane items like office furniture) that had been designed for use on a battlefield against enemy combatants to be used on American streets, in American neighborhoods, against American citizens.

━

NOT ALL POLICE OFFICIALS SHARED DARYL GATES'S APPROACH to the use of force. Norm Stamper still remembers the case that changed his mind about police militarization. Stamper joined the San Diego Police Department in 1966 as a beat cop. By March 12, 1987, he had worked his way through the ranks to the position of field operations chief. That was the evening Tommie DuBose died.[18]

"We were serving a series of high-risk warrants all over the city that day," Stamper says. "They were going on all day. My guys who were serving the warrants weren't a SWAT team, but undercover field operations cops who had been working with narcotics. At around six or seven in the evening, they hit a house in east San Diego."

It was the home of DuBose, a fifty-six-year-old civil servant who had worked for over twenty years for the US Navy. Their warrant was for Tommie's son, Charles, who was wanted for drug distribution. Tommie DuBose knew his son had a drug problem. Consequently, he was an outspoken opponent of drug use and abuse. "But he had nothing to do with that himself," Stamper says. "Perhaps somewhat naively, I don't think he had any suspicion that his son was doing anything more than using."

According to subsequent reports, the police knocked and announced themselves, then forced entry when an officer claimed to have seen DuBose run to the back of the house. Once they made their way inside, DuBose threw a glass of wine into the face of Officer Andy Rios. Police say the two men then engaged in a struggle over Rios's gun. Officer Carlos Garcia then opened fire, shooting DuBose five times, four times in the back. DuBose died in his home.

"I wasn't personally involved, but these were my guys," Stamper says. "They called me in. I showed up shortly afterward, and I saw this man lying dead in his own living room. He was just watching TV. He had no criminal record. All he knew was that some armed men were breaking into his house."

The incident hit Stamper hard. "Just overwhelming heartsickness. I mean, this man wasn't armed, he was not named in the warrant. He spoke out against drug use because he saw what it had done to his kid. And you know, God knows how many other times we scared the bejesus out of innocent people. You hit the wrong house. Or you hit the right house, but there are wives, girlfriends, kids inside completely unaware of what's going on. They could be completely ignorant of any drug-related criminal activity, but a girl-friend's home or apartment might have a stash that their male part-ner has secreted away. And so they'd get raided too. When one of these raids would just scare the hell out of women, children, family pets, it just made me wonder what in the world we were doing, and why the hell we were doing it."

Tommie DuBose's wife, brother-in-law, and twenty-five-year-old son Brett were all in the house at the time of the raid. None of them heard either the knock or the announcement. One neighbor who saw the entire raid estimated that only about fifteen seconds expired from the time the police pulled up until he heard gunshots. Others said that they never heard any announcement. Brett Du-Bose said that he first saw the police pull up from the window in an-other room, but that they were in the house before he had time to say anything.

The San Diego County District Attorney's Office eventually cleared the raiding officers of any wrongdoing, but the report did question their tactics. It found that the yellow jackets they wore dur-ing raids didn't make it clear enough to citizens that they were po-lice. And in the DuBose raid specifically, the DA found that the officers didn't properly announce themselves and didn't wait long enough after the announcement before entering.

The San Diego Police Department eventually acknowledged that DuBose was an innocent victim. Assistant Chief Bob Burgreen even acknowledged that the police had made some mistakes. "The offi-cers did not allow enough time or enough notice," he told the *Los Angeles Times*. "They did not give the DuBose family enough time to answer the door adequately before they went into the house. The entry that quickly was not justified." But Burgreen added that be-cause their mistakes were made in good faith, none of the officers would be disciplined. And the officers involved would continue to serve high-risk drug warrants.

The problem was that this wouldn't be the only mistake. On March 2, 1988, San Diego police conducted a 2:20 AM raid on the home of John Taylor, his brother George, and George's wife. Forty-four-year-old George Taylor was thrown to the floor with a gun to his head. An officer then stepped on his neck to keep him in place while they searched the house. He'd had spinal surgery a year earlier. The police apologized when they realized they had intended to raid the house next door. But a week later the Taylors were *again* awoken by San Diego police. The cops were again raiding the house next door. This time one officer mistakenly smashed out the windows to the Taylors' home, then pushed the barrel of his gun inside.[19]

Eighteen months after the DuBose raid, San Diego police stormed the home of Adelita Pina and her three daughters. They expected to find a major drug operation, including "kilos" of marijuana, firearms, and ammunition. They found nothing. Lt. Dan Berglund, head of the city's narcotics team, refused to admit that they had made a mistake, and retreated to the now-familiar excuse that though Pina may have been innocent, someone else must have been selling drugs from her house. Of course, that excuse completely missed the point—and showed how the drug war could blind police to the rights and well-being of the people they were supposed to be serving. Berglund's defense of the raid was that his officers had correctly raided the house where undercover cops had bought drugs from a man named "Pete." That Pete didn't actually live at the house, or that three young girls, their aunt, and their uncle were subjected to a terrifying raid that turned up nothing, was all beside the point. Technically, Berglund's cops were probably right. That was all that mattered. Therefore the raid was justified.[20]

Five months later, another mistaken raid. Police said that they knocked on Ken Fortner's door, then decided to break it down when they heard noises inside indicating that someone was destroying evidence. But as Commander Larry Gore told the *Los Angeles Times,* during the pre-raid briefing someone "inadvertently wrote down the wrong number." Fortner was thrown face-first into a flight of stairs. His friend Kelly McAloon was tossed onto a concrete patio and suffered injuries to his ribs that required a trip to the emergency room for X-rays. Like Berglund, Gore's justification once again glossed over the harm done. "They went to this location with the best of intentions," he said. "They were armed with all the correct information, and they had a legitimate reason to do what they did. They just had the wrong address."[21]

But unlike other parts of the country, things did improve in San Diego. In response to the mistaken raids and a number of questionable police shootings, Stamper spearheaded a series of reforms to move the department to a more community-oriented style of policing. By the early 1990s, San Diego police officials and city leaders were in regular contact with civil rights and minority leaders. The city set up a hotline to report police abuse, and persuaded a local TV station to host a telethon in which viewers could call in to have on-air conversations with city leaders.

In 1993 the *Los Angeles Times* credited those efforts with saving the city from the riots that hit Los Angeles after the verdict in the Rodney King beating case in 1992.[22] City and police officials in San Diego were quick to denounce the acquittal of the LAPD officers who beat Rodney King, but more importantly, they had direct lines to the city's minority communities when the verdict was announced. They could build a strategy around empathy, not antagonism. Consequently, city officials knew that angry people would want to vent. So rather than suppress demonstrations, they allowed them—and in fact encouraged them.

They then sent police officers out into the city's minority neighborhoods. City officials later acknowledged that this was to prevent the protests from getting out of hand and turning violent. But because of the city's embrace of true community policing, dispatching cops to their beats en masse looked more like a show of support than a show of force. The cops knew the neighborhoods they were sent out to keep calm—not just the street grids and landmarks but the pastors, the school principals, and the community leaders. One local activist told the *Times,* "One of the reasons we survived is that people from the mayor to the City Council to the arts organizations got out into the streets immediately and sided with the people, not against them."[23]

While paramilitary police raids—and botched raids—continued to soar in large cities around the country throughout the 1990s and 2000s, in my own research I've found only one mistaken raid by San Diego police since the 1990 raid at the home of Ken Fortner. Interestingly, since the late 1980s, San Diego has also boasted one of the lowest crime rates in the country. It consistently ranks among the five safest big cities in America.[24] Crime in the city has been falling for the last two decades, just as it has in the rest of the country. San Diego's crime rate peaked in 1989, however, just as the new policies were taking hold in the city.[25] The national crime rate peaked in 1991.[26] As we'll see, there were a few other places that for at least a time bucked the trend toward more militarized police. As with San Diego in the 1990s—and even Washington, DC, in the early 1970s—not only were none of them overrun by drug dealers and gangs as a result, but there's good evidence that their lower crime rates outperformed comparable cities and the country at large.

GEORGE H. W. BUSH TROUNCED THE DEMOCRATIC CANDIDATE, Massachusetts governor Michael Dukakis, in the 1988 presidential election, when he did it with a campaign that exploited the fear of crime like none since Nixon in 1968. The most notorious example was the racially loaded television commercial about Willie Horton, a black convict who raped and stabbed a white woman while on furlough from a Massachusetts prison. Bush and campaign manager Lee Atwater relentlessly attacked Dukakis as soft on crime, hitting him with Horton, his opposition to the death penalty, and his ties to the ACLU. Three years later, Atwater—then fighting an inoperable brain tumor—would apologize to Dukakis.[27] But Bush's victory was a green light for a whole new slate of tough-on-crime initiatives.

One of his first moves was to appoint William Bennett to be his drug czar. Bennett had practically begged for the job, calling Bush and Bush's chief of staff, John Sununu, several times after the election to ask for the position. Bennett had headed up the National Endowment for the Humanities and then the Department of Education under Reagan. He had run both agencies as a proud moral scold. Which isn't to say he was a prude. Bennett was an obese man, a chain-smoker, and, the country would learn years later, he had a pretty serious jones for video poker. But those weren't culture war issues. Bennett was also a fierce drug warrior and a favorite of Christian Coalition types. After leaving office, he'd basically appoint himself the country's guardian of virtue.

Bennett's main contribution to the drug war was to infuse it with morality. "The simple fact is that drug use is wrong," he wrote in a 1990 essay for *Reader's Digest*. "And in the end, the moral argument is the most compelling argument."[28] That was the lingering irony of Bennett's reign in the Office of National Drug Control Policy (ONDCP). The man who often struggled to control his own indulgences was ready to unleash a full federal arsenal of force on people whose indulgences he personally found immoral. Of course, Bennett's indulgences were legal. But when pressed on the morality question—*Why is marijuana immoral, but alcohol and nicotine aren't?*—the best he and his surrogates could do was point to the fact that pot was illegal. When confronted with the legalization question, Bennett would return to the argument that pot was immoral. The transparently circular bit of argumentation—it's immoral because it's illegal, and it's illegal because it's immoral—would have been amusing if not for the fact that it had some very real consequences, up to and including ruining and ending lives.

For all the war rhetoric to have come from politicians' mouths over the previous twenty years of drug prohibition, Bennett's somehow managed to reach new heights of bellicosity. Embedded in his morality approach to drug prohibition was a new effort at dehumanizing drug users. Bennett demanded that drug warriors in the administration stop talking about addicts as "sick" and stop referring to addiction as a health problem. Going forward, the federal government would simply view them as bad people. Fundamentally bad people aren't cured or mended. The only real question is how best to remove them from the good people.[29]

On his first day in office, Bennett took a page from Nixon and designed a plan for the nation's capital. He wanted "a massive wave of arrests" of drug offenders, and proposed converting abandoned buildings into temporary prisons to house the arrestees until he could get more money to build more prisons. He didn't mince words about his intent. "I'm not a person who says that the first purpose of punishment is rehabilitation," Bennett said. "The first purpose is moral, to exact a price for transgressing the rights of others." It's a line Bennett and other drug warriors would use over and over again for the next decade.[30] Of course, Bennett was advocating mass punishment for consensual crimes, which by definition don't violate the rights of others. But Bennett was never one for consistency—just force. Bennett and some members of Congress briefly even considered declaring martial law in DC and bringing in the National Guard to enforce it. He did impose an 11:00 PM curfew, which was later overturned by a federal judge. In 1990 Bennett floated the idea of suspending *habeas corpus* for drug offenders. "It's a funny war when the 'enemy' is entitled to due process of law and a fair trial," he told *Fortune*. Lest that seem too extreme, he hedged a bit. "By the way, I'm in favor of due process. But that kind of slows things down."[31] Later he told Larry King that he'd be up for beheading drug dealers. He conceded that doing so might be "legally difficult," but said that, "morally, I have no problem with it."[32]

Bennett even urged children to turn in their friends who used drugs to police. Doing so, he said, was "an act of true friendship."[33] The country seemed to agree. One poll found that 83 percent of respondents would call the police on a drug-using relative.[34] Urging families to turn one another in to the government for victimless crimes was once an idea we associated with Iron Curtain regimes. But the drug war encouraged it. Back in 1983, Daryl Gates had started the Drug Abuse Resistance Education (DARE) program, which sent cops into Los Angeles schools to talk to students about drugs. The program swept the country, and by the mid-1990s there were numerous reports of children who had turned in their parents for small amounts of drugs after attending DARE lectures. DARE officials denied that the program encouraged such behavior, but in most cases the children were commended by police and DARE for "doing the right thing" after watching their parents marched into squad cars and taken to jail for what were usually possession charges.[35]

Despite consistent data showing that drug use and addiction were abating, Bennett's *Drug Strategy* report of 1989 declared drugs to be a "deepening crisis" that presented "the gravest threat to our national well-being." Bennett's appointment and subsequent hard line instigated a new round of drug war hysteria from other public officials. Sen. Phil Gram, Republican of Texas, and Republican Georgia representative Newt Gingrich introduced a bill to convert unused army centers into mass detention centers for drug offenders. Republican representative Richard Ray of Georgia proposed that drug offenders be exiled to Midway and Wake Islands. With no distractions, Ray argued, it would be easier for them to rehabilitate. Ray's proposal even passed the House Armed Services Committee. He said that when he proposed the idea to a conference of sheriffs and police chiefs, he received a standing ovation. FBI director William Sessions declared that the country would need to "strike a new balance between order and individual liberties." Joint Chiefs of Staff chairman Adm. William Crowe went further, stating that with the new antidrug offensive, "you're probably going to have to infringe on some human rights." In testimony before Congress, Darryl Gates proclaimed that casual drug use was "treason," then recommended that users be "taken out and shot." It was an especially odd comment given that Gates's own son had a history of problems with drug abuse.[36] On several occasions in the 1980s, the House and Senate also flirted with extending the death penalty to convicted drug dealers.

In terms of actual policy, Bush and Bennett proposed huge increases in funding to build new prisons. Their plan proposed three times more funding for law enforcement than for treatment, and shifted much of the enforcement emphasis from smugglers and dealers to casual users. The plan nudged states to raise penalties on users, to seize their cars, and to send them to military-like "boot camps" for rehabilitation, regardless of whether or not they were actually addicted.

As part of the 1988 crime bill, Congress also created a new set of federal grants called "Byrne grants" through the Justice Department's Justice Assistants Grants (JAG) program.[37] Over the next twenty-five years, Byrne grants would send billions of federal dollars to police departments across the country to fight crime in what amounted to a larger, better-funded, more ingeniously planned, and thus more successful attempt at what Nixon tried to do with the LEAA.

The Byrne grant program gave the White House another way to impose its crime policy on local law enforcement. As local police departments were infused with federal cash, members of Congress got press release fodder for bringing federal money back to the police departments in their districts. No one gave much thought to the potential unintended consequences of such a program because there was no reason to—for everyone who mattered, the program was a winner. The program's losers would become apparent in the 1990s.

The careless mixing of cops and soldiers continued too. In 1989 President Bush created yet more regional "joint task forces" to further coordinate between the military and law enforcement agencies across the country—but again, only for drug policing. One of the few voices of sanity in the Reagan years was Secretary of Defense Caspar Weinberger, who spoke out against his own boss's attempt to enlist the military in drug policing. Bush's secretary of Defense, Dick Cheney, had no such reservations. He'd write in a DoD publication a few years later, "The detection and countering of the production, trafficking, and use of illegal drugs is a high priority national security mission at the Department of Defense."[38]

Democrats in Congress savaged Bennett and Bush's drug plan—*for not going far enough*. Senate Judiciary Committee chairman Joe

Biden told the Associated Press that, "quite frankly," the Bush-Bennett plan "is not tough enough, bold enough, or imaginative enough to meet the crisis at hand."[39] Representative Larry Smith of Florida lamented the lack of more funding to hire more drug warriors. "This is a war that is being fought without very many troops," he said.[40] The most pointed criticism came from Representative Charlie Rangel of New York. A March 1989 profile of Rangel in *Ebony* magazine ran under the headline, "Charles Rangel: The Front-Line General in the War on Drugs." Rangel told the magazine: "All these people are talking about protecting the world against communism and the Soviets. . . . How dare they let this happen to our children and not scream with indignation!" It isn't clear just whom Rangel was criticizing. Just about everyone running for office had been screaming with indignation for ten years. Yet Rangel called the federal drug war "lackadaisical" and "indifferent" and said that it suffered from "a lack of commitment." He damned methadone treatment as "a crime" and snapped that anyone who even mentioned legalization was committing "moral suicide."[41]

By the late 1980s, the policies, rhetoric, and mind-set of the Reagan-Bush all-out antidrug blitzkrieg had fully set in at police departments across the country. Nearly every city with a population of 100,000 or more either had a SWAT team or was well on its way to getting one. The tactics that ten years earlier had been reserved for the rare, violent hostage-taking or bank robbery were by now employed daily by large police departments from coast to coast. "I wonder where the United States is heading," Federal District Court judge Richard Matsch, a Nixon appointee, told *USA Today* in 1989. "My concern is that the real victim in the war on drugs might be the United States Constitution." Another federal judge, Reagan appointee John Conway, worried that "police practices of this nature raise the grim specter of a totalitarian state."[42] The free market economist Milton Friedman, who had worked in both the Nixon and Reagan administrations, was so concerned that he wrote an open letter to Bennett in the *Wall Street Journal:*

This plea comes from the bottom of my heart. Every friend of freedom, and I know you are one, must be as revolted as I am by the prospect of turning the United States into an armed camp, by the vision of jails filled with casual drug users and of an army of enforcers empowered to invade the liberty of citizens on slight evidence. A country in which shooting down unidentified planes "on suspicion" can be seriously considered as a drug-war tactic is not the kind of United States that either you or I want to hand on to future generations.[43]

The public appeared to side with Bennett. In a September 1989 poll conducted by the *Washington Post* and ABC News, 62 percent of the country said that they would "be willing to give up a few of the freedoms we have in this country if it meant we could greatly reduce the amount of illegal drug use." Another 52 percent agreed that police should be allowed "to search without a court order the houses of people suspected of selling drugs, even if houses of people like you are sometimes searched by mistake."[44]

In Boston, police cracked down with "Terry" searches—the "stop-and-frisk" searches that were borne of *Terry v. Ohio*—of any suspected drug offenders "who cause fear in the community," a broad enough justification to let them search anyone at will. Suffolk Superior Court judge Cortland Mathers described the new policy as, "in effect, a proclamation of martial law in Roxbury for a narrow class of people, young blacks." A *Boston Globe* article in September 1989 described how what was essentially an occupation of some neighborhoods was degrading an entire generation's opinion of police. One woman who worked with preteens at a city community center told the paper that the children "have a negative sense of a police officer. They see the television version of a police officer, who is knocking down doors for the bad guys, then they see their friends, innocent people, getting stopped and searched. They see innocent people getting harmed by police for no reason. When I talk to 9- and 10-year-olds, they think all police are bad." A thirteen-year-old girl at the center told the *Globe* reporter, "Some officers let guns and badges go to their heads. They want respect, but if they don't give respect, they don't get respect. Like when they jumped to the conclusion to shoot that 30-year-old man." (She was referring to an incident in which a Boston police officer shot Rolando Carr during a stop-and-frisk. Carr was unarmed.) An eight-year-old added, "Sometimes, they should look more into the situation before they do anything."[45]

William Bennett supported what was going on in Boston and in a number of other cities that had passed "anti-loitering" laws, which had the same effect—to give police the power to essentially declare martial law in many neighborhoods. Such law enforcement saturations of mostly minority neighborhoods were merely due to "the overriding spirit and energy of our front-line enforcement officers," Bennett said. "We should be extremely reluctant to restrict [them] within formal and arbitrary lines."

Meanwhile, the pile of collateral damage was growing. In Riverside, California, police staged fourteen simultaneous raids over a two-and-a-half-block area. The raid turned up very little contraband. In one of the raids, fifty-year-old Richard Sears and his wife Sandra woke up to flash-bang grenades and armed men in their bedroom. Unaware that the men were police, Sears resisted and was repeatedly struck in the face with the butt of a rifle. When Sandra Sears attempted to escape the detonating grenades, she was pulled back into the room and thrown to the floor. Sears was arrested and charged with interfering with a police officer and resisting arrest. The charges were later dropped, and the sheriff's department admitted that the Searses had done nothing wrong.[46]

In March 1989, police in Gardena, California, raided the home of Lorine Harris on suspicion of drug activity. By the occupants' account of the raid, Officer Davie Mathieson mistook the sound of a flash-bang grenade for hostile gunfire and shot Harris's twenty-year-old son, Dexter Herbert, in the back, killing him. According to Mathieson's account of the raid, another man, Mack Charles Moore, had run out of a bedroom holding a shotgun. Officer Mathieson attempted to shoot Moore, but shot and killed Herbert instead. By both accounts, Herbert was unarmed. Prosecutors twice attempted to try Moore for Herbert's death, arguing that his wielding of the shotgun provoked Mathieson to shoot Herbert. The first attempt ended in a mistrial, the second in an acquittal.[47]

Though law enforcement officials would often defend the paramilitary tactics as critical to preserving officer safety, cops were dying in these raids too.

Boston detective Sherman Griffiths died after he was shot through the door while preparing to raid a suspected drug house. In May 1988, the *Washington Post* ran an article under the headline "Show of Force."[48] The piece profiled the new, particularly aggressive antidrug police units at the Prince George's County, Maryland, police department. The article noted that the department was conducting more raids, more "jump outs" on suspected drug dealers, and making many, many more arrests than it had in the past. Three months later, one of those teams conducted a drug raid on an apartment in the town of Riverdale. Cpl. Patrick Murphy, thirty-five years old, crouched in front of the door to position a hydraulic ram designed to blow the door open. As he did, someone inside opened the door. Two of Murphy's colleagues responded by opening fire. One suspect was shot in the face. Murphy was struck in the back of the head. He later died at the hospital. The police first claimed that someone inside the house fired at them. But it was later revealed that the only gun in the house hadn't been fired that night. Murphy himself had shot an unarmed, fleeing suspect during a drug raid in 1982.[49]

Officer Keith Neumann, twenty-four years old, was also killed by a fellow police officer during a predawn drug raid on August 4, 1989, in Irvington, New York. The raid turned up an eighth of an ounce of cocaine and no weapons. Neumann had been married just three weeks before his death.[50]

And in February 1989, black-clad police wearing face masks broke into the Titusville, Florida, home of fifty-eight-year-old Charles DiGristine, his wife, and their four children. They staged the no-knock raid after an informant told police someone was dealing drugs from the house and was protecting the drug supply with armed guards. DiGristine first heard an explosion (the flash-bang grenade), then his wife's scream. He ran to his bedroom to get his handgun. Officer Stephen House entered DiGristine's bedroom with his gun drawn. The two exchanged gunfire. House was struck and killed. The police found no large supply of drugs, only less than a gram of marijuana that belonged to DiGristine's sixteen-year-old son. DiGristine was arrested and initially charged with murder, which could have brought a death sentence. A grand jury lowered the charge to second-degree murder, which still could have sent him to prison for the rest of his life. But the following August, a Titusville jury acquitted him on all charges. DiGristine later filed suit against the city. During discovery, his attorney found prior incidents of botched raids and excessive force, including one incident where, as police approached a house, the homeowner opened the door and invited them inside. They tossed flash-bang grenades through the doorway anyway. Titusville city manager Randy Reid called the lawsuit part of an "overall plan of greed and publicity."[51]

Forty-three-year-old Richard Elsass was sleeping in a trailer outside the Ripon, California, truck stop where he worked when on the morning of October 20, 1989, black-clad SWAT teams from San Joaquin and Stanislaus Counties swarmed the building as part of a predawn drug raid. According to police, they knocked and announced themselves several times, after which Elsass said, "Wait a minute." When he didn't answer the door, Sgt. Deighton Little of the San Joaquin County Sheriff's Department went around to the back and smashed a window with his flashlight. When Little looked inside, Elsass shot him, killing him. The other officers then opened fire into the trailer, killing Elsass.

Friends and coworkers said Elsass was both a heavy sleeper and hard of hearing. They also told local media that he had mentioned having some safety concerns about some of the people and activity near the truck stop. The police found no drugs in Elsass's trailer, nor any evidence linking him to a drug crime. Officials from both police departments promised a full and impartial investigation, even as they assured the public that their officers had followed all the proper procedures and done nothing wrong. Not surprisingly, the subsequent internal reviews at both departments cleared all of the raiding. The police conducted a violent, volatile drug raid on the home of an innocent man, killed him, and got one of their own killed in the process. Yet by their own measure, they followed all the proper procedures, and nothing about those procedures needed to be changed. The inescapable conclusion: raiding and killing innocent people is an acceptable outcome of drug policing. In 1994 a jury found the officers negligent and awarded Elsass's family $175,000 in damages. [52]

UNDER THE OPEN FIELDS DOCTRINE, THE SUPREME COURT had already given its approval to law enforcement officers trespassing on private property without a warrant to search for criminal activity, even when they had to scale fences, open gates, and ignore NO TRESPASSING signs to do so. The Court then broadened the doctrine to include aerial inspections and photographs from fixed-wing aircraft from one thousand feet or higher. In 1989 the Court capped a rather ignoble decade of drug war decisions with a gobsmacker: the Court gave its approval for police to hover in helicopters at low altitudes in order to see behind the walls of structures built on the private property of private citizens. All without a warrant. In 1988 a law enforcement officer in Florida got a tip that marijuana was being grown in a private greenhouse. When the investigating deputy was unable to see into the greenhouse on foot, he used a police helicopter to fly over the property. After lowering the helicopter to just four hundred feet from the ground, the deputy was able to peer into an open roof panel and spot some marijuana plants. In January 1989, by a 5–4 vote, the Supreme Court ruled that the deputy's actions did not constitute a "search" under the Fourth Amendment, and therefore did not require a warrant.[53] The plurality opinion focused mainly on whether Federal Aviation Administration (FAA) regulations permitted a helicopter to fly that low. Justice Sandra Day O'Connor wrote a concurring opinion arguing that the standard shouldn't be FAA regulations, but whether it was common for aircraft to fly that low. If it was uncommon, then the defendant would have a reasonable expectation of privacy. But because the defendant didn't argue the point, O'Connor provided the deciding vote for the majority.

*Florida v. Riley* was one of the last cases that William Brennan would hear. His dissent reads like a man with outrage fatigue. "The plurality undertakes no inquiry into whether low-level helicopter surveillance by the police activities in an enclosed backyard is consistent with the 'aims of a free and open society,'" Brennan wrote. He then returned to a running theme in his dissents in such cases—that the Court was creating a drug war exception to the Fourth Amendment. He noted that the plurality opinion suggested that the Court might have viewed the case differently if the officer had seen "intimate details" from the helicopter. "Where in the Fourth Amendment . . . [is there] a requirement that the activity observed must be 'intimate' in order to be protected by the Constitution?" Brennan wrote. "If the Constitution does not protect Riley's marijuana garden against such surveillance, it is hard to see how it will prohibit the government from aerial spying on the activities of a law-abiding citizen on her fully-enclosed outdoor patio." Brennan then quoted from a law review article by Fourth Amendment scholar Anthony Amsterdam: "The question is not whether you or I must draw the blinds before we commit a crime. It is whether you and I must discipline ourselves to draw the blinds every time we enter a room, under pain of surveillance if we do not." Fittingly, Brennan closed with a passage from George Orwell's *1984:* "In the far distance, a helicopter skimmed down between the roofs, hovered for an instant like a bluebottle, and darted away again with a curving flight. It was the Police Patrol, snooping into people's windows."[54]

The Court's last real civil libertarian retired a month later.

## The Numbers

○ Number of drug raids conducted in 1987 by the San Diego Police Department: 457

○ Number of drug raids conducted by the Seattle Police Department in 1987: approximately 500

○ Value of the assets in the Justice Department's forfeiture fund in 1985: $27 million

○ Value of the assets in the Justice Department's forfeiture fund by 1991: $644 million

○ Percentage of US cities with populations over 50,000 that had a SWAT team in 1982: 59 percent

 . . . in 1989: 78 percent

 . . . in 1995: 89 percent

○ Percentage of those SWAT teams that trained with active-duty military personnel: 46 percent

○ Average annual number of times each of those SWAT teams was deployed in 1983: 13

 . . . in 1986: 27

 . . . in 1995: 55

○ Percentage of those deployments in 1995 that were only to serve drug warrants: 75.9 percent

○ Percentage of cities with populations between 25,000 and 50,000 that had a SWAT team in 1980: 13.3 percent

 . . . in 1984: 25.6 percent

 . . . in 1990: 52.1 percent

○ Average annual number of times each SWAT team in a city with a population between 25,000 and 50,000 was deployed in 1980: 3.7

 . . . in 1985: 4.5

 . . . in 1990: 10.3

 . . . in 1995: 12.5[55]

# THE 1990S—IT'S ALL ABOUT THE NUMBERS

> Why serve an arrest warrant to some crack dealer with a .38? With full armor, the right shit, and training, you can kick ass and have fun.
>
> —US MILITARY OFFICER WHO CONDUCTED TRAINING SEMINARS FOR CIVILIAN SWAT TEAMS IN THE 1990S

The 1990s kicked off with a familiar debate: Congress wanted the military to be more involved with the drug war. At the urging of drug czar William Bennett, the Bush administration was waging aggressive antidrug campaigns in Latin America, the most notable of which was the 1989 invasion of Panama to capture military governor Manuel Noriega, who was wanted in the United States for drug trafficking. That action was made possible by an opinion from the Justice Department's Office of Legal Counsel; issued a month before the invasion, the opinion concluded that the Posse Comitatus Act didn't apply outside of US borders. Members of

Congress followed by calling for more policelike actions by US troops to arrest suspected drug dealers in other countries.

Secretary of Defense Dick Cheney had led the Republican push for the 1988 drug bill that included the death penalty for drug dealers and widespread use of the military for drug interdiction. One Cheney lieutenant, Assistant Secretary of Defense Stephen Duncan, said at a 1991 conference, "We look forward to the day when our Congress . . . allows the Army to lend its full strength toward making America drug free."[1] Even some career military officials were starting to come around, mostly out of fear that after the fall of communism in Europe, the military could suffer a loss of stature if it didn't find a new enemy to engage. "The Soviet threat is being taken away from us," one DC military scholar explained to the *Chicago Tribune*. "The Department of Defense had better develop some social-utility arguments that match the requirements of the American people."[2]

Even Cheney drew the line at using active-duty troops for civilian policing inside of US borders—but that didn't seem to stop it from happening. The *Christian Science Monitor* reported in August 1990 that 58 active-duty Army troops had assisted in Operation Clean Sweep, the latest marijuana eradication program in northern California, and another 225 infantry soldiers and aviators and nine UH-60 Blackhawk helicopters from Fort Lewis, Washington, helped find pot plants in Operation Ghost Dancer in Oregon.[3]

The early 1990s also saw a new push to find a greater drug war role for the National Guard. "When you have the equipment and trained personnel, you might as well put them to work," said Rep. Nick Mavroules, a Massachusetts Democrat serving on the House Armed Services Committee. When asked about the traditional line separating the military from domestic policing, Republican representative Duncan Hunter of California snapped, "It depends on which is more sacred, that line or your children's lives." One influential Capitol Hill staffer gave an especially confused justification. "We have to take some kind of action, not because it's going to solve the problem . . . but because of the fact that the druggies have gotten their fingers into an awful lot of pies."

Part of the reason why so many politicians were enthusiastic was that National Guard involvement brought increased funding to their states. In 1989, the first year of the program, Congress appropriated $40 million for the National Guard's drug interdiction efforts. The next year funding jumped to $70 million. Two years later it was up to $237 million.[4] Any congressman or senator who opposed Guard troops fighting the drug war out of principle risked leaving his state out of the bounty. In Washington State, for example, the state's National Guard received just under $1 million for antidrug operations. The next year the state's congressional delegation signed a letter requesting seven times that amount.

In 1989 in Portland, Oregon, Herb Robinson of the *Seattle Times* noted, fully armed Guard troops had recently been stationed in front of suspected drug houses in a series of drug raids.[5] In Kentucky local residents became so enraged by frequent Guard sweeps in low-flying helicopters that they blew up a radio tower used by the Kentucky State Police. In Oklahoma, Guard troops dressed in battle garb rappelled down from helicopters and fanned out into rural areas in search of pot plants to uproot.

National Guard units flew antidrug surveillance helicopters and boarded up crack houses in Washington, DC; flew surveillance helicopters and cruised the streets with infrared gear to spot drug houses in Brooklyn; sealed crack houses in Philadelphia; were sent to support drug raids in Baltimore; and helped serve ninety-four drug warrants during a massive, citywide raid in Pittsburgh. Members of the Pennsylvania Guard assisted in raids of two factories that produced small glass vials. There were no drugs in the vials, but under state law the vials were still illegal because they were primarily used by drug dealers to package crack cocaine.[6] In the summer of 1990, an Army helicopter circled overhead as Massachusetts National Guard troops—some in uniform, some undercover—assisted police in Foxboro in identifying potential drug offenders at a Grateful Dead show.[7]

In rural Maine, the National Guard was assisting in Humboldt County–style raids in rural parts of the state. Guard helicopters would perform flyovers, then raid teams consisting of federal and state officials would swoop in. "The standard operating procedure is to come in with battering rams, weapons out and cocked, shouting profanities," a marijuana legalization activist in the town of Chesterville told the Associated Press in 1992.[8]

By the end of 1992, the National Guard's role in the drug war was fully operational. In that year alone, National Guard troops across the country assisted in nearly 20,000 arrests, searched 120,000 automobiles, entered 1,200 private buildings without a search warrant, and stepped onto private property to search for drugs (also without a warrant) 6,500 times.[9]

Col. Richard Browning III, head of the organization's drug interdiction effort, declared that year, "The rapid growth of the drug scourge has shown that military force must be used to change the attitudes and activities of Americans who are dealing and using drugs. The National Guard is America's legally feasible attitude-change agent."[10]

Symbolically, the National Guard bridges the gap between cop and soldier. Guard troops train like soldiers and dress like soldiers, and they are regularly called up to fight in wars overseas. But when they are acting under the authority of a state governor, Guard troops aren't subject to the restrictions of the Posse Comitatus Act. Giving the Guard a more prominent role in the drug war not only escalated the drug fight, it further conditioned the country to the idea of using forces that looked and acted quite a bit like soldiers for domestic law enforcement.

⌐╼

WITH MORE AND MORE FUNDS FLOWING TOWARD DRUG eradication, police agencies began to step on each other's toes to grab grants and shares of the money earmarked for various antidrug programs. That produced tragic outcomes for any citizens caught in the middle. In January 1990, for example, President Bush initiated a new plan to crack down on drug smugglers at the border. He designated five border regions as "high-intensity drug-trafficking areas," making each region eligible for a cut of the $10.6 billion he had requested to fund the plan.

One of the regions included the San Diego area. About three years into the program, forty-one-year-old Fortune 500 executive Donald Carlson awoke at around midnight to a pounding at his front door. He asked several times who was there. No one answered. Carlson became frightened. He walked back to his bedroom in the pitch dark to retrieve his gun, while nervously fumbling with a cordless phone as he attempted to call the police.

Carlson then heard the glass window in his den shatter. That was followed by what he'd later describe as "a thunderous explosion." Someone then yelled, "He's got a gun!" Now terrified, Carlson fired at the door, hoping to scare the intruders away. Instead, they fired back. The first bullet flayed his upper thigh, severing his femoral artery. Carlson discarded the gun. He had just made it back to his bedroom when he dropped to the floor. He'd been hit by two more bullets.

Carlson looked up and saw figures staring down at him, darkened behind the flashlights they were pointing in his face. One of them screamed at him, "Don't move, motherfucker, or I'll shoot!"

But the pain in Carlson's arm began to overcome his adrenaline, so he attempted to adjust it. Again: "Don't move, motherfucker, or I'll shoot!" The men then rolled him over and handcuffed him. None of them attempted to give him medical attention. They left him to bleed in his own bedroom until paramedics arrived a half-hour later. Carlson later said that on the way to the hospital, he prayed for God to let him die.

Fortunately, Carlson survived. What happened to him was a direct consequence of President Bush's new drug policy. The DEA and Customs had always had a bitter rivalry, going back to the Nixon years. Bush's 1990 border plan had shifted a great deal of the federal government's antidrug strategy toward the border, putting Customs in charge. That angered the careerists at the DEA, and only intensified the rivalry between the two agencies. Because they were competing for the same pot of money, pressure mounted for agents to make big busts, skim over constitutional protections, and play fast and loose with procedure.

"The Carlson shooting is an example of how competition between federal law enforcement works to the detriment of the public," one federal agent later told the *San Diego Union-Tribune*. A local judge agreed. "There's no question that when you have turf wars between law enforcement agencies, you're going to have potential for disaster." The Carlson raid was part of Operation Alliance, which itself was part of a border interdiction effort in which Customs and the DEA were supposed to have been working together. Subsequent reports would show that the project only inflamed tensions. Customs officials were so eager to make a big bust that they had neglected to investigate the informant whose tip was their sole source of information for the raid. If they had done so, they'd have discovered that he had a history of lying. According to the *Union-Tribune*, the DEA had been paying him $2,000 a month to work as an informant but had dropped him two weeks prior to the Carlson raid because he was unreliable. According to one agent, "When a DEA agent says, 'This guy is no good,' the first thing a Customs agent wants to do is prove the DEA wrong." Odder still, because the two agencies were supposed to be working together, there were actually DEA agents who participated in the Carlson raid, which was based on a tip from the informant the DEA had just let go for being untrustworthy.

The police found no drugs or any evidence of any criminal activity in Carlson's home. They had also raided another home on the same night, based on information from the same informant. That raid didn't turn up any contraband either. Nevertheless, Carlson spent the first several days of his convalescence shackled to his bed with an armed guard outside his room. By the time he testified before Congress the following June, he had been cleared of any wrongdoing. But the government still refused to give him the names of the agents who raided his home and who worked on the investigation. No one from the government had contacted him about taking care of his medical bills, which by then had topped $350,000, or covering the costs of repairing his house. No one had even bothered to apologize. And no agents had been disciplined or reprimanded, much less criminally charged. Only the informant had been charged, and those charges were later dismissed. Carlson and his attorney were told that neither Customs, nor the DEA, nor any of the local police agencies involved in the raid saw any reason to change their procedures as a result of what happened.

In its report on the bureaucratic bumbling that led to the Carlson raid, the *Union-Tribune* found evidence of other mistaken raids wrought by the same misplaced incentives. Midlevel managers and federal law enforcement agencies faced constant pressure to keep their statistics: "Impressive seizures allow these managers of the drug wars to ask for, and receive, larger staffs—and higher pay." So long as performance was measured with raw seizure and arrest figures, drug agents told the paper, mistaken raids would remain "a fact of life in drug work." Added a San Diego–era narcotics cop, "Every narc, at one time or another, has hit a wrong door."

In December 1994, Carlson accepted a $2.75 million settlement from the federal government. He never got an apology.[11]

~

PROPONENTS OF NO-KNOCK RAIDS AND FORCED-ENTRY RAIDS HAD always argued that scrutiny from judges and prosecutors would keep abuses and excesses in check. Yet the police officers interviewed for this book unanimously told me that beginning in about the mid-1980s, judges almost never denied their requests for a search warrant. Some judges asked questions now and then, but even then they rarely denied a warrant. As the sheer volume of drug cases picked up in the late 1980s and into the 1990s, many judges stopped asking questions too. A few officers said that they had known that some judges looked more closely at affidavits for no-knock warrants, but added that knock-and-announce requests were never a problem, even when everyone knew the warrant would be served with a dynamic entry.

In 1992 University of Minnesota law professor Myron Orfield sent a questionnaire to Chicago judges, prosecutors, and defense attorneys to determine the state of the Fourth Amendment in that city. Even cynics would find the results dispiriting. More than one-fifth of Chicago judges believed that police lie in court more than half the time when questioned about searches and seizures. *Ninety-two percent* of judges said that police lie "at least some of the time," and 38 percent of judges said that they believed that police superiors encourage subordinates to lie in court. More than 50 percent of respondents believed that at least "half of the time" the prosecutor "knows or has reason to know" that police fabricate evidence. Another 93 percent of respondents (including 89 percent of the prosecutors) reported that prosecutors have knowledge of perjury "at least some of the time." Sixty-one percent of respondents, including half of the surveyed prosecutors, believed that prosecutors know or have reason to know that police fabricate evidence in case reports, and half of prosecutors believed the same to be true when it comes to warrants. Prosecutors also described the unspoken understandings they often shared with cops, including prosecutors articulating cases to police in terms like, "If this happens, we win. If that happens, we lose." Yet Chicago judges went on approving search warrants with little to no scrutiny. Orfield asked one more question. Did the Exclusionary Rule really deter police misconduct? Every judge, every defense attorney, and every prosecutor but one answered yes.[12]

Former narcotics cop Russ Jones says it wasn't always like that. "When I first started writing search warrants, I had to take it to the DA, who would thoroughly review it. Then I'd take it to the judge, who'd also give it a close look. Then the judge always read the warrant, always asked questions. By the time I left law enforcement, and certainly since, it had gotten to the point where the DEA no longer needed to have warrants reviewed by a federal prosecutor, and often the judge wouldn't even read it. It just became a rubber-stamp process. And I understand it's happening more and more."[13]

In many jurisdictions, search warrants can be approved by magistrates who needn't even have any legal training. A 1984 study of the warrant process in seven US cities by the National Center for State Courts found that magistrates spend an average of two minutes and forty-eight seconds reviewing warrant affidavits before (almost always) approving the warrant. The study also found evidence that police "magistrate shop"—they seek out magistrates with a reputation for approving warrants quickly and with no hassles, and avoid those who ask questions. In one city, a single magistrate approved 54 percent of the search warrants over the period the study was conducted. The most popular magistrate in another city had rejected just one search warrant in fifteen years on the bench. Not surprisingly, "most police officers interviewed could not remember having a search warrant turned down."[14]

After the botched raid that ended the life of Ismael Mena in 1999, the *Denver Post* looked into how judges in the Mile High City handled requests for no-knock warrants. Again, the results were unsettling. Over a twelve-month period, police in Denver requested 163 no-knock warrants. The city's judges granted 158 of them. Defense attorneys told the paper they were surprised to learn that the judges had rejected even five. Perhaps Denver police had come to the judges with more than adequate probable cause? Perhaps. But the paper also found that, astonishingly, many of the city's judges would sign off on no-knock warrants *even though the police hadn't requested one*. In fact, about 10 percent of the no-knock warrants were changed from knock-and-announce warrants merely by the judge's signature—the police hadn't presented any additional information establishing exigent circumstances. The paper also found that in eight of ten raids over that period, police assertions in affidavits that they would find weapons during the search turned out to be wrong. In only seven of the 163 no-knock affidavits did police present any evidence that the suspect had been seen with a gun. Of those seven raids, just two turned up an actual weapon. The Denver Police Department requires that all no-knock raids be preapproved by the DA's office. In about one-third of the raids, that never happened. And nearly all the no-knock warrants were granted on little more than a police officer's assertion that a confidential informant had told him the suspect was

armed or likely to dispose of drug evidence, with no additional corroborating information.

When confronted with the results of the investigation, the presid-
ing judge over Denver's criminal court system wasn't particularly re-
assuring. "We are not fact gatherers," Judge Robert Patterson said.
"It's pretty formulaic how it's done." On how a judge could possibly inadvertently approve a no-knock warrant when the police
hadn't even asked for one, Patterson said, "If you sign your name
100 times, you can look away and sign in the wrong place. We read
a lot of documents. We may, just like anyone else, sign something
and realize later that it's the wrong place or the wrong thing. Is it
wrong not to be paying attention? No. It's just that we're doing
things over and over again."[15]

Hearing Patterson's explanation, you'd think he was talking
about the elementary school teacher who might occasionally mis-
grade one of dozens of homework assignments. This was about giving armed law enforcement officers permission to break into homes
in the middle of the night, detonate flash-bang grenades, and point
their guns at Denver citizens. Patterson, astonishingly, was calmly
explaining how the city's judges couldn't even be bothered to pay
attention to where they signed their names.

Judges and prosecutors weren't just neglecting their responsibility to protect the Fourth Amendment. They were nearly conspiring
against it.

THE EARLY 1990s WEREN'T KIND TO THE FATHER OF SWAT.
In response to the Rodney King beating of May 1991, Los Angeles
mayor Tom Bradley asked Warren Christopher to chair a commission looking into the LAPD's use of excessive force. The commission's report was damning. It found that a small but significant
group of police officers within the department regularly used excessive force—and that LAPD leadership did little to stop them. Between 1986 and 1990, the city had faced eighty-three lawsuits that
resulted in settlements of awards of over $15,000. The commission

found that even though officer misconduct in those cases had often been egregious, it had usually resulted in "light and often nonexistent" discipline. The commission reviewed radio transmissions of LAPD officers referring to a drug roundup in a black neighborhood as "monkey slapping time" or fantasizing about driving down one particular street with a flamethrower—"We would have a barbecue."

The comments themselves would have been bad enough. Even worse was the fact that a culture existed within the department in which officers felt free to make them over police radio. The LAPD's focus on reacting to crime instead of preventing it, the commission found, had isolated officers from the communities they patrolled. Cops were rewarded for putting up impressive arrest statistics and for being "hard-nosed." The report found that drug and gang sweeps of the late 1980s had alienated LAPD cops from the community, creating reciprocal hostility and resentment. The LAPD did a poor job of screening applicants for violent backgrounds, and the department's training put far too much emphasis on force and too little on communication and problem-solving. The commission found that when academy students went out in the field, they were quickly schooled to view the world from a "we/they" perspective. It also found that many of the field training officers who gave new cops their first experiences on the street themselves had histories of misconduct or excessive use of force.

The commission's finding on how the LAPD handled citizen complaints was perhaps the most disturbing and enlightening part of the Christopher report. Of the 2,152 complaints filed against LAPD cops between 1986 and 1990, just 42 had been found credible by the department. Most were handled by the accused officer's supervisors, not by Internal Affairs. Intake officers "actively discouraged" citizens who tried to file complaints, often with verbal harassment or by making them wait for long periods of time. Investigating officers made no attempt to find independent witnesses, meaning that the "investigations" often came down to the officer's word against the complainant's. After shootings, officers were usually granted an unrecorded "pre-interview" before they were questioned on tape. The officers involved were also usually interviewed as a group, not individually. All of which gave them opportunity to work out any inconsistencies or contradictions in the story. Perhaps most tellingly, the commission found that when officers were disciplined, the punishment given to officers who had embarrassed the department (drug use, corruption, theft) was much more severe than the punishment given to officers who used excessive force or violated a citizen's constitutional rights—again reflecting a culture of "us versus them."[16]

The Christopher Commission made a number of recommendations, but one made much more of a splash than the others: it recommended that Daryl Gates be removed as chief of police. Gates announced his intent to resign on July 13, 1991, three days after the Christopher report came out. But by the time the LA riots broke out the following April, Gates was still in office.

Sparked by a jury's decision to acquit the LAPD officers who beat Rodney King, the riots themselves lasted four days, although there were flare-ups of violence in the days that followed. In all, 13,500 troops from the California National Guard, the Third Battalion First Marine, and the Fortieth Infantry Division and Seventh Infantry Division of the US Army were sent in to stop the violence. There were 53 fatalities, over 2,000 injured, and property damage of more than $1 billion.

The Watts riots in 1965 had made Daryl Gates a rising star within the LAPD. The helplessness that Gates and his officers felt while getting shot at by snipers in what had become an urban war zone had inspired him to create and push for the SWAT team, his most influential and lasting legacy. Twenty-seven years later, the riots after the Rodney King verdict effectively ended Gates's career. By then, SWAT teams across America numbered in the thousands. Most of them weren't responding to riots or Black Panther barricades or shootings like the one on Surry Street—most SWAT teams were spending most of their time breaking down doors on drug raids.

Though rioting gave birth to Gates's legacy in 1965, his proudest legacy was powerless to stop the rioting in 1992. Order wasn't restored until the National Guard showed up. One other big difference between Watts and the 1992 riots: far more Americans were beginning to see problems with police brutality. When Gallup asked, "Do you think there is police brutality in your area?" in 1967, just 6 percent said yes. In July 1991, it was 39 percent.[17]

On June 28, 1992, Gates resigned from the Los Angeles Police Department—this time for real.

AS NOTED PREVIOUSLY, AFTER IMPLEMENTING MANY OF the community policing practices proposed by Norm Stamper, San Diego was seeing some progress. Crime had started to go down in the city even as it continued to rise elsewhere in the country, and police-community relations were improving. By 1992, Stamper was Burgreen's right-hand man. Burgreen asked Stamper to conduct an audit of the entire department, instructing his top deputy to "concentrate on our warts." After conducting his audit, Stamper made a number of proposals, but one of them was particularly interesting. He wanted to "demilitarize" the department.

Stamper knew of a few smaller police departments that had tried demilitarizing to various degrees, with mixed results. Back in 1970 the town of Lakewood, Colorado, built a new department from the ground up. Police Chief Pierce Brooks wanted a department that looked more like it was part of the community than an outside force charged with keeping the community in line. So the cops wore slacks and blazers instead of military-like uniforms. Instead of using Army ranks like sergeant or lieutenant, they took titles like "field advisor." Rank-and-file cops were called "agents." The Lakewood experiment was short-lived: by 1973, they were back to using traditional titles and the conventional police blues. Similar efforts in Menlo Park and Beverly Hills, California, hadn't gone quite as far, but had been somewhat more successful.

Stamper's proposal was relatively mild by comparison. As he writes in his book *Breaking Rank:*

I knew there'd be a shit-rain of opposition—military titles are a cultural icon in civilian policing, as much a part of the cop culture as mustaches, sidearms, and doughnuts. But, win or lose, I thought it was important to air the *rationale* behind "demilitarization." I hoped to encourage a departmentwide dialog on the principles of a more "democratic," less militaristic police force. And since *language structures reality,* I was convinced that our military nomenclature stood between us and the community.[18]

Stamper's idea was to change the titles of "sergeant," "lieutenant," and "captain" to titles less evocative of the military. He suggested looking to federal law enforcement: the FBI, for instance, had "agents," "special agents," and "supervisors." Burgreen was dubious, not because he necessarily disagreed, but because he knew the idea would be dead on arrival within the department. He gave Stamper two months to try it out.

Burgreen was right. The department erupted in protest. Letters to the editor of the department's internal newsletter howled with derision. The *San Diego Union-Tribune* got wind of the idea and spat on it in an editorial.

Stamper had a few supporters, but only a few. (One of them, oddly enough, was former Reagan attorney general Ed Meese.) Stamper writes in his book about one lieutenant who initially scoffed at the proposal, but later came around. "The more I thought about it the more I realized, we're *not* the military, we're cops. We're *community* cops. We ought to have titles that make sense to the community. What does 'lieutenant' or 'sergeant' mean to the average citizen?"

A related question: what effect do such titles have on the average cop? Still, as Stamper writes, of the department's 2,800 employees, "the lieutenant's change of heart brought the number of converts up to approximately eleven."

Stamper's proposal didn't involve demilitarizing police tactics. He wasn't suggesting that they disband the SWAT teams, or get rid of their guns, or even switch to slacks and blazers. All he was proposing was that they ditch the military titles and jargon. And there was no way it was ever going to happen.[19]

But Stamper wasn't the only high-ranking law enforcement official growing concerned about militarization in the 1990s. In a 1993 article for the FBI's *Law Enforcement Bulletin,* Lt. Tom Gabor of the Culver City, California, Police Department argued that SWAT teams were becoming too ubiquitous and being used in ways that were inappropriate for police work. Gabor wrote that the massive rise in deployments of SWAT teams across the country was more about "justifying the costs of maintaining [the] units" than about maintaining public safety. Even as early as 1993, Gabor had already noticed that "in many organizations, patrol leaders feel pressured to call for SWAT assistance on borderline cases, even though field supervisors believe that patrol personnel could resolve the incident."[20]

In Wisconsin, Marquette County sheriff Rick Fullmer actually disbanded his department's SWAT team in 1996. "Quite frankly, they get excited about dressing up in black and doing that kind of thing," Fullmer told the *Madison Capital Times.* "I said, 'This is ridiculous.' All we're going to end up doing is getting people hurt."[21]

In New Haven, Connecticut, Police Chief Nick Pastore was facing growing pressure to collect military gear from the Pentagon and to use his SWAT team in situations where he thought it was inappropriate. Pastore told the *New York Times* that outfitting cops in battle garb "feeds a mind-set that you're not a police officer serving a community, you're a soldier at war. I had some tough-guy cops in my department pushing for bigger and more hardware. They used to say, 'It's a war out there.' They like SWAT because it's an adventure." Pastore also worried about the martial rhetoric. "If you think everyone who uses drugs is the enemy, then you're more likely to declare war on the people."[22] In another interview, with *The Nation,* Pastore pointed out that before he took over, New Haven's SWAT team was being called out several times a week. "The whole city was suffering trauma," he said. "We had politicians saying 'The streets are a war zone, the police have taken over,' and the police were driven by fear and adventure. SWAT was a big part of that."[23] After Pastore took over, New Haven's SWAT team was called out just four times in all of 1998. Lo and behold, reserving the SWAT team for true emergencies didn't lead to a criminal takeover of New Haven. In fact, the city's crime rate dropped at a brisker pace than that of the rest of Connecticut (which also dropped)—from 13,950 incidents in 1997 to 9,455 in 2000.[24]

In Colorado, the *Denver Post* ran an article in 1995 about three area deaths from no-knock drug raids in the area in thirty-three months—including a sixteen-year-old boy, a deputy sheriff, and a fifty-four-year-old grandfather of eight. "Such raids are very dangerous," said Pitkin County sheriff Robert Braudis. "They are the closest thing I can think of to a military action in a democratic society." Braudis explained that it was far safer to conduct surveillance, to learn a suspect's routine, and to then do "a quick, quiet arrest when a suspect is in the open." As for possible destruction of evidence, he said that his department would have the water shut off before serving a warrant (by knocking at the door and waiting for an answer). In some cases, they had arranged for a plumber to set up a "catch net" to capture anything flushed after police arrived to serve the warrant. But Braudis said that his concern went beyond the SWAT tactics. "The 'war on drugs' is an abysmal failure," he said. "Even the term creates a dangerous war mentality."[25]

In 1998 the city of Albuquerque, New Mexico, commissioned an outside investigation after a series of questionable shootings and SWAT incidents. In one case that made national news, a SWAT officer said to his colleagues, "Let's go get the bad guy," just before the team went to confront thirty-three-year-old Larry Walker. The "bad guy" wasn't a terrorist, a killer, or even a drug dealer, but a depressed man whose family had called the police because they feared he might be contemplating suicide. The SWAT team showed up in full battle attire, including assault rifles and flash-bang grenades. They found Walker "cowering under a juniper tree," the *New York Times* later reported, then shot him dead from forty-three feet away. The city brought in Sam Walker, a well-regarded criminologist at the University of Nebraska, to evaluate the police department's use of lethal force. Walker was astonished by what he found. "The rate of police killings was just off the charts," Walker told the *Times.* The city's SWAT team, he said, "had an organizational structure that led them to escalate situations upward rather than de-escalating." The city then brought in Toledo, Ohio, police chief Jerry Galvin to take over its police department. Galvin immediately disbanded the SWAT team, toned down the militarism, and implemented community policing policies. He told the *Times,* "If cops have a mindset that the goal is to take out a citizen, it will happen."[26]

THE ELECTION OF BILL CLINTON IN 1992 GAVE HOPE TO some in the drug reform community that an admitted pot smoker who had some ties to the counterculture during his college days might bring a less aggressive and less militaristic approach to federal drug policy. Those hopes were dashed pretty quickly.

Clinton and his appointees weren't as bellicose as Reagan and Bush or Meese and Bennett, but the policies that Clinton implemented showed little understanding or appreciation of the Symbolic Third Amendment. In 1993, for example, the Justice Department and the Defense Department entered into a formalized technology and equipment sharing agreement. Not only were American police forces becoming more militarized, the thinking went, but in places like Korea the US military was taking on more of a policing role. It only made sense for the two institutions to work more closely together. Attorney General Janet Reno explained this strategy in a speech to defense and intelligence specialists. "So let me welcome you to the kind of war our police fight every day," Reno said. "And let me challenge you to turn your skills that served us so well in the Cold War to helping us with the war we're now fighting daily in the streets of our towns and cities across the nation."

In 1997 the resulting Department of Justice and Department of Defense Joint Technology Program released a report on the new agency's anniversary. Many of the projects the program developed seem relatively innocuous, such as using police and military experience to develop better body armor or developing technology to locate snipers, which could be of benefit to both institutions. But the report also includes some more troubling projects, such as developing "less lethal, faster acting pyrotechnic devices such as flash-bang grenades" and "a gas-launched, wireless, electric stun projectile with a self-contained power supply" that "adheres to clothing and imparts a strong electric shock." The report discusses developing sound cannons for use in crowd control and a project to develop "miniature, low-cost, wireless, modular devices that can locate, identify, and monitor the movement of selected individuals."

Most concerning, however, is the language in which the report describes the relationship between the police and the military. While acknowledging at the outset that the two institutions have very different roles, the report asserts that those distinctions are eroding, particularly with respect to the war on drugs and the war on terrorism.

In one particularly troubling passage, the report cautions that both institutions need to be *less transparent* about the use of force. Another factor in how the military and law enforcement apply force, the report notes, is the greater presence of members of the media, who are observing, if not recording, situations in which force is applied. Even the lawful application of force can be misrepresented to or misunderstood by the public. More than ever, the report concludes, the police and the military need to be highly discreet to keep applications of force out of the public eye.[27]

There were other indications that Clinton didn't appreciate the distinction between the military and civilian policing. He nominated Barry McCaffrey—an actual retired general—to be his drug czar. There was also his "troops to cops" program, which subsidized police departments for hiring returning veterans. While there is nothing inherently wrong with allowing veterans to apply to become police officers, providing a federal grant enabling them to do so risked incentivizing police departments to give a pass to vets hardened or traumatized by war who might be psychologically unfit for the job. But more broadly, the program demonstrated a belief that the two jobs are similar—that because both troops and cops carry guns, wear uniforms, and are authorized to use force, anyone trained as a soldier naturally makes a good cop. This is certainly possible. But there's little about military service that would make a soldier a better candidate to become a police officer than other applicants—at least as the job of police officer is properly understood. And there's a good argument to be made that soldiers who have seen combat ought to get *extra* scrutiny before they're given a badge and a gun.

Clinton was also responsible for one policy in particular that not only encouraged paramilitary raids on low-level offenders—even users—but by its very nature also directed such raids *only* at the poor. In March 1996, an ABC News crew went along on a no-knock SWAT raid in Toledo, Ohio. The fourteen-member squad performed a "dynamic entry" into the house, threw its occupants to the ground at gunpoint, then tore the place apart in a drug search. They found less than an ounce of pot in the bedroom of a teenager who lived in the house with his family. You might think that ABC News broadcast the raid to show an abuse of police power, that the raiding SWAT team felt embarrassed about using such force for such a petty crime. But in fact the raid was broadcast because it was considered a successful enforcement of a new federal policy.

The home the police had raided was public housing. Under the Clinton administration's new "one strike and you're out" policy, any drug offense—even a misdemeanor—committed in public housing supported by federal funding was grounds for eviction. The policy applied even if the drug offense was committed by someone who didn't live in the home or was committed without the tenant's knowledge.[28] It was a popular idea. After all, why should taxpayers subsidize the drug habits of people on public assistance? Of course, there was no similar policy for recipients of corporate welfare, or for elected officials who received government paychecks. No matter. The ABC News report characterized the raid as a small victory in the war on drugs.[29]

PRIOR TO 1995, THE US SUPREME COURT HAD ALWAYS considered cases involving the knock-and-announce rule (and there hadn't been very many of them) either under the rule's common-law tradition or under the section of the US Criminal Code describing the conditions under which a federal agent is permitted to force his way into a private residence.[30] Though the knock-and-announce requirement is included in that law, the Court had yet to state that the rule—and thus the Castle Doctrine—was included in the protections against unreasonable search and seizure afforded by the Fourth Amendment. Justice Brennan had argued for that position in *Ker v. California* but fell one vote short of getting a majority.

In the 1995 case *Wilson v. Arkansas,* the Court unanimously ruled that the rule is part of the tapestry of the Fourth Amendment.[31] Justice Clarence Thomas relayed the long common-law history of the rule, as well as the events prior to the American Revolution that gave rise to the Fourth Amendment. But Thomas also noted the common-law exceptions to the rule—exceptions that, as Brennan pointed out in *Ker,* didn't really exist prior to 1962 but that US courts, Congress, and state legislatures had since recognized anyway. Thomas cautioned that the Court's ruling "should not be read to mandate a rigid rule of announcement that ignores countervailing law enforcement interests." Here he was referring to the two most widely recognized "exigent circumstances" that allow police to ignore the knock-and-announce rule: destruction of evidence and the threat of harm to police officers. After waxing historic on the long and storied tradition of the Castle Doctrine and the knock-and-announce rule, Thomas had finally ruled—with unanimous agreement from his colleagues—that the rule is part and parcel of the Fourth Amendment . . . but then took note of the exceptions to the rule that would allow police to all but ignore it.

Thomas didn't get into specifics about the conditions that would qualify as exigent circumstances, but in a series of cases over the next ten years the Court would begin to hash them out. The next case to address the issue was *Richards v. Wisconsin* in 1997. After *Wilson,* several states gave police permission to conduct no-knock raids in *any* narcotics investigation, on the theory that drugs were easy to destroy in a hurry, generally by flushing them down the toilet. In *Richards,* the Wisconsin Supreme Court ruled just that—narcotics cases by their very nature merit a blanket exception to the knock-and-announce rule on the theory that all drugs can be easily and quickly disposed. The Supreme Court overruled, but the opinion by Justice John Paul Stevens was narrowly written. Stevens came up with a couple of examples of cases where the destruction of evidence rule wouldn't apply, such as "a search . . . conducted at a time when the only individuals present in a residence have no connection with the drug activity and thus will be unlikely to threaten officers or destroy evidence," or when "police could know that the drugs being searched for were of a type or in a location that made them impossible to destroy quickly."[32] The first scenario seems unlikely. Police usually say that they need to serve warrants when the suspect is home in order to tie him to the drugs. It also makes it easier to make an arrest. Ironically, the second scenario gives more protection to major drug dealers than to small-time dealers or people who possess drugs for personal use. Cases involving drugs "of a type" unlikely to be quickly disposable would be cases involving large quantities of drugs. And drugs "in a location" that makes them impossible to destroy quickly would probably be drugs that aren't in a building with a toilet or sink nearby. As a result, Stevens's opinion offered more protection for people suspected of storing drugs in warehouses or businesses than for people suspected of storing them in their homes. The Court rejected a blanket narcotics exception to knock-and-announce, but Stevens's opinion seemed to indicate that only a small selection of drug cases could fall outside the exception. (The Court actually upheld the conviction against Richards.)

The Court also put some limits on judicial oversight over forced-entry raids, ruling that "a magistrate's decision not to authorize a no-knock entry should not be interpreted to remove the officers' authority to exercise independent judgment concerning the wisdom of a non-knock entry at the time the warrant is being executed." So even when denied a no-knock warrant, police could go ahead and decide at the scene to do a no-knock raid anyway. The Court also ruled that police only need to have "reasonable suspicion" that one of the three exigent circumstances exists in order to dispense with the announcement requirement, and that the standard of evidence for that reasonable suspicion is "not high." Like *Wilson, Richards* appeared to be another "victory" for the Castle Doctrine that also threatened to ruin it.

After *Richards,* state courts fell back on the "particularity approach" to determine when a no-knock raid was or wasn't merited. Judges determined whether a suspect was likely to destroy evidence on a case-by-case basis. There was no reliable, predictable standard. As we've seen, in the absence of such guidelines, and as judges were increasingly swamped with drug cases and drug warrants, the default position tended to defer to the judgment of police, even when the language in search warrant affidavits began to look like boilerplate.

It's worth noting here that on the rare occasions when warrants are challenged, the challenges necessarily occur, of course, *after* the warrant has been served. It would be ludicrous to notify a suspect of a surprise search warrant ahead of time so that he could challenge its legitimacy in court. But it's also worth remembering that these warrants give police permission to mete out extraordinary violence on people still only *suspected* of nonviolent crimes. When police get the right house with a questionable warrant, at worst the evidence they collect will be ruled inadmissible. In cases where questionable warrants lead to wrong-door raids, mistaken shootings, or some other calamitous outcome, the suspect's opportunity to challenge the warrant comes only *after* the harm has been done. That augurs for a system in which judges play an enormously important role in ensuring the validity and soundness of warrants, as well as for a clear set of guidelines and high evidentiary standards under which they would make those decisions. Instead, the Supreme Court has consistently ruled that judges should err on the side of putting their faith in the police.

In the 1999 case *United States v. Ramirez,* the Court did what it stopped short of doing in *Wilson*—it formally ruled that the "destruction of evidence" exception, the "threat to a police officer" exception, and the "useless gesture" exception all permitted police to break into a home without first knocking and announcing.[33] The Court also ruled that those exceptions apply to the section of the US Criminal Code on forced entry for federal officers, even though the law itself makes no mention of such exceptions. This was a curious undertaking by the Court's conservatives. They were adding exceptions to a law that it seems likely would have been included in the original language had its authors and the Congress at the time actually intended the exceptions to be included. And the Court was doing so by putting more value on the common law than on the plain language of the statute—and even *this* was based on a flawed understanding of the common law. The Court's conservative wing has always believed in original intent—except when it hasn't.

By the end of the 1990s, the Court seemed to have all but sunk the Castle Doctrine. Yet in the following decade, the justices would find yet more ways to give police yet more discretion to bring more violence into Americans' living rooms and bedrooms.

*⌐⌐*

"NOW, IF THE BUREAU OF ALCOHOL, TOBACCO AND FIREARMS comes to disarm you and they are bearing arms, resist them with arms. Go for a head shot; they're going to be wearing bulletproof vests. . . . They've got a big target on there, ATF. Don't shoot at that, because they've got a vest on underneath that. Head shots, head shots. . . . Kill the sons of bitches."[34]

That was G. Gordon Liddy, giving his listeners home defense advice on his syndicated radio show in August 1994. It was some remarkable language to be coming from the guy who helped create ODALE, the Nixon-era office that sent narcotics task forces barreling into homes to make headline-grabbing drug busts. And Giddy was still suffering from cognitive dissonance. In the same interview, he lamented that it wasn't a federal felony to possess a personal use amount of illicit drugs.[35] And of course narcotics cops hit the wrong house many, many more times than ATF agents did. Liddy wasn't offended by the tactics as much as he was by the mission (gun control) and the people who were calling the shots at the time (Bill Clinton and Janet Reno).

Still, this was part of something new. Outside of Liddy, other figures on the right were also starting to speak out against the lurch toward militarism among federal law enforcement agencies. A few high-profile incidents seemed to instigate the concern on the right, including the gunfights in Ruby Ridge, Idaho, in 1992; the raid on the Branch Davidian compound in Waco, Texas, in 1993; and the raid to seize Cuban refugee Elián González from his Miami relatives in 2000.

The Ruby Ridge fiasco began in 1989 when Randy Weaver sold an ATF informant two sawed-off shotguns that had been cut shorter than was allowed under federal law.[36] Weaver was no doubt an odd duck. He and his wife Vicki had moved their family to rural Idaho in 1983 to escape what they believed to be the coming Armageddon. He associated with white supremacists and in fact met the ATF informant at a meeting of the Aryan Nations. The informant's handler at the ATF didn't think Weaver was much of a threat, so rather than charge Weaver, the ATF attempted to leverage the gun charges to get him to work as an informant. When Weaver refused, the agent filed federal gun charges.

On August 21, 1992, a team of US marshals dressed in camouflage and carrying M-16s went to Weaver's home on a reconnaissance mission to determine an appropriate place and manner to capture him. Once there, one of the marshals threw rocks at the Weaver cabin to see how the family's dogs would react. The dogs went nuts. Hearing them, Weaver's fourteen-year-old son Sammy went out with family friend Kevin Harris to see what the commotion was about. Accounts of the incident differ here, but at some point one of the agents shot and killed one of the Weavers' dogs. Sammy Weaver responded by firing his own gun at the source of the gunfire, then fled toward the house. One of the marshals then shot him in the back as he ran. Sammy Weaver was dead. Harris then exchanged fire with the marshals, killing one of them.

A twelve-day siege ensued, featuring hundreds of cops, agents, and troops from the ATF, the FBI, the US Marshals, the Idaho State Police, the local sheriff's department, the Idaho National Guard, and—for some reason—the US Border Patrol. On day two of the siege, FBI sniper teams were told that their rules of engagement were, basically, to shoot on sight, instructions usually reserved for the battlefield and virtually unheard of in civil law enforcement. When Randy Weaver left the house to visit the body of his son, which they had put in a guest cabin, an FBI sniper shot him in the chest. As Weaver, Harris, and one of Weaver's daughters fled back into the house, the agent fired again at the front door. That bullet went through the door, then through Vicki Weaver's head, killing her instantly. She was holding her ten-month-old daughter at the time. The baby fell to the floor. Weaver and Harris were eventually tried in federal court for murder, attempted murder, and other felonies. They were acquitted on all of the serious charges. The federal government eventually settled with the Weaver family for over $3 million, and with Weaver for $380,000.

The raid in Waco the next year involved many of the same agencies—indeed, many of the same agents.[37] The ATF was investigating the Branch Davidians and their leader, David Koresh, for weapons violations. Koresh went jogging every day and could conceivably have been picked up peacefully. Instead, the agency drew up plans for a heavily armed raid on the Branch Davidian compound, even knowing that there were women and children inside. In fact, ATF officials learned ahead of time from an agent who had infiltrated the compound that Koresh and his followers knew the raid was coming. Their plan depended on the element of surprise. They went through with it anyway.

The raid began on February 28, 1993, as cattle trailers of federal agents pulled up to the compound. The raid planners hadn't bothered to instruct any individual agent announce their presence or purpose, nor had they made any plans for even the possibility of serving their warrants peacefully. The initial confrontation ended with two hours of gunfire, four dead federal agents, and six dead Branch Davidians, but no resolution. Both sides claimed the other started shooting first.

The subsequent siege went on for six weeks. Finally, on April 19, Attorney General Janet Reno gave orders to flush the Branch Davidians out of the compound. Federal agents used tanks to smash holes in the building, into which they then injected tear-gas canisters. They next used grenade launchers to shoot 350 "ferret rounds" of gas through windows and doors. A fire broke out, which eventually consumed the building and nearly everyone inside. In all, seventy-six Davidians died, including twenty-six children.

Waco and Ruby Ridge made militarization a political issue. Perhaps counterintuitively, the laws the agents were enforcing—federal gun control laws—put conservatives in the unprecedented role of criticizing federal cops for overkill, and liberals in the position of defending the aggressive tactics. (One fact about Waco that conservative ATF critics often overlook: the military presence at the compound was only made possible by the drug war. The ATF told the leaders of Joint Task Force 6—one of the many military-civilian police antidrug task forces set up during the Reagan and Bush administrations—that David Koresh was running a methamphetamine operation. The evidence for this was suspect at best.)

As for the ATF itself, the agency appeared to be suffering from the same afflictions that a decade of "warring" on drugs and crime had brought out in other federal police agencies. Back in 1991, for example, sixty agents from the ATF, the DEA, the US Forest Service, and the National Guard—the latter wearing face paint and camouflage—raided three homes in New Mexico based on an unsubstantiated tip from a confidential informant that they would find drugs and weapons. The ATF led the investigation because of federal laws prohibiting the use of guns by drug offenders. They found nothing. Later the same year, sixty ATF agents invited television crews to film them while they raided the Oklahoma home of John Lawmaster. They had received a tip that Lawmaster had illegally converted one of his semiautomatic weapons to an automatic. They ripped Lawmaster's home to shreds, but found no evidence that he'd broken any law. Lawmaster wasn't home at the time. When he returned, he found his doors open, his house in ruins, and a note from the federal agency that read, "Nothing found." And just three weeks before the raid in Waco, ATF agents raided a woman's home in Portland. They held her at gunpoint for several hours and wouldn't let her call her attorney. They finally admitted that they had raided the wrong home.

These were just a few examples of the agency's excesses.[38] The ATF abuses that came to light in the 1990s were a good indication that the warriorlike, us-against-them mentality wasn't limited to drug policing. Those police actions also gave some momentum to a new militia movement—or at least caused the media to take notice of them. The militia movement was vast and fairly diverse, but most groups had views about government, guns, and property that were well to the right of the rest of the country. Very few espoused violence, but the new attention on the few that did, along with anger from the National Rifle Association (NRA), Gun Owners of America, and the rants of right-wing personalities like Liddy, inspired more reactionary opposition from the left. Then, on April 19, 1994, Timothy McVeigh set off a fertilizer bomb outside the Arthur Murrah Federal Building in Oklahoma City, killing 164 people. McVeigh claimed that he bombed the building in retaliation for the events at Waco.

McVeigh's act gave fresh fuel to the ATF's defenders—not so much to defend the agency, but to attack its critics. Four days after the bombing, President Bill Clinton laid part of the blame at the feet of right-wing critics of federal law enforcement officials. "We hear so many loud and angry voices in America today whose sole goal seems to be to try to keep some people as paranoid as possible and the rest of us all torn up and upset with each other," Clinton said. "They spread hate. They leave the impression that, by their very words, that violence is acceptable."

Of course, just as it was possible to think David Koresh was a madman *and* be appalled by the federal government's siege at Waco, it was also possible to believe the ATF deserved sharp criticism for its handling of both Ruby Ridge and Waco *and* be appalled at Timothy McVeigh's retaliatory murder of 164 innocent people. But McVeigh's actions seemed to cement partisian battle lines for years to come, at least when it came to ATF abuses.

The final event to nudge the right to question the militarization of police—at least at the federal level—was the raid to wrest five-year-old Cuban refugee Elián González from the home of his relatives in Miami.[39] In November 1999, González had fled to Florida on a boat with his mother and her boyfriend. His mother drowned when the boat sank, but González was picked up by a Florida fisherman, then handed over to Immigration and Naturalization Service (INS) officials, who initially placed him with the Miami relatives. When word of his rescue made it back to Cuba, González's father said that his mother had taken the boy without his permission, and he immediately began agitating for his son's return. A legal battle ensued, culminating with a decision by the Eleventh Circuit Court of Appeals on April 19 that González was to be returned to Cuba. When informed of the decision by a Justice Department official, Elián's cousin Marisleysis González allegedly responded, "You think we just have cameras in the house? If people try to come in, they could be hurt." The Justice Department cited that statement and other threats from the family's supporters as the reason for its decision to send a 130-member INS team to take custody of the boy, headed by a heavily armed, eight-member INS SWAT team. The resulting raid produced an iconic, Pulitzer Prize–winning photo by Associated Press photographer Alan Diaz in which an INS agent points a semi-automatic weapon at the crying, terrified boy while he's being held by Donato Dalrymple, one of the fishermen who found him.

Once again, reactions to the raid and the photo broke down along partisan lines. Conservatives lined up behind the Miami relatives, who were part of the city's large community of generally conservative, anti-Castro, anti-Communist Cuban immigrants. Liberals tended to line up behind Bill Clinton, Janet Reno, and the Justice Department, who were trying to enforce the Eleventh Circuit ruling.

Then-presidential candidate George W. Bush declared that "the chilling picture of a little boy being removed from his home at gunpoint defies the values of America." Bush would go on to win the presidency, a position from which he would order heavily armed SWAT teams to raid AIDS and cancer patients who used medical marijuana in states that had legalized the drug for medicinal purposes. The conservative *Washington Times* compared the INS agents to the Nazi brownshirts in the movie *Schindler's List*. And conservative bomb-thrower (and drug war cheerleader) Ann Coulter deplored "the predawn raid with masked, machine-gun-toting federal agents" breaking into a private home.

Yet as *Chicago Tribune* columnist Clarence Page pointed out, heavily armed INS SWAT teams had been breaking into private homes and businesses to snatch up nonviolent but undocumented immigrants for years, thanks to policies passed and funded by the Republican Congress, and with the full support of anti-immigration conservatives.[40] Meanwhile, on the left, former Clinton solicitor general Walter Dellinger pointed out that *of course* SWAT teams like the one in the González photo look scary. That's the whole point. "A great show of force can often avoid violence," Dellinger said on ABC's *This Week*. "It allowed [the INS agents] to get in and out in three minutes. . . . Look again at that iconographic picture and you will see that Mr. Dalrymple . . . is stunned by the officer in his display of a weapon. . . . His jaw goes slack, his arm loses its grip, and that avoided a physical tug-of-war."[41] *Slate* writer Will Saletan explained that the INS agents were "heavily armed because Justice Department officials had heard there might be weapons in the house. They were wrong. But they weren't reckless."[42] These are the very same justifications SWAT teams across the country give for conducting violent, heavily armed raids on people suspected of nonviolent drug crimes.

As police militarization began to creep beyond the drug war into other police actions in the 1990s, the country's major political ideologies continued to react through the prism of partisan affiliation. When George W. Bush moved into the White House in 2001, conservatives stopped caring about police heavy-handedness (though there were a few exceptions). Progressives then rose up to decry the raids on medical marijuana clinics and the disproportionate use of SWAT teams and paramilitary tactics against minority groups, on immigration raids, and at political protests.

Both sides were capable of righteous anger when the opposing party was in power and using big guns to enforce policies they found objectionable. And at the same time, both sides were more than willing to endorse the use of heavy-handed police tactics on their political opponents. It's a trend that continues today, and further enables domestic police militarization to continue to flourish.

In 1989 A FRIEND ASKED PETER KRASKA IF HE WANTED TO TAG along for a US Coast Guard exercise on Lake Erie.[43] Kraska is a criminologist at the University of Eastern Kentucky; his students describe him as demanding, whip-smart, and, in the words of one female student, "a strangely hot lumberjack." He agreed to go along, mostly out of curiosity. While on that trip, Kraska learned that the Coast Guard worked closely with the US Navy on drug interdiction efforts. The Navy itself would intercept boats or ships that fit drug courier profiles, but would then have Coast Guard personnel on board to conduct the actual searches, seizures, and arrests. One Coast Guard officer flatly admitted to Kraska that the procedure was a way of getting around the Navy's policy prohibiting its personnel from participating in civil police actions.

Kraska was both alarmed and intrigued. The experience started him down a road of scholarship focused on examining the ways in which the US military was increasingly being drawn into enforcing drug laws. In particular, Kraska began looking into indirect militarization: the rise of SWAT teams and other paramilitary police teams; what might be called the criminal-justice-industrial complex; and the increasing tendency of public officials to address social problems with martial rhetoric and imagery and to suggest military-like solutions,

from the "wars" on crime and drugs, to the heavy weaponry and vehicles that police were beginning to use, to the proposals that juve-
nile offenders be punished in "boot camps." Kraska obtained funding
to conduct two broad surveys of police departments on their use of
SWAT teams. His resulting reports systematically documented a previously unheeded, two-decade insurgence of militarism into just
about every city and county in America.

The numbers were staggering. By 1995, 89 percent of American
cities with 50,000 or more people had at least one SWAT team,
double the percentage from 1980. Among smaller cities (populations between 25,000 and 50,000), 65 percent had a SWAT team
by 1995, a 157 percent increase over ten years. Nearly 20 percent of
all police officers in these towns served on the SWAT team, a phenomenon that Kraska dubbed "the militarization of Mayberry." By
1995, combining these figures for cities and towns, 77 percent of all
American cities with over 25,000 people had a SWAT team.

Kraska then asked police departments that had maintained SWAT
teams going back to the early 1980s to report how many times the
teams had been deployed over the years, and for what reasons.
Again, the numbers were jaw-dropping. In the early 1980s, the ag-
gregate annual number of SWAT deployments was just under
3,000. By 1995 it was just under 30,000. In fifteen years, the number of annual SWAT team deployments in America had jumped by
937 percent. Some SWAT teams, Kraska found, were conducting up
to 700 raids per year. What was precipitating the surge in SWAT
activity? The drug war, almost exclusively.

Logan, Utah, is a typical example of the phenomenon. As of
2011, the city had just under 50,000 people, hadn't had a murder
in five years, and had recently been rated the "safest city in America." Yet, since the mid-1980s, Logan has had its own SWAT team.
What does a SWAT team do in a city with no violent crime? It creates violence out of nonviolent crime. "We haven't really had a
whole lot of barricaded subjects, and certainly we haven't had an
active gunman shooter," a department spokesman told the local paper. But it was nice to have the SWAT team around just in case. In

the meantime, he said, it's "mostly used for assistance on high-risk search warrants"—"high-risk" meaning all or most drug warrants. "We've destroyed some doors over the years that maybe wouldn't have gotten destroyed if there wasn't a SWAT team, but it's all in the name of trying to make a high-risk situation more safe for everyone."[44]

Some 43 percent of the police departments in Kraska's survey told him they had used active-duty military personnel to train the SWAT team when it was first started, and 46 percent were training on a regular basis "with active-duty military experts in special operations," usually the Army Rangers or Navy Seals. This was the goal of the joint task forces set up during the Bush administration—to encourage cooperation between local police, federal police, and the military in order to foster a battlefield approach to drug enforcement. In a follow-up interview, one department's SWAT commander told Kraska:

> We've had special forces folks who have come right out of the jungles of Central and South America. These guys get into the real shit. All branches of military service are involved in providing training to law enforcement. US Marshals act as liaisons between the police and military to set up the training—our go-between. . . . We've had teams of Navy Seals and Army Rangers come here and teach us everything. We just have to use our judgment and exclude the information like: "at this point we bring in the mortars and blow the place up."[45]

The commander added that he had received a letter from a four-star general expressing concern about the sort of training the department was getting. Back in the 1850s, the Cushing Doctrine had allowed federal marshals to summon US troops to enforce domestic law. More than a hundred years after the controversial policy was repealed by the Posse Comitatus Act, federal marshals were now soliciting elite US military personnel again—not to enforce domestic law themselves, but to teach civilian police officers how to enforce the laws *as if they* were in the military.

Perhaps most disturbing was Kraska's finding that these paramilitary police teams and aggressive tactics were increasingly being used even for regular patrols. By 1997, 20 percent of the departments he surveyed used SWAT teams or similar units for patrol, mostly in poor, high-crime areas. This was an increase of 257 percent since 1989.

SWAT proponents argued that all of this buildup was in response to a real problem—after all, violent crime had soared in the 1980s and early 1990s. But the SWAT teams weren't generally responding to violent crime. They were usually serving drug warrants. When Kraska and colleague Louie Cubellis compared changes in violent crime rates to changes in the use of SWAT teams in the jurisdictions they surveyed, they found that only 6.63 percent of the rise in SWAT deployments could be explained by the rising crime rate.[46]

Kraska's findings prompted a surge of media interest in the phenomenon of police militarization. The *New York Times, Washington Post, Boston Globe, National Journal,* and ABC News all covered Kraska's study—and also ran their own investigations into the issue. But nothing really changed. Politicians and policymakers didn't seem to notice—or if they did, they didn't much care. Kraska noted the fizzling out of the issue in a self-deprecating footnote in a book he edited a few years later. "What exactly all this media attention accomplished is not quite clear. It resulted in no fame, no money, and no appreciable difference in the phenomenon itself."[47] Of course, that wasn't Kraska's fault. Congress, state legislatures, and other politicians either weren't paying attention or just didn't find the reports particularly troubling.

In fact, the phenomenon only continued to pick up momentum. The year before Kraska's reports were published, Congress had passed the National Defense Authorization Security Act of 1997, the biennial bill to fund the Pentagon. One provision in the bill created what is now usually called "the 1033 program," named for the section of US Code assigned to it. The provision established the Law Enforcement Support Program, an agency headquartered in Fort Belvoir, Virginia. Its mission? To further grease the pipeline through which hard-core military gear flows to civilian police agencies.

It certainly accomplished its mission. In its first three years, the office handled 3.4 million orders for Pentagon gear from 11,000 police agencies in all fifty states. By 2005, the number of police agencies serviced by the office hit 17,000. *National Journal* reported in 2000 that between 1997 and 1999 the office doled out $727 million worth of equipment, including 253 aircraft (notably, six- and seven-passenger airplanes and UH-60 Blackhawk and UH-1 Huey helicopters), 7,856 M-16 rifles, 181 grenade launchers, 8,131 bulletproof helmets, and 1,161 pairs of night-vision goggles.[48]

With all that military gear, plus the federal drug policing grants and asset forfeiture proceeds, just about anyone running a police department who wanted a SWAT team could now afford to start and fund one. And so the trend crept into smaller and smaller towns. By the mid-2000s, SWAT had come to Middleburg, Pennsylvania (population: 1,363); Leesburg, Florida (17,000); Mt. Orab, Ohio (2,701); Neenah, Wisconsin (24,507); Harwich, Massachusetts (11,000); and Butler, Missouri (4,201), among others. In research for his ethnography on militarization, Kraska spent a good deal of time with cops and SWAT teams in these smaller cities. One general dynamic he observed was a kind of masculinity-infused arms race between police agencies that could often lead to an inferiority complex at smaller departments. "These officers strongly believed that small municipalities and county police were being left behind by not having special tactical teams," Kraska writes. Smaller departments may have started acquiring SWAT teams not because of a sudden surge in violence, or hostage takings, or even drug activity. The towns' police departments simply saw that other police departments had them, so they wanted one too.

Neill Franklin, a former narcotics cop in Maryland, also witnessed the dynamic over the course of his career. "It's almost like they would get their own high off the money and the equipment. And then the agencies would get competitive. If a city department had a SWAT team, the county wanted one. If one department upgraded to a more powerful gun, or got an APV, all the departments nearby had to get the same thing."[49] Stephen Downing, who worked in the same LAPD patrol bureau as Daryl Gates while Gates was developing his SWAT idea, explains how the move to smaller police departments makes already dangerous SWAT raids even more perilous. "You'd have this 'I want one too' phenomenon," Downing says. "And so the SWAT teams get bigger, and they start to spread. And standards would start to drop. You have to be very careful about who you put on the SWAT team. The guys who want it most are the last ones who should be given a spot. At LAPD, you were choosing from a force of nine thousand strong. You're getting elite, disciplined officers, and the pool is big enough that you can screen them. For fitness and marksmanship and all the usual stuff. But also for attitude and psychology."

Choosiness isn't a luxury at smaller police agencies. "Right now, I'm preparing to testify in a lawsuit stemming from a wrongheaded raid by a SWAT team in a twenty-eight-man police department," Downing says. "How do you even begin to select from twenty-eight people?" Several officers interviewed for this book made the intuitive point that the officers who want to be on the SWAT team are the last officers who should be selected for it. "And how do they find time to train? At LAPD, the SWAT team will spend at least half their on-duty time in training. In these smaller towns, the SWAT team is something these guys do on the side. They're patrol officers. And so what happens is that they train by practicing on the people."[50]

In the September 2011 issue of *Tactical Edge* magazine, Ed Sanow, a SWAT leader in Benton County, Indiana, and a well-published author and consultant on police tactics, suggests doing exactly that— practicing SWAT raids on low-level offenders. "Team commanders must raise the profile of their teams," Sanow writes. "Stay active. Yes, I mean do warrant service and drug raids even if you have to poach the work. First, your team needs the training time under true callout conditions. If all your team does is train, but seldom deploy, you will end up training just to train. You need to train to fight. . . . Make deploying SWAT something that is routine, not something only done after much hand-wringing."[51]

As had been happening throughout the drug war, this mass militarization brought with it a new wave of dehumanization. In one follow-up interview to his survey, a SWAT commander told Kraska, referring to the use of his team for routine patrols, "When the soldiers ride in, you should see those blacks scatter." Former San Jose police chief Joseph McNamara told *National Journal* in 2000 that at a recent SWAT conference he had attended, "officers . . . were wearing these very disturbing shirts. On the front, there were pictures of SWAT officers dressed in dark uniforms, wearing helmets, and holding submachine guns. Below was written: 'We don't do drive-by shootings.' On the back, there was a picture of a demolished house. Below was written: 'We stop.'"[52]

Kraska found more evidence of the mind-set problem in a separate ethnography study he conducted. As part of the study, he had been invited to sit in on an informal (and probably illegal) training session for police officers. The session was taught by two members of an elite military unit with whom he had become friendly and who worked with several police departments that were developing or in the process of developing SWAT-like units. The actual "training" turned out to be little more than a group of cops and soldiers gathering in a remote area to shoot big guns. But before the police officers arrived, Kraska talked to the trainers about the proliferation of SWAT teams. "This shit is going on all over," one of them said. "Why serve an arrest warrant to some crack dealer with a .38? With full armor, the right shit, and training, you can kick ass and have fun." The other trainer jumped in. "Most of these guys just like to play war; they get a rush out of search-and-destroy missions instead of the bullshit they do normally."

When the "trainees" arrived—all active-duty cops either on a SWAT team or soon to be—Kraska described what he saw:

> Several had lightweight retractable combat knives strapped to their belts; three wore authentic army fatigue pants with T-shirts; one wore a T-shirt that carried a picture of a burning city with gunship

helicopters flying overhead and the caption "Operation Ghetto Storm"; another wore a tight, black T-shirt with the initials "NTOA" (for National Tactical Officers Association). A few of the younger officers wore Oakley wraparound sunglasses on heads that sported either flattops or military-style crew cuts.

The Oakleys and crew cuts were part of a muscle-bound, mechanistic look popular with younger police officers. The look was usually accessorized with sensory-enhancement gear like night-vision goggles to achieve what Kraska calls a "techno-warrior" image. He notes that one purveyor of SWAT gear and clothing calls its line "Cyborg 21st."

Later, Kraska wrote, a guy who had served as a sniper both in the military and on a SWAT team put on a demonstration for the group. The rest of the officers sat in awe as he popped off "head-sized" jugs of water sitting behind plates of glass. The sniper, Kraska observed, was held in especially high esteem in the paramilitary subculture because he embodied "the skill, discipline, endurance, and mind-set necessary to execute people from long distances in a variety of situations."

Most interesting are Kraska's observations about his own state of mind during the training session. There's a point in his narrative where one of the trainers asks him if he wants to take a turn with an MP5. Kraska is reluctant, but after some prodding, gives the weapon a try. "I fired at a body-sized target, and, just as this officer surely anticipated, I made all the mistakes of someone who had never fired an automatic." He took some ribbing, and then was surprised to hear himself defending his masculinity to the group of virtual strangers by pointing out that he had grown up hunting with shotguns. Presented with a shotgun, he then redeemed himself with what he calls "a personally satisfying demonstration." Kraska found himself working hard to fit in and win the approval of the officers, even though he was there as an observer and likely would never see them again. He also felt a rush of power.

I had an intense sense of operating on the boundary of legitimate and illegitimate behavior. Clearly much of the activity itself was illegal, although reporting it would never have resulted in it being defined as "criminal." . . . I felt at ease and in some ways defiant. I've had this experience in the past when field-researching police officers, and I realize that in a sense I am basking in the security of my temporary status as a beneficiary of state-sanctioned use of force. This is likely the same intoxicating feeling of autonomy from the law that is experienced by an abusive police officer. . . .

On a personal level, what disturbed me most was how I, as a person who had so thoroughly thought out militarism, could have so easily enjoyed experiencing it. This study illustrates the expansive and seductive powers . . . of a deeply embedded ideology of violence.[53]

The officers with SWAT and dynamic-entry experience interviewed for this book say raids are orders of magnitude more intoxicating than anything else in police work. Ironically, many cops describe them with language usually used to describe the drugs the raids are conducted to confiscate. "Oh, it's a huge rush," Franklin says. "Those times when you do have to kick down a door, it's just a big shot of adrenaline." Downing agrees. "It's a rush. And you have to be careful, because the raids themselves can be habit-forming." Jamie Haase, a former special agent with Immigration and Customs Enforcement who went on multiple narcotics, money laundering, and human trafficking raids, says the thrill of the raid may factor into why narcotics cops just don't consider less volatile means of serving search warrants. "The thing is, it's so much safer to wait the suspect out," he says. "Waiting people out is just so much better. You've done your investigation, so you know their routine. So you wait until the guy leaves, and you do a routine traffic stop and you arrest him. That's the safest way to do it. But you have to understand that a lot of these cops are meatheads. They think this stuff is cool. And they get hooked on that jolt of energy they get during a raid."[54]

THE 1996 ELECTION MAY HAVE REPRESENTED A TURNING point in public opinion about marijuana. Despite heavy campaigning by the office of Clinton's drug czar, Barry McCaffrey, and the federal government in general, California voters overwhelmingly passed a ballot initiative to legalize marijuana for medical purposes. Arizona voters passed an even more permissive law, but the state legislature effectively repealed it the following year. Over the next sixteen years, seventeen more states and the District of Columbia would pass medical marijuana laws—eleven of them through ballot initiatives. And all of this led to the historic 2012 election results, in which voters in Washington State and Colorado legalized the drug outright.

But the federal government wasn't about to let sick people just start smoking pot without a fight. After the 1996 election, McCaffrey called a press conference to denounce California voters. "Nothing has changed," McCaffrey said. "This is not a medical proposition. This is the legalization of drugs that we're concerned about. . . . This is not medicine. This is a Cheech and Chong show. And now what we are committed to doing is to look in a scientific way at any proposition that would bring a new medicine to the assistance of the American medical establishment."[55] Naturally, there was no such medicine in the offing.

Months later the Clinton administration announced that doctors who recommended pot to their patients would not only lose their DEA licenses, but could also face criminal charges. In 2000 a federal judge chastised the Clinton administration for threatening doctors who even mentioned the medical benefits of marijuana to their AIDS and cancer patients.

The medical marijuana fight also began what would become a new and especially disturbing chapter in the story of police militarization in America—the use of heavy-handed paramilitary raids to send a political message. When the DEA began raiding marijuana suppliers in California, and then also in the states that subsequently legalized the drug, they generally raided suspects who were either well-known supporters of pot or people who they believed had enormous supplies of the drug. The latter were people running businesses, operating openly under state law. Many of them had obtained business licenses and permits, as well as permission from local law enforcement. These were not dangerous people. The use of tactical teams and frightening raids to shut down medical marijuana suppliers in California was about sending a clear, unambiguous message to other pot suppliers around the state: openly defy the federal government, and you can expect the blunt force of federal power to be brought down upon you.

One of those early raids was on a medical marijuana farm run by Todd McCormick and Peter McWilliams in the Los Angeles neighborhood of Bel Air. Both men had become advocates of the drug after using it to treat symptoms of their own serious illnesses. McCormick smoked pot to treat the pain associated with a cancer treatment that had fused two of his vertebrae. McWilliams had both AIDS and non-Hodgkin's lymphoma brought on by AIDS. Smoking marijuana relieved his nausea, which helped him keep down the medication he took both to manage his AIDS and during his chemotherapy for the cancer. McWilliams was also a self-help author, and had become an outspoken civil liberties activist. With respect to pot, he made no attempt to hide the fact that while it was saving his life, it also made him feel good. The pot helped him keep down his medicine, dulled the pain associated with his conditions, and took his mind off the fact that he was suffering from them.

None of that was enough to get McCormick and McWilliams out from under the boot of the federal government. McWilliams describes the first moments of the raid:

A hard pounding on the door accompanied by shouts of "Police! Open up!" broke the silence, broke my reverie, and nearly broke down the door. I opened the door wearing standard writer's attire, a bathrobe, and was immediately handcuffed. I was taken outside while Drug Enforcement Administration (DEA) agents ran through my house, guns drawn, commando-style. They were looking, I suppose, for the notorious, well-armed, highly trained Medical Marijuana Militia. To the DEA, I am the Godfather of the Medicine

Cartel. Finding nothing, they took me back into my home, informed me I was not under arrest, and ordered me—still in handcuffs—to sit down. I was merely being "restrained," I was told, so the DEA could "enforce the search warrant."[56]

The two men were unquestionably growing marijuana—the police found some four thousand plants. The entire operation was legal under California law, but because they were brought up on federal charges and tried in federal court, a jury wouldn't be allowed to hear anything about California law. McWilliams was also barred from telling the jury that, according to his doctors, marijuana was keeping him alive.

Because all of that information would be kept from any potential jury, McWilliams really had no choice but to plead guilty and hope for leniency. After his arrest, McWilliams's mother put her house up as collateral to help post his bail. One of the conditions of McWilliams's bail was that he refrain from smoking marijuana. Federal prosecutors told McWilliams's mother that if he failed a drug test or was caught with even a trace of pot in his possession, they'd take her house. So to protect his mother, McWilliams refrained from using the drug.

He died before he could be sentenced. McWilliams was found dead in his apartment on June 14, 2000. Overcome with nausea, he had choked and aspirated on his own vomit. Tributes popped up all over the political spectrum—conservative icon and pot champion William F. Buckley devoted a column to eulogizing McWilliams. Drug war reformers and libertarians snapped up his book—and probably his most lasting legacy—*Ain't Nobody's Business if You Do,* an eloquent defense of John Stuart Mill's harm principle.

And yet to those on the other side—the federal prosecutors who went after him, the DEA agents who raided him, Barry McCaffrey, Janet Reno, and Bill Clinton—Peter McWilliams was just more collateral damage.[57]

WHEN BILL CLINTON TOOK OFFICE IN 1993, CRIME IN America was still climbing. The concept of *community policing* was growing increasingly popular. Ideally, community policing is the sort of thing implemented by law enforcement officials like Norm Stamper in San Diego, Nick Pastore in New Haven, and, as we'll see, Joseph McNamara in San Jose. Rather than taking a "call-and-response" approach to policing—which focuses on aspects of policing like increasing response times to 911 calls—cops walk regular beats. They go to community meetings. They know the names of the principals of the schools in their district, and they know and consult with community and neighborhood leaders. It's a more proactive form of policing, but one that stresses making cops a part of the places they work.

In 1994 Clinton started a new grant program under the Justice Department called Community Oriented Policing Services, or COPS. For its inaugural year, Clinton and leaders in Congress (most notably Sen. Joe Biden) funded it with $148.4 million. The next year funding jumped to $1.42 billion, and it stayed in the neighborhood of $1.5 billion through 1999. COPS grants were mostly intended to go to police departments to hire new police officers, ostensibly for the purpose of implementing more community-oriented policing strategies.

The problem was that there was no universal definition of community policing. Most law enforcement officials and academics agree that community policing is a more proactive approach to policing than call-and-response, but within that general agreement is a huge range of approaches.

The style of community policing embraced by officials like Pastore and Stamper aims to make police a helpful presence in the community, not an occupying presence. But theirs is not the only way to be proactive about law enforcement. Street sweeps, occupation-like control of neighborhoods, SWAT raids, and aggressive anti-gang policies are also proactive. These police activities are aggressive, often violent, and usually a net loss for civil liberties, but they *are* proactive.

When Clinton, Biden, and other politicians touted the COPS program, they did so with language that evoked the Peace Corps approach (though both Clinton and Biden also supported policies that promoted militarization). Although Clinton described the goal of COPS as "build[ing] bonds of understanding and trust between police and citizens," it wasn't clear if he or any other politician really believed this. The majority of the funding in COPS grants was given simply to hire more police officers. The program said little about how those officers should be used, or what sort of attitude they should bring to the job.

Moreover, while Congress regularly makes federal funding contingent on states passing a particular law or policy (think speed limits or drunk driving laws tied to federal highway funding), it's much more difficult to dictate how a police department puts a big federal grant to work in day-to-day operations. And so as the COPS program threw billions at police departments under the pretense of hiring whistling, baton-twirling Officer Friendlies to walk neighborhood beats, rescue kittens, and maybe guest-umpire the occasional Little League game, many police agencies were actually using the money to militarize.

One of the first to notice what was going on was Portland journalist Paul Richmond. "The unfortunate truth about community policing as it is currently being implemented is that it is anything but community based," Richmond wrote in a 1997 article for the alternative newspaper *PDXS*.[58] Instead, he wrote, in Portland the grants had resulted in "increased militarization of the police force." Richmond also found in Portland that, ironically (or perhaps not), a federal program touted as a way to encourage local police to get more involved with local communities was actually federalizing local law enforcement. At the same time Clinton was pushing COPS, the administration and Democrats in Congress were pushing policies like "troops to cops" bills, management training programs for police agencies based on federal models of policing, and a bill that would allow local police departments to fund community policing programs with asset forfeiture money obtained through the Justice Department's Equitable Sharing Program—the program that allows local police departments to ignore state forfeiture laws by teaming up with the federal government. Another bill would have established a 2,500-person "Federal Rapid Deployment Force"—essentially a small standing army—that states and cities could call upon to swoop in for special crime- and drug-fighting missions. The same bill would also have directed yet more funding to create joint federal-state-local antidrug task forces.

Richmond found that while the overall cops-to-citizens ratio fell in the early 1990s, in Portland, between 1989 and 1994, the number of officers in the city's tactical operations department jumped from two to fifty-six. The two officers in charge of the city's tactical teams had formerly been in charge of the city's Department of Community Policing. Richmond also obtained a copy of the city's "Community Policing Strategic Plan," passed by the city council in 1994. Among the plan's objectives was to increase the police department's involvement with the federal ATF and the Oregon National Guard. It included implementing at a local level Clinton's "one strike and you're out" plan for drug use in public housing, which allowed for raids on public housing tenants, followed by their possible eviction, based on no more than an anonymous tip. Richmond was alarmed that so many progressives in the city were embracing the community policing plan based on little more than its pleasant-sounding name and that it was coming from a Democratic administration in Washington and administered by a progressive city government. The devil was in the details, and no one had bothered to look at the details.

Little of this would have surprised Peter Kraska. All of the police departments he surveyed that had a SWAT team "also claimed to place high emphasis on the democratic approach to community policing."[59] Kraska found that when most law enforcement officials heard "community policing," they thought of the militarized zero-tolerance model. To them the idea of a police agency simultaneously militarizing and implementing community policing policies was perfectly reasonable.

In fact, two out of three departments Kraska surveyed said their SWAT team *was actually part of their community policing strategy.* Surprising as that may seem at first glance, it went hand in hand with the increasing use of these tactical teams for routine patrols.

In 2001 a *Madison Capital Times* investigation found that sixty-five of Wisconsin's eighty-three local SWAT teams had come into being since 1980—twenty-eight of them since 1996, and sixteen in just the previous year. In other words, more than half of the state's SWAT teams had popped up since the inaugural year of the COPS program. The newer tactical units had sprung up in absurdly small jurisdictions like Forest County (population 9,950), Mukwonago (7,519), and Rice Lake (8,320). Many of the agents who populated these new SWAT teams, the paper found, had been hired with COPS grants. A local criminologist was incredulous: "Community policing initiatives and stockpiling weapons and grenade launchers are totally incompatible."[60] Perhaps that was true in theory, but not in how community policing was being practiced.

Of course, Byrne grants and the 1033 program had also contributed to the SWAT-ification of the Dairy State. The paper found that in the 1990s, Wisconsin police departments hauled in over 100,000 pieces of military equipment valued at more than $18 million. Columbia County alone—home to all of 52,000 people—made out with 5,000 military items valued at $1.75 million. Some of the bounty was benign, items like computers and office equipment, but it also included "11 M-16s, 21 bayonets, four boats, a periscope, and 41 vehicles, one of which was converted into a mobile command center for the SWAT team." Columbia County also received "surveillance equipment, cold weather gear, tools, battle dress uniforms, flak jackets, [and] chemical suits." The county put its tactical team to use by sending it to "Weedstock" in nearby Saulk County, an event where cops in full SWAT attire intimidatingly stood guard while "hundreds of young people gather[ed] peacefully to smoke marijuana and listen to music."

Moreover, the *Capital Times* found that the state distributed the Byrne grants, COPS grants, and block law enforcement grants it received from Washington to local police agencies based *solely* on their drug policing statistics. The size of the disbursements was directly tied to the number of city or county drug arrests. Each drug-related arrest, the paper found, brought in $153 to each local police department. Jackson County quadrupled its drug arrests between 1999 and 2000. Correspondingly, the county's state-distributed federal law enforcement subsidies quadrupled too. Several jurisdictions brought in enough in grants alone to more than cover the cost of starting a SWAT team.

This is how the game is played. Drug arrests brought in federal money. Federal money and 1033 let police departments buy cool battle garb to start a SWAT team, which they justify to local residents by playing to fears of terrorism, school shootings, and hostage takings. But those sorts of events are not only rare, they don't bring in any additional money. Drug raids bring in more federal funding, plus the possibility of asset forfeiture. All in the name of community policing.

During the 2008 campaign, Barack Obama and Joe Biden—but especially Biden—credited the COPS program as the reason behind America's historic crime drop that began in 1994. Biden's campaign website during the 2008 primaries exclaimed, "In the 1990s, the Biden Crime Bill [an incarnation of the final bill establishing COPS] added 100,000 cops to America's streets. As a result, murder and violent crime rates went down eight years in a row." The Justice Department's inspector general put the new cops number closer to 60,000, and a Heritage Foundation analysis found that, accounting for attrition, the total number of cops on the streets increased between 6,000 and 40,000. More to the point, there's little evidence that the crime drop was a result of the program. A 2005 report by the Government Accountability Office found that while the violent crime rate dropped 32 percent between 1993 and 2000, at most, the COPS program accounted for 2.5 percent of that decrease, and at a cost of $8 billion. A 2007 analysis in the peer-reviewed academic journal *Criminology* concluded that "COPS spending had little to no effect on crime."[61]

In 2007 I was asked to speak about police militarization at a "crime summit" hosted by Rep. Bobby Scott of Virginia, the Democratic chairman of the House Subcommittee on Crime. During a question-and-answer session, someone asked about community policing and the possibility of restoring full funding to the COPS grants. (The Bush administration had phased the program out.) Everyone seemed to be in favor of the "Peace Corps" model of community policing, and they also seemed to believe that this was what the COPS grants were funding. Pointing to the *Madison Capital Times* investigation and Kraska's research, I explained that these idealized visions of community policing didn't appear to have much to do with how the grants were actually being used. Representative Scott stopped me.

"Are you telling me that our community policing grants are being used to start and fund . . . SWAT teams?"

I responded that, yes, that was what Kraska and the Madison paper had found.

Scott replied, with a bit of whimsy, "Well, *that's* not really what we intended."

The room had a good chuckle. The next year the Democrats increased funding to the COPS program by $40 million. The following year, with Obama in the White House, the program's budget increased 250 percent, to $1.55 billion.

⌐

Early Monday morning, the chief of detectives requests an urgent meeting with the police chief. At the meeting he tells the police chief that the department's op narc, Detective Eveready, has gathered intelligence indicating that "Mad Dog Brown," one of the city's more well-known drug dealers, has obtained a large shipment of rock cocaine. Mad Dog, who is credited by police with killing a number of rival dealers after giving them a mad dog look, has said he will never be taken alive. The intelligence indicates that Mad Dog has obtained enough rock cocaine to supply the city's drug users for a month. He is reportedly held up in a fortified apartment on the third floor of a public housing project and surrounded by colleagues armed with military-type assault rifles.

That was the scenario Joseph McNamara set up to kick off the afternoon panel he was moderating for a groundbreaking drug policy conference in 1997 at the Hoover Institution. McNamara was a fellow at Hoover, the conservative think tank affiliated with Stanford University. More than one hundred police chiefs, judges, prosecutors, civil rights and civil liberties leaders, drug treatment professionals, and academics had gathered for the event, which was covered by C-SPAN. It was likely the first event of its kind—and if not, it was certainly the most high-profile. McNamara—who had thirty-five years' experience in law enforcement—himself had become a critic of the drug war and police militarization. But the Hoover name gave the event some credibility with conservatives and law enforcement officials. Speakers included Milton Friedman, former secretary of State George Schultz, Baltimore mayor Kurt Schmoke, Baltimore police commissioner Thomas Frazier, Ed Meese, California judge James Gray, and San Jose, California, mayor Susan Hammer.

McNamara himself started his career as a patrol officer in Harlem in the 1960s, where he walked one of the highest-crime beats in the country. He worked his way up through the NYPD, achieving the rank of lieutenant before accepting a criminal justice fellowship at Harvard. Under the fellowship, he studied the operations of a methadone clinic back in Harlem, which spurred his interest in drug policy. McNamara went on to earn a doctorate in public administration. His dissertation was an examination of how law enforcement handled drug use in America before and after the 1913 Harrison Narcotics Act. After completing his doctorate, he returned to the NYPD as a deputy inspector in charge of crime analysis.

In 1973, McNamara was appointed police chief in Kansas City. Three years later, he was appointed police chief for San Jose, California. He headed that department for fifteen years. McNamara resisted the aggressive, militaristic trends brought on by the drug war in the 1980s. He embraced community policing, and showed little tolerance for police misconduct and excessive force. By the time he retired in 1991, San Jose had surpassed San Francisco to become the most populous city in northern California. Among cities with a population of 400,000 or more, San Jose also had the lowest crime rate in the country for the last three years of McNamara's tenure. The city's crime rate in 1990 was 60 percent of San Diego's, half that of San Francisco, and one-quarter of the rate in Los Angeles. McNamara pulled this off with one of the smallest per capita police departments in America.

That record (and his own conservative politics) won McNamara clout with the right, despite his vocal criticism of the war on drugs, police abuse, and police militarization. It also helped him land his post–law enforcement position with Hoover shortly after retirement. In 1995, McNamara won funding to conduct four drug policy conferences at Hoover. The first was in 1995. The panel he was moderating in 1997 was the second.

McNamara's co-panelists for the militarization session were Los Angeles police chief Bernard Parks, US district judge Robert Sweet, San Jose mayor Hammer, defense attorney Ron Rose, San Francisco district attorney Terence Hallinan, ACLU executive director Ira Glasser, former Santa Clara, California, NAACP director Tommy Fulcher, and Robert Garner of the Drug Abuse Services Bureau in Santa Clara.

After laying out the hypothetical above, McNamara turned to Chief Parks. What was his next move? Parks responded that he'd attempt to verify the tip. If it checked out, he'd send in the SWAT team. McNamara asked about the sort of ammunition the SWAT team used. Weren't their bullets capable of going through walls? "They'll go through a car engine two blocks away," Parks answered. McNamara then changed the hypothetical. What if it wasn't crack, but marijuana? Would he still send in an armed-to-the-teeth SWAT team? Parks said he would. What if it was a shipment of bootlegged Valium? Still with the SWAT team. Black market booze? SWAT team.

Mayor Hammer was up next. What was her role in overseeing the police department? Would she be comfortable with her own police department conducting a heavy-handed SWAT raid in a crowded housing complex over illegal Valium? Hammer replied that her job was "to support the chief," not to question him. If the raid had gone over poorly with the public, she might go on TV to reassure the city. She added that she doubted whether such raids did anything at all to reduce the drug supply, but that the raid needed to be carried out anyway. "I don't know how you don't do the raid and have any credibility with the community."

McNamara then turned to DA Hallinan. He too said it wasn't his job to question police tactics. Even if he thought the raid was too dangerous or an unnecessary use of force, he'd keep his opinions to himself. It just wasn't his job to tell the police chief whether or not he thought a raid was appropriate.

McNamara also asked Sweet, the federal judge, if he'd sign a warrant to make the raid a "no-knock" in each of the various hypotheticals. Since Nixon first pushed the no-knock policy, politicians and police officials had stated over and over again that the tactic would be monitored and patrolled by the judges who must sign off on the search warrants. Sweet said that while he worried about the drug war's erosion of the Fourth Amendment, he and most judges typically didn't second-guess or provide much scrutiny to affidavits requesting no-knock search warrants. After the fact, they might hear a defendant's argument that contraband seized in the raid should be suppressed because the raid was unreasonable, but in his experience, judges rarely gave any consideration to whether the use of a SWAT team and paramilitary, "volatile entry" tactics were an appropriate use of force for the crime under investigation.

It went on like that. Even Glasser and Fulcher, the civil liberties activists, said they'd become involved only if they received complaints from residents of the housing complex about police misconduct after the raid. They likely wouldn't devote any resources to criticizing the tactics themselves. Garner, the panelist who had an extensive public health background and who ran Santa Clara's public addiction clinic, added that police in his community had never in his career consulted him about the extent of the drug problem in Santa Clara, be it about which drugs were most prevalent, which drugs presented more of a public health threat than others, or what sorts of policies would best minimize the harm caused by addiction.

Finally, McNamara asked the panel: if the drug raid was a complete and total success, resulting in a confiscation of Mad Dog's entire stash, with no casualties to police, suspects, or citizens, would it have any impact on drug abuse in your city? All but Chief Parks said no.

The police chief of the second-largest city in America had just told the audience that he was willing to use extraordinary force to confiscate a supply of illegal drugs. It was a level of force that could well result death or injury to innocents—and indeed by that point already had, countless times. What's more, he added that what drug he was pursuing and how much actual harm that particular drug caused *had no relevance* on the amount of force he elected to use. Every public official on the panel who had the power to check that decision then told the same audience that they had no interest in second-guessing him. During a question-and-answer session after the panel, the public officials in the audience basically reaffirmed what the panelists had already said.

"It really showed the extent of the problem," McNamara says. "You get this robot mentality with these officials. The mayor said she knew nothing about these raids and didn't want to know anything about them until they were over. The judge wasn't interested in scrutinizing the raid until it was over—when any damage would already be done. Everyone else said it wasn't their job to worry about it. And so you end up with this dangerous decision that gets made by people of lower rank with little training, with little incentive to care much about constitutional rights, with no oversight—no checks or balances. Collateral damage is just part of the game."

In a paper on the conference that McNamara later submitted to the International Congress on Alcohol and Drug Dependence, he concluded:

> The session revealed that public officials, judges, mayors, district attorneys, police chiefs, public health directors, and community leaders rarely, if ever, meet as a group to discuss urban drug control

goals and problems. And they never meet to discuss police drug raids unless something goes awry. . . . Each of the panelists indicated a sensitivity to problems of drug control, appropriate police conduct, and public safety but felt that his or her role was basically compartmentalized.

Another troubling theme to emerge from the 1997 conference is that police, judges, and prosecutors—the people most closely connected with the drug war other than drug offenders themselves—were afraid to speak openly and honestly, even in an academic setting. One police chief cornered McNamara to voice his displeasure with McNamara inviting media to cover the conference. He said the presence of reporters made him and other drug war critics reluctant to talk candidly. In responses to a questionnaire about overall impressions of the conference, one police chief wrote, "The conference reinforced my feelings that we need to change." A prosecutor wrote that the event "confirmed my views that the war on drugs cannot be justified logically or economically. New approaches are needed and soon." Another police chief wrote, "The conference gave me a strong sense of the need for changing drug policies," and still another wrote, "It is risky for us to even attend a conference which could lead to an accusation of being soft on drugs." A judge wrote that the conference "challenged many of my views." But all of them requested anonymity.[62]

THERE'S A STRONG ARGUMENT THAT LARRY PHILLIPS JR. AND Emil Mătăsăreanu did more to advance the militarization of American police forces than anyone short of Daryl Gates. Phillips and Mătăsăreanu, a Romanian immigrant, met at a Gold's Gym in the late '80s, struck up a friendship, and embarked on a decade-long crime spree together. By the time they were preparing a heist of a Bank of America in North Hollywood, California, in early 1997, they had robbed two armored cars and two other branches of Bank of America. On the morning of February 28, the two suited up in body armor and loaded a Chevrolet Celebrity with six guns and over 3,000 rounds of ammunition. The robbery went down with no casualties, though the two were disappointed to make out with only a little over $300,000, less than half of what they were expecting. But as they left the bank at around 9:30 AM, several LAPD patrol cars had already showed up and formed an embankment, the officers taking cover behind their squad cars. Phillips and Mătăsăreanu fired off several rounds at one of the cars. The police fired back. The shoot-out was on.

The officers hit the two men several times, but the patrol officers' weapons—including one shotgun—couldn't penetrate the body armor. About twenty minutes later, an LAPD SWAT team showed up. At around ten minutes before 10:00 AM, Phillips's rifle jammed. He started firing with a pistol, then dropped that too after he was struck in the hand. He picked up the pistol and, about twenty minutes after the shoot-out began, shot himself in the head.

Mătăsăreanu tried to mount an escape in the Celebrity, but police had shot out the tires. He managed to move it a few blocks, where he attempted to commandeer a pickup truck. When he couldn't get it started, he took cover behind it just as the SWAT team arrived. He exchanged fire with them for a few more minutes before surrendering. By then, he'd been shot at least twenty times—in his legs, and other parts of his body unprotected by armor. He died before the ambulance arrived. By the end of the shoot-out, more than 300 law enforcement personnel fired approximately 650 total rounds at each of the two men. Phillips and Mătăsăreanu fired 1,100 rounds between them. The shoot-out lasted forty-four minutes. Eleven police officers and seven citizens were wounded. Phillips and Mătăsăreanu were the only fatalities. Nearly all of the shoot-out was broadcast on live television by several local news helicopters.

If you wanted to create an incident to win sympathy for police militarization, you couldn't do much better than the North Hollywood Shoot-out. A live, televised shoot-out between hundreds of cops and two career criminals, heavily armed and armored, and who refused to go down, was a tailor-made poster case for soldiering up

America's police forces. The following September, the Pentagon sent six hundred M-16s to the Los Angeles Police Department for officers to put in their patrol cars. The department also authorized patrol officers to carry .45-caliber semiautomatic pistols. The incident moved other police departments across the country to upgrade patrol officer sidearms as well.[63]

In the fifteen years since it happened, the North Hollywood Shoot-out has become the go-to incident for proponents of police militarization. For years now it has been regularly cited as the prime example of why cops need bigger guns, and why police departments need SWAT teams. There's some merit to these arguments. A strong argument could be made, for example, for allowing patrol officers to store powerful weapons in the trunks of their squad cars in the event that they're the first on the scene of such an incident—and the SWAT team is still ten or twenty minutes away. But the incident isn't an argument for the proliferation of SWAT teams to small towns, for more militarized uniforms, or for using increasingly militarized tactics for increasingly petty crimes.

Given that the only two fatalities at North Hollywood were the criminals themselves and that the incident happened fifteen years ago, the incident's staying power as an anecdote is in some ways puzzling. But in other ways, perhaps it isn't. That the best anecdote defenders of police militarization can come up with is fifteen years old may attest to the rarity of such incidents. In any case, even most critics of the SWAT phenomenon acknowledge that there are some situations where a paramilitary police response is appropriate—and a heavily armed bank robbery would be right at the top of that list. The criticism of SWAT proliferation is that the overwhelming majority of SWAT deployments today are to break into private residences to serve search warrants for nonviolent crimes. Phillips and Mătăsăreanu committed armed robberies, crimes for which violence is a prerequisite.

The other major incident from the late 1990s that proponents of militarization often cite in justifying SWAT teams is the 1999 mass shooting at Columbine High School in Littleton, Colorado. But if the justification for SWAT teams is to have a team of brave, highly trained, highly professional, well-armed, and well-protected cops to intervene in such tragedies, Columbine is a particularly unfortunate example. Though there were eventually eight hundred police officers and eight SWAT teams on the Columbine campus, the SWAT teams held off from going inside to stop shooters Dylan Klebold and Eric Harris because they deemed the situation too dangerous. A spokesman for the Jefferson County Sheriff's Department justified the SWAT team's actions after the shooting. "A dead police officer would not be able to help anyone." Added SWAT team leader Donn Kraemer, "If we went in and tried to take them and got shot, we would be part of the problem." David Kopel of the Independence Institute in Colorado explained how that panned out for the victims:

> While one murder after another was being perpetrated, a dozen police officers were stationed near [the] exit. These officers made no attempt to enter the building, walk 15 steps, and confront the murderers. (According to police speaking on condition of anonymity, one Denver SWAT officer did begin to enter but was immediately "ordered down" by commanders.)
>
> Twenty minutes after the rampage began, three SWAT officers were finally sent into the building—on the first floor, on the side of the building furthest from the library, where killings were in progress. Finding students rushing out of the building, they decided to escort students out, rather than track down the killers. This began a police program to "contain the perimeter."

Instead of confronting the killers, then, the SWAT team frisked the victims. They then passed on another chance to confront Harris and Klebold.

> The two murderers eventually tired of the library killings, and went downstairs to the cafeteria. More students were hiding in a room nearby, with the door locked. The two murderers attempted to shoot off the lock, and enter that room.

Students in the room had called 911 and the line was open, so again the killers' location was known. Many officers were massed near the cafeteria door. They knew where the murderers were. They knew that the murderers were attempting to get into a room to kill more people. The police stood idle.

Harris and Klebold killed themselves in the library. Not knowing that, and still considering it too dangerous to enter the portions of the building where there had been known gunfire, it took more than three hours for the SWAT team to finally reach the victims. In the meantime, science teacher David Sanders bled to death on the second floor. He might have survived had he received reasonably prompt medical attention—he was still alive when police finally reached him, three hours after he'd been shot. He died during the additional forty-five minutes it took paramedics to reach him. Students in his classroom had put up a sign in the window to alert the police to his condition. It read: "1 bleeding to death."

The LAPD SWAT team was later asked to review the actions of their colleagues in Jefferson County. They found that the officers had followed standard procedure. Perhaps that was just an act of professional courtesy. If not, consider the implications. Columbine was precisely the sort of incident for which the SWAT team had been invented. It was the sort of incident often cited by defenders of SWAT teams to justify their existence. And it was the sort of incident for which even critics of SWAT teams concede the use of a SWAT team would be appropriate. Yet not only did the SWAT teams at the scene not confront the killers, potentially costing innocent lives, but the most respected SWAT team in the country then reviewed the Jefferson County team's actions and found their actions were appropriate.[64]

In the following years, Littleton and North Hollywood would be cited ad nauseam by police officials in towns and counties across the country agitating for their own SWAT team, or defending or arguing for more weaponry for the one they already had. When the town of Ithaca, New York, reformulated its SWAT team in 2000, for example, Assistant Commander Peter Tyler was asked why a college town with virtually no violent crime needed a SWAT team in the first place. He pointed to Columbine and similar mass shootings. "I think it's naive for anyone to think it couldn't happen here in Ithaca," he said. Perhaps. But in a different context, Ithaca Police Chief Richard Basile later explained that the reformulated SWAT team would save taxpayers money because its smaller size made it more efficient at its primary duty—serving drug warrants.[65] A 2002 *Miami Herald* article on the spread of SWAT teams in Florida noted that "police say they want [SWAT teams] in case of a hostage situation or a Columbine-type incident. But in practice, the teams are used mainly to serve search warrants on suspected drug dealers. Some of these searches yield as little as a few grams of cocaine or marijuana."[66] As recently as July 2012, Portland, Maine, police chief Michael Sauschuck cited both incidents to justify his department's acquisition of a military-grade armored truck.[67]

There have, of course, been a number of other school shootings since Columbine, on both high school and college campuses. And some, like Virginia Tech, have ended with horrifically high body counts. But most such shootings are also over within seconds, far less time than it would take a typical SWAT team to scramble to the scene. (One possible exception is Newtown, where a Connecticut State Police SWAT team arrived quickly, and their presence reportedly persuaded shooter Adam Lanza to kill himself instead of killing more children.) It's also important to note that though they make huge headlines and spark weeks of breathless coverage, school shootings (and mass shootings in general) are exceedingly rare. University of Virginia psychologist and education professor Dewey Cornell, who studies violence prevention and school safety, has estimated that the typical school campus can expect to see a homicide about once every several thousand years—hardly justification to rush out to get a SWAT team.[68] Yet many college campuses now have their own paramilitary police teams, and many cited Columbine and Virginia Tech as the reason they needed one. A recent example is the

University of North Carolina–Charlotte Campus Police Department, which started a SWAT team in 2011. Lt. Josh Huffman explained why it was necessary: "The purpose for creating the UNCC SWAT Team is to protect the community and prevent the loss of life. We must be prepared to respond to high risk situations such as those tragedies that occurred at Virginia Tech and Columbine."[69]

The number of campuses that will ever host a mass shooting or hostage taking may be vanishingly small, but most campuses produce more than enough pot smokers—and thus dealers to supply them—to keep the SWAT team busy once it's up and running.

ODDLY ENOUGH, THE MOVE TOWARD AGGRESSIVE EVEN preventative crackdowns on protesters by cops decked out in riot gear kicked into high gear during protests in a city whose police chief was a self-described "progressive hippie." The head of the Seattle Police Department during the 1999 World Trade Organization (WTO) protests was Norm Stamper, the same guy who pioneered community policing and tried to demilitarize the police in San Diego.

It wasn't that the police in Seattle weren't prepared. The police department had gone through ten thousand hours of training in the weeks leading up to the event. The state-of-the-art riot gear they had ordered gave them a look that Stamper likened, in his book *Breaking Rank*, to Darth Vader. When the police come to a protest dressed like that, armed, and expecting confrontation, both police and protesters start to think that a confrontation is inevitable. This was why, at the height of the often-violent protests of the 1970s, Washington, DC, police chief Jerry Wilson put cops in traditional police blues on the front lines, but kept his riot squad on buses parked on side streets—ready, but out of sight.

Stamper says today that he didn't have the luxury of keeping the cops clad in riot gear off to the side while putting uniformed guys on the front lines; he simply didn't have enough personnel to do both. It was a large event for a city of Seattle's size, but there were also reports that law enforcement officials (and there were at least a dozen agencies handling security at the conference) vastly overestimated the size of the protests—again, an indication that *over*preparation by the security planners may have given the cops who worked the event a distorted impression of what they were about to face, an impression that then became self-fulfilling. After all the training the department had gone through was done and the event was just days away, Stamper writes, *he,* as a commander, was feeling confident. *We've got this sucker covered,* he recalls thinking. But the cops themselves were less assured. "They appreciated the training, they loved the new equipment," Stamper writes, "but they were convinced that the city was in for a real shitstorm."

And that's what they got. Midmorning on the first day, demonstrators surged into an intersection and took a seat, locking arms to form what Stamper called "one massive knot of humanity." A police department field commander told them they'd be arrested. When they didn't move, he warned them again—and several more times. Then he hit them with gas.

Despite the hours and hours of training, the cops lobbed the tear-gas canisters behind the frontline protesters, giving them the option of either running into plumes of gas, or surging into a line of police officers. That created chaos.

By the time the first day turned to evening, Seattle mayor Paul Schell had declared a state of emergency, imposed a curfew, and banned protests in and around the conference. He also made it a crime to possess a gas mask, an order that almost certainly exceeded his authority and was probably unconstitutional. Rioters and cops continued to clash. The next day Washington governor Gary Locke called in the National Guard.

A Seattle City Council investigation would later find that the police who handled the event were panic-stricken, driven by exaggerated crowd estimates and unfounded rumors. (One such rumor later determined to be untrue was that protesters were tossing Molotov cocktails.) The riots resulted in $20 million in damage to local businesses. But even the vandals, looters, and anarchists never turned violent. There were no fatalities and fewer than 100 injuries, the most serious of which was a broken arm. In 2004 the city reached a financial settlement with 157 protesters who had been illegally arrested. And in 2007 a federal jury found that the city had violated the Fourth Amendment rights of 170 more.

Norm Stamper took responsibility for the disaster and resigned as Seattle police chief. Though he defended the decision to tear-gas peaceful protesters in his 2005 book, he now says he was wrong. In fact, he says, it was the worst mistake of his career.

"I changed my mind during my book tour," Stamper says. "After I had given a talk in Seattle to promote the book, a guy who had been gassed at the protests in Seattle came up to me and said to me in a soft voice, 'I had such hope and such respect for you, and I just lost it. I just can't accept your explanation for why you used tear gas on nonviolent people. I just can't accept that.'"

Stamper told the man they'd just have to agree to disagree. But when the tour was over, he says he began to question his own rationale. "I finally turned the corner shortly before a speech to an ACLU gathering at the University of Washington. I told the story about the protests, about the man who had come up to me during my book tour, and I talked about how I had changed my mind. And I said the more I thought about it, the more I thought it was the worst professional mistake I had ever made. I didn't realize it, but the same guy was in the audience that night. He came up to me afterward in tears."

The "Battle for Seattle" is commonly considered the start of the modern antiglobalization movement. But it was also a landmark event in the way police and city officials react to protests. In spite of the fact that there were few injuries and no fatalities, the images that emerged from Seattle depicted a city that had lost control. Going forward, "control" would be the prevailing objectives for police handling protests. In the years to come, the Darth Vader look would become the standard police presence at large protests. Cities and police officials would commit mass violations of civil and constitutional rights and deal with the consequences later. There would be violent, preemptive SWAT raids, mass arrests, and sweeping use of police powers that ensnared violent protesters, peaceful protesters, and people who had nothing to do with the protest at all.

That's why Stamper calls his decisions in Seattle "the worst mistake" of his career. He's seen how the police response to protest has changed since 1999. "We gassed fellow Americans engaging in civil disobedience," Stamper says. "We set a number of precedents, most of them bad. And police departments across the country learned all the wrong lessons from us. That's disheartening. So disheartening. I mean, you look at what happened to those Occupy protesters at UC Davis, where the cop just pepper sprays them down like he's watering a bed of flowers, and I think that we played a part in making that sort of thing so common—so easy to do now. It's beyond cringeworthy. I wish to hell my career had ended on a happier note."[70]

## The Numbers

- Number of SWAT raids conducted by the Minneapolis Police Department in 1987: 36
- Number of SWAT raids conducted by the Minneapolis Police Department in 1996: over 700
- Number of raids carried out by the Bureau of Alcohol, Tobacco, and Firearms from 1993 to 1995: 523
- Percentage of these ATF raids that used dynamic entry: 49 percent
- Percentage of these ATF raids that turned up weapons of any kind: 18 percent
- Approximate number of paramilitary police raids in the United States in 1980: 3,000
- Approximate number of paramilitary police raids in 1995: 30,000
- Approximate number of paramilitary police raids in 2001: 45,000
- Number of SWAT deployments in Orange County, Florida, from 1993 to 1997: 619
- Percentage of those SWAT deployments undertaken to serve drug warrants: 94 percent

- Number of police officers in the tactical operations branch of the Portland, Oregon, Police Department in 1989: 2
- Number of Portland police officers in the tactical operations branch in 1994: 56
- Percentage of police departments in cities of 100,000 or more that had a SWAT team in 1982: 59 percent
    . . . in 1995: 89 percent
- Average number of times each of those SWAT teams was deployed in 1980: 13
    . . . in 1989: 38
    . . . in 1995: 52
- Percentage increase in the number of police departments using tactical units for proactive patrol from 1982 to 1997: 292 percent[71]

# CHAPTER 8

# THE 2000S—
# A WHOLE NEW WAR

Blessed are the peacemakers: for they shall be called the children of God.

—SHERIFF LEON LOTT OF RICHLAND COUNTY,
SOUTH CAROLINA, QUOTING MATTHEW 5:9 IN A PRESS
RELEASE ANNOUNCING HIS ACQUISITION OF A TRACK-
PROPELLED ARMORED PERSONNEL CARRIER WITH A
BELT-FED ROTATING MACHINE GUN TURRET CAPABLE
OF FIRING .50-CALIBER ROUNDS OF AMMUNITION

Betty Taylor still remembers the night it all hit her.

As a child, Taylor had always been taught that police officers were the good guys. She learned to respect law enforcement, as she puts it, "all the time, all the way." She went on to become a cop because she wanted to help people, and that's what cops did. She wanted to fight sexual assault, particularly predators who take advantage of children. To go into law enforcement—to become one of the good guys—seemed like the best way to accomplish that. By the late 1990s, she'd risen to the rank of detective in the sheriff's department of Lincoln County, Missouri—a sparsely populated farming community about an hour northwest of St. Louis. She eventually started a sex crimes unit within the department. But it was a small department with a tight budget. When she couldn't get the money she needed, Taylor was forced to give speeches and write her own proposals to keep her program operating.

What troubled her was that while the sex crimes unit had to find funding on its own, the SWAT team was always flush with cash. "The SWAT team, the drug guys, they always had money," Taylor says. "There were always state and federal grants for drug raids. There was always funding through asset forfeiture." Taylor never quite understood that disparity. "When you think about the collateral effects of a sex crime, of how it can affect an entire family, an entire community, it just didn't make sense. The drug users weren't really harming anyone but themselves. Even the dealers, I found much of the time they were just people with little money, just trying to get by."

The SWAT team eventually co-opted her as a member. As the only woman in the department, she was asked to go along on drug raids in the event there were any children inside. "The perimeter team would go in first. They'd throw all of the adults on the floor until they had secured the building. Sometimes the kids too. Then they'd put the kids in a room by themselves, and the search team would go in. They'd come to me, point to where the kids were, and say, 'You deal with them.'" Taylor would then stay with the children until family services arrived, at which point they'd be placed with a relative.

Taylor's moment of clarity came during a raid on an autumn evening in November 2000. Narcotics investigators had made a controlled drug buy a few hours earlier and were laying plans to raid the suspect's home. "The drug buy was in town, not at the home," Taylor says. "But they'd always raid the house anyway. They could never just arrest the guy on the street. They always had to kick down doors." With just three hours between the drug buy and the raid, the police hadn't done much surveillance at all. The SWAT team would often avoid raiding a house if they knew there were children inside, but Taylor was troubled by how little effort they put into seeking out that sort of information. "Three hours is nowhere near enough time to investigate your suspect, to find out who might be inside the house. It just isn't enough time for you to know the range of things that could happen."

That afternoon the police had bought drugs from the stepfather of two children, ages eight and six. Both were in the house at the time of the raid. The stepfather wasn't.

"They did their thing," Taylor says. "Everybody on the floor, guns and yelling. Then they put the two kids in the bedroom, did their search, then sent me in to take care of the kids."

Taylor made her way inside to see them. When she opened the door, the eight-year-old girl assumed a defense posture, putting herself between Taylor and her little brother. She looked at Taylor and said, half fearful, half angry, "What are you going to do to us?"

Taylor was shattered. "Here I come in with all my SWAT gear on, dressed in armor from head to toe, and this little girl looks up at me, and her only thought is to defend her little brother. I thought, How can we be the good guys when we come into the house looking like this, screaming and pointing guns at the people they love? How can we be the good guys when a little girl looks up at me and *wants to fight me?* And for what? What were we accomplishing with all of this? Absolutely nothing."

Taylor was later appointed police chief of the small town of Winfield, Missouri. Winfield was too small for its own SWAT team, even in the 2000s, but Taylor says she'd have quit before she ever created one. "Good police work has nothing to do with dressing up in black and breaking into houses in the middle of the night. And the mentality changes when they get put on the SWAT team. I remember a guy I was good friends with, it just completely changed him. The us-versus-them mentality takes over. You see that mentality in regular patrol officers too. But it's much, much worse on the SWAT team. They're more concerned with the drugs than they are with innocent bystanders. Because when you get into that mentality, there are no innocent people. There's us and there's the enemy. Children and dogs are always the easiest casualties."

Taylor recently ran into the little girl who changed the way she thought about policing. Now in her twenties, the girl told Taylor that she and her brother had nightmares for years after the raid. They slept in the same bed until the boy was eleven. "That was a difficult day at work for me," she says. "But for her, this was the most traumatic, defining moment of this girl's life. Do you know what we found? We didn't find any weapons. No big drug operation. We found three joints and a pipe."[1]

⌒

POLICE MILITARIZATION WOULD ACCELERATE IN THE 2000S. The first half of the decade brought a new and lucrative source of funding and equipment: homeland security. In response to the terrorist attacks of September 11, 2001, on the World Trade Center in New York City and the Pentagon in Washington, the federal government opened a new spigot of funding in the name of fighting terror. Terrorism would also provide new excuses for police agencies across the country to build up their arsenals and for yet smaller towns to start up yet more SWAT teams. The second half of the decade also saw more mission creep for SWAT teams and more pronounced militarization even outside of drug policing. The 1990s trend of government officials using paramilitary tactics and heavy-handed force to make political statements or to make an example of certain classes of nonviolent offenders would continue, especially in response to political protests. The battle gear and aggressive policing would also start to move into more mundane crimes—SWAT teams have recently been used even for regulatory inspections.

But the last few years have also seen some trends that could spur some movement toward reform. Technological advances in personal electronic devices have armed a large percentage of the public with the power to hold police more accountable with video and audio recordings. The rise of social media has enabled citizens to get accounts of police abuses out and quickly disseminated. This has led to more widespread coverage of botched raids and spread awareness of how, how often, and for what purpose this sort of force is being used. Over just the six years I've been covering this issue, I've noticed that media accounts of drug raids have become less deferential to police. Reporters have become more willing to ask questions about the appropriateness of police tactics and more likely to look at how a given raid fits into broader policing trends, both locally and nationally. Internet commenters on articles about incidents in which police may have used excessive force also seem to have grown more skeptical about police actions, particularly in botched drug raids.

It's taken nearly a half-century to get from those Supreme Court decisions in the mid-1960s to where we are today—police militarization has happened gradually, over decades. We tend not to take notice of such long-developing trends, even when they directly affect us. The first and perhaps largest barrier to halting police militarization has probably been awareness. And that at least seems to be changing. Whether it leads to any substantive change may be the theme of the current decade.

*⌒*

BY THE MID-1990S, THE BYRNE GRANT PROGRAM CONGRESS had started in 1988 had pushed police departments across the country to prioritize drug crimes over other investigations. When applying for grants, departments are rewarded with funding for statistics such as the number of overall arrests, the number of warrants served, or the number of drug seizures. Those priorities, then, are passed down to police officers themselves and are reflected in how they're evaluated, reviewed, and promoted. Perversely, actual success in reducing crime is generally not rewarded with federal money, on the presumption that the money ought to go where it's most needed—high-crime areas. So the grants reward police departments for making lots of easy arrests (i.e., low-level drug offenders) and lots of seizures (regardless of size), and for serving lots of warrants. When it comes to tapping into federal funds, whether any of that actually reduces crime or makes the community safer is irrelevant—and in fact, successfully fighting crime could hurt a department's ability to rake in federal money.

But the most harmful product of the Byrne grant program may be its creation of hundreds of regional and multijurisdictional narcotics task forces. That term—"narcotics task force"—pops up frequently in the case studies and horror stories throughout this book. There's a reason for that. While the Reagan and Bush administrations had set up a number of drug task forces in border zones, the Byrne grant program established similar task forces all across the country. They seemed particularly likely to pop up in rural areas that didn't yet have a paramilitary police team (what few were left).

The task forces are staffed with local cops drawn from the police agencies in the jurisdictions where the task force operates. Some squads loosely report to a state law enforcement agency, but oversight tends to be minimal to nonexistent. Because their funding comes from the federal government—and whatever asset forfeiture proceeds they reap from their investigations—local officials can't even control them by cutting their budget. This organizational structure makes some task forces virtually unaccountable, and certainly not accountable to any public official in the region they cover.

As a result, we have roving squads of drug cops, loaded with SWAT gear, who get more money if they conduct more raids, make more arrests, and seize more property, and they are virtually immune to accountability if they get out of line. In 2009 the Justice Department attempted a cost-benefit analysis of these task forces but couldn't even get to the point of crunching the numbers. The task forces weren't producing any numbers to crunch. "Not only were data insufficient to estimate what task forces accomplished," the report read, "data were inadequate to even tell what the task forces did for routine work."[2]

Not surprisingly, the proliferation of heavily armed task forces that have little accountability and are rewarded for making lots of busts has resulted in some abuse.

The most notorious scandal involving these task forces came in the form of a massive drug sting in the town of Tulia, Texas. On July 23, 1999, the task force donned black ski-mask caps and full SWAT gear to conduct a series of coordinated predawn raids across

Tulia. By 4:00 AM, forty black people—10 percent of Tulia's black population—and six whites were in handcuffs. The *Tulia Sentinel* declared, "We do not like these scumbags doing business in our town. [They are] a cancer in our community, it's time to give them a major dose of chemotherapy behind bars." The paper followed up with the headline "Tulia's Streets Cleared of Garbage."

The raids were based on the investigative work of Tom Coleman, a sort of freelance cop who, it would later be revealed, had simply invented drug transactions that had never occurred.

The first trials resulted in convictions—based entirely on the credibility of Tom Coleman. The defendants received long sentences. For those who were arrested but still awaiting trial, plea bargains that let them avoid prison time began to look attractive, even if they were innocent. Coleman was even named Texas lawman or the year.

But there were some curious details about the raids. For such a large drug bust, the task force hadn't recovered any actual drugs. Or any weapons, for that matter. And it wasn't for a lack of looking. The task force cops had all but destroyed the interiors of the homes they raided. Then some cases started falling apart. One woman Coleman claimed sold him drugs could prove she was in Oklahoma City at the time. Coleman had described another woman as six months pregnant—she wasn't. Another suspect could prove he was at work during the alleged drug sale. By 2004, nearly all of the forty-six suspects were either cleared or pardoned by Texas governor Rick Perry. The jurisdictions the task force served eventually settled a lawsuit with the defendants for $6 million. In 2005, Coleman was convicted of perjury. He received ten years' probation and was fined $7,500.[3]

The following year, it all happened again. In November 2000, SWAT teams from the Byrne-funded South Central Texas Narcotics Task Force rolled into Hearne, a town of about five thousand people in Robertson County, to wage another series of coordinated raids. The raids netted twenty-eight arrests—twenty-seven of the suspects were black. One of them was Regina Kelly, a single mother. Kelly wasn't home when her house was raided, she was waiting tables at a local diner. The police marched her off the job in handcuffs and tossed her in a jail cell. She first thought she had been arrested for unpaid parking tickets. Kelly's court-appointed attorney encouraged her to take a plea bargain. Plead guilty, and she'd get eighteen years' probation. She'd get no prison time and wouldn't lose her kids. She refused. "I wasn't going to plead guilty to something I didn't do," she told me in a 2007 interview. The attorney went back to DA John Paschall, who then offered five years' probation. Kelly again refused, and told her attorney to ask for the evidence they had used to indict her. Her attorney brought back a tape recording the DA's office claimed was evidence of her drug sales. The tape recording was a conversation between two men. There were no female voices, and Kelly's name was never mentioned. Kelly's bail was then reduced from $70,000 to $10,000. Her parents were able to post bond, and she never had to go to court again. She was eventually cleared of any criminal wrongdoing.

In part because of Kelly's courageous refusal to accept a plea bargain for a crime she didn't commit, we now know that all twenty-eight indictments were based on the word of a single confidential informant. Paschall's office was forced to admit that the informant had both tampered with evidence and failed a polygraph test. At the civil trial for the lawsuit brought by Kelly and other defendants, the informant testified that Paschall had given him a list of twenty black men. He promised leniency for the informant's own burglary charge if he helped Paschall convict the men on the list. The informant also testified he was promised $100 for every suspect he helped convict beyond that list of twenty. The lawsuit was settled in 2005. Of the twenty-eight people charged, seventeen were later exonerated. The 2008 movie *American Violet* was based on Kelly's experience after she was arrested.

But similar mass round-up raids had been going on in Hearne for fifteen years. "They come on helicopters, military-style, SWAT style," Kelly told me. "In the apartments I was living in, in the projects, there were a lot of children outside playing. They don't care. They throw kids on the ground, put guns to their heads. They're kicking in doors. They just don't care."[4]

In the following years, there were numerous other corruption scandals, botched raids, sloppy police work, and other allegations of misconduct against the federally funded task forces in Texas. Things got so that by the middle of the 2000s Gov. Rick Perry began diverting state matching funds away from the task forces to other programs. The cut in funding forced many task forces to shut down. The stream of lawsuits shut down or limited the operations of others. In 2001 the state had fifty-one federally funded task forces. By the spring of 2006, it was down to twenty-two.[5]

Funding for the Byrne grant program had held steady at about $500 million through most of the Clinton administration. Just as it had done with the cops program, the Bush administration began to pare the program down—to about $170 million by 2008. This was more out of an interest in limiting federal influence on law enforcement than concern for police abuse or drug war excesses.

But the reaction from law enforcement was interesting. In March 2008, Byrne-funded task forces across the country staged a series of coordinated drug raids dubbed Operation Byrne Blitz. The intent was to make a series of large drug seizures to demonstrate how important the Byrne grants were to fighting the drug war. In Kentucky alone, for example, task forces uncovered 23 methamphetamine labs, seized more than 2,400 pounds of marijuana, and arrested 565 people for illegal drug use.[6] Of course, if police in a single state could simply go out and find 23 meth labs and 2,400 pounds of marijuana in twenty-four hours just to make a political point about drug war funding, that was probably a good indication that twenty years of Byrne grants and four decades of drug warring hadn't really accomplished much.

During the 2008 presidential campaign, Barack Obama criticized Bush and the Republicans for cutting Byrne, a federal police program beloved by his running mate Joe Biden. Despite Tulia, Hearne, a growing pile of bodies from botched drug raids, and the objections of groups as diverse as the ACLU, the Heritage Foundation, La Raza, and the Cato Institute, Obama promised to restore full funding to the program, which, he said, "has been critical to creating the anti-gang and anti-drug task forces our communities need." He kept his promise. The 2009 American Recovery and Reinvestment Act resuscitated the Byrne grants with a whopping $2 billion infusion, by far the largest budget in the program's twenty-year history.[7]

———

EARLY IN THE MORNING OF SEPTEMBER 13, 2000, AGENTS from the DEA, the FBI, and a Stanislaus County, California, narcotics task force conducted raids on fourteen homes in and around Modesto—the culmination of a nineteen-month investigation. One of the homes was that of Moises Sepulveda and his family. According to the *Los Angeles Times,* the DEA and FBI asked that the local SWAT teams enter each home unannounced in order to secure the area ahead of the federal agents, who would then come to serve the warrants and search for evidence. Federal agents warned the SWAT teams that the targets of the warrants should be considered armed and dangerous. When local police asked if there were any children in the Sepulveda home, the feds answered, "Not aware of any."

There were. Moises Sepulveda had three children—a daughter and two sons. After the police forcibly entered the Sepulveda home, Moises, his wife, and his children were ordered to lie face-down on the floor with their arms outstretched. They were then told to remain still as officers pointed guns at their heads. Eleven-year-old Alberto was doing just that—lying still under the gun of Officer David Hawn. But shortly after the raid began, Hawn's gun went off. The boy died instantly.

There were no drugs or guns in the Sepulveda home. A subsequent internal investigation by the Modesto Police Department found that the DEA's evidence against Moises Sepulveda—who had no previous criminal record—was "minimal." The city of Modesto and the federal government settled a lawsuit brought by the Sepulvedas for the death of their son for $3 million.

In response to the incident, California attorney general Bill Lockyer assembled a blue ribbon commission to review the procedures, guidelines, and performance of the state's hundreds of SWAT teams.

The *Modesto Bee* reported in 2001 that the commission would look at the way SWAT teams were deployed, the use of intimidating clothing and equipment, and, in the words of one commissioner, the "overbearing-type attitudes" of SWAT teams.

Unsurprisingly, the commission found that while SWAT teams were generally justified, defended, and regarded as responders to emergency situations like hostage crises and terror attacks, they were most commonly being used to serve drug warrants. Nevertheless, the panel's final recommendations did little to address the number of SWAT teams, how they were being used, or police militarism in general. The panel's chief complaint was that SWAT teams were undertrained and underfunded, suggesting that local, state, and federal government should be throwing *more* funding and resources at SWAT teams, not less. The other recommendations consisted largely of standardizing procedures, definitions, and guidelines and communicating better with the public. The commission didn't address any of the more urgent problems that had plagued the state's SWAT teams over the previous twenty years, such as SWAT teams launching raids based on uncorroborated tips from informants, asset forfeiture incentivizing the use of aggressive policing, or prosecutors and judges neglecting their duty to scrutinize the warrants authorizing these violent raids.

In the end, even if every SWAT team in the state had implemented the panel's recommendations (and they were by no means obligated to), it's unlikely that much would have changed. In fact, if the suggestions had been implemented in the 1990s, it seems unlikely that they would have prevented the death of Alberto Sepulveda, the reason for Lockyer's panel in the first place.

Back in the early 1970s, nationwide outrage over a series of wrong-door drug raids had inspired furious politicians to hastily call congressional hearings; as a consequence, the law that had authorized those raids was repealed. Now, in 2000, an eleven-year-old boy had just been obliterated at close range with a shotgun as his parents and siblings lay on the ground beside him. And even that wasn't enough to stop his *own town* from discontinuing the aggressive tactics that caused his death. The mistakes, the terrorizing of innocents, and the unnecessary fatalities would continue.[8]

THE GEORGE W. BUSH ADMINISTRATION QUICKLY MADE IT clear that the drug war would once again be fought as a culture war. Bush appointed only one drug czar in his two terms. John Walters was a longtime aide to William Bennett who, like Bennett, took a hard-line, zero-tolerance approach to drugs. But when the 9/11 attacks happened eight months after Bush was inaugurated, they presented a new opportunity. Instead of exploiting the fear of crime or tapping into what remained of anti-counterculture sentiment, they could now exploit the fear of terrorist attacks. They would use the 9/11 attacks for drug war propaganda.

And so, starting in the February following the attacks, the Office of National Drug Control Policy (ONDCP) started the "I helped . . . " campaign, which consisted of commercial and print ads claiming that casual drug users in the United States were supporting the very sorts of terrorists that had attacked America. The television commercials featured a series of young people portrayed as casual drug users. One by one, the young actors rattled off the varieties of atrocity allegedly funded by recreational drug use. "I helped kill a policeman," one said. "I helped murder families," said another. "I helped kidnap people's dads," said still another. The ads aired during the 2002 Super Bowl, just after a September 11–themed halftime show that featured a running scroll of the names of the 9/11 victims, accompanied by a performance by the band U2.

The campaign was not only shamefully exploitative, it was simply false. The claim that casual drug users supported terrorism was dubious at best. To the extent that black market drug purchases in the United States did support terror groups, it was the "black market" part that made it possible. Nearly all of the terror attacks listed on the DEA's website at the time had been attacks by drug-smuggling groups related to the drug trade, and nearly all had taken place in Latin America and Mexico. The only widely used drug in the United

States with any tangible connection to terrorism of the 9/11 variety was heroin, and even that link was tenuous. By the federal government's own estimates, 82 percent of US heroin came from Mexico and South America. A small percentage was domestically grown, and much of the rest came from a slew of countries in Asia, only a few of which were host to active anti-American terrorist groups. There was just no evidence that Al Qaeda operatives were selling pot to Americans to fund their schemes to slam airplanes into buildings. But that was the line the government was pushing. The DEA would later put on a touring museum exhibit with the same themes. It included pieces of rubble from the World Trade Center.

If anything, there was a stronger argument that the country's *antidrug* efforts were sponsoring terrorism. In May 2001—just four months before September 11—the US State Department announced a $43 million aid gift to Afghanistan, which at the time was ruled by the Taliban. The grant was intended to be used to compensate Afghan farmers who had been hurt by a Taliban edict (encouraged by the United States) banning the cultivation of opium poppies. Of course, the edict didn't really stop the heroin from flowing out of Afghanistan. It simply enabled the Taliban to consolidate heroin production so that more of the revenue went directly to the regime. The United States had also given aid to support a drug war in Thailand that included government "death squads" that human rights groups accused of carrying out as many as four thousand extrajudicial executions of suspected drug offenders. US aid had also gone to right-wing paramilitary groups in Colombia that were accused of mass human rights abuses.

From a broader view, the ads weren't all that different from prior attempts to associate drugs and intoxicants with whatever bogeyman the country happened to be facing at the time. But by tying even casual drug users to terrorism so soon after one of the most horrific attacks on US soil in the country's history—particularly an attack that took the lives of so many police officers—the federal government afforded drug cops yet more moral license to treat suspected drug offenders as enemy combatants not as citizens with rights.[9]

Bush also continued Clinton's assault on medical marijuana. In the 2000 campaign, Bush had promised a federalist approach to the issue—he had said he would leave it to the states to decide. That promise didn't last long. It quickly became clear that, like Clinton before him, Bush would give no quarter to sick people using pot in states that had legalized it for treatment. The aggressive raids that began during the Clinton administration increased, in both number and intensity.[10]

The result was the perverse spectacle of armed federal cops taking down medical facilities and their patients. On September 5, 2002, for example, federal agents raided the Wo/Men's Alliance for Medical Marijuana in Santa Cruz, California. Suzanne Pfeil, a post-polio patient who couldn't walk without leg braces and crutches, told columnist Mitch Albom that she awoke to find federal agents pointing assault rifles at her head. They yelled at her to get up. She said she couldn't. They yelled at her some more. She explained, again, that she was crippled. They finally handcuffed Pfeil to her bed, then moved on to other patients. Because she was allergic to many classes of drugs, Pfeil smoked marijuana to alleviate muscle and nerve pain brought on by her condition.[11]

On the same day, federal agents also raided the home of the facility's owners, Valerie and Michael Coral. A DEA SWAT team decked out in flak jackets and M-16s stormed the house, shoved Valerie Coral to the ground, and put a gun to her head. She was cuffed, arrested, and taken to a federal detention center, still wearing her pajamas. When asked if such heavy-handed tactics were necessary given that Valerie Coral was hardly a dangerous drug kingpin, DEA spokesman Will Glaspy replied, "We target drug traffickers. There is no such term as 'medical marijuana,' except as created by the marijuana lobby."[12] A week later, agents raided the Genesis 1:29 medical cannabis dispensary and the grower that supplied it. California attorney general Bill Lockyer was angry, protesting, "A medical marijuana provider such as the Santa Cruz collective represents little danger to the public and is certainly not a concern which would warrant diverting scarce federal resources."[13]

The heavy-handed federal enforcement on medical providers wasn't limited to marijuana. As fears about prescription opioid painkillers started to take root in the media in the early 2000s, the DEA began targeting doctors, and it has been doing so ever since. These are professionals with medical degrees, practices, offices, and patients, singled out for allegedly overprescribing a certain class of drugs. There's still a debate over whether overprescribing these drugs—as defined by drug cops, not other doctors—should even be a crime, and whether some of the doctors were even overprescribing in the first place.[14] Those questions aside, it's hard to fathom why it would be necessary to send SWAT teams to storm their homes and offices, subjecting their families and patients to the violence and volatility of a typical raid.[15]

The federal government wasn't even pretending anymore. Alleged "states' rights" supporters like Asa Hutchison, the head of DEA appointed by Bush in 2001, and Attorney General John Ashcroft were making an example of these doctors, these dispensaries, and the people who owned, supplied, and patronized them. The guns and commando tactics were completely unnecessary. No reasonable person believed that Suzanne Pfeil or Valerie Coral was going to take out a couple of DEA agents in a suicidal blaze of glory. Most of the dispensaries were operating openly, within state law. Bush, Walters, Hutchison, Ashcroft, and the rest of the administration's drug policy team were using state-sanctioned violence to make a political point.

~

"WE'RE GOING TO HAVE OUR OWN TANK," KEENE, N.H., Mayor Kendall Lane whispered to Councilman Mitch Greenwald during a December 2011 city council meeting.

It wasn't quite a tank. But the quaint town of 23,000—home to just two murders since 1999—had just accepted a $285,933 grant from the Department of Homeland Security to purchase a Bearcat, an eight-ton armored personnel vehicle made by Lenco Industries, Inc. Since the September 11 attacks, Homeland Security has been handing out anti-terrorism grants like parade candy, giving cities and towns across the country funds to buy military-grade armored vehicles, guns, armor, aircraft, and other equipment. Companies like Lenco have thrived, creating yet another class of government hardware contractors, and a new interest group to lobby Washington to ensure the process of police militarization continues.

These DHS grants have dwarfed the 1033 program. At the end of 2011, the Center for Investigative Reporting (CIR) found that Homeland Security had given out at least $34 billion in anti-terror grants since its inception, many of which went to such unlikely terrorism targets as Fargo, N.D.; Fon du Lac, Wisc.; and Canyon County, Idaho. Defense contractors that had previously served the Pentagon exclusively, CIR reported, have since shifted their focus to police departments, hoping to tap a new homeland security market bounty expected to be worth $19 billion annually by 2014. Police agencies have a whole new source of funding for their war gear. Just as they'd done with the 1033 program, they'd initially argue that the equipment was necessary "just in case" of the rare school shooting or Al Qaeda attack in Fon du Lac. But once they get the gear, they use it for drug raids.

But in Keene, there was some resistance to the Bearcat. It began with Mike Clark, a 27-year-old handyman. Clark, who'd had a couple encounters with Keene police that he described as "negative," read about the Homeland Security grant in the newspaper. "The police are already pretty brutal," Clark told me in February 2012. "The last thing they need is this big piece of military equipment to make them think they're soldiers."

On Feb. 9, 2012, more than 100 people packed a meeting of a city council committee, nearly all to oppose equipping the Keene Police Department and its 45 sworn officers with a Bearcat. One speaker quoted in the *Keene Sentinel* was Roberta Mastrogiovanni, owner of a newsstand downtown. "It promotes violence," Mastrogiovanni said. "We should promote more human interaction rather than militarize. I refuse to use money for something this unnecessary when so many people in our community are in need."

Lenco spokesman Jim Massery dismissed critics who asked why a town with almost no crime would need a $300,000 armored truck. "I don't think there's any place in the country where you can say, 'That isn't a likely terrorist target,'" Massery told me. "How would you know? We don' t know what the terrorists are thinking . . . Our trucks save lives. They save police lives. And I can't help but think that the people who are trying to stop this just don't think police officers' lives are worth saving."

It's a line of argument defenders of militarization use often. Oppose the arming of cops as if they were soldiers, and you must be secretly want cops to be killed on the job. But the video Lenco was using to market the vehicle to police departments didn't exactly emphasize negotiation. The camera viewpoint in the video was similar to that of a shooter video game. The soundtrack was AC/DC's "Thunderstruck." Cops dressed in camouflage toted assault weapons, piled in and out of the Bearcat, and took aim at targets from around and behind the vehicle. They then attached a battering ram to the front of the vehicle, which they then used to punch a hole in the front door of a house, into which they injected canisters of tear gas.

Lenco wasn't stupid. The company had chosen the images and music used in the video because they felt it would appeal to those police departments in the market for a Bearcat.

Dorrie O'Meara, a 13-year resident of the town told me, "Keene is a beautiful place. It's gorgeous, and it's safe, and we love it here. We just don't want to live in the kind of place where there's an armored personnel carrier parked outside of City Hall . . . It's just not who we are."

According to CIR's research, DHS gave out $2 billion in grants in 2011, about four times the value of equipment given out through the 1033 program. As with the Byrne and COPS grants, the DHS grant program also got a big boost in President Obama's 2009 economic recovery package. The CIR investigation also found that DHS makes little effort to track how the grants are spent once they're sent, nor does it track how the equipment is used once it has been purchased. The agency also doesn't seem to care if the recipients of the grants are places that face any tangible threat of terrorism. Hence, a city like Fargo, North Dakota has been able to get its hands on $8 million in grants, which the police department has used to buy assault rifles, kevlar helmets, and an armored truck with a rotating turret.

Fargo Police Lt. Ross Renner attempted to defend the city's armament. "It's foolish to not be cognizant of the threats out there," he said, "whether it's New York, Los Angeles, or Fargo." But until the day when the next Muhammad Atta casts rage-filled eyes on North Dakota, the department hasn't made much use of its gun-fitted armored truck. CIR reported that it's mostly used for show, including at the annual city picnic, where police parked it near the children's bouncy castle.

Elsewhere, CIR found that "In Augusta, Maine, with fewer than 20,000 people and where an officer hasn't died from gunfire in the line of duty in more than 125 years, police bought eight $1,500 tactical vests. Police in Des Moines, Iowa, bought two $180,000 bomb-disarming robots, while an Arizona sheriff is now the proud owner of a surplus Army tank." And in Montgomery County, Texas, "the sheriff's department owns a $300,000 pilotless surveillance drone, like those used to hunt down al Qaeda terrorists in the remote tribal regions of Pakistan and Afghanistan." A couple months before the CIR report, the sheriff in Montgomery County had broached the possibility of arming his drone with rubber bullets, or possibly teargas. "No matter what we do in law enforcement, somebody's going to question it, but we're going to do the right thing, and I can assure you of that," he said. Five months later, the department made headlines when its DHS-funded drone accidentally crashed into its DHS-funded Bearcat.

Lenco's Massery told me he was certain that the Keene protesters' efforts would ultimately be in vain. "We have Bearcats in 90 percent of the 100 or so largest cities in America," Massery said. "This is going to happen. It has already happened. To resist now would be like saying police officers should scrap the Glock and go back to the revolver. It's a fantasy."

Massery was right. In November 2012, Lenco accepted its check from DHS, and delivered a shiny new Bearcat to the town of Keene.[16]

⌒

ON NOVEMBER 2, 2002, A LARGE GROUP OF POLICE OFFICERS in tactical gear descended on a rave party in Racine, Wisconsin. The cops kicked in doors, dragged young people from bathroom stalls, threw others to the floor, and held dozens more at gunpoint. The police issued more than 450 citations of $968 each to partygoers merely for attending an event where some attendees were breaking the state's drug laws. Only three people were arrested on actual drug charges. With help from the ACLU, the city of Racine eventually dismissed the charges against all attendees who hadn't yet pleaded guilty.[17]

The trendy new drug throwing the media and politicians into hysterics was Ecstasy. Raves were the new, weird, and different dance parties where teenagers were allegedly taking this crazy sex drug. Cue the moral panic, political grandstanding, and ensuing aggressive crackdown. Prior to the raid in Racine, Sen. Joe Biden of Delaware seemed particularly obsessed with rave parties. Politicians seemed to think that any party with techno music, pulsing lights, and neon inevitably degenerated into underage kids getting high on Ecstasy and engaging in mass orgies. In the summer of 2002, Biden was pushing his RAVE Act, an absurdly broad law that would have made venue and club owners liable for running a drug operation if they merely sold the "paraphernalia" common to parties where people took Ecstasy— accessories like bottled water and glow sticks. After attempting to sneak the bill through Congress with various parliamentary maneuvers, Biden was finally able to get a slightly modified version folded into the bill that created the Amber Alert for missing children. Once again a politician had demagogued worries over a mostly harmless drug into a climate of fear. And once again that fear led to aggressive, wholly disproportionate crackdowns across the country.[18]

A few years later one of rave raids was captured on video. In August 2005, more than 90 police officers from several state and local SWAT teams raided 1,500 people at a peaceful, outdoor dance party in Spanish Fork Canyon, Utah. The police were armed with assault weapons, full SWAT attire, police dogs, and tear gas. Many in attendance say that police beat, abused, and swore at partygoers. Police denied the allegations, though amateur video/audio clearly showed the police barking out orders punctuated with profanity. In truth, the party appeared to have been pretty well run. Private security guards had been stationed outside the event, and confiscated any illegal drugs they found on attendees. The raiding SWAT cops then arrested the private security guards for the drugs they had confiscated, and charged them with possession.[19]

The other new concept at work in Racine and Spanish Fork was the willingness to subject large groups of people to commando tactics in hopes of catching even a few offenders. By the late 2000s, SWAT teams were increasingly called out to raid entire bars and nightclubs for drug activity. A search warrant for a bar's owner or a description of the place as a drug market could allow police to go in and give the SWAT treatment to everyone inside. And it wasn't just bars and nightclubs that were treated this way. In November 2003, police in Goose Creek, South Carolina, raided an entire high school, conducting a blanket commando-style raid on Stratford High School. Students were ordered at gunpoint to lie facedown on the floor while police searched their lockers and persons for drugs. Some were handcuffed, while K-9 units deployed dogs to search their lockers, backpacks, and bodies. Oddly, media reports indicated that the school had a stellar academic reputation.[20]

Le'Quan Simpson, a fourteen-year-old, was forced to kneel at gunpoint. His father had once served on a SWAT team. "They hit that school like it was a crack house," he said. "Like they knew that there were crack dealers in there armed with guns." The raid was based on a tip from the school's principal that a single student might have been selling pot. The raid turned up no illicit drugs, and the police made no arrests.[21]

Still, though these raids of schools and parties were somewhat new, drug cops had been conducting massive drug sweeps of entire neighborhoods for years, subjecting innocent people to violent tactics simply because of where they happened to live. There were more of those police actions too. In February 2002, for example, one hundred Durham police officers, two National Guard helicopters, and ten North Carolina Bureau of Investigation agents seized an entire neighborhood on Cheek Road, then engaged in a series of forced-entry drug raids. They called the whole episode Operation TAPS, short for The Aggressive Police Strategy. The police arrested thirty-five people and confiscated an "undisclosed" amount of drugs, plus two pistols. Superior Court judge Orlando Hudson later threw out all the arrests and evidence, ruling that the entire operation was unconstitutional and "partially illegal" and that some of the officers' behavior amounted to "criminal conduct."[22]

One particularly aggressive action peppered with war rhetoric occurred in April 2006, when police in Buffalo, New York, staged a series of drug raids throughout the city under the moniker Operation Shock and Awe. They borrowed the phrase from the US military, which had used it to describe its strategy in the early days of the Iraq War. Shock and Awe in Buffalo meant thirty-eight SWAT raids over three days. The cops even invited along a couple of reporters from the *Buffalo News* to cover the invasion.

A month later, the *Buffalo News* ran a follow-up report. The original six pounds of marijuana police claimed to have found was actually four pounds, thirteen ounces. Three and a half pounds of that came by way of an unrelated traffic stop on the same day that had nothing to do with the raids. They found all of five guns. Not surprisingly, the revised haul wasn't enough contraband to keep the seventy-eight people in jail. Sixteen were immediately released with no criminal charges. Another thirty-two were out of jail within twenty-four hours due to insufficient evidence.

City leaders were furious, not because city police had just terrorized innocent people with fruitless SWAT raids, but because so many petty offenders were let off. City officials demanded tougher drug laws, and discussed the possibility of sending drug cops and SWAT teams out with housing code inspectors to clean up suspected crack houses without those pesky Fourth Amendment warrant requirements.

Buffalo's chief of detectives, Dennis Richards, told the newspaper that Operation Shock and Awe was "just the beginning." "There will certainly be more raids in the future," he said. "You can count on that. . . . We're looking at small-scale, large-scale, street-level. . . . We're looking at top to bottom."[23]

‿

IN THE 2000S, THE US SUPREME COURT SOMEHOW MANAGED to inflict more damage on the already crippled Castle Doctrine. It began with *United States v. Banks*.[24] In 1998 a raid team in North Las Vegas knocked and announced themselves while serving a drug warrant. The suspect was in the shower at the time, and claimed he didn't hear them. They waited an estimated fifteen to twenty seconds, then forced their way inside. The search turned up illicit drugs and illegal weapons.

In 2003 the Supreme Court unanimously ruled that fifteen to twenty seconds is sufficient time for police to wait after knocking before forcing entry, though they conceded that it was a "close call." The search warrant for Banks was served on a Wednesday afternoon, a time of day when fifteen to twenty seconds might seem like enough time. But a warrant served at night, while everyone is asleep—most likely in a bedroom removed from the front door (where bedrooms usually are)—would be quite a bit different. The opinion, written by Justice David Souter, made no such distinction. Souter also indicated that even shorter wait times might be justified in narcotics cases because of the disposableness of the evidence. Here again, a US Supreme Court opinion had taken a position that makes it easier to use violent dynamic-entry tactics on low-level drug offenders than major ones (because smaller quantities are easier to destroy than larger ones) and for nonviolent offenses like drugs or gambling (where the incriminating evidence is generally disposable) than for crimes like weapons violations or murder (guns and bodies being tougher to destroy quickly).

By Souter's analysis, "what matters is the opportunity to get rid of cocaine, which a prudent dealer will keep near a commode or kitchen sink. The significant circumstances include the arrival of the police during the day, when anyone inside would probably have been up and around, and the sufficiency of 15 to 20 seconds for getting to the bathroom or the kitchen to start flushing cocaine down the drain. . . . It is imminent disposal, not travel time to the entrance, that governs when the police may reasonably enter."

As discussed earlier, the knock-and-announce rule arose out of the common-law tradition and the Castle Doctrine valued so highly by the American Founders. To protect the sanctity of the home, the police were obligated to give a homeowner the opportunity to grant them entrance in order to prevent a violent confrontation, the destruction of his door and property, and the infliction of terror upon him and his family. Souter's direction to police to consider *disposal time* instead of the time it would take an occupant to come to the door not only does away with the notion that the purpose of the knock-and-announce rule is to give citizens the opportunity to avoid a violent confrontation, it also presupposes that *all* drug suspects are guilty. Souter's *only* concern was with making sure the knock-and-announce requirement doesn't give drug offenders the opportunity to destroy evidence. And every other justice agreed with him.

In *Banks,* a unanimous Court decided that preserving the evidence needed to convict people suspected of nonviolent, consensual drug crimes was more important than protecting innocent people from the violence of a paramilitary-style police raid. Thirty years after it began, the modern drug war had finally killed the Castle Doctrine.

Next up was the 2006 case *Hudson v. Michigan,* in which the Supreme Court effectively erased its own recognition of the knock-and-announce requirement ten years earlier.[25] By a 6–3 vote, the Court decided that even when police conduct a clearly illegal no-knock raid, any illegal evidence they seize can still be used against the defendant at trial. Writing for the majority, Justice Antonin Scalia took aim at that old conservative nemesis, the Exclusionary Rule. Scalia wrote that the rule is excessive and inappropriate in such cases. He added that there are other ways of holding police officers accountable when they violate the knock-and-announce requirement. Scalia explained that police management and internal affairs departments could, for instance, bring disciplinary action against offending officers, or innocent victims of illegal raids could sue the offending officers in court. He also cited the existence of civilian review boards. If you've read this far into this book, it should be clear that those solutions haven't been particularly effective at preventing these abuses.

In pointing to these other possible remedies for knock-and-announce violations, Scalia cited the work of criminologist Sam Walker, who has done extensive research on the development of police professionalism. In the study Scalia cited, Walker concluded that there has been enormous progress "in the education, training and supervision of police officers."[26] Scalia argued that this progress was gradually making the Exclusionary Rule obsolete. But Walker's thesis was that this progress has come about in part *because* of Supreme Court decisions applying the Exclusionary Rule, particularly during the Warren years.

Walker was horrified. Shortly after the *Hudson* decision came down, in an op-ed in the *Los Angeles Times* headlined "Thanks for Nothing, Nino" (Nino is Scalia's nickname), Walker wrote:

> Scalia's opinion suggests that the results I highlighted have sufficiently removed the need for an exclusionary rule to act as a judicial-branch watchdog over the police. I have never said or even suggested such a thing. To the contrary, I have argued that the results reinforce the Supreme Court's continuing importance in defining constitutional protections for individual rights and requiring the appropriate remedies for violations, including the exclusion of evidence.[27]

The Court wasn't finished. In 2011, another 8–1 vote found that police officers may forcibly enter a home without a warrant if exigent circumstances exist even if police create the exigent circumstance themselves. In the case before the Court, an informant had conducted a cocaine buy while working for police in Lexington, Kentucky. The police then followed their suspect into an apartment complex, at which point they lost him. They claimed, however, that while they were there they smelled marijuana coming from an unrelated apartment. They knocked, and when they heard "rustling" inside, kicked down the door. Inside, they found marijuana and cocaine. The Kentucky Supreme Court threw out the conviction, writing that in this case "police have created their own exigency, and cannot rely on the fear of evidence being destroyed as a justification for a warrantless entry."[28]

The US Supreme Court disagreed. Writing for the majority, Justice Samuel Alito found that so long as the police conduct itself is lawful before the exigent circumstances manifest, the subsequent search is legal.[29] The Court has a history of assuming good intent on the part of police officers (see the "good-faith exception" to the Exclusionary Rule). But as the lone dissenter, Justice Ruth Bader Ginsburg, explained, decisions like these can become a how-to guide for cops to undermine the Fourth Amendment. "The court today arms the police with a way routinely to dishonor the Fourth Amendment's warrant requirement in drug cases. In lieu of presenting their evidence to a neutral magistrate, police officers may now knock, listen, then break the door down, never mind that they had ample time to obtain a warrant."[30]

⌐

THINGS WERE GETTING BAD IN NEW YORK CITY. BY 2002, the New York Police Department (NYPD) was conducting over 450 drug raids per month, the vast majority under no-knock warrants. In October 2002, Norman Siegel, former director of the New York Civil Liberties Union, held a press conference to announce that he was representing the victims of three such raids—all of them involving raids on wrong addresses—in a lawsuit against the city. Siegel pleaded with police to use more caution. "We must do a better job of no-knock search warrants," he warned. "Otherwise, someone might wind up dead as a result of how we implement this procedure." Less than a year later, his prediction came to pass.

On May 16, 2003, a dozen New York City police officers stormed an apartment building in Harlem on another no-knock warrant.

They were acting on a tip from a confidential informant who told them a convicted felon was dealing drugs and guns from the sixth floor. But there was no felon. The only resident in the building was Alberta Spruill, a fifty-seven-year-old city employee described by friends as a "devout churchgoer." Before breaking in, the raid team set off a "flash-bang" grenade—a nonlethal weapon that emits a bright flash and deafening thud used to shock and disorient criminal suspects or the enemy in combat situations. The explosion of bright white light and accompanying thunderous boom stunned Spruill. She fell to the ground. Once the police figured out their mistake, an officer attempted to help Spruill to her feet. But she went limp and slipped into cardiac arrest. She died two hours later.

The ensuing investigation found that the NYPD's informant had flat-out lied and that the officers who conducted the raid had done no investigation whatsoever to corroborate the tip. A police source later told the *New York Daily News* that, in fact, the informant's record was so poor, he was due to be dropped from the city's informant list.[31] Yet somehow an uncorroborated tip from an informant with a prior success rate somewhere around 0 percent was still enough to get the Manhattan district attorney's office and a state magistrate to sign off on a no-knock warrant. The entire process—from the conversation with the informant until the moment Alberta Spruill's heart stopped beating—took only a matter of hours. In an article the following June, the *New York Times* noted another horribly botched raid, on Timothy Brockman, a frail, sixty-eight-year-old former Marine. The raid was so violent that "next-door neighbors, afraid that the building had been bombed by terrorists, fled with their pajama-clad children." The police had the wrong house. Sources interviewed by the paper said the operation was "muddled by erroneous information" and "the belief in a phantom informant." The assault on Brockman's home illustrated "not only the ways that aggressive police work can go wrong, but also the willingness—or hesitance—of the authorities to take responsibility for preventing such errors. At the time, the incident received no publicity and no serious attention from the police leadership." Brockman was raided two days before Alberta Spruill.[32]

In its own follow-up piece, the *Village Voice* found that reports of botched no-knocks had been pouring into the NYPD for years. "Until Spruill's death, the NYPD had done nothing to stem the number of incidents," the *Voice* wrote, "despite receiving a memo from the Civilian Complaint Review Board in January noting the high number of raid complaints. Last March, the NAACP also approached NYPD commissioner Raymond W. Kelly about the raids." The raids were straining already tense relations between police and minority communities. One of the wrongly raided, Orlando Russell, told the *Voice* that while he had once been an "upstanding citizen," he was fed up with the number of no-knock raids on low-income and minority communities. "Any cop walking [into his home] without an invitation better have a body bag."[33]

That 1998 *New York Times* story ran under the headline "As Number of Police Raids Increase, So Do Questions." The article noted that the number of narcotics search warrants issued in New York City had doubled from 1994 to 1998, from 1,447 to 2,977. And most of these raids, according to the *Times*, were drug raids done with no-knock warrants.

Despite ongoing media reports of "wrong-door" raids throughout the late 1990s, city officials continued to insist that such incidents were uncommon and nothing to be alarmed about. And yet, in February 1998, the NYPD circulated a memo among the city's police officers instructing them on how to contact locksmiths and door repair services should they break down in the wrong home. Outwardly, the claim was that these were isolated incidents, rare as a lightning strike. Inwardly, the department knew they were common enough that officials had established procedures for fixing wrongly raided doors.

Though complaints about botched raids came in regularly, the city's Civilian Complaint Review Board (CCRB) could do little to stop them. The board was hamstrung by bureaucracy, limited jurisdiction, and antagonism from the police union. The review board was only permitted to review cases in which the raiding cops themselves had acted improperly. It couldn't look at the substance of an individual warrant to determine, for example, if it was proper for a judge to have issued it in the first place. The board also couldn't give victims the information they needed to seek compensation—or even an official apology and admission of error, which some needed to appease landlords or employers who were unpersuaded by their protestations of innocence. And so, as the number of no-knock raids in New York City soared, NYPD officials would tell victims that their only recourse was the CCRB, knowing full well that there was little the CCRB could actually do. With its jurisdiction limited to the conduct of police in specific raids after the warrant was issued, the review board not only was unable to investigate whether a raid should ever have been conducted in the first place, it also couldn't look into the use and abuse of informants, whether the same cops were conducting too many raids, or whether the same raid teams were making the same mistakes.

In 2003 Police Chief Raymond Kelly estimated that at least 10 percent of the city's more than 450 monthly no-knock drug raids were served on the wrong address, were served under bad information, or otherwise didn't produce enough evidence for an arrest. Incredibly, Kelly made that estimate in *defense* of the way the NYPD was handling these raids. Some forty-five times per month, innocent New Yorkers were getting raided, terrorized, sometimes injured, and nearly killed. (Police officials would argue that in a significant percentage of cases where a raid came up empty the suspects weren't actually innocent; they were just successful at moving their stash before police could serve the warrant.) And the city's police chief found that figure acceptable. It was just more collateral damage. Kelly also admitted that the NYPD didn't keep track of botched raids, leading one city council member to speculate that the percentage could be even higher.

So what about the city's judges, the public servants charged with protecting the Fourth Amendment? *Newsday* found that many courts in the city didn't even keep no-knock warrants on file after they were issued and executed. That is, not only did the courts not notice or care about what was happening, but they made it impossible for anyone else to investigate possible patterns of abuse. The paper reported that Judge Juanita Bing Newton, who oversaw all the city's criminal courts at the time, said "she doesn't necessarily believe the court's role in record-keeping is as a 'Big Brother,' to check the police and district attorney," a statement that not only showed an astonishing lack of concern for the rights of New Yorkers, but suggests that Newton didn't actually know the origin of the phrase "Big Brother."

After Spruill's death, New York State Supreme Court judge Brenda Soloff refused to unseal the affidavit and search warrant authorizing the raid—there was "no significant need," she found. Apparently the death of an innocent fifty-seven-year-old woman and the city government's regular terrorization of its citizens weren't "significant" concerns. In favor of keeping the documents sealed, Soloff cited concern for the safety of the confidential informant—the same informant who had given nothing but bad information in the past, and whose tip was the reason an innocent woman was dead. (The concern wasn't valid anyway—the documents could have been released with the informant's identity redacted.)

A day after the New York City Council held hearings on no-knock raids in response to Spruill's death, Manhattan borough president Virginia Fields held hearings of her own. According to the *Village Voice:*

> Dozens of black and Latino victims—nurses, secretaries, and former officers—packed her chambers airing tales, one more horrifying than the next. Most were unable to hold back tears as they described police ransacking their homes, handcuffing children and grandparents, putting guns to their heads, and being verbally (and often physically) abusive. In many cases, victims had received no follow-up from the NYPD, even to fix busted doors or other physical damage.
>
> Some complainants reported that they had filed grievances with the [Civilian Complaint Review Board] and were told there was no police misconduct. Unless there is proven abuse, the CCRB disregards complaints about warrants that hold a correct address but are faulty because of bad evidence from a [confidential informant].[34]

Perhaps no one was more victimized by the battlefield mentality that had set in at the NYPD than Walter and Rose Martin. The Brooklyn couple, both in their eighties, were wrongly raided *more than fifty times* between 2002 and 2010. The couple filed numerous complaints with the police department. They wrote letters to Mayor Michael Bloomberg and NYPD commissioner Ray Kelly. They were ignored. In 2007 they at least got someone at the NYPD to try to wipe their address out of the department's computer system. But the raids continued. It wasn't until the couple went to the media in 2010 that the city finally looked into the problem. Back in 2002, someone had used the Martins' address as a dummy address to test the department's new computer system. When the new system was implemented, no one removed their address. So anytime NYPD cops in certain precincts used the system for a warrant and forgot to remove the dummy address to put in the correct one, the police would end up at the Martins' door.

At least that was the official explanation. But the *New York Daily News* tracked down the previous owner of the house, who said he too had been frequently visited by cops, going back to 1994. It seems safe to say that NYPD cops weren't repeatedly terrorizing an elderly couple deliberately. But the Martins' inability to stop the raids until they went to the media is more evidence that even after the Spruill incident, the department just wasn't all that concerned about mistaken raids and the rights of New Yorkers.

"They should have listened to us all those years when we tried to tell them something was happening," Rose Martin told the *Daily News*. That was certainly true in her case. It was also true of the dozens, probably hundreds, of complaints from victims going back to the early 1990s.[35]

Despite public outcry, intense media coverage, and promises for reform by public officials, change after Alberta Spruill's death was slow and sparse. The key recommendation from the Fields report was that the NYPD produce an annual report detailing "all statistics regarding the execution of warrants." Fields believed that such a report would provide some transparency and accountability in the issuance and execution of drug warrants, particularly those authorizing no-knock raids. The NYPD issued no such report in 2005.

There were a few positive developments. The city did implement some procedures that increased the amount of time it takes to obtain a drug raid warrant from two to twenty-four hours. Consequently, the total number of drug raids did drop, from 5,117 in 2002 to 3,577 in 2003. That decrease isn't insignificant, but the post-reform figure in 2003 was still 250 percent higher than the number of annual raids just ten years earlier. Judges and police were also required to attend training workshops on proper drug investigation techniques and the issuance of narcotics warrants. The city also restricted the use of flash-bang grenades, and finally prohibited them completely in 2010.

It would be hard to come up with a more sympathetic drug raid victim than Alberta Spruill. But even after her death, after the revelation of dozens of similar botched raids, after intense media exposure in the country's largest city, and after promises for substantive reforms to prevent similar incidents from happening again, it wasn't long before drug policing in the city returned to business as usual—and the mistaken raids started up again.[36] By 2006, the number of citizen complaints about residential search warrant raids had swelled to 1,065, a 49 percent jump over 2002, the year *before* the Spruill raid.[37] If it couldn't happen in New York City after this incident, real reform would be a long, tough slog, if it was possible at all.[38]

JUST BEFORE THE FEDERAL ASSAULT WEAPONS BAN WAS SET to expire in 2004, the National Institute for Justice released a study looking at the use of assault weapons in violent crimes. Drawing on crime data from several American cities, the report found that assault weapons were "rarely used in gun crimes, even before the ban" was put in place. Moreover, because assault weapons are so rarely used by criminals, NIJ found that, "should it be renewed, the ban's effects on gun violence were likely small at best, and perhaps too small for reliable measurement." The report also found that the use of such high-powered weaponry to kill police officers was "very rare."[39]

The NIJ study was used by gun rights groups to argue against renewing the assault weapons ban. But it was also a strong piece of evidence undercutting the common argument from law enforcement officials that SWAT teams and military gear were essential because the police were in a nonstop arms race with drug dealers and other criminals—call it the North Hollywood Shoot-out Argument.

And in fact, the 2004 NIJ study was only the most recent to cut against that argument. In 1995 the Justice Department had released a study showing that 86 percent of violent gun crimes in the United States involved a handgun. The most popular weapon used in homicides at the time wasn't an automatic weapon but a large-caliber revolver. Just 3 percent of murders in 1993 were committed with rifles, and just 5 percent with shotguns.[40] A 1997 *Palm Beach Post* investigation of area SWAT raids found that of 309 recent arrests made by the twelve SWAT teams in Palm Beach County, Florida, only 60—or 19 percent—produced weapons of *any* kind.[41] A five-year investigation in Orange County, Florida, in the mid-1990s likewise found that just 13 percent of SWAT raids turned up weapons.[42]

In 2007 I asked David Doddridge, a retired narcotics cop and LAPD veteran, about the argument that SWAT tactics are necessary because drug dealers are increasingly well armed. "It just isn't true," he said. "In twenty-one years at LAPD, I never once saw any assault weapons on a drug raid. Drug dealers prefer handguns, which are easier to conceal. Occasionally you'll find a shotgun. But having a bunch of high-powered weaponry around is just too much trouble for them. It's too much for them to worry about."[43] Doddridge's experience isn't universal, but it is common among drug cops I've talked to. There do seem to be more higher-powered arms around the border, and obviously cops who investigate the sale and smuggling of illegal guns will tend to find a greater quantity of more powerful weapons in the course of their work.

But even when the crime rate was peaking in the late 1980s and early 1990s, there was little evidence that murderers were using high-powered weapons. In a 1991 paper for the Independence Institute (a libertarian think tank), researchers David Kopel and Eric Morgan ran a survey of dozens of American cities and found that, in general, fewer than 1 percent of the weapons seized by police fit the definition of an "assault weapon." Nationally, they found that fewer than 4 percent of homicides involved rifles of any kind. And fewer than one-eighth of 1 percent of homicides involved weapons of military caliber. Even fewer homicides involved weapons commonly called "assault" weapons. The proportion of police fatalities caused by assault weapons was around 3 percent, a number that remained relatively constant throughout the 1980s.

Kopel and Morgan also interviewed police firearms examiners. In Dade County, Florida—where *Miami Vice* had propagated the image of machine gun–toting drug dealers spraying bullets all over the city—Kopel and Morgan found that the use of assault weapons in shootings and homicides in the city actually *declined* throughout the decade. A police lieutenant in Washington, DC—the most violent city in the country at the time—told the authors that the preferred weapon of criminals in the nation's capital was the pistol.[44]

But more generally, the argument that well-armed criminals have made cops' jobs more dangerous than ever just isn't backed up by the data. The job of police officer has been getting progressively safer for a generation. The number of officer fatalities peaked in 1974 and has been steadily dropping since. In fact, 2012 was the safest year for police officers since the 1950s. According to the FBI's Uniform Crime Reports, the homicide rate for police officers in 2010 (the last year for which data is available) was about 7.9 per 100,000 officers. That's about 60 percent higher than the overall homicide rate in America, which is 4.8. But it's lower than the homicide rates in many large cities, including Atlanta (17.3), Boston (11.3), Dallas (11.3), Kansas City (21.1), Nashville (8.9), Pittsburgh (17.3), St. Louis (40.5), and Tulsa (13.7). In fact, of the seventy-four US cities with populations of 250,000 or more, thirty-six have murder rates higher than that of police in America. You're more likely to be murdered just by living in these cities than the average American police officer is to be murdered on the job.

Proponents of police militarization will argue that these figures show that militarization is working—it's making cops safer. It's a convenient way to frame the debate. If police fatalities go up, it's an indication that criminals are getting more dangerous and cops need more firepower. If police fatalities go down, it means militarization is working. But it's far from clear that bigger guns and more aggressive tactics are responsible for the drop. For example, assaults on police officers have also been dropping, a statistic that isn't explained by cops in SWAT gear performing more drug raids. The most likely explanation is that killings of police officers have declined for the same reasons the overall crime rate has dropped over roughly the same period. (Criminologists are still fighting over what those reasons are.)

The more important questions are why these myths persist, and what effect they have on the way police officers approach the job. As for why the myths persist, one explanation is that the public rarely takes an optimistic view of crime and public safety. For example, polls still consistently show that most Americans think crime in the country is getting *worse*, even though, as noted, it has been dropping quite dramatically for nearly twenty years.

But law enforcement officials themselves help perpetuate the perception that cops' jobs are fraught with peril. At the end of every calendar year, the National Law Enforcement Officers Memorial Fund puts out the police mortality figures for the year about to end. The figures always generate a good amount of media coverage. But whether the figures are up or down, the quotes in these stories from the law enforcement community are always the same. They always stress that police officers have incredibly dangerous jobs and that every cop's next day on the job could be his last. But from the figures above, that's like saying every day a Bostonian spends in Boston could be his last. Technically both statements are true. But they convey a false sentiment about risk. The problem is that there are plenty of incentives for law enforcement leaders to play up the risks to the job. It moves the public debate over issues like militarization, police discretion, use of force, and police budgets more in their favor. The "heavily armed criminals" angle also tends to find favor with gun control advocates in the media.

But playing up the risks and dangers of the job, even in spite of overwhelming evidence that things are getting better, almost certainly has an impact on the mind-set of the average cop. If you approach the job as if every day could be your last, you're going to approach every citizen encounter as if it could be your last. That makes everyone a potential enemy. The job becomes about survival, not public service. Hence, the unofficial motto of the job you often hear from cops, or see posted on police discussion boards: "Whatever I need to do to get home safe at the end of the day."

In a 2006 op-ed in the *Wall Street Journal* written in reaction to the killing of twenty-three-year-old Sean Bell—who went down in a storm of fifty bullets fired by NYPD cops—Joseph McNamara looked at the gradual change in the average cop's mind-set since he walked a beat in New York.

> Simply put, the police culture in our country has changed. An emphasis on "officer safety" and paramilitary training pervades today's policing, in contrast to the older culture, which held that cops didn't shoot until they were about to be shot or stabbed. Police in large cities formerly carried revolvers holding six .38-caliber rounds. Nowadays, police carry semi-automatic pistols with sixteen high-caliber rounds, shotguns, and military assault rifles, weapons once relegated to SWAT teams facing extraordinary circumstances. Concern about such firepower in densely populated areas hitting innocent citizens has given way to an attitude that the police are fighting a war against drugs and crime and must be heavily armed.
>
> Yes, police work is dangerous, and the police see a lot of violence. On the other hand, 51 officers were slain in the line of duty last year, out of some 700,000 to 800,000 American cops. That is far fewer than the police fatalities occurring when I patrolled New York's highest-crime precincts, when the total number of cops in the country was half that of today. Each of these police deaths and numerous other police injuries is a tragedy and we owe support to

those who protect us. On the other hand, this isn't Iraq. The need to give our officers what they require to protect themselves and us has to be balanced against the fact that the fundamental duty of the police is to protect human life and that law officers are only justified in taking a life as a last resort.[45]

On the other side, it's difficult to even get an estimate of the number of times police officers shoot citizens. Some states require police departments to keep those figures, but national data is difficult to come by. The *New York Times* reported in 2001, "Despite widespread public interest and a provision in the 1994 Crime Control Act requiring the attorney general to collect the data and publish an annual report on them, statistics on police shootings and use of nondeadly force continue to be piecemeal products of spotty collection, and are dependent on the cooperation of local police departments." The paper added, "No comprehensive accounting for all the nation's 17,000 police departments exists."[46] University of South Carolina criminology professor Geoffrey Alpert called the lack of reporting "a national scandal," adding, "These are public servants who work for us and are paid to protect us."[47] The *Las Vegas Review Journal* also looked for national figures for its 2011 series on a rise in local police-involved shootings. Little had changed since the *New York Times* report a decade earlier.

> The nation's leading law enforcement agency collects vast amounts of information on crime nationwide, but missing from this clearinghouse are statistics on where, how often, and under what circumstances police use deadly force. In fact, no one anywhere comprehensively tracks the most significant act police can do in the line of duty: take a life.
>
> "We don't have a mandate to do that," said William Carr, an FBI spokesman in Washington, DC. "It would take a request from Congress for us to collect that data."[48]

Congress, it seems, hasn't asked.

Americans, then—both police officers and others—are regularly reminded about the inherent danger faced by police officers, even though the job is getting safer. But not only aren't figures about how many times cops shoot at, injure, or kill citizens publicized, the figures themselves haven't been tabulated. The federal government has been arming American cops with military-grade guns, vehicles, and other weaponry, but has little interest in knowing if all of that is affecting how and when police use lethal force against American citizens. Cops are told all the time that the public presents a threat to them, and that the threat grows more dire by the day. But as for what sort of threat cops pose to the public, the public isn't permitted to know.

These policies have given us an increasingly armed, increasingly isolated, increasingly paranoid, increasingly aggressive police force in America, and a public shielded from knowing the consequences of it all.

THE EXPLOSION HAPPENED WITHOUT WARNING AROUND 4 AM IN West Chester, Pennsylvania. FBI agent Donald Bain was sitting in his car in a parking lot with two other agents. He was armed and wore a Kevlar vest. He was also carrying a "flash-bang" grenade, a nonlethal weapon that emits a bright flash and deafening bang that's used to shock and disorient criminal suspects or the enemy in combat situations.

The three agents—Bain, Thomas Scanzano, and James Milligan—were waiting for developments in a kidnapping that had turned into a hostage stakeout.

That's when, Bain says, the flash-bang grenade in his vest just blew up.

"The car is on fire," Bain recalled. "I was told later I was on fire. Smoke billowing in the car. It was obviously chaos."[49]

That was the introduction to a 2008 CNN report about an incident that happened in 2004. The federal government subsequently issued criminal indictments against Pyrotechnic Specialties Inc. (PSI), alleging that the company knew that its flash-bang grenades were defective but continued to sell them to the federal government anyway.

CNN also interviewed Dean Wagner, a US Army sergeant who lost a hand in Iraq when a flash-bang grenade prematurely detonated as he was holding it. "They don't have a clue what it's like," Wagner told the network, referring to PSI. "If they could experience that, or someone close to them would have to go through that experience, I'm sure it would be a different story and maybe they wouldn't have allowed it to happen."

A few years later, in February 2011, Fred Thornton, a member of the Charlotte-Mecklenburg SWAT team, was killed when a flash-bang grenade went off as he was organizing his SWAT gear in his garage. The next month, in Alice, Texas, SWAT commander Richard DeLeon was critically injured when a flash-bang grenade went off as he was putting gear into his car.[50] And in 2001 an FBI agent in Buffalo, New York, was burned on his hands and upper body when a flash-bang grenade went off unexpectedly.[51]

These incidents are tragic and unfortunate. But they're also rather chilling. Every day SWAT teams across the country use the very same explosives that injured agents Bain, Scanzano, Milligan and killed Officer Thornton—and they use them against American citizens. Granted, they aren't deployed in quite as tight an area as an enclosed car. But garages? Certainly. Also bedrooms, kitchens, hallways, and living rooms. This could be perhaps justified if the devices were only used against people actively taking hostages or robbing a bank or violent fugitives on the run. But the vast majority of the time they're used in the service of warrants for nonviolent crimes— and not even against people convicted of those crimes, but people merely suspected of them. They're also used against anyone else who happens to be in the house at the time of the raid. And against the victims of wrong-door raids.

Clay Conrad, a criminal defense attorney in Houston, has argued that flash-bang grenades are unconstitutional because, by design, they're intended to inflict injury on people who have yet to even be charged with a crime, much less convicted of one. "It's just an assault," Conrad told me in a 2010 interview. "These things are designed to blind and deafen. They produce a shock wave of 136 decibels or more. You're intentionally injuring people."[52]

Conrad once mounted a challenge to flash-bang grenades in a drug case, based on a Texas law that prevents evidence from being admitted in trial if the police commit a crime while obtaining it. He argued in a brief that the use of flash-bangs during drug raids constitutes a criminal assault. Conrad says that the prosecution offered a generous plea before that issue could be hashed out in court. "We were prepared to argue that if these things are as harmless as the state claims, we should be able to detonate one in the courtroom," Conrad says. "That would have been fun." (Of course, it could also be argued that nearly everything about these raids inflicts punishment on people who have yet to be charged with a crime.)

The same year the CNN story came out, a state judge in New Jersey tossed the conviction of a man suspected of dealing meth because police used flash-bang grenades and paramilitary tactics to serve the warrant, including waking a seventeen-year-old (who was not the suspect) by pointing their guns at him. "This was a commando raid–like scenario," Superior Court judge James J. Morley said, "and my decision was based on the overall way they approached the case—at 5 AM with 29 police officers in commando gear and pointing a weapon at a sleeping 17-year-old."[53]

"The argument is that it shocks the conscience," Conrad says. "That argument has some validity to it in the right cases, where you're using these volatile tactics against someone who's suspected of nothing more than drug dealing. It's excessive to the point of violating the Fourth Amendment."

The CNN report called flash-bang grenades "nonlethal," but that term only refers to the officers' intent when using them; it doesn't mean the devices can't kill, as the families of Officer Thornton and Alberta Spruill would attest. More recently, in late 2012, a twelve-year-old Montana girl suffered severe burns after police on a drug raid tossed a flash-bang grenade through her window.[54] The following month the city of St. Paul, Minnesota, paid out a $400,000 settlement to a woman set on fire by a flash-bang grenade thrown by police during a drug raid.[55]

Fires aren't uncommon. In 1994 a flash-bang grenade detonated during a raid in Dallas burned the surrounding building to the ground, leaving fifteen people homeless.[56] In 2001 a flash-bang deployed during a raid on a Florida house that was home to a small record label ignited the foam rubber put in the walls for soundproofing. The fire destroyed the studio's master recordings and $100,000 worth of equipment. Sgt. Gary Robbins said afterward, "It's unfortunate those guys packed that house with materials that were flammable."[57] In 1996 a SWAT team in Fitchburg, Massachusetts (population 39,102) burned down an entire apartment complex with a flash-bang they used during a drug raid. Six police officers were injured and twenty-four people were left homeless. Several of the officers were later cited for bravery.[58] More recently, police in San Antonio rendered a home a total loss when, on a drug raid, they tossed a flash-bang grenade that ignited a mattress, which then set the rest of the house aflame.

There are other problems with the use of flash-bang grenades beyond their potential to inflict injuries and start fires. By design, the devices are intended to confuse, stun, and bewilder everyone in the room where they're detonated. That may make sense if you're apprehending a suspect who poses an immediate threat to other people—again, bank robbers, hostage takers, active shooters, and so on. But in raids for nonviolent offenses, sowing confusion only *increases* the potential for violence. On numerous occasions, police have detonated a flash-bang grenade in the course of a raid, then claimed that a suspect who subsequently grabbed a gun or a knife or who physically attacked one of the officers should have known that it was the police raiding the home. But you can't first claim that the use of flash-bang grenades to stun and confuse people is critically important, then claim that seconds after the device goes off, those same people (many of whom have also just woken up) should be cognizant, collected, and alert enough to make sense of the chaos around them. Well, you can't *logically* make both claims. In practice, police make both claims all the time. Courts and public officials rarely question the contradiction.

The fact that flash-bang grenades are usually detonated before, during, or just after the police break down a door creates yet more problems. Sometimes they're tossed through a window before the door comes down, or detonated shortly after police make an announcement but before they force entry. "The whole psychological philosophy behind them is contradictory," says Joseph McNamara, the former police chief of Kansas City and San Jose. "Knock-and-announce is to give the person inside time to voluntarily surrender. When you're waiting just fifteen seconds, setting off flash grenades, then using a battering ram, you're *diverting* attention from the front door. You're scaring people into running in the other direction."[59] It also decreases the likelihood that the occupants inside will recognize the armed intruders as police officers. In 2006 a Florida state appeals court found that a SWAT team had violated a man's Fourth Amendment rights because although they waited fifteen seconds after announcing before forcing entry, the officers began counting only after detonating a flash-bang grenade and included in their count the time they spent bashing the door with a battering ram.[60]

But only a few other courts have either questioned the use of flash-bang grenades or put restrictions on their use, and even then only in limited circumstances.[61] Generally speaking, the courts give police an enormous amount of leeway in deciding how to serve a search warrant. Even in the rare case when a court has found that the use of the grenades was unreasonable, and therefore a violation of a plaintiff's constitutional rights, the same court inevitably finds that the police officers are protected by qualified immunity, which means that the person injured by the grenade won't even get his case in front of a jury. In 2004, for example, the US Court of Appeals for the Ninth Circuit found that "blindly" tossing a flash-bang grenade into a house or room with no certainty as to who and how many people might have been inside was unreasonable. But because it wasn't so unreasonable as to be established law or obvious to a layperson, the officers in that case still couldn't be held liable.[62]

The flash-bang grenade issue has never been of much interest to politicians either. During congressional hearings on the Branch Davidian raid, Democratic representative Charles Schumer of New York asked Dick DeGuerin, an attorney for David Koresh, if the Branch Davidians had stockpiled grenades. DeGuerin responded that the only grenades he had seen were thrown by ATF agents. Schumer derisively dismissed the idea that flash-bang grenades were harmful. "Mr. DeGuerin said flashbangers can kill, injure, maim," Schumer said. "Anyone who knows anything about these things knows they can't." Schumer went on to win a US Senate seat in 1998. Which means that when New York City resident Alberta Spruill died from the effects of a flash-bang grenade in 2003, she was one of Schumer's constituents.

SAL CULOSI IS DEAD BECAUSE HE BET ON A FOOTBALL GAME— but it wasn't a bookie or a loan shark who killed him. His local government killed him, ostensibly to protect him from his gambling habit.[63]

Several months earlier at a local bar, Fairfax County, Virginia, detective David Baucum overheard the thirty-eight-year-old optometrist and some friends wagering on a college football game. "To Sal, betting a few bills on the Redskins was a stress reliever, done among friends," a friend of Culosi's told me shortly after his death. "None of us single, successful professionals ever thought that betting fifty bucks or so on the Virginia–Virginia Tech football game was a crime worthy of investigation." Baucum apparently did. After overhearing the men wagering, Baucum befriended Culosi as a cover to begin investigating him. During the next several months, he talked Culosi into raising the stakes of what Culosi thought were just more fun wagers between friends to make watching sports more interesting. Eventually Culosi and Baucum bet more than $2,000 in a single day. Under Virginia law, that was enough for police to charge Culosi with running a gambling operation. And that's when they brought in the SWAT team.

On the night of January 24, 2006, Baucum called Culosi and arranged a time to drop by to collect his winnings. When Culosi, barefoot and clad in a T-shirt and jeans, stepped out of his house to meet the man he thought was a friend, the SWAT team began to move in. Seconds later, Det. Deval Bullock, who had been on duty since 4:00 AM and hadn't slept in seventeen hours, fired a bullet that pierced Culosi's heart.

Sal Culosi's last words were to Baucum, the cop he thought was a friend: "Dude, what are you doing?"

In March 2006, just two months after its ridiculous gambling investigation resulted in the death of an unarmed man, the Fairfax County Police Department issued a press release warning residents not to participate in office betting pools tied to the NCAA men's basketball tournament. The title: "Illegal Gambling Not Worth the Risk." Given the proximity to Culosi's death, residents could be forgiven for thinking the police department believed wagering on sports was a crime punishable by execution.

In January 2011, the Culosi family accepted a $2 million settlement offer from Fairfax County. That same year, Virginia's government spent $20 million promoting the state lottery.

The raid on Sal Culosi was merely another red flag indicating yet more SWAT team mission creep in America. It wasn't even the first time a Virginia SWAT team had killed someone during a gambling raid. In 1998 a SWAT team in Virginia Beach shot and killed security guard Edward C. Reed during a 3:00 AM raid on a private club suspected of facilitating gambling. Police said they approached the tinted car where Reed was working security, knocked, and identified themselves, then shot Reed when he refused to drop his handgun. Reed's family insisted the police story was unlikely. Reed had no criminal record. Why would he knowingly point his gun at a heavily armed police team? More likely, they said, Reed mistakenly believed the raiding officers were there to do harm, particularly given that the club had been robbed not long before the raid. Statements by the police themselves seem to back that account. According to officers at the scene, Reed's last words were, "Why did you shoot me? I was reading a book."[64]

As the Texas Hold 'Em craze picked up momentum in the mid-2000s, fans of the game started hosting tournaments at private clubs, bars, and residences. Police in many parts of the country responded with SWAT raids. In 2011, for example, police in Baltimore County, Maryland, sent a tactical unit to raid a $65 buy-in poker game at the Lynch Point Social Club.[65] From 2006 to 2008, SWAT teams in South Carolina staged a number of raids to break up poker games in the suburbs of Charleston. Some were well organized and high-stakes, but others were friendly games with a $20 buy-in. "The typical police raid of these games . . . is to literally burst into a home in SWAT gear with guns drawn and treat poker players like a bunch of high-level drug dealers," an attorney representing poker players told a local newspaper. "Using the taxpayers' resources for such useless Gestapo-like tactics is more of a crime than is playing of the game."[66]

In 2007 a Dallas SWAT team actually raided a Veterans of Foreign Wars outpost for hosting charity poker games. Players said the tactics were terrifying. One woman urinated on herself.[67] When police raided a San Mateo, California, poker game in 2008, card players described cops storming the place "in full riot gear" and "with guns drawn." The games had buy-ins ranging from $25 to $55. Under California law, the games were legal so long as no one took a "rake," or a cut of the stakes. No one had, but police claimed the $5 the hosts charged players to buy refreshments qualified as a rake. In March 2007, a small army of local cops, ATF agents, National Guard troops, and a helicopter raided a poker game in Cary, North Carolina. They issued forty-one citations, all of them misdemeanors. A columnist at the *Fayetteville Observer* remarked, "They were there to play cards, not to foment rebellion. . . . [I] wonder . . . what other minutiae, personal vices and petty crimes are occupying [the National Guard's] time, and where they're occupying it. . . . Until we get this sorted out, better not jaywalk. There could be a military helicopter overhead."[68]

Police have justified this sort of heavy-handedness by claiming that people who run illegal gambling operations tend to be armed, a blanket characterization that absurdly lumps neighborhood Hold 'Em tournaments with Uncle Junior Soprano's weekly poker game. And in any case, if police know that people inside an establishment are likely to be armed, it makes even less sense to come in with guns blazing. Police have also defended the paramilitary tactics by noting that poker games are usually flush with cash and thus tend to get robbed. That too is an absurd argument, unless the police are afraid they're going to raid a game at precisely the same moment it's getting robbed. Under either scenario, the police are acknowledging that the people playing poker when these raids go down have good reason to think that the men storming the place with guns may be criminals, not cops.

Indeed, that's exactly what happened to seventy-two-year-old Aaron Awtry in 2010. Awtry was hosting a poker tournament in his Greenville, South Carolina, home when police began breaking down the door with a battering ram. Awtry had begun carrying a gun after being robbed. Thinking he was about to be robbed again, he fired through the door, wounding Deputy Matthew May in both arms. The other officers opened fire into the building. Miraculously, only Awtry was hit. As he fell back into a hallway, other players reporting him asking, "Why didn't you tell me it was the cops?" The raid team claimed they knocked and announced several times before putting ram to door, but other players said they heard no knock or announcement. When Awtry recovered, he was charged with attempted murder. As part of an agreement, he pleaded guilty and was sentenced to five years in prison. Police had broken up Awtry's games in the past. But on those occasions, they had knocked and waited, he had let them in peacefully, and he'd been given a $100 fine.[69]

The poker raids have gotten bad enough that the Poker Players Alliance, an interest group that lobbies to make the game legal, has established a network of attorneys around the country to help players who have been raided and arrested.

But the mission creep hasn't stopped at poker games. By the end of the 2000s, police departments were sending SWAT teams to enforce *regulatory law*. In August 2010, for example, a team of heavily armed Orange County, Florida, sheriff's deputies raided several black- and Hispanic-owned barbershops in the Orlando area. More raids followed in September and October. The *Orlando Sentinel* reported that police held barbers and customers at gunpoint and put some in handcuffs, while they turned the shops inside out. The police raided a total of nine shops and arrested thirty-seven people.

By all appearances, these raids were drug sweeps. Shop owners told the *Sentinel* that police asked them where they were hiding illegal drugs and weapons. But in the end, thirty-four of the thirty-seven arrests were for "barbering without a license," a misdemeanor for which only three people have ever served jail time in Florida.

The most disturbing aspect of the Orlando raids was that police didn't even attempt to obtain a legal search warrant. They didn't need to, because they conducted the raids in conjunction with the Florida Department of Business and Professional Regulation. Despite the guns and handcuffs, under Florida law these were licensure inspections, not criminal searches, so no warrants were necessary.[70]

That such "administrative searches" have become an increasingly common way for police to get around the Fourth Amendment is bad enough. More disturbing is the amount of force they're opting to use when they do. In the fall of 2010, police in New Haven, Connecticut, sent a SWAT team to a local bar to investigate reports of underage drinking. Patrons were lined up at gunpoint while cops confiscated cell phones and checked IDs.[71] There have been similar underage drinking SWAT raids on college fraternities. The Atlanta City Council recently agreed to pay a $1 million settlement to the customers and employees of a gay nightclub after a heavy-handed police raid in which police lined up sixty-two people on the floor at gunpoint, searched for drugs, and checked for outstanding warrants and unpaid parking tickets. Police conducted the September 2009 raid after undercover vice cops claimed to have witnessed patrons and employees openly having sex at the club. But the police never obtained a search warrant. Instead, the raid was conducted under the guise of an alcohol inspection. Police made no drug arrests, but arrested eight employees for permit violations.[72]

Federal appeals courts have upheld these "administrative searches" even when it seems obvious that the real intent was to look for criminal activity as long as the government can plausibly claim that the primary purpose of the search was regulatory. In the case of the Orlando raids, simply noting the arrests of thirty-four unlicensed barbers would be enough to meet the test.

But the Fourth Amendment requires that searches be "reasonable." If using a SWAT team to make sure a bar isn't serving nineteen-year-olds is a reasonable use of force, it's hard to imagine what wouldn't be. At least a couple of federal appeals courts have recognized the absurdity. In 2009 the US Court of Appeals for the Fifth Circuit struck a small blow for common sense, allowing a civil rights suit to go forward against the sheriff's department of Rapides Parish, Louisiana, after a warrantless SWAT raid on a nightclub thinly veiled as an administrative search.[73] And in 1995 the US Court of Appeals for the Eleventh Circuit made an even broader ruling, finding that having probable cause and a warrant for the arrest of one person in a club did not justify a SWAT raid and subsequent search of the entire club and everyone inside.[74]

But other legal challenges to paramilitary-style administrative searches have been less successful. Consider the bizarre case of David Ruttenberg, owner of the Rack 'n' Roll pool hall in Manassas Park, Virginia. In June 2004, local police conducted a massive raid on the pool hall with more than fifty police officers, some of whom were wearing face masks, toting semi-automatic weapons, and pumping shotguns as they entered. Customers were detained, searched, and zip-tied. The police were investigating Rutten-berg for several alleged drug crimes, although he was never charged. The local narcotics task force had tried unsuccessfully to get a warrant to search Ruttenberg's office but were denied by a judge. Instead, they simply brought along several representatives of the Virginia Department of Alcoholic Beverage Control and claimed that they were conducting an alcohol inspection. Ruttenberg was cited only for three alcohol violations, based on two bottles of beer a distributor had left that weren't clearly marked as samples, and a bottle of vodka they found in his private office.

In June 2006, Ruttenberg filed a civil rights suit alleging that, among other things, using a SWAT team to conduct an alcohol inspection was an unreasonable use of force. (The town's vendetta against Ruttenberg stretched on for years and is one of the strangest cases I've ever encountered. He eventually sold his bar and moved to New York.) In 2010, the US Court of Appeals for the Fourth Circuit denied his claim. So for now, in the Fourth Circuit, sending a SWAT team to make sure a bar's beer is labeled correctly is not a violation of the Fourth Amendment.[75]

By the end of the decade, state and local SWAT teams were regularly being used not only for raids on poker games and gambling operations but also for immigration raids (on both businesses and private homes) and raids on massage parlors, cat houses, and unlicensed strip clubs. Today the sorts of offenses that can subject a citizen to the SWAT treatment defy caricature. If the government wants to make an example of you by pounding you with a wholly disproportionate use of force, it can. It's rare that courts or politicians even object, much less impose consequences.

Another example is the use of these tactics on people suspected of downloading child pornography.

Because people suspected of such crimes are generally considered among the lowest of the low, there's generally little objection to using maximum force to apprehend them. But when police use force to demonstrate disgust for the crimes the target is suspected of committing, there's always a risk of letting disgust trump good judgment. In one recent case in West Virginia, police violently stormed a house after a Walmart employee reported seeing an image of a man's genitals near a child's cheek in a set of photos a customer had left at the store to be developed. After terrorizing the customer's family (he was out of town), the police learned that the cheek in the photo wasn't a child's but that of a thirty-five-year-old Filipino woman.[76]

Given that most child pornography investigations today involve people who use the Internet to find or distribute the offending images and videos, the investigations can be fraught with problems. There have been several instances in recent years of police waging child porn raids on people after tracing IP addresses, only to learn after the fact that the victims of the raid had an open wireless router that someone else had used to download the pornography. Inevitably, the lesson drawn by police and by the media covering these stories is not that a SWAT raid may be an inappropriate way to arrest someone suspected of looking at child porn on a computer, or that police who insist on using such tactics should probably factor the possibility of an open router into their investigation before breaking down someone's door, but rather that we should all make sure our wireless routers are password-protected—so we too don't get wrongly raided by a SWAT team, too.[77]

It can also be difficult to trace an IP address to a physical address, which can lead to yet more mistaken raids. An example of that problem manifested in one of the more bizarre botched raids in recent years. It took place in September 2006, when a SWAT team from the Bedford County sheriff's department stormed the rural Virginia home of A. J. Nuckols, his wife, and their two children. Police had traced the IP address of someone trading child porn online to the Nuckols' physical address. They had made a mistake. As if the shock of having his house invaded by a SWAT team wasn't enough, Nuckols was in for another surprise. In a letter to the editor of the *Chatham Star Review,* he described the raid: "Men ran at me, dropped into shooting position, double-handed semi-automatic pistols pointed at me, and made me put my hands against my truck. I was held at gunpoint, searched, taunted, and led into the house. I had no idea what this was about. I was scared beyond description."

He then looked up, and saw . . . *former NBA star Shaquille O'Neal.*

O'Neal, an aspiring lawman, had been made an "honorary deputy" with the department. Though he had no training as a SWAT officer, Shaq apparently had gone on several such raids with other police departments around the country. The thrill of bringing an untrained celebrity along apparently trumped the requirement that SWAT teams be staffed only with the most elite, most highly qualified and best-trained cops. According to Nuckols, O'Neal reached into Nuckols's pickup, snatched up his (perfectly legal) rifle, and exclaimed, "We've got a gun!" O'Neal told *Time* that Nuckols's description of the raid on his home was exaggerated. "It ain't no story," he said. "We did everything right, went to the judge, got a warrant. You know, they make it seem like we beat him up, and that never happened. We went in, talked to him, took some stuff, returned it—bada bam, bada bing."[78]

Incidentally, there have been other strange incidents of SWAT teams with star power. Matt Damon accompanied SWAT officers on several raids while preparing for the movie *The Departed*. And after police mistakenly shot and killed immigrant and father Ismael Mena on a raid in Denver in 1999, they revealed that Colorado Rockies first baseman Mike Lansing had gone along for the ride. Denver police added that it was fairly common to take sports stars on drug raids.

In 2010 a massive Maricopa County SWAT team, including a tank and several armored vehicles, raided the home of Jesus Llovera. The tank in fact drove straight into Llovera's living room. Driving the tank? Action movie star Steven Seagal, whom Sheriff Joe Arpaio had recently deputized. Seagal had also been putting on the camouflage to help Arpaio with his controversial immigration raids. All of this, by the way, was getting caught on film. Seagal's adventures in Maricopa County would make up the next season of the A&E TV series *Steven Seagal, Lawman*.

Llovera's suspected crime? Cockfighting. Critics said that Arpaio and Seagal brought an army to arrest a man suspected of fighting chickens to play for the cameras. Seagal's explanation for the show of force: "Animal cruelty is one of my pet peeves." All of Llovera's chickens were euthanized. During the raid, the police also killed his dog.[79]

In the end, while the Supreme Court has laid down some avoidable requirements for obtaining a no-knock warrant (or deciding to conduct a no-knock raid at the scene), there are few court decisions, laws, or regulations when it comes to when it is and isn't appropriate to use a SWAT team and all the bells and whistles of a dynamic entry. The decision is almost always left to the discretion of the police agency—or in the case of the multi-jurisdictional task forces, to the SWAT team itself. The mere fact that there's actually a split in the federal court system over the appropriateness of using SWAT teams *to perform regulatory alcohol inspections* at bars shows just how little attention the courts pay to the Fourth Amendment's reasonableness requirement.

In other words, if the DEA wants to stick it to medical marijuana users because they're flouting federal law, they can. If Steven Seagal wants to drive a tank into a man's living room to demonstrate his love of animals, he can. If the Consumer Products Safety Commission (CPSC) wants to send a SWAT team to a physicist's house to show that it's cracking down on illegal bottle rockets, it can.[80] At worst, the DEA, the CPSC, and Steven Seagal will be chastised by a judge after the fact, though that seldom happens. Even on the rare occasions when someone actually gets into court and wins an excessive-force lawsuit stemming from a raid, the damages are usually borne by taxpayers, not by the cops who used excessive force. In some cases, community outrage and bad press have persuaded police agencies to change a policy here or there regarding the deployment of their SWAT teams. But if they want to reneg and go back to breaking down the doors of people suspected of stealing decorative fish, there's very little to stop them.[81]

⌇

TOWARD THE END OF THE 2000S, THERE WERE HINTS THAT the public was beginning to want a change, though that desire could manifest in unexpected ways. A former colleague at the Cato Institute, Tim Lynch, has told me that when he gives talks about the Waco raid, he finds that people are somewhat sympathetic to the argument that the government overreacted, but that they still can't get past the weirdness of the Branch Davidians themselves—their stockpile of weapons and the claims of sexual abuse and drug distribution in the community. Even the children who died are sometimes dismissed with guilt by association. But when he mentions that the ATF agents killed the Davidians' dogs, Lynch tells me, people become visibly angry. I have found the same thing to be true in my reporting on drug raids.

At first, that may seem to indicate that people callously value the lives of pets more than the lives of people. But the fact that killing the dog during these raids has become nearly routine in many police agencies demonstrates just how casually those agencies have come to accept drug war collateral damage. When I started logging cop-shoots-dog incidents on my blog (under the probably sensational term "puppycide"), people began sending me new stories as they happened. Cops are now shooting dogs at the slightest provocation. As of this writing, I'm sent accounts of a few incidents each week.

It's difficult to say if this is happening more frequently. There are no national figures, and estimates are all over the map. One dog handler recently hired to train a police department in Texas esti-mates there are up to 250,000 cop-shoots-dog cases each year. That seems high. In 2009 Randal Lockwood of the American Society for the Prevention of Cruelty to Animals (ASPCA) told the *Las Vegas Review-Journal* that he sees 250 to 300 incidents per year in media reports, and he estimates that another 1,000 aren't reported. The *Indianapolis Star* reported that between 2000 and 2002 police in that city shot 44 dogs. A recent lawsuit filed by the Milwaukee owner of a dog killed by cops found that police in that city killed 434 dogs over a nine-year period, or about one every seven and a half days. But those figures aren't all that helpful. They don't say how many of those dogs were actually vicious, how many were strays, or how many were injured and perhaps killed as an act of mercy versus how many were unjustified killings of pets.[82]

What is clear is that police are almost always cleared of any wrongdoing in these shootings. An officer's word that he felt a dog posed a threat to his safety is generally all it takes. Whether or not the officer's fear was legitimate doesn't seem to matter. Thanks to smart phones and surveillance cameras, a growing batch of these in-cidents have been caught on video have shown that officers' claims that the dog was threatening often aren't matched by the dog's body language. In recent years, police officers have shot and killed chihuahuas, golden retrievers, labs, miniature dachshunds, Wheaton terriers, and Jack Russell terriers. In 2012 a California police officer shot and killed a boxer puppy and pregnant chihuahua, claiming the boxer had threatened him. The chihuahua, he said, got caught in the crossfire. Police officers have also recently shot dogs that were chained, tied, or leashed, going so far as to kill pets while merely questioning neighbors about a crime in the area, cutting across private property while in pursuit of a suspect, and after responding to false burglar alarms.

It's possible that these incidents could just be attributed to rogue cops. But the fact that the police are nearly always excused in these cases—even in the more ridiculous examples—suggests there may be an institutional problem. So does the fact that only a handful of police departments give their cops any training at all when it comes to reading and handling the dogs they may encounter. In a 2012 article for the *Huffington Post*, my intern J. L. Greene and I looked at twenty-four recent cases of "puppycide" and called the relevant police departments to inquire about training. Only one department could confirm that its officers received training at the time of the incident in question. (Eleven departments did not return our phone calls.) That jibes with an earlier article I wrote for *The Daily Beast* in which both the ASPCA and the Humane Society told me that they offer such training to any police department that wants it, while few take advantage of the offer. Joseph Pentangelo, the ASPCA's assistant director for law enforcement, who also served twenty-one years with the NYPD, told me, "New York is the only state I know of that mandates formalized training, and that's during academy. There are some individual departments in other parts of the country that avail themselves of our training, but not many. Not enough."[83]

Given how likely it is that police officers will often interact with animals, you would think that such training would be common. It is at the US Postal Service. A spokesman for the USPS told me that while dog bites do happen on occasion, serious dog attacks on mail carriers are almost nonexistent. Postal workers are given regular training in distracting dogs with toys, subduing them with voice commands, or, at worst, incapacitating them with Mace. Mail carriers are shown a two-hour video and then given annual instruction on topics like recognizing and reading a dog's body language and differentiating between aggressive charging and playful bounding, and between a truly dangerous dog and a merely territorial one.

The fact that the Postal Service offers such training and most police departments don't lends some credence to the theory that dog shootings are part of the larger problem of a battlefield mentality that lets police use lethal force in response to the slightest threat—usually with few consequences. "It's an evolving phenomenon," says Norm Stamper, the former Seattle police chief. "It started when drug dealers began to recruit pit bulls to guard their supply. These dogs weren't meant to attack cops. They were meant to attack other drug dealers who came to rob them. But of course they did attack cops. And yes, that's awfully scary if one of those things latches on to your leg."

But Stamper says that like many aspects of modern policing, dog shootings may have had a legitimate origin, but the practice has since become a symptom of the mind-set behind a militarized police culture. "Among other things, it really shows a lack of imagination. These guys think that the only solution to a dog that's yapping or charging is shooting and killing it. That's all they know. It goes with this notion that police officers have to control every situation, to control all the variables. That's an awesome responsibility, and if you take it on, you're caving to delusion. You no longer exercise discrimination or discretion. You have to control, and the way you control is with authority, power, and force. With a dog, the easiest way to take control is to simply kill it. I mean, especially if there are no consequences for doing so."[84]

A handful of police departments do now mandate dog training, including Nashville, Omaha, and Milwaukee. Police departments in Austin, Fort Worth, and Arlington, Texas, do too. All began offering training after public backlash over one or more cop-shoots-dog incidents.

"In my ten years in law enforcement on the street, I can't re-member one case where a police officer shot a dog," says Russ Jones, the former narcotics cop with the San Jose Police Department and the DEA. "I don't understand it at all. I guess somewhere along the line a cop shot a dog under questionable circumstances and got away with it. Word got out, and now it seems like some cops are just looking for reasons to take a shot at a dog. Maybe it just comes down to that—we can get away with it, therefore we do it."[85]

ON THE FRIDAY AFTERNOON BEFORE THE 2009 G-20 SUMMIT was to begin in Pittsburgh at the David L. Lawrence Convention Center, a reader in the city sent me a photo he'd snapped moments earlier. The photo was of a police officer standing in the middle of an intersection. He was wearing a military-green top, camouflage pants, and combat boots. He had a gun strapped to his thigh and looked to be carrying another one. The camouflage in particular seemed odd—as it does whenever it's worn by a police officer in an urban area. It was unclear why this cop would have wanted to hide, and even if he did, how camouflage would help him do so in the city. There seemed to be little purpose for it other than to mimic the military. In any case, it was a sign of what was to come.

This is how the country that gave the world the First Amend-ment now handles protest. There's a disquieting ease now with which authorities are willing to crush dissent—and at the very sorts of events where the right to dissent is the entire purpose of protect-ing free speech—that is, events where influential policymakers meet to make high-level decisions with far-reaching consequences. In fact, the more important the policymakers and the more consequential the decisions they'll be making, the more likely it is that police will use more force to keep protesters as far away as possible. As Norm Stamper said, this unfortunately was the lesson the country's law en-forcement agencies took from the 1999 WTO protests in Seattle.

A number of police departments from across the country had sent officers to Pittsburgh to help police the 2009 summit. Nearly all were dressed in similar paramilitary garb. In one widely circulated video from the summit, several police officers dressed entirely in camouflage emerged from an unmarked car, apprehended a young backpack-toting protester, stuffed him into the car, then drove off. It evoked the sort of "disappearance" you might envision happening in a Latin American country headed by a junta, or one of the countries of the Soviet bloc. Matt Drudge linked to the video with a headline describing the officers in it as members of the military. They weren't, though it's certainly easy to understand how someone might make that mistake.

Another video showed a police unit with a handcuffed protester. Officers surrounded the protester, propped him up, then posed with him while another officer snapped a trophy photo. (YouTube later removed the video, citing a terms of use violation.) It was later revealed that the police unit was from Chicago. They had taken vacation time to come to Pittsburgh to provide "freelance security" for the G-20 summit.[86]

As the summit went on, Twitter feeds and uploaded photos and videos claimed (and sometimes provided some evidence to prove) that police fired tear-gas canisters into dorm rooms, used sound cannons, and fired bean bags and rubber bullets. One man was arrested for posting the locations of riot police to his Twitter feed. The charges were later dropped.

Emily Tanner, a grad student at the University of Pittsburgh who described herself as a "capitalist" who didn't agree with the general philosophy of the antiglobalization protesters, covered the summit, the protests, and the fallout on her blog. The most egregious police actions seemed to take place on the Friday evening before the summit, around the university, when police began ordering students who were in public spaces to disperse, despite the fact that they had broken no laws. Students who moved too slowly were arrested, as were students who were standing in front of the dormitories where they lived.

A University of Pittsburgh spokesman later said that the tactic was to break up crowds that "had the potential of disrupting normal activities, traffic flow, egress and the like. . . . Much of the arrests last night had to do with failure to disperse when ordered." Note that no one needed to have broken any actual laws to get arrested. The *potential* to break a law was more than enough. That standard was essentially a license for the police to arrest anyone, anywhere in the city, at any time, for any reason.

Pennsylvania ACLU legal director Vic Walczak said the problem was that police didn't bother to attempt to manage the protests. They simply suppressed them. In the process, they rounded up not only innocent protesters but innocent students who had nothing to do with the protests at all. In all, 190 people were arrested. One of the arrestees was a reporter from the left-leaning organization Indy-Media. When they apprehended her, the police took her camera. When they returned her camera, it was broken, and the police had deleted her photos and videos of the protests and police reaction. The police presence "seemed to focus almost exclusively on peaceful demonstrators," Walczak said. "On [Friday] night they didn't even have the excuse of property damage going on or any illegal activity. It's really inexplicable."[87]

Inexcusable perhaps, but not inexplicable. Since Seattle, this had become the template. At the 2008 Republican National Convention in Minneapolis, police conducted *peremptory* raids on the homes of protesters before the convention had even started. Police broke into the homes of people known to be activist rabble-rousers before they had any evidence of any actual crime. Journalists who inquired about the legitimacy of the raids and arrests made during the convention were also arrested. In all, 672 people were put in handcuffs. The arrest of *Democracy Now* journalist Amy Goodman was captured on a widely viewed video. She was charged with "conspiracy to riot." That charge against Goodman was later dropped. So were the charges against most of the others arrested. The *Minneapolis Star-Tribune* reported the following February that charges were dropped or dismissed for 442 of the 672 people arrested.[88]

There were similar problems at the 2008 Democratic National Convention. Police in Denver showed up for the protests decked out in full riot gear. One particularly striking photo from Denver showed a sea of cops in shiny black armor, batons in hand, surrounding a small, vastly outnumbered group of protesters. The most volatile night of the convention featured one incident in which Jefferson County, Colorado, deputies unknowingly clashed with and then pepper-sprayed undercover Denver cops *posing as violent protesters*. The city later paid out $200,000 to settle a lawsuit alleging that a Denver SWAT team was making indiscriminate arrests, rounding up protesters and bystanders alike.[89]

Perhaps the best insight into the mentality the police brought to the DNC protests could be found on the T-shirts the Denver police union had printed up for the event. The shirts showed a menacing cop holding a baton. The caption: DNC 2008: WE GET UP EARLY, TO BEAT THE CROWDS. Police were spotted wearing similar shirts at the 2012 NATO summit in Chicago.[90] At the 1996 DNC convention in Chicago, cops were seen wearing shirts that read: WE KICKED YOUR FATHER'S ASS IN 1968 . . . WAIT 'TIL YOU SEE WHAT WE DO TO YOU!

This default militaristic response to protest of overkill was then given an extended national stage during the Occupy protests of 2011. In the most infamous incident, now forever captured in countless Internet memes and mashups, Lt. John Pike of the University of California–Davis campus police casually hosed down a peaceful group of protesters with a pepper-spray canister. But that was far from the only incident. Police across the country met protesters in riot gear, once again anticipating—and in too many instances seemingly even craving—confrontation. In Oakland, the skull of Iraq War veteran Scott Olsen was fractured by a tear-gas canister that the police had fired into the crowd.[91] In New York, NYPD officer Anthony Bologna pepper-sprayed a group of helpless protesters who had been penned in by police fencing.[92]

One thing the Occupy crackdowns did seem to do was focus renewed attention on police tactics and police militarization. Big-picture stories about the Pentagon buildup, Department of Homeland Security (DHS) funding for antiterror gear, and the proliferation of SWAT teams started streaming out of media outlets, giving the militarization issue the most coverage it had received since Kraska's studies came out in the late 1990s. Part of that was due to social media. The ubiquity of smart phones and the viral capacity of Twitter, Facebook, Tumblr, and blogs were already bringing unprecedented accountability to police misconduct and government oppression, be it a Baltimore cop screaming obscenities at a kid on a skateboard, a transit cop in Oakland shooting a man who lay handcuffed on his stomach, or government paramilitaries in Iran gunning down a young woman in cold blood during Arab Spring democracy protests. But the Occupiers, who tended to be young, white, and middle- to upper-middle-class, knew social media like few other demographics. They knew how to live-stream video directly to the Internet. They *all* had smart phones, so police couldn't suppress incriminating video by confiscating one or two or ten phones—someone was bound to have video of not only the original incident but also of police trying to confiscate phones to cover it up.

The political reaction to the Occupy crackdowns was interesting to watch. In the 1990s, it had been the right wing—particularly the far right—that was up in arms over police militarization. Recall the outrage on the right over Waco, Ruby Ridge, and the raid to seize Elián González. The left had largely either remained silent or even defended the government's tactics in those cases. But the right-wing diatribes against jackbooted thugs and federal storm-troopers all died down once the Clinton administration left office, and they were virtually nonexistent after September 11, 2001. By the time cops started cracking heads at the Occupy protests, some conservatives were downright gleeful. The militarization of federal law enforcement certainly didn't stop, but the 9/11 attacks and a friendly administration seemed to quell the conservatives' concerns. So long as law enforcement was targeting hippie protesters, undocumented immigrants, suspected drug offenders, and alleged terrorist sympathizers, they were back to being heroes.

Steven Greenhut, a conservative-leaning columnist for the *Orange County Register* and editor of the investigative journalism site CalWatchdog, was dismayed by the right's reaction. "What's really disgusting is the natural instinct of so many conservatives to stick up for the police," Greenhut wrote. "They don't like the Occupy protesters, so they willingly back brutality against them, without considering the possibility that conservatives at some point might be on the receiving end of this aggression."[93]

Unfortunately, consistent voices like Greenhut's have been rare. Partisan reaction to aggressive police actions against opponents tends to fall somewhere between indifference and schadenfreude.

After the December 2012 shooting massacre in Newtown, Connecticut put the issue of gun control back into the political discourse, some progressives again dredged up the right's criticism of the ATF in the early 1990s. In one lengthy segment, MSNBC host Rachel Maddow aired old footage from Waco and Ruby Ridge while making some tenuous connections between gun rights politicians and activists and Weaver, McVeigh, and Koresh. She referred to a "conspiracy-driven corner of the gun world's paranoia about federal agents," without paying much heed to the fact that the ATF was inflicting the same sort of abuse on suspected gun offenders that Maddow herself has decried when used against suspected undocumented immigrants or Occupy protesters. More tellingly, Maddow added that there's nothing wrong with wanting to give more power to the ATF *based only on the politics of the people opposed to doing so.* "Sometimes the character of the opposition defines why something ought to be the most politically viable thing in the world," she said.

But even before Newtown, progressives have been advocating for the use of more government force against political factions they find unsavory. In 2009 the Department of Homeland Security issued a controversial report on what the author—DHS analyst Daryl Johnson—called a resurgence of right-wing extremism and the threat it posed to domestic security. The report was widely criticized on the right and was eventually criticized and revoked by DHS secretary Janet Napolitano. But after a spate of mass killings in the following years by assailants with political views that in some cases could loosely be characterized as right-wing, Johnson became something of a progressive hero. Most of the incidents involved clearly mentally ill attackers whose politics were all over the place. Even Johnson acknowledged that the incident most in line with his thesis—the massacre at a Sikh Temple in Oak Creek, Wisconsin, by a white supremacist named Wade Michael Page—was the work of a "lone wolf" attacker and likely would not have been prevented by the recommendations in his report.

Still, he was celebrated on the left. The progressive advocacy group Media Matters declared him "vindicated." Similar sentiment popped up on progressive outlets like ThinkProgress, Salon, Rachel Maddow's MSNBC blog, and *Democracy Now*.

In truth, attacks by groups on the fringes of the right wing have actually dropped in recent years, despite some claims that they've increased in response to the election of a black president. Attacks from groups on the fringes of the left wing are in decline too, as are alleged attempted terrorist attacks by fringe Muslim groups.[94]

In a 2012 interview with the *Idaho Spokesman Review*, Johnson showed why it may not have been such a great idea for progressives to embrace him simply because he wanted to shut down opinions they found distasteful. Johnson was interviewed for an article on the twentieth anniversary of the Ruby Ridge fiasco, and he took one step further Rachel Maddow's idea of supporting government force simply because you don't like the factions opposing it. Johnson in fact suggested that merely having concerns about police militarization is a worry only borne by extremists. In fact, he appeared to have suggested that even *recognizing that militarization is happening* is an indication of fringe extremism.

"For American extremists, the siege at Ruby Ridge symbolizes the 'militarized police state,'" said Johnson. The US government, through its Department of Homeland Security in particular, he said, "has unintentionally fostered, and even solidified, Orwellian conspiracies concerning an overzealous, oppressive federal government and its perceived willingness to kill to ensure citizen compliance. . . . In the minds of modern-day extremists, [Homeland Security] has enhanced the lethal capability of many underfunded, small-town po-lice forces through its grant programs." Using federal grants, state and local law enforcement agencies have been able to buy expensive equipment and training that are "commonly associated with the mil-itary," he said, adding that "extremists view such a security buildup as a continuation of the Ruby Ridge legacy." That legacy is a con-tinuing drumbeat for extremists and white supremacists who recruit with the message of "big government versus the little guy" and "the government set me up." These extremist ideas continue as messages and even recruiting themes among various radical groups in the United States, Johnson said.[95]

I attempted to contact Johnson to ask if he'd like to clarify his comments. He didn't return my calls. As they stand, these quotes are striking, particularly from someone who once worked for the Department of Homeland Security and now runs a consulting firm that works with law enforcement agencies. They certainly appear to dismiss police militarization—a phenomenon documented by a wide range of media outlets and criticized by interests all across the polit-ical spectrum—as merely a fantasy cooked up by extremists to boost their recruiting. Incidentally, the publications and advocacy groups who have recently expressed concerns about police militarization in-clude ThinkProgress, *Wired, Salon,* MSNBC, and *Democracy Now*— all of them also ran articles praising Johnson.

So long as partisans are only willing to speak out against aggres-sive, militarized police tactics when they're used against their own and are dismissive or even supportive of such tactics when used against those whose politics they dislike, it seems unlikely that the country will achieve enough of a political consensus to begin to slow down the trend.

JUST AS WITH BILL CLINTON, THERE WAS HOPE AMONG progressives that Barack Obama would take a more conciliatory, less militaristic approach to the drug war. And just as with Bill Clinton, Obama has come up short. According to a tally by Current TV, by the end of his first term, Obama had overseen more federal raids on medical marijuana dispensaries in four years than George W. Bush had presided over in eight. Obama also stepped up immigration raids and continued the raids on doctors and pain clinics suspected of overprescribing opioids. He continued to encourage Mexico's policy (aided by US foreign aid and weapons) of fighting its drug war with the military, despite the horrifying carnage caused by that policy. And as previously discussed, Obama and Democratic leaders in Congress re-funded the Byrne grant and COPS programs that contributed to the rise in SWAT teams and multi-jurisdictional anti-drug and anti-gang task forces—and at record levels.

The 1033 program has also soared to new heights under Obama. In its October 2011 newsletter—which carries the revealing tagline "From Warfighter to Crimefighter"—the Law Enforcement Support Office (LESO), the agency that oversees the Pentagon giveaways, boasted that fiscal year 2011 was the most productive in its history—by a lot. "FY 11 has been a historic year for the program," wrote LESO program manager Craig Barrett. "We reutilized more than $500M, that is million with an M, worth of property in FY 11. This passes the previous mark by several hundred million dollars. . . . Half a billion dollars in reutilization was a monumental achievement in FY 11 but I believe we can exceed that in FY 12."[96]

The take in 2011 alone was equivalent to about 18 percent of the total value of the equipment the program had given away in its history. In fiscal year 2011, the program gave away eight hundred Humvees, a 700 percent increase over 2010. In Los Angeles County, the sheriff's department put four semi-trailers on standby so that as a new piece of desirable war gear became available, the department could be en route to pick it up before another police department could claim it. The investigative journalism site California Watch reported that by 2011 the department was taking in $3 to 4 million worth of military gear annually, including "M16 rifles, helicopters, microwaves, survival kits, workout equipment, bayonet knives, [and] ammunition cans." During the record year for 1033 in the state as a whole, California police agencies raked in over 163,000 total items in

2011 worth over $26 million, "from bath mats acquired by the sheriff of Sonoma County to a full-tracked tank for rural San Joaquin County." Police in San Joaquin County had already purchased a $500,000 armored "mobile command center" with a DHS grant. California Watch reported that in "Rio Dell—a small Humboldt County town with just four full-time officers, not including the chief—the police department has used the program to pick up two vehicles [and] two M-16 rifles."[97]

In Richland County, South Carolina, Sheriff Leon Lott was so pleased with his new acquisition that he posed with it, along with his SWAT team, and then put out a press release. He called it "The Peacemaker," explaining in his release that "the Bible refers to law enforcement in Matthew 5:9, 'Blessed are the peacemakers: for they shall be called the children of God.'" The "Peacemaker" is an M113A1 armored personnel carrier. The vehicle moves on tanklike tracks and features a belt-fed, turreted machine gun that fires .50-caliber rounds. Richland County includes the city of Columbia and its northern suburbs. It's also home to the University of South Carolina. What it *isn't* is a battlefield.

According to Charles Earl Barnett, a US Marine veteran and retired police major who has served on several United Nations and NATO military and peacekeeping missions, a .50-caliber machine gun is "completely inappropriate" for domestic police work. It "causes mass death and destruction," Barnett told me in 2008. "It's indiscriminate. I can't think of a possible scenario where it would be appropriate."[98]

But Richland County isn't the only jurisdiction that can fire off rounds of that size. Sheriff Joe Arpaio in Maricopa County, Arizona, also has a gun that shoots .50-caliber ammunition. So does Chattanooga, Tennessee; Anne Arundel County, Maryland; and Cuyahoga County, Ohio. In Bossier Parish, Louisiana, the .50-caliber gun is mounted to an armored vehicle that the sheriff calls his "war wagon." At least after the sheriff's department in Faulkner County, Arkansas, used nearly $12,000 in asset forfeiture funds to purchase a .50-caliber gun, they had the good sense to decide they shouldn't use it. "It shoots through buildings," Sheriff Karl Byrd told a local newspaper. "There is absolutely no legitimate law enforcement use of this rifle."[99]

There have been at least a few other voices of sanity. In Massachusetts, Gov. Deval Patrick ordered the state's police agencies to stop using the program pending an investigation, after a *Boston Globe* report found—well, basically what similar investigations all over the country had found. From the *Globe:*

> Police in Wellfleet, a community known for stunning beaches and succulent oysters, scored three military assault rifles. At Salem State College, where recent police calls have included false fire alarms and a goat roaming the campus, school police got two M-16s. In West Springfield, police acquired even more powerful weaponry: two military-issue M-79 grenade launchers.[100]

In June 2012, the Pentagon suspended the entire 1033 program—not because of any concern about the militarization of civilian policing, but because of recent press reports of mismanagement by some of the participating law enforcement agencies. An *Arizona Republic* investigation had found that the Pinal County sheriff's department transferred some of the Pentagon equipment to nonpolice agencies, and was planning to sell some other equipment at auction. A broader AP report found that police departments had kept poor records about their use of the equipment obtained through the program, including high-powered weapons that could no longer be accounted for. As of November 2012, however, the program was back up and running.

Finally, the Obama administration has continued to defend in court the use of military-like violence to enforce the drug laws. In *Avina v. US*, DEA agents pointed their guns at an eleven-year-old and a fourteen-year-old during a mistaken drug raid. The agents had apparently misidentified the license plate of a suspected drug trafficker for the plate on a car owned by Thomas Avina, the father of the children. The Obama administration argued in federal court that the lawsuit should be dismissed before even being heard by a jury—that the agents' actions were reasonable under the Fourth Amendment.

Of course, it's not at all unusual for an administration to defend the actions of federal drug agents. But this was an administration whose drug czar had suggested that perhaps it was time to tone down the battle rhetoric that government officials often used when enforcing the drug laws. He was right about that. But on the front lines, the administration was arguing in court that there's nothing unreasonable about government agents pointing guns at the heads of children whose parents are suspected of drug crimes—and that even when said gun-pointing is done in the service of a mistaken raid, the agents should be shielded from any liability.[101]

⌇

"THERE'S ALWAYS A GOOD TIME TO USE A TASER."

So said Andrea, an attractive single mom and one of the four stars of the TLC reality show *The Police Women of Broward County*, which debuted in 2009. In the trailer that included the Taser quip, the video then cut to the show's stars tackling suspects, slamming knees into kidneys, pointing guns, and generally kicking ass. Judging from other clips on the TLC website, some of which featured shots of the female officers in bikinis, it seemed that the network couldn't make up its mind whether these women were sexpots with handcuffs or girl cops who were just as rough and tough as the boys. A poster ad campaign for the show only reinforced the identity crisis. One read: "Taser Time." Another: "Cavity Search, Anyone?"

Pop culture has always had a big influence on police culture, sometimes reflecting prevailing sentiment and sometimes driving it. In his chronicle of the 1970s *How We Got Here*, conservative pundit David Frum argues that the decade's parade of renegade cops who skirt the law but still abide by a familiar moral code (think Dirty Harry) reflected the prevailing opinion at the time that bad court decisions and criminal-coddling procedures were preventing well-meaning cops from getting the bad guys.[102] Ed Burns, the former narcotics cop and co-creator of HBO's *The Wire*, thinks the influence might have been the other way around. In a 2008 interview, Burns said that the Gene Hackman movie *The French Connection* had a big influence on the culture of drug cops. "In *The French Connection*, [detective] Popeye Doyle had this very cynical, harsh, rough, law-breaking type of drug style that sort of set the tone in how street narcotics guys work. Very flippant. What the movie didn't pick up, and what you didn't see, is all the intense surveillance and hard work that would go into a drug bust back then. But they put out the idea of this guy who cracks heads, especially in that scene they went and they shook the bar down. That became iconic. And that is the way the cops were afterward. I mean, you'd see white cops in black neighborhoods looking like Serpico, and they're not undercover. It was just this mind-set that took over of how you're supposed to dress and act and the way you're supposed to be."[103]

*The French Connection*, it's worth noting, came out in 1971. The series of botched ODALE raids in Collinsville and elsewhere began in 1973.

In the 1980s, the TV show *Miami Vice* nurtured the belief that south Florida was teeming with drug lords armed with more guns than most Third World armies, while *Hill Street Blues* offered the grittiest, most realistic portrayal of a big city police department yet aired on television. The show cast most of its cops in a sympathetic light, but, also took on issues like racism, corruption, and brutality.

For the better part of a generation, the Fox hit *Cops* was the only reality police show on TV. For twenty years, America watched as patient patrol officers broke up domestic disputes, arrested sunburned wife beaters, and chased petty drug offenders down darkened allies. Though the departments depicted in the show always had veto power over the footage that made it on the air, *Cops* generally did well to depict the monotonies of police work, be it walking a beat, calmly talking down a jealous husband, or driving a long, all-night neighborhood patrol in a squad car.

It was really the expansion of cable TV in the 1990s and 2000s that blew out the cop reality genre with shows that tended to emphasize confrontation and celebrate a culture of police militarism. A&E broke in first with *Dallas SWAT,* which sent a camera crew with the city's elite paramilitary police unit to document drug raids and standoffs. The show's success spawned *Detroit SWAT* and *Kansas City SWAT*. Court TV then jumped in with *Texas SWAT* and *SWAT U.S.A.*

Testosterone-infused Spike TV joined the mix in 2008 with *DEA*. Produced by jolly weatherman–cum–drug warrior Al Roker, the first season followed a group of federal agents, also in Detroit (the city's crumbling badlands provide great backdrop for reality shows), as they planned and carried out drug raids. (It also produced an unintentionally hilarious moment when self-proclaimed pot smoker and legalization advocate Joe Rogan was forced to conduct a reverent, promotional interview with one of the show's drug-agent stars while hosting one of Spike's mixed martial arts events.)

The obvious criticism of such shows is their exploitation and general tackiness. Not that anyone expects much dignity from most of the cable networks, but you'd think, for example, that the Broward County Sheriff's Department might object to the sexualization of its female officers, or to a national ad campaign insinuating that they're sporting itchy Taser fingers.

But these shows may have a more sinister effect. In emphasizing the more aggressive, confrontational aspect of police work over community service—hurting people instead of helping people—they may be shifting the profile of the typical young person attracted to police work. Browse the dozens of police recruitment videos on YouTube, for example, and you'll find that many of them feature images of cops tackling suspects, rappelling out of helicopters, shooting guns, kicking down doors, and siccing dogs on people. The images are often set to blaring guitars or heavy metal music. These are the videos that police departments send to high schools and colleges to attract new recruits. At the very first step in the process of staffing their departments, then, these agencies are deliberately appealing to people who are likely to be lured by the thrill-seeking, adrenaline-producing, butt-kicking aspects of law enforcement. Build an entire police force of people who fit that description and you have a force of cops who seek confrontation instead of avoiding it and who look to escalate volatile situations instead of resolving them peacefully. These are the sort of cops who volunteer for the SWAT team for the very reasons they should be excluded from it—cops like the two Maricopa County SWAT officers who talked to CBS News reporter Jim Stewart in 1997. The best part of being on the SWAT team, one of the officers said, was that "you get to play with a lot of guns. That's what's fun. You know, everybody on this team is—you know, loves guns." The second cop then chimed in. "Hey, the bottom line is it's friggin' fun, man. That's the deal. Nobody wants to take burglary reports."[104]

Even the wrong-door raid has become well established in pop culture. The first depiction of one I could find on network television was in a 1990 episode of the NBC drama *LA Law*. But it's become more common in the last decade or so. In one episode of *The Simpsons*, Chief Wiggum mistakenly raids the home of Reverend Lovejoy in search of a cattle rustler. The shot then pans down the street to show loose cattle grazing in the front yard of Springfield's well-known career criminal. One particularly pointed skit on Comedy Central's *Chapelle's Show* depicted the discrepancy between police raids on white people suspected of white-collar crimes and black people suspected of drug crimes. In the skit, a white CEO is subjected to a drug raid in which the cops set off a flash grenade, shoot the man's dog, sexually assault his wife, and beat him as they yell at him to "stop resisting." Coming full circle, in 2009 a viral video posing as an ad for a search engine parodied the SWAT reality shows by following "Fresno SWAT" as they mistakenly raid a day care center, a family eating dinner, and an elderly couple. It ends with the statement: "Imagine if dispatch gave out as much bad information as search engines do."

And so here we are. The wrong-door raid has now been normalized to the point where it can be parodied in a viral Internet commercial for a search engine.

## The Numbers

○ Number of drug raids in New York City in 1994: 1,447
  . . . in 1997: 2,977

. . . in 2002: 5,117

o Approximate number of raids each year by the Toledo, Ohio, SWAT team, as of 2008: 400

o Percentage of towns between 25,000 and 50,000 people with a SWAT team in 1984: 25.6 percent

. . . in 1990: 52.1 percent

. . . in 2005: 80 percent

o Approximate number of SWAT raids in the United States in 1995: 30,000

. . . in 2001: 45,000

. . . in 2005: 50,000–60,000

o Total number of federal agencies employing law enforcement personnel in 1996: 53

. . . in 2008: 73

o Total number of federal law enforcement officers as of 1996: 74,500 (28 per 100,000 citizens)

. . . in 2008: 120,000 (40 per 100,000 citizens)

o Number of SWAT teams in the FBI alone in 2013: 56

o Unlikely federal agencies with SWAT teams: US Fish and Wildlife Service, Consumer Product Safety Commission, National Aeronautics and Space Administration, Department of Education, Department of Health and Human Services, US National Park Service, Food and Drug Administration

o Value of surplus military gear received by Johnston, Rhode Island, from the Pentagon in 2010–2011: $4.1 million

o Population of Johnston, Rhode Island, in 2010: 28,769

o Partial list of equipment given to the Johnston police department: 30 M-16 rifles, 599 M-16 magazines containing about 18,000 rounds, a "sniper targeting calculator," 44 bayonets, 12 Humvees, and 23 snow blowers[105]

# CHAPTER 9

# REFORM

There is no crueler tyranny than that which is perpetu-
ated under the shield of law and in the name of justice.
—CHARLES DE MONTESQUIEU

Cheye Calvo only intended to be home long enough to grab a
bite to eat and walk his dogs.[1] Calvo worked full-time at an ed-
ucational foundation in Washington, DC, but he also had an unusual
part-time job: he was mayor of the small town of Berwyn Heights,
Maryland. In 2004, at age thirty-three, he was the youngest elected
mayor in the history of Prince George's County, Maryland. Now
thirty-seven, he lived with his wife, Trinity Tomsic, her mother, Georgia Porter, and their two black labradors, Payton and Chase. Calvo
was due back in town later that night for a community meeting.

As Calvo took the dogs out for a walk the evening of July 29,
2008, his mother-in-law told him that a package had been delivered
a few minutes earlier. He figured it was something he had ordered
for his garden. "On the walk, I noticed a few black SUVs in the
neighborhood, but thought little of it except to wave to the drivers," he would later recall. When Calvo and the dogs returned, he

picked up the package, brought it inside, then went upstairs to change for his meeting.

The next thing Calvo remembers is the sound of his mother-in-law screaming. He ran to the window and saw heavily armed men clad in black rushing his front door. Next came the explosion. He'd later learn that this was when the police blew open his front door. Then there was gunfire. Then boots stomping the floor. Then more gunfire. Calvo, still in his boxers, screamed, "I'm upstairs, please don't shoot!" He was instructed to walk downstairs with his hands in the air, the muzzles of two guns pointed directly at him. He still didn't know it was the police. He described what happened next at a Cato Institute forum six weeks later. "At the bottom of the stairs, they bound my hands, pulled me across the living room, and forced me to kneel on the floor in front of my broken door. I thought it was a home invasion. I was fearful that I was about to be executed." I later asked Calvo what might have happened if he'd had a gun in his home for self-defense. His answer: "I'd be dead." In another interview, he would add, "The worst thing I could have done was defend my home."

Calvo's mother-in-law was face-down on the kitchen floor, the tomato-artichoke sauce she was preparing still sitting on the stove. Her first scream came when one of the SWAT officers pointed his gun at her from the other side of the window. The police department would later argue that her scream gave them the authority to enter the home without knocking, announcing themselves, and waiting for someone to let them in.

Rather than obeying the SWAT team demands to "get down" as they rushed in, Georgia Porter simply froze with fear. They pried the spoon from her hand, put a gun to her head, and shoved her to the floor. They asked, "Where are they? *Where are they?*" She had no idea what they were talking about. She told them to look in the basement. She would later tell the *Washington Post,* "If somebody puts a gun to your head and asks you a question, you better come up with an answer. Then I shut my eyes. Oh, God, I thought they were going to shoot me next."

Calvo's dogs Payton and Chase were dead by the time Calvo was escorted to the kitchen. Payton had been shot in the face almost as soon as the police entered the home. One bullet went all the way through him and lodged in a radiator, missing Porter by only a couple of feet. Chase ran. The cops shot him once, from the back, then chased him into the living room and shot him again.

Calvo was turned around and put on his knees in front of the door the police had just smashed to pieces. He heard them rummaging through his house, tossing drawers, emptying cabinets.

Calvo and Porter were held for four hours. Calvo asked to see a search warrant. He was told it was "en route." The police continued to search the house. At one point, a detective got excited when she found an envelope stuffed with cash. According to Porter, the detective was deflated when she found only $68 inside and noticed that the front of the envelope read: "Yard Sale." At one point, Porter overheard a detective call to ask a relative to schedule a veterinary appointment. The sight of the dogs' bodies apparently reminded her that she need to make an appointment for her own pet.

Even after they realized they had just mistakenly raided the mayor's house, the officers didn't apologize to Calvo or Porter. Instead, they told Calvo that they were both "parties of interest" and that they should consider themselves lucky they weren't arrested. Calvo in particular, they said, was still under suspicion because when armed men blew open his door, killed his dogs, and pointed their guns at him and his-mother-in-law, he hadn't responded "in a typical manner."

Trinity Tomsic came home about an hour later to find a blur of flashing police lights and a crowd gathering on her front lawn. She was told that her husband and mother were fine. Then she was told that her dogs were dead. She broke down in tears. When she was finally able to enter her home, she found her dogs' blood all over her house. The police had walked through the two large pools of blood that collected under Payton and Chase, then tracked it all over the home. Even once the police realized they had made a mistake, they never offered to clean up the blood, to put the house back together, or to fix the front door.

As Calvo and Porter were being interrogated, one of Calvo's own police officers saw the lights and stopped to see what was going on. Berwyn Heights officer Amir Johnson knew this was his mayor's house, but had no idea what the commotion was about because the Prince George's County Police Department hadn't bothered to contact the Berwyn Heights police chief, as they were required to do under a memorandum of understanding between the two agencies. Johnson told the *Washington Post* that an officer at the scene told him, "The guy in there is crazy. He says he is the mayor of Berwyn Heights."

Johnson replied, "That *is* the mayor of Berwyn Heights."

Johnson then called Berwyn Heights police chief Patrick Murphy. Eventually, Murphy was put in touch with the supervising officer, Det. Sgt. David Martini. Murphy recounted the conversation to the *Post:* "Martini tells me that when the SWAT team came to the door, the mayor met them at the door, opened it partially, saw who it was, and then tried to slam the door on them," Murphy recalled. "And that at that point, Martini claimed, they had to force entry, the dogs took aggressive stances, and they were shot."

If that indeed was what Martini told Murphy, he was either lying or repeating a lie told to him by one of his subordinates. There was never any further mention of Calvo shutting the door on the SWAT team—because it never happened. Calvo later had his dogs autopsied—the trajectories the bullets took through the dogs' bodies weren't consistent with the SWAT team's story.

But the lies, obfuscations, and stonewalling were only beginning.

The police department would first claim that they had obtained a no-knock warrant for the raid. They then backtracked and blamed Calvo's mother-in-law, arguing that when her scream blew their cover, they were no longer obligated to knock and announce themselves. (This was an interesting theory, given that the knock-and-announce requirement, by definition, would have required them to blow their own cover. That's the point of the requirement.) Maj. Mark Magaw, commander of the Prince George's County narcotics enforcement division, claimed that the SWAT team couldn't have obtained a no-knock warrant if they had wanted to, because the state of Maryland doesn't allow them. This too was false. The state had passed a bill allowing for no-knock warrants in 2005.[2] It's the sort of law that one would think would have a day-to-day impact on the drug unit of a police department that conducts several raids each week. Yet the head narcotics unit in Prince George's County was completely ignorant of it.[3] Three years later, Magaw would be promoted to Prince George's County police chief.[4]

The affidavit for the search warrant was prepared by Det. Shawn Scarlata. It is incredibly thin. In a few paragraphs, Scarlata relates that he intercepted a FedEx package containing thirty-two pounds of marijuana at one of the company's warehouses. The package was addressed to Trinity Tomsic at her home address. A police officer disguised as a delivery man then took the package to Calvo's house, where it was accepted by Georgia Porter. There was also a one-paragraph description of Calvo's home. That's the only information in the warrant specific to Calvo and his family. The remainder of the six-page affidavit is a cut-and-paste recitation of Scarlata's training, qualifications, and assumptions he felt he could make based on his experience as a narcotics officer. As Calvo described the warrant in an online chat, "It talks about all the stuff a drug trafficker should have in his or her home and then says something like, 'Although we know that the police have no evidence of these things, they can be *inferred* from the very nature of the charge.' It is circular reasoning that says because we are suspicious of you, there must be evidence of your guilt."

On August 7, police arrested a FedEx driver and an accomplice and charged them with various crimes related to drug trafficking. Trinity Tomsic was never supposed to receive that package of marijuana. A drug distributor in Arizona had used her address to get the package into the general Prince George's County area, at which point an accomplice working for the delivery company was supposed to intercept it. The police had found several similar packages. Worse, county police *knew* the scheme was going on and knew some packages had been delivered to residences unbeknownst to the people who lived in them. The *Washington Post* reported a couple of months later on cases in which innocent people had been arrested. "Defense lawyers who practice in the county said authorities appear to arrest and charge anyone who picks up a package containing marijuana without conducting a further investigation,"[5] the *Post* reported. "The more I think about that, the angrier I get," Calvo later told *Post* columnist Marc Fisher. "They knew this scheme was going on, yet it never occurred to them from the moment they found out about that package that we were anything but drug dealers."[6] Prince George's County police chief Melvin High still couldn't bring himself to rule out the Calvos as suspects, telling the *Washington Post*, "From all the indications at the moment, they had an unlikely involvement, but we don't want to draw that definite conclusion at the moment."[7]

Two days later, after the raid had made national and international news, the Prince George's County Police Department finally cleared Cheye Calvo and his family of any wrongdoing. They did it by way of a press release they put out at 4:30 PM on a Friday, the time and day of the week when bad news is typically buried. It also happened to be the night of the opening ceremonies for the 2008 Summer Olympics in Beijing.[8]

Perhaps even more baffling, officials continued to insist that the raid *shouldn't* have happened any other way. Even as they acknowledged that Calvo and his family were innocent, in the months and years following the raid they would repeat again and again that not a single officer did anything wrong, and that no one had any reason for remorse. In 2010 Sheriff Michael Jackson was asked during his campaign for Prince George's County executive if he had any regrets about the raid. His response: "Quite frankly, we'd do it again. Tonight." Even when Chief High called Calvo to tell him that he had been cleared of any criminal suspicion, High made sure to explicitly tell the mayor that the call should not be interpreted as an apology. The statements from county officials over the next several months were also astonishingly callous. A day after he called Calvo, High told the press that the raiding cops showed "restraint and compassion" and insisted that they should be *credited* for not arresting Calvo or members of his family. (The only incriminating evidence found in the home was the unopened box of marijuana that the deputies themselves had delivered.)[9] Months later, Prince George's County executive Jack Johnson said something even more preposterous. He insisted that once Prince George's County police agencies had cleared themselves, that was the only apology necessary—and in fact that they deserved praise for clearing Calvo's name after nearly killing him. "Well, I think in America that is the apology, when we're cleared," Johnson said. "At the end of the day, the investigation showed [Calvo] was not involved. And that's, you know, a pat on the back for everybody involved, I think."[10] On September 8, about five weeks after the raid, Sheriff Jackson's office announced that his internal investigation had cleared his deputies of any wrongdoing. Everything was done according to procedure. Or, as Jackson put it, "the guys did what they were supposed to do."[11] Nine months later, Jackson's office would conclude another investigation, again clearing his deputies. Neither outcome was surprising, given that Jackson had been defending his deputies since the night of the raid. It's probably also worth noting that the father of Det. Shawn Scarlata—the officer who initiated the investigation leading to the raid—was on the internal affairs team that conducted the investigations.

The officials in Prince George's County, two of them elected, openly and without reservation stated that they had no problem with the collateral damage done to the Calvo family. It was part of the war against getting high—which even they had to know is a war that can't be won. They didn't even really think it was something to regret or learn from, or to try to avoid in the future. As Calvo himself pointed out on several occasions, this isn't a problem that can be laid at the feet of the police officers who raided his home. This problem can't be fixed by firing the police involved. This is a political problem. It's a policy problem.

Calvo understood all of this almost immediately. Someone sent him a copy of *Overkill: The Rise of Paramilitary Police Raids in America*, the paper on police militarization I had written for the Cato Institute two years earlier. A policy wonk at heart, Calvo devoured the paper, reading it on his subway rides to and from work. Still traumatized from the raid, his wife didn't like the image on the cover—a close-up of a SWAT officer with his hand on a machine gun. Calvo then began reading up on the case law behind these raids. Within a few weeks, the charismatic, accessible small-town mayor had become a compelling advocate for reform. I moderated a forum about the raid at the Cato Institute in September 2008. As Calvo spoke about what he had gone through—and particularly about his dogs, and how angry he was that the police tried to blame the dogs for their own deaths—about a fourth of the audience was in tears. He told his story on CNN, the morning network talk shows, and the BBC. And to his credit, he recognized that what had specifically happened to him was part of a broader problem of policy, not of individual cops.

"The reality is that this happens all the time in this country, and disproportionately in Prince George's County," Calvo told CNN. "Most of the people to whom it happens don't have the community support and the platform to speak out. So I appreciate you paying attention to our condition, but I hope you'll also give attention to those who may not have the same platform and voice that we have."[12]

As Calvo continued to advocate for reform, he started to hear from other victims of mistaken police raids, both in Prince George's County and around the state of Maryland. Several included the routine, sometimes callous killing of the family dog. Within a week of the raid, for example, Prince George's County residents Frank and Pam Myers came forward to say that they too were raided by sheriff's department deputies. Indeed, that raid the previous November had been covered by some local media. When the couple told the deputies that the address on the warrant was two doors down, the police refused to leave. They continued to look around the couple's house for another forty-five minutes. Then two shots rang out from the backyard. A deputy had gone into the backyard and shot the couple's five-year-old boxer, Pearl. He claimed that he feared for his life. Pam Myers told a local news station, "I said, 'You just shot my dog.' I just wanted to go out and hold her a bit. They wouldn't even let me go out."[13]

Amber James, another Prince George's County resident, also came forward. Police raided her home in May 2007 looking for her sister, who didn't live in the house. According to James, when their search came up empty, they promised to return the next day—and to kill James's dog when they did.[14]

A series of police raid horror stories from Howard County, Maryland, also emerged. Kevin and Lisa Henderson said they were the victims of a mistaken raid in January 2008. At 10:00 PM the night of January 18, a raid team opened the family's unlocked front door. Inside were the couple, a twenty-eight-year-old houseguest, their two teenage sons, and their sons' friend. The police first met the family dog, a twelve-year-old lab/rottweiler mix named Grunt. According to the lawsuit, one officer distracted the dog while another shot it point-blank in the head. When one of the couple's sons asked why they had shot the dog, one officer pointed his gun at the boy's head and said, "I'll blow your fucking head off if you keep talking." The police found marijuana in a jacket pocket of the Hendersons' house guest. He was arrested. Four days later, after Lisa Henderson called to complain about the raid, she and her husband were also arrested for possession of marijuana, even though the police hadn't found any drug anywhere else in the house. Ten months later, a state judge acquitted the couple of all charges. The Hendersons believe that the police intended to raid a different house in the neighborhood that looked a lot like their own. A subsequent raid on that house turned up marijuana, scales, and cash.[15]

Karen Thomas, also a resident of Howard County, told a Maryland State Senate hearing in 2009 that police shot and killed her dog during a mistaken raid on her home in January 2007. Even after they had surrounded her in her bedroom, she said they still hadn't yet identified themselves, and she thought the gunshot had been directed at her son. "In my mind, terrorists had just killed my son, and they were going to kill me next." Boyd Petit told the same committee, "Our collective lives flashed before our eyes" during a mistaken raid on him and his family in April 2008.[16] Mike Hasenei, his wife, and their twelve-year-old daughter were subjected to a nighttime raid when police received a tip that Hasenei's stepson and a friend might have stolen items from a police car, including a rifle and ammunition. They also raided the home where the stepson actually lived, as well as the friend's home. They found none of the stolen items and made no arrests. Hasenei and his wife Phyllis told the *Baltimore Sun* that they were still reeling from the trauma. "They had their guns drawn, Angel and I were screaming," Phyllis Hasenei said. "They had their black-on-black uniforms. All you could see were their eyeballs." Hasenei added that had police done a bit more investigating, "they would have found out that neither of us are violent criminals, we don't have criminals records at all."[17]

Armed with these incidents, Calvo went to the Maryland legislature to push for reform. The bill he proposed was modest. It required every police agency in Maryland with a SWAT team to issue a quarterly report—later amended to twice yearly—on how many times the team was deployed, for what purpose, and whether any shots were fired during the raid. It was a simple transparency bill. It put no limits or restrictions on how often or under what circumstances SWAT teams could be used.

Yet it was the only bill of its kind in the country. And it was opposed by every police organization in the state. One Maryland lawmaker attempted to amend the bill to prohibit the use of SWAT teams in cases involving known misdemeanors, a seemingly reasonable restriction. That measure was rejected after more lobbying from police groups.

But the main bill passed the Maryland house in March 2009 by a vote of 126–9, and the state's senate in April by a vote of 46–0. It was signed into law by Gov. Martin O'Malley. Calvo sent the media a response to the legislation.

> Although the botched raid of my home and killing of our dogs, Payton and Chase, have received considerable attention in the media, it is important to underscore that this bill is about much more than an isolated, high-profile mistake. It is about a growing and troubling trend where law enforcement agencies are using SWAT teams to

perform ordinary police work. Prince George's County police acknowledges deploying SWAT teams between 400 and 700 a year—that's twice a day—and other counties in the state have said that they also deploy their special tactical units hundreds of times a year. The hearings on these bills have brought to light numerous botched and ill-advised raids in Anne Arundel, Baltimore, Carroll, Howard, Montgomery, and Prince George's counties that also have had devastating effects on the lives of innocent people and undermined faith in law enforcement. . . .

Although I applaud lawmakers for passing this bill over the objections of law enforcement, I was disappointed that state law enforcement groups decided to oppose this measure rather than embrace it as an opportunity to restore the public trust. I remain especially concerned with the argument put forward that only law enforcement should police itself and that it is somehow inappropriate for elected leaders to legislate oversight and accountability. I cannot disagree with this argument more. As elected officials, we must take full responsibility for the law enforcement departments that we fund and authorize, and we must hold our law enforcement officials to the highest standards and ideals.[18]

By the following spring, the Maryland Governor's Office of Crime Control and Prevention released the first batch of statistics. They were predictably unsettling. For the last half of 2009, SWAT teams were deployed 804 times in the state of Maryland, or about 4.5 times a day. In Prince George's County alone, which has about 850,000 residents, a SWAT team was deployed about once a day. According to an analysis by the *Baltimore Sun*, 94 percent of the state's SWAT deployments were to serve search or arrest warrants, leaving just 6 percent that were raids involving barricades, bank robberies, hostage takings, and other emergency situations. Half of Prince George's County's SWAT deployments were for what were called "misdemeanors and nonserious felonies." More than one hundred times over a six-month period, Prince George's County sent police barreling into private homes for nonserious, nonviolent crimes.[19] Calvo pointed out that the first set of figures confirm what he and others concerned about these tactics have suspected: SWAT teams are being deployed too often as the *default* way to serve search warrants, not as a last resort.

In January 2011, Calvo settled his lawsuit with Prince George's County. Although the details haven't been made public, we know that it involved a substantial sum of money as well as reforms to the way Prince George's County uses its SWAT teams, the types of cases in which the teams are deployed, and better training in dealing with the pets they encounter in raids, as well as treating them more humanely.[20]

⌒

HOW DO WE RETURN TO A MORE ROBUST EMBRACE OF THE Castle Doctrine, the Fourth Amendment, and an unbreachable divide between the police and the military? Overcoming a trend that has extended across two, possibly three, generations sounds like an impossibly difficult task. And indeed, some of the people interviewed for this book are skeptical that it can be done. Donald Santarelli, the now-regretful father of the no-knock raid, says, "I don't think it's possible to roll any of this back now. . . . It would take serious leadership, probably from nobody less than the president. It would take a huge scandal, which doesn't seem likely. . . . But we're not given to revolutionary action in this country. Each generation is a little more removed from the deep-seated concerns about liberty of the generation before. We just don't seem to value privacy and freedom anymore."[21]

Cheye Calvo's example shows that change is possible—even though much more of it is in order. Despite falling crime rates, and even after the public outrage and media scrutiny engendered by the Calvo raid and other high-profile incidents, the number of SWAT raids continues to rise.

Still, even if the will to bend the arc of police militarization doesn't currently exist, there are some policy reforms that would at least improve the current state of affairs. In particular, the concerned police officers and public officials interviewed for this book have suggested a number of possible reforms—some abstract, some concrete, some within reach, and some that at least at the moment seem unattainable.

## The Drug War

To begin at the *least likely* end of the spectrum, the best reform to scale back the overly militarized, dangerously civil liberties–averse style of policing that prevails in this country would be to end the drug war altogether. Complete legalization is, of course, never going to happen. But even something short of legalization, like decriminalization, would remove many of the reasons why we're fighting the drug war as if it were an actual war. President Obama's drug czar, Gil Kerlikowske, at least seemed to understand the value of rhetoric when he made a point in 2010 of stating that he didn't think it was appropriate to use the phrase "drug war." Unfortunately, he didn't change any of the actual tactics used to enforce the federal drug laws. As indicated earlier, the raids, grants, and giveaways of Pentagon gear have all only increased since Obama took office.

But just ending the federal drug war and the federal incentives toward militarization would help. SWAT teams would probably continue to exist and, at least in the short term, would find other, probably equally objectionable missions. But ending the federal drug war could begin to unwind the violent paramilitary task forces and the us-versus-them, black-and-white drug-war mentality. If the federal government were to end the Byrne grants, cut off federal funding tied to drug enforcement, end the Pentagon giveaway program, and get rid of the federal equitable sharing program that lets local police departments get around state asset forfeiture laws and makes drug warring more lucrative (and therefore a higher priority), we'd see more of these tactical teams begin to disband because of the expense of maintaining them. We'd almost certainly see the multi-jurisdictional task forces start to dry up, since they're often funded exclusively through federal grants and forfeiture. Those tactical teams that remained would no longer be incentivized to go on drug raids. Perhaps some still would. But without the money to lure them, it seems likely that the expense of deploying them would persuade police departments to reserve them for the sorts of missions for which they were originally intended.

At the very least, the federal government should respect the states that have already expressed a desire to ease up on the drug war and stop sending in heavily armed battle teams to raid medical marijuana dispensaries and growers who are licensed and regulated under state law.

Legislatures or city councils could also pass laws restricting the use of SWAT teams to those limited, rare emergencies in which there's an imminent threat to public safety. They could prohibit the use of no-knock raids or even forced entry to serve warrants on people suspected of violent crimes. Failing that, policymakers could simply put more restrictions on search warrants. For example, they could prohibit the use of dynamic-entry tactics for any warrant obtained with only the word of an informant. The records of informants should be made available to defense attorneys and attorneys in civil suits, with the stipulation that any identifying information be redacted. (Informants' records could simply be a set of numbers indicating their success rate.)

Ending any of the federal drug war policies that set all of this in motion would be a step in the right direction.

## Halt the Mission Creep

There is no need for regulatory agencies at any level to be conducting SWAT raids. The Department of Education and the Food and Drug Administration don't need their own SWAT teams. SWAT teams shouldn't be raiding American Legion halls to break up charity poker games. They shouldn't be raiding *any* poker games. Nor should they be used to confront Tibetan monks who have overstayed their visas, or sent to storm the offices of doctors suspected of overprescribing painkillers.[22] And the idea of SWAT teams enforcing underage drinking laws, performing occupational licensing inspections, or checking that beer bottles are adequately labeled ought to be so self-evidently preposterous as to be laughable.

That heavily armed assault forces are sent to perform such tasks ought to shock the conscience. The people making these kinds of decisions should lose their jobs. More broadly, the amount of force the government uses to enforce a given law should be based on a reasonable assessment of the threat posed by the person suspected of committing the crime, not by what sort of message the government wants to send about how seriously it takes whatever crime it happens to be enforcing.

## Transparency

Cheye Calvo's bill in Maryland is a good start toward greater transparency. Other states should duplicate it. But there are other policies that would make police departments more transparent and less isolated and detached from their communities. The remarkable advances in and democratization of smart-phone technology have enabled a large and growing portion of the population to record the actions of on-duty police officers. Rather than fighting it, police officials and policymakers ought to embrace this development. Legislatures should pass laws that not only clearly establish a citizen's right to record on-duty cops but provide an enforcement mechanism so that citizens wrongly and illegally arrested have a course of action. As even many police officials have pointed out, such policies not only expose police misconduct, leading to improvements, but can also provide exonerating evidence in cases where police officers have been wrongly accused.

All forced-entry police raids should be recorded in a tamper-proof format, and the videos should be made available to the public through a simple open records request. If the political will to do so existed, this could be done efficiently and inexpensively. Even better: equip the officers participating in a raid with cameras mounted on their helmets, jackets, or guns. Not only would recording all raids help clear up disputes about how long police waited after knocking, whether police knocked at all, or who fired first, but the knowledge that every raid would be recorded would also encourage best practices among the SWAT teams. Additionally, recordings of raids would provide an accurate portrayal of how drug laws are actually enforced. It's likely that many Americans aren't fully aware of just how violent these tactics can be. Perhaps many would still support tactical raids for drug warrants even after being exposed to videos of actual drug raids. But if the drug war is being waged to protect the public, the public should be able to see exactly how the war is being waged.

Police departments should track warrants from the time they're obtained to the time they're executed, in a database that's accessible to civilian review boards, defense attorneys, judges, and, in some cases, the media (acknowledging that the identities of confidential informants need not be revealed). Botched raids should be documented, including warrants served on the wrong address, warrants based on bad tips from informants, and/or warrants that resulted in the death or injury of an officer, a suspect, or a bystander. Police departments should also keep running tabs of how many warrants are executed with no-knock entry versus knock-and-announce entry, how many required a forced entry, how many required the deployment of a SWAT team or other paramilitary unit, and how many used diversionary devices like flash-bang grenades. They should also make records of what these raids turned up. If these tactics are going to be used against the public, the public at the very least deserves to know how often they're used, why they're used, how often things go wrong, and what sort of results the tactics are getting.

Local police departments that receive federal funding should also be required to keep records on and report incidents of officer shootings and use of excessive force to an independent federal agency such as the National Institute for Justice or the Office of the Inspector General.

We also need easy-to-find, publicly accessible records of judges and search warrants (and where applicable, prosecutors). The public deserves to know if all the narcotics cops in a given area are going to the same judge or magistrate with their narcotics warrants, or if a given judge hasn't declined a warrant in twenty years. As more and more courts use computer software to process warrants, it will get easier to compile this sort of information and make it available to the public.

## Community Policing

Police departments and policymakers should embrace real community policing. That doesn't mean sending off millions of dollars in federal grants that merely say "Community Policing" on the envelope. Nor does it mean calling the deployment of SWAT teams to clear out entire neighborhoods "community policing" because such actions involve both "police" and a "community." Instead, it means taking cops out of patrol cars to walk beats and become a part of the communities they serve. It means ditching statistics-driven policing, which encourages the sorts of petty arrests of low-level offenders and use of informants that foment anger and distrust.

"The emphasis on statistics in the war on drugs is really what encourages the Fourth Amendment cheating," says Stephen Downing, the former deputy chief at the LAPD. "Everyone wants to be successful at what they do. Police officers are no different. But we have this drug war. And in order to get the goods—the grants and such, which earn you good reviews and promotions—you have to meet your quotas. So you want to get in before the drugs are flushed down the toilet. So you lie about what goes on at the door. You take shortcuts to get your warrant before the drugs are moved. It's the bad policy that forces that to happen. The big shots will say to the public, 'We have all these rules and we enforce them. There are no quotas.' But then internally they'll say, 'Why do you only have two arrests this month?' It's a system that creates cheaters. The quota system just doesn't work without cheating."[23]

## Changing Police Culture

Changing a culture sounds like a tall order. And it probably is. "I think there are two critical components to policing that cops today have forgotten," says the former Maryland cop Neill Franklin. "Number one, you've signed on to a dangerous job. That means that you've agreed to a certain amount of risk. You don't get to start stepping on others' rights to minimize that risk you agreed to take on. And number two, your first priority is not to protect yourself, it's to protect those you've sworn to protect. But I don't know how you get police officers today to value those principles again. The 'us and everybody else' sentiment is strong today. It's very, very difficult to change a culture."[24]

But high-ranking police officials and the policymakers who oversee them could start by simply not perpetuating the problem. Consider those recruitment videos discussed previously. Think back to high school or college and consider who among your classmates would have been excited by that sort of video. Now think about who among your classmates would have been attracted to a video depicting cops walking a beat, attending meetings of neighborhood groups, or learning the skills necessary to deescalate a potentially dangerous situation instead of shooting the problem away. These are two very different personality types.

"It's really about a lack of imagination and a lack of creativity," says Norm Stamper. "When your answer to every problem is more force, it shows that you haven't been taught and trained to consider other options."[25]

The thing is, when law enforcement officials face suspects who present a genuine threat to officer safety, they *do* tend to be more creative. When the FBI finally located Whitey Bulger in 2010 after searching for him for sixteen years, the reputed mobster was suspected in nearly twenty murders and was thought to be armed with a huge arsenal of weapons. Of all the people who might meet the criteria for arrest by a SWAT team, you'd think Bulger would top the list. He was also aging, in poor physical health, and looking at spending the rest of his life in prison. If ever there was a candidate to go out in a blaze of cop-killing glory, it was Whitey Bulger. And yet instead of sending a tactical team in to tear down Bulger's door, the FBI did some investigating and learned that Bulger rented a public storage locker. They called him up, pretending to be from the company that owned the facility, and told Bulger someone might have broken into his locker. When he went to the facility to investigate, he was arrested without incident.

Why can't investigators handle common drug offenders the same way? A big reason is a lack of resources. If your department is serving several drug warrants a day, you just aren't going to have the personnel to come up with that sort of plan for each one. A second reason is that drug offenders simply aren't all that likely to shoot at cops, and it's easier to use violent tactics against people who aren't going to fire back. It's by no means a universal rule, but often when police do face a genuinely violent suspect like an escaped fugitive with a violent history, a suspect in a series of violent crimes, or a barricade or hostage situation, they *don't* immediately storm the place. They set up a perimeter or try to figure out other ways to make the arrest safely. This again isn't possible with drug warrants—there are just too many of them. But because drug dealers aren't all that dangerous, it works out to raid them instead.

Police today are also given too little training in counseling and dispute resolution, and what little training they do get in the academy is quickly blotted out by what they learn on the street in the first few months on the job. When you're given an excess of training in the use of force but little in using psychology, body language, and other noncoercive means of resolving a conflict, you'll naturally gravitate toward force. "I think about the notion of *command presence*," Stamper says. "When you as a police officer show up at a chaotic or threatening or dangerous situation, you need to demonstrate your command presence—that you are the person in command of this situation. You do this with your bearing, your body language, and your voice. What I see today is that this well-disciplined notion of command presence has been shattered. Cops today think you show command presence by yelling and screaming. In my day, if you screamed, if you went to a screaming, out-of-control presence, you had failed in that situation as a cop. You'd be pulled aside by a senior cop or sergeant and made to understand in no uncertain terms that you were out of line. The very best cops I ever worked around were quiet. Which isn't to say they were withdrawn or passive, but they were quiet. They understood the value of silence, the powerful effect of a pause."

Stamper adds that these things aren't emphasized anymore. "Verbal persuasion is the first tool a police officer has. The more effective he or she is as a communicator, the less likely it is he or she is going to get impulsive—or need to."[26]

Neill Franklin suggests that deteriorating physical fitness at police departments can also lead to unnecessary escalations of force—another argument in favor of foot patrols over car patrols. "When I was commander of training in Baltimore, one of the first things I did was evaluate the physical condition of the police officers themselves," Franklin says. "The overweight guys were the guys who knew very little about arrest control and defensive strategy. Being a police officer is a physically demanding job. You can't be so out of shape. When you are, you're less confident about less lethal force. It can get so that the only use of force you're capable of using is a firearm. You also fear physical confrontation, so you're more likely to reach for your firearm earlier. Getting cops in shape is a confidence builder, and it gets people away from relying too much on the weapons they have on their belt."[27]

More generally, politicians should also be held accountable when they use war rhetoric to discuss crime and illicit drugs. Words do have an impact on the way police officers approach their jobs, and the way they view the people with whom they interact while on patrol. If we want to dissuade them from seeing their fellow citizens as the enemy, we need to stop our political leaders—the people who set the policies and appropriate the budgets for those officers—from referring to their fellow citizens as the enemy.

### Accountability

In numerous states across the country, police unions have lobbied legislatures to pass variations on a "law enforcement bill of rights." Though they vary from state to state, the general thrust of these laws is to afford police officers accused of crimes additional "rights" above and beyond what regular citizens get. Or as *Reason* magazine's Mike Riggs puts it, the intent of such laws is "to shield cops from the laws they're paid to enforce." These laws have made it nearly impossible to fire bad cops in many jurisdictions, and worse, they have instilled in them the notion that they're above the law—and above the regular citizens they're supposed to serve. Investigations of how bad cops are able to stay on the job have become a perennial newspaper undertaking. Recent exposés have tackled the flawed systems in Florida, Georgia, Louisiana, West Virginia, and Chicago.

Part of the problem is that union-management negotiations in law enforcement are decidedly different from those in the private sector. For one, there's little downside for a mayor or city council to give everything away. Voters rarely get angry at politicians for being too generous with the police. But when city officials face tight budgets, they can use accountability as a negotiating chip, offering more job protections for cops accused of wrongdoing in exchange for concessions on pay or benefits. A CEO who negotiates away his ability to hold his employees accountable is likely to feel the repercussions on his bottom line—it affects him directly. When city officials make it more difficult to fire bad cops, they are rarely affected that way. At worst, a lawsuit might take a bite out of a city budget. But no cops will be harassing or beating the politicians themselves. That happens to other people.

Police unions also help enforce the "Blue Code of Silence," the unwritten rule that police officers never rat out or testify against other police officers. A stark example from several years ago in New Mexico involved, oddly enough, former race car driver Al Unser Sr. In 2006 Albuquerque police officer Sam Costales testified against some deputies from the Bernalillo County Sheriff's Department. The deputies had gotten into a confrontation with Unser that resulted in Unser's arrest and criminal charges. Costales had witnessed the incident. At Unser's trial, he testified that Unser did not assault or threaten officers from the Bernalillo County Sheriff's Department, as claimed in police reports. Costales's testimony helped Unser win an acquittal.

None of the Bernalillo deputies was disciplined. But one officer was: Sam Costales. His own chief opened an internal affairs investigation of him. Costales's transgression: he wore his police uniform when he testified in Unser's case. Albuquerque cops apparently are permitted to wear the uniform when they're testifying for the prosecution, but not when they're testifying for the defense. At that point, the Albuquerque police union got involved—but not to protect Officer Costales. He may have been disciplined for telling the truth, but for the union he committed the far more serious offense of telling an unflattering truth about his fellow cops. James Badway, secretary of the Albuquerque Police Officers Association, apologized for Costales's actions in an email message to the Bernalillo sheriff:

> As Secretary of the APOA I feel it is my duty and responsibility to apologize to you and your officers. Ofc. Sam Costales does not represent APD/APOA. The majority of our officers look at the BCSO as our brother and sisters in blue. We are embarrassed and ashamed of Ofc. Costales's testimony in the Unser trial. If there is anything we can do to rebuild the damage caused by Sam please let me know.[28]

Only in law enforcement would a union rep apologize to the management for the actions of one of its members. Former narcotics cop Russ Jones says that unions reinforce the notion among cops that it's just them and their brother cops against the world. "Police unions have really gotten to the point where they protect bad police officers, and they shield management from having to take any responsibility," Jones says. "Everybody involved in the bargaining wins. The citizens end up the losers, in all aspects."[29]

Perhaps the biggest problem with police unions, however, is that they present a major obstacle to real reform. Their political clout is difficult to surmount. Democrats don't cross them because of the traditional alliance of unions and public employees. Republicans rarely cross them because of the party's law-and-order reputation. But awareness of their formidable influence and likely opposition to any accountability efforts is at least a start.

Good ideas for accountability policies include civilian review boards, but only if they have subpoena power, are granted the authority to impose discipline, and can't be overruled by arbitrators.

Unfortunately, there aren't many in the country that have those powers. And as we saw with the death of Alberta Spruill and other cases, even a major, headline-grabbing scandal isn't enough to establish credible civilian oversight.

The most productive accountability policy—and thus the most controversial and least likely to be adopted—would be to impose more liability on police officers who make egregious errors. Under the qualified immunity from civil lawsuits currently afforded to police under federal law, a police officer can't be sued for mere negligence—or even for gross negligence that results in a fatality. To even get into court against a police officer, a plaintiff must show not only that a police officer intentionally violated the plaintiff's constitutional rights, but that said rights were well established at the time they were violated. With this protection, police officers aren't required to keep informed on the latest court decisions that pertain to their job. In fact, in a perverse way, it even *discourages* police departments and officers from doing so. A cop who is aware that he was violating someone's rights is much more likely to be found liable than a cop who isn't.

Some commentators like University of Tennessee law professor Glenn Reynolds have suggested that SWAT teams that conduct forced-entry raids be held to a strict liability standard. If they raid the wrong house, they're liable for damages no matter what; whether the mistake was due to a bad informant, a mistyped address, or just a bad investigation wouldn't matter. Such a policy would be difficult to apply in many cases. For example, if police claim in the affidavit that they're looking for a large stash of heroin but raid a house that turns up only a small amount of pot, would that be considered a "wrong house" raid? Still, adopting the policy just for cases of clear, unambiguous mistakes would probably encourage more caution, more restraint, and fewer errors.

THE MOST DIFFICULT CHANGE IS THE ONE THAT'S PROBABLY necessary to make any of these others happen. The public needs to start caring about these issues. The proliferation of "cop watch" sites, citizen-shot video of police misconduct, and coverage of police abuse incidents by a bevy of online media is encouraging. Another good sign is the fact that this growing skepticism of police has been accompanied by a decline in violence against police officers themselves. Activists are fighting police abuse with technology and information, not with threats and violence. But while exposing individual incidents of misconduct is important, particularly to the victim of the misconduct, it's more important to expose the policies that allow misconduct to flourish. Bad systems will continue to turn out bad results. And bad systems will never be reformed until and unless policymakers and politicians (a) are convinced there is a problem, and (b) pay a political price for not addressing it. Yes, trends that develop over years or decades can gradually normalize things that we might not have tolerated had they been imposed on us all at once. But it's still rather remarkable that domestic police officers are driving tanks and armored personnel carriers on American streets, breaking into homes and killing dogs over *pot*. They're subjecting homes and businesses to commando raids for white-collar and even regulatory offenses, and there's been barely any opposition or concern from anyone in Congress, any governor, or any mayor of a sizable city. That, more than anything, is what needs to change.

# CONCLUSION

The war on drugs . . . I liken it to the Vietnam War. Hit
and miss, there is no clear win—we don't know if we're
gaining ground or not. What we want to do is we want to
change our strategy. We want to make this more like a
Normandy invasion.

—Former Clayton County,
Georgia Sheriff Victor Hill

The way these people were treated has to be judged in
the context of a war.

—Hallandale, Florida, attorney Richard Kane,
after city police mistakenly raided
Edwin and Catherine Bernhardt

I have my own army in the NYPD—the seventh largest
army in the world.

—New York City Mayor Michael Bloomberg

Officers' safety comes first, and not infringing on
people's rights comes second.

—Philadelphia Police Department
spokesperson Fran Healy

333

> My message to my troops is if you see anybody carrying
> a gun on the streets of Milwaukee, we'll put them on the
> ground, take the gun away and then decide whether you
> have a right to carry it.
>
> —MILWAUKEE POLICE CHIEF ED FLYNN,
> DESCRIBING HOW HIS OFFICERS WOULD
> HARASS LEGAL GUN OWNERS, IN
> SPITE OF WISCONSIN STATE LAW

Given that the Founders could never have anticipated police as they exist today, maybe *Are cops constitutional?* is the wrong question. A better one might be *Are today's police forces consistent with the principles of a free society?*

It's difficult to say that they are. Police today are armed, dressed, trained, and conditioned like soldiers. They're given greater protections from civil and criminal liability than normal citizens. They're permitted to violently break into homes, often at night, to enforce laws against nonviolent, consensual acts—and even then, often on rather flimsy evidence of wrongdoing. Negligence and errors in judgment that result in needless terror, injury, and death are rarely held accountable. Citizens who make similar errors under the same circumstances almost always face criminal charges, usually felonies.

Police today share a bond tighter than that shared by soldiers who fight in wars together. There's a strict code of omerta that's enforced more ruthlessly and thoroughly than in any other non-criminal profession. Cops who rat out other cops tend not to remain cops for very long. Lying and exaggerating in police reports and on the witness stand isn't just common, it's routine and expected. It's a part of the job.

Today, there are entire communities in which a large percentage of residents refuse to talk to police, under any circumstances. These so-called "Stop Snitch'n" movements are often derided by politicians and police officials, but there's a pretty astonishing revelation driving them: There are large swaths of the population who fear the people who are supposed to protect them from criminals more than they fear the criminals.

As I've written and spoken on this issue over the years, I've even had current and former members of the military tell me the object to the word *militarization*—not because they disagree with the basic premise of what's happened to police departments in recent years, but because from their own experience, the military is more accountable and disciplined than many police departments today. Several have even told me that military raids on residences where they suspected insurgents may be hiding are done more carefully and with more deference to the rights of potential innocents than some of the SWAT raids they see and read about today. The police today may be more militarized than the military.

Police officers today are a protected class, one no politician wants to oppose. Law enforcement interests may occasionally come up short on budgetary issues, but legislatures rarely if ever pass new laws to hold police more accountable, to restrict their powers, or to make them more transparent.

In short, police today embody all of the threats the Founders feared were posed by standing armies, plus a few additional ones they couldn't have anticipated.

This isn't to say we're in a police state, a term that's often misused. Generally speaking, we're free to travel. We don't face mass censorship. We still have habeus corpus. And the odds of any single person being victimized by a wrong-door raid, shot or beaten by a cop, or otherwise victimized by militarized police violence are slim to nil. But perhaps we *have* entered a police state writ small. At the individual level, a police officer's power and authority over the people he interacts with day to day is near complete. Absent video, if the officer's account an incident differs from that of a citizen—even several citizens—his superiors, the courts, and prosecutors will nearly always defer to the officer. If other officers are nearby, there are policies in place—official and unofficial—to encourage them to back one another up. Even if the officer *does* violate the citizen's rights, the officer is protected by qualified immunity.

In the Introduction, I noted that this is not an anti-cop book. And it isn't. Despite all of this, there are still good cops. A lot of them. But we have passed laws and policies that have elevated police officers above the people they serve. As Tim Lynch of the Cato Institute has written, you could make a good argument that police should be held to a *higher* standard than regular citizens. And you could make a good argument they should be held to the same standard. But it's hard to conceive of a convincing argument that they should be held to a lower one. But that's exactly what we've done.

Systems governed by bad policies and motivated by incentives will produce bad outcomes. Today, laws, policies, and procedures select for personalities attracted to aggressive, antagonistic policing; isolate police from the communities they serve; and condition police officers to see the people they serve—the people with whom they interact every day—as the enemy. We shouldn't then be surprised when cops then begin to see a world divided between cops and their families . . . and everybody else.

Perhaps most distressing of all, not only does the military continue to provide surplus weapons to domestic police agencies, but thanks to the Department of Homeland Security grants, military contractors are now shifting to market resources toward police agencies. Worse, a new industry appears to be emerging just to convert those grants into battle-grade gear. That means we'll soon have powerful private interests, funded by government grants, who will lobby for more government grants to pay for further militarization—a police industrial complex. It's a threshold that will be difficult to un-cross.

No, America today isn't a police state. Far from it. But it would be foolish to wait until it becomes one to get concerned.

# NOTES

## Introduction

1. Roger Roots, "Are Cops Constitutional?" *Seton Hall Constitutional Law Journal* 11 (2001): 685–757.

2. Ibid., p. 757.

3. Samuel Walker, *Popular Justice: A History of American Criminal Justice* (New York: Oxford University Press, 1998), pp. 25–28.

4. Roots, "Are Cops Constitutional?" p. 689.

5. Ibid., p. 692.

6. Timothy Egan, "Soldiers of the Drug War Remain on Duty," *New York Times,* March 1, 1999.3.

## Chapter 1: From Rome to Writs

1. The Rome narrative is from Sandra J. Bingham, "The Praetorian Guard in the Political and Social Life of Julio-Claudian Rome," PhD diss., University of British Columbia (August 1997); Robert H. Langworthy and Lawrence F. Travis III, *Policing in America,* 3rd ed. (Englewood Cliffs, NJ: Prentice-Hall, 2003), pp. 40–42; and "Praetorian Guard," Globalsecurity.org, available at: http://www.globalsecurity.org/military/world/spqr/army-praetorian-guard.htm (last accessed December 26, 2012).

2. The history of British policing through the nineteenth century is from Langworthy and Travis, *Policing in America,* pp. 54–58; and Erik H. Monkkonen, "History of Urban Police," in *Modern Policing,* ed. Michael Tonry and Norval Morris (Chicago: University of Chicago Press, 1992), pp. 547–580.

3. Cicero quoted in William Blackstone, "Of Offenses Against the Habitations of Individuals," ch. 16 in *Commentaries on the Laws of England,* book 4 (1753).

4. Olmstead v. United States, 277 US 438 (1928) (Brandeis, dissenting).

5. Semayne's Case, 77 Eng. Rep. 194, 195 (KB 1603).

6. Richard Burn, *Justice of the Peace and Parish Officer 87,* 6th ed. (1758).

7. Case of Richard Curtis, 168 Eng. Rep. 67 (Crown 1757).

8. The Otis narrative is summarized from James M. Farrell, "The Writs of Assistance and Public Memory: John Adams and the Legacy of James Otis," *New England Quarterly* 79 (4, 2006): 533–556; and James R. Ferguson, "Reason in Madness: The Political Thought of James Otis," *William and Mary Quarterly* 36 (1979): 194–214.

9. John Adams, *The Works of John Adams, Second President of the United States,* vol. 2, app. A (Boston: Little, Brown & Co., 1850), pp. 523–525. The Adams quote also appears in Jedidiah Morse, *Annals of the American Revolution* (s.n., 1824), p. 225.

## Chapter 2: Soldiers in the Streets

1. Engblom v. Carey, 677 F.2d 957 (1979). The US Court of Appeals for the Second Circuit ruled that the Third Amendment is incorporated to the states, that under the amendment National Guard troops are "soldiers," and that tenants are included as "owners."

2. See Tom W. Bell, "'Property' in the Constitution: The View from the Third Amendment," *William and Mary Bill of Rights* 20 (2012); and Tom W. Bell, "The Third Amendment: Forgotten but Not Gone," *William and Mary Bill of Rights* 2 (1, 1993): 117.

3. Robert A. Gross, "Public and Private in the Third Amendment," *Valparaiso University Law Review* 26 (1, 1991): 215–221.

4. The history of quartering in England is from William S. Fields and David T. Hardy, "The Third Amendment and the Issue of Standing Armies," *American Journal of Legal History* (Temple) 35 (4, 1991): 393–431.

5. Gary B. Nash, *The Unknown American Revolution: The Unruly Birth of Democracy and the Struggle to Create America* (New York: Viking, 2005), p. 44.

6. Fields and Hardy, "The Third Amendment and the Issue of Standing Armies," p. 416.

7. John Philip Reid, *Constitutional History of the American Revolution* (Madison: University of Wisconsin Press, 1986), p. 194.

8. Oliver Morton Dickerson, *Boston Under Military Rule, 1768–1769: As Revealed in a Journal of the Times* (Chapman & Grimes, 1936).

9. Alexander Hamilton, "Federalist No. 8: The Consequences of Hostilities Between the States," November 20, 1787.

10. The standing army debate is from Fields and Hardy, "The Third Amendment and the Issue of Standing Armies"; and from *The Debates in the Several State Conventions on the Adoption of the Federal Constitution as Recommended by the General Convention at Philadelphia in 1787*, 2nd ed., vol. 3, ed. Jonathan Elliot (Burt Franklin, 1888).

11. The Shays' Rebellion narrative is from Christopher Collier and James Lincoln Collier, *Decision in Philadelphia: The Constitutional Convention of 1787* (New York: Ballantine Books (1987), pp. 12–13.

12. Charles G. Loring, closing argument in the Thomas Sims hearing, April 8, 1851, available at: http://archive.org/stream/trialthomassims00 circgoog#page/n4/mode/2up (accessed September 5, 2012).

13. Jacqueline Jones, *Saving Savannah: The City and the Civil War* (New York: Random House, 2008), p. 9. As a tradesman, Sims had received better treatment than most slaves and could earn wages for his work. Even though he was required to give his wages to his mother, who was required to give them to Potter, he could have accumulated enough money before running away to bribe enough crew members to get himself to Boston.

14. The text of the Fugitive Slave Act of 1850 is available at: http://www.usconstitution.net/fslave.html (accessed September 1, 2012).

15. For an excellent history of the hearings of Thomas Sims and Anthony Burns and of the consequences of the Fugitive Slave Act of 1850, see Stanley W. Campbell, *The Slave Catchers: Enforcement of the Fugitive Slave Law, 1850–1860* (Chapel Hill: University of North Carolina Press, 1970).

16. The Burns narrative is from Charles Emery Stevens, *Anthony Burns: A History* (John P. Jewett and Co., 1856), available at: http://docsouth.unc.edu/neh/stevens/stevens.html (accessed September 16, 2012); Albert J. Von Frank, *The Trial of Anthony Burns: Freedom and Slavery in Emerson's Boston* (Cambridge, MA: Harvard University Press, 1998); and Chuck Leddy, "Boston Combusts: The Fugitive Slave Case of Anthony Burns," *Civil War Times* (May 2007).

17. Robert W. Coakley, *The Role of Federal Military Forces in Domestic Disorders, 1789–1878* (DIANE Publishing, 1996), p. 134.

18. Ibid.

19. Puleo, *A City So Grand*, p. 33.

20. Coakley, *The Role of Federal Military Forces*, p. 137.

21. Ibid., p. 136.

22. Ibid.

23. "Official Opinions of the Attorneys General of the United States, Advising the President and Heads of Departments in Relation to Their Official Duties," vol. 6 (R. Farnham, 1856), pp. 466–474, available at: http://books.google.com/books?id=xY5JAQAAIAAJ&dq (accessed September 16, 2012).

24. The Reconstruction narrative is from Coakley, *The Role of Federal Military Forces*, pp. 129–140.

### Chapter 3: A Quick History of Cops in America

1. Samuel Walker, *Popular Justice*, 2nd ed. (New York: Oxford University Press, 1998), p. 16.

2. Ibid., p. 170.

3. Eric Burns, *Spirits of America: A Social History of Alcohol* (Philadelphia: Temple University Press, 2004) p. 229.

4. Burns, *Spirits of America*, p. 229.

5. The history of early policing in the United States is from Walker, *Popular Justice*; Roger Lane, "Urban Police and Crime in Nineteenth-Century America," and Eric H. Monkkonen, "History of Urban Police," both in *Modern Policing*, ed. Michael Tonry and Norval Morris (Chicago: University of Chicago Press, 1992); Robert H. Langworthy and Lawrence F. Travis III, *Policing in America* (Englewood Cliffs, NJ: Prentice-Hall, 2003); Burns, *Spirits of America*; and Samuel Walker and Charles M. Katz, *The Police in America*, 7th ed. (New York: McGraw-Hill, 2011).

6. See Walker, *Popular Justice*, pp. 173–175.

7. Clayton Laurie and Ronald Cole, *The Role of Federal Military Forces in Domestic Disputes, 1877–1945* (Washington, DC: US Army, Center for Military History, 1997), p. 324.

8. The Bonus March is summarized from Roger Daniels, *The Bonus March: An Episode of the Great Depression* (Westport, CT: Greenwood Publishing, 1971).

9. "The Bonus Army: How a Protest Led to the GI Bill," *Radio Diaries*

(National Public Radio), November 11, 2001, available at: http://www
.npr.org/2011/11/11/142224795/the-bonus-army-how-a-protest-led
-to-the-gi-bill (accessed August 10, 2012).

10. "1932 Bonus March," GlobalSecurity.org, available at: http://
www.globalsecurity.org/military/ops/bonus-march.htm (accessed September 1, 2012).

11. George S. Patton, "Federal Troops in Domestic Disturbances"
(1932), available at: http://www.pattonhq.com/textfiles/federal.html.

12. Ibid.

13. Douglas MacArthur, remarks at a news conference, Washington,
DC, July 28, 1932, transcript available at: http://www.wwnorton.com
/college/history/america7/content/multimedia/ch29/research_01c.htm
(accessed September 15, 2012).

14. US War Department, *Basic Field Manual,* vol. 7, *Military Law,*
August 1, 1935, pt. 3, "Domestic Disturbances," pp. 14, 31–67, cited and
summarized in Laurie and Cole, *The Role of Federal Military Forces,* p. 364.

15. Laurie and Cole, *The Role of Federal Military Forces,* p. 364.

16. Ibid.

17. Ibid., p. 365.

18. See Robert W. Coakley, *The Role of Federal Military Forces in Domestic Disorders, 1789–1878* (DIANE Publishing, 1996), pp. 17–38.

19. Farnsworth Fowle, "Little Rock Police, Deployed at Sunrise, Press
Mob Back at School Barricades," *New York Times,* September 24, 1957.

20. Steve Barnes, "Federal Supervision of Race in Little Rock Schools
Ends," *New York Times,* February 24, 2007.

21. W. H. Lawrence, "Eisenhower Irate; Says Federal Orders 'Cannot
Be Flouted with Impunity'; Protection of Laws Denied; President Warns
He'll Use Troops; Queried on Force Drafted in Washington," *New York
Times,* September 24, 1957. For a thorough analysis of Eisenhower's de-
liberation, decision, and motives about sending troops to Little Rock, see
Walker, *Popular Justice,* pp. 174–176.

## Chapter 4: The 1960s—From Root Causes to Brute Force

1. Miller v. California, 357 US 301 (1958).

2. Ibid.

3. Ker v. California, 374 US 23 (1963) (Brennan, dissenting).

4. Ibid.

5. Layhmond Robinson, "Assembly Votes Anticrime Bills," *New York
Times,* February 12, 1964.

6. Martin Arnold, "NAACP and CORE to Fight Bills Increasing Police Powers," *New York Times,* February 29, 1964.

7. Douglas Dales, "Rockefeller Signs Bills Increasing Powers of Police," *New York Times,* March 4, 1964.

8. Fred P. Graham, "Why Cops May Knock That 'No-Knock' Law," *New York Times,* February 1, 1970.

9. Richard Bartlett, interview with the author, June 2012.

10. The Watts narrative is from Daryl F. Gates, with Diane K. Shah, *Chief: My Life in the LAPD* (New York: Bantam, 1993), pp. 101–119; Valerie Reitman and Mitchell Landsberg, "Watts Riots, 40 Years Later," *Los Angeles Times,* August 11, 2005; Darrell Dawsey, "To CHP Officer Who Sparked Riots, It Was Just Another Arrest," *Los Angeles Times,* August 19, 1990.

11. "Military Support of Law Enforcement During Civil Disturbances: A Report Concerning the California National Guard's Part in Suppressing the Los Angeles Riot," California Office of State Printing, August 1965, available at: http://www.militarymuseum.org/watts.pdf (accessed September 15, 2012).

12. "One person threw a rock, and then, like monkeys in a zoo, others started throwing rocks." See "Past Police Chiefs," *Los Angeles Times,* April 17, 1992.

13. Daryl Gates, *Chief: My Life in the LAPD* (New York: Bantam, 1992), p. 104.

14. Mapp v. Ohio, 367 US 643 (1961).

15. Robinson v. California, 370 US 660 (1962).

16. Gideon v. Wainwright, 372 US 335 (1963).

17. Brady v. Maryland, 373 US 83 (1963).

18. Escobedo v. Illinois, 378 US 478 (1964).

19. Miranda v. Arizona, 384 US 436 (1966).

20. Katz v. United States, 389 US 347 (1967).

21. William F. Buckley, "The Court and the Fifth" (syndicated), *Sarasota Herald-Tribune,* June 18, 1966.

22. James J. Kilpatrick, "Judicial Activists Gain Full Control" (syndicated), *Evening Independent,* June 9, 1967.

23. Editorials summarized in "Opinion in the United States," *New York Times,* June 19, 1966.

24. Terry v. Ohio, 392 US 1 (1968).

25. Norm Stamper, *Breaking Rank: A Top Cop's Exposé of the Dark Side of American Policing* (New York: Nation Books, 2005), p. 66.

26. See Barry Friedman and Dahlia Lithwick, "Watch as We Make This Law Disappear: How the Roberts Court Disguises Its Conservatism," *Slate,* October 4, 2010; Susan A. Bandes, "The Roberts Court and the Future of the Exclusionary Rule," American Constitution Society for Law and Policy issue brief, April 1, 2009; Adam Liptak, "Justices Step Closer to Repeal of Evidence Ruling," *New York Times,* January 30, 2009; David A. Moran, "The End of the Exclusionary Rule, Among Other Things: The Roberts Court Takes on the Fourth Amendment," *Cato Supreme Court Review* (2006): 283–309.

27. The Texas clock tower shooting narrative is from Pamela Colloff, "96 Minutes," *Texas Monthly* (August 2006); Gary M. Lavergne, *A Sniper in the Tower: The Charles Whitman Murders* (Denton: University of North Texas Press, 1997); and William J. Helmer, "The Madman in the Tower," *Texas Monthly* (August 1986).

28. Ricardo Gandara, "Casting Off Shadow of UT Tower Shooting," *Austin American-Statesman,* May 13, 2011.

29. David Eagleman, "The Brain on Trial," *The Atlantic* (July-August 2011).

30. Robert L. Snow, *SWAT Teams: Explosive Face-offs with America's Deadliest Criminals* (New York: Plenum Press, 1996), p. 7.

31. Sid Heal, "Minimum Performance Standards," *The Tactical Edge* (Winter 1991): 19–21, quoted in Snow, *SWAT Teams,* p. 7.

32. Rick Tejada-Flores, "The United Farmworkers Union," for *The Fight in the Field: Cesar Chavez and the Farmworkers' Struggle,* PBS, 1997, available at: http://www.pbs.org/itvs/fightfields/cesarchavez1.html (accessed September 12, 2012).

33. "Community Response Unit," City of Delano, California website, available at: http://www.cityofdelano.org/index.aspx?NID=140 (accessed September 15, 2012); and Charles Bennett, "The Birth of SWAT," February 25, 2010, available at: http://www.officer.com/article/10232858/the-birth-of-swat (accessed September 29, 2012).

34. Gates, *Chief,* pp. 124–125.

35. Ibid., pp. 125–126.

36. Michael Newton, "Thomas Reddin," in *The Encyclopedia of American Law Enforcement* (New York: Infobase Publishing, 2007), p. 288.

37. Gates, *Chief,* p. 129.

38. LAPD, "Metropolitan Division," available at: http://www.lapdonline.org/metropolitan_division (accessed September 30, 2012).

39. Newton, "Thomas Reddin."

40. Gates, *Chief,* p. 129.

41. Ibid., p. 130.

42. Ibid., p. 131.

43. Ibid.

44. Ibid., pp. 131–132.

45. Ibid., p. 133.

46. "Police Stockpiling Weapons for Riots," Associated Press, March 2, 1968.

47. George Gallup, "Civil Rights Holds Top Concern in US" (syndicated), April 15, 1965.

48. See, for example, David Lawrence, "War on Crime Goes Even Worse Than in Viet Nam," *New York Herald Tribune,* July 28, 1965; and Richard L. Strout, "Crime Data Challenge High Court: The Supreme Court of the United States Returns to Its Cozy Marble Palace in the Capital with a Storm Against 'Coddling the Criminal' Raging Outside," *Christian Science Monitor,* October 8, 1965.

49. "Lyndon Johnson, the Campaigner," *New York Times,* July 24, 1966.

50. See Gallup, "Presidential Approval Ratings—Gallup Historical Statistics and Trends," available at http://www.gallup.com/poll/116677/presidential-approval-ratings-gallup-historical-statistics-trends.aspx#2 (accessed October 3, 2012.)

51. Lyndon B. Johnson, "Remarks to the Members of the President's Commission on Law Enforcement and Administration of Justice," September 8, 1965, available at: http://www.presidency.ucsb.edu/ws/?pid=27242 (accessed September 30, 2012).

52. US President's Commission on Law Enforcement and Administration of Justice, *The Challenge of Crime in a Free Society* (Washington, DC: US Government Printing Office, 1967); proposals summarized in Associated Press, "Needs Are Cited by Commission for War on Crime," February 19, 1967.

53. "Administrative History," Records of the Law Enforcement Assistance Administration (LEAA), US National Archives, record 423.1.

54. Dan Baum, *Smoke and Mirrors: The War on Drugs and the Politics of Failure* (Boston: Little, Brown, 1996), p. 9.

55. Donald Santarelli, interview with the author, July 2012.

56. Ibid.

57. Ibid.

58. William C. Eckerman, *Drug Usage and Arrest Charges: A Study of*

*Drug Usage and Arrest Charges Among Arrestees in Six Metropolitan Areas of the United States* (Washington, DC: US Bureau of Narcotics and Dangerous Drugs, Drug Control Division, 1971). The study didn't look at drug *dealers,* who are more likely to be violent; their violence stems from the fact, however, that the drugs they're dealing are prohibited.

59. Baum, *Smoke and Mirrors,* p. 11.

60. Todd Gitlin, *The Sixties: Years of Hope, Days of Rage* (New York: Bantam, 1987), p. 337. The remark was also referenced in the trial of the "Chicago Seven" DNC protesters. Transcript available at: http://law2 .umkc.edu/faculty/projects/ftrials/chicago7/chicago7.html (accessed October 1, 2012). Daley has denied that this is what he said.

61. "56 Percent Defend Police in Chicago Strife," *New York Times,* September 18, 1968.

62. David Farber, *Chicago '68* (Chicago: University of Chicago Press, 1988), p. 206; "Gallup Poll Finds Nixon Is Maintaining Large Lead," *New York Times,* October 10, 1968.

63. "The Troubled American: A Special Report on the White Majority," *Newsweek,* October 6, 1969.

64. "Many Americans Fear Anarchy, Poll Shows," United Press International, October 8, 1968.

65. Baum, *Smoke and Mirrors,* pp. 10–11.

66. Richard Nixon, speech delivered September 16, 1968, quoted in ibid., p. 12.

67. Baum, *Smoke and Mirrors,* pp. 13–14.

68. Edward Jay Epstein, *Agency of Fear: Opiates and Political Power in America* (London: Verso, 1990), p. 64.

69. Ibid., p. 65; Baum, *Smoke and Mirrors,* pp. 15–16.

70. Epstein, *Agency of Fear,* p. 65.

71. Baum, *Smoke and Mirrors,* pp. 15–16.

72. Milton Heumann and Lance Cassak, *Good Cop, Bad Cop: Racial Profiling and Competing Views of Justice* (New York: Peter Lang, 2003), p. 28.

73. Baum, *Smoke and Mirrors,* p. 16.

74. Epstein, *Agency of Fear,* pp. 66–67.

75. Richard Nixon, "Special Message to the Congress on Control of Narcotics and Dangerous Drugs," July 14, 1969, available at: http://www.presidency.ucsb.edu/ws/index.php?pid=2126 (accessed October 1, 2012).

76. Ibid.

77. "Interview: Dr. Robert DuPont," *Frontline,* PBS, 2000, available at: http://www.pbs.org/wgbh/pages/frontline/shows/drugs/interviews /dupont.html (accessed September 27, 2012).

78. Noel Greenwood, "Father, 22, Killed by Officer's Accidental Shot into Ceiling," *Los Angeles Times,* October 4, 1969; "Calif. Man Killed in Drug Raid Mixup," United Press International, October 5, 1969.

79. Catherine Ellis Smith and Stephen Drury Smith, eds., *Say It Loud! Great Speeches on Civil Rights and African American Identity* (New York: New Press, 2010), p. 70.

80. Gates, *Chief,* pp. 134–136.

81. Matthew Fleischer, "Policing Revolution: How the LAPD's First Use of SWAT—a Massive, Military-Style Operation Against the Black Panthers—Was Almost Its Last," *LA Times Magazine,* April 2011.

82. *41st & Central: The Untold Story of the LA Black Panthers,* directed by Gregory Everett, Ultra Wave Vision (2009).

83. Fleischer, "Policing Revolution."

84. Gates, *Chief,* pp. 138–139.

85. "Gallup Poll Sees Concern on Crime," *New York Times,* February 16, 1969; Joseph Carroll, "Most Americans Approve of Interracial Marriages," Gallup News Service, August 16, 2007, available at: http:// www.gallup.com/poll/28417/most-americans-approve-interracial-marriages.aspx (accessed October 1, 2012); "56% Defend Police in Chicago Strife," *New York Times,* September 18, 1968; "Gallup Poll Sees Concern on Crime," *New York Times,* February 16, 1969; Norman E. Zinberg and John A. Robertson, *Drugs and the Public* (New York: Simon & Schuster, 1972), pp. 29–30.

## Chapter 5: The 1970s—Pinch and Retreat

1. Sen. Samuel Ervin Jr., address to the Civil War Round Table of the District of Columbia (Washington, DC: US Government Printing Office, 1961).

2. Mallory v. United States, 354 US 449 (1957).

3. "Senator Samuel J. Ervin, Jr. Defends Law Enforcement Officers in the United States," *Congressional Record,* vol. 104, no. 44, August 19, 1958.

4. Herbert L. Packer, "A Special Supplement: Nixon's Crime Program and What It Means," *New York Review of Books,* October 22, 1970.

5. Paul R. Clancy, *Just a Country Lawyer: A Biography of Senator Sam Ervin* (Bloomington: Indiana University Press, 1974), p. 221.

6. Dan Baum, *Smoke and Mirrors: The War on Drugs and the Politics of Failure* (Boston: Little, Brown, 1996), pp. 29–47.

7. Clancy, *Just a Country Lawyer*, pp. 221–222.

8. The narrative on the 1969 DC no-knock vote is taken from Leonard Downie Jr., "Nixon Submits Bills to Fight Crime in City," *Washington Post*, July 12, 1969; David A. Jewell, "Senate Unit Narrows City Crime Bill," *Washington Post*, November 4, 1969; David A. Jewell, "Senate Votes Wiretap Bill for District," *Washington Post*, December 6, 1969; and Clancy, *Just a Country Lawyer*, pp. 220–222.

9. Packer, "A Special Supplement: Nixon's Crime Program and What It Means."

10. "The Censure Case of Thomas J. Dodd of Connecticut (1967)," available at: http://www.senate.gov/artandhistory/history/common/censure_cases/135ThomasDodd.htm (accessed October 1, 2012).

11. Wickard v. Filburn, 317 US 111 (1942).

12. The narrative of the January 1970 no-knock debate and the votes is taken from Clancy, *Just a Country Lawyer*, pp. 222–224; Sam Ervin, *Preserving the Constitution: The Autobiography of Senator Sam Ervin* (Charlottesville, VA: Michie Co., 1984), pp. 281–292; "Ervin Hits 'No-Knock' Power in Drug Act," Associated Press, January 25, 1950; "Senate Leaders Back No-Knock Raid Section of Pending Drug Bill," Associated Press, January 28, 1970; "'No-Knock' Section Backed by Leaders," Associated Press, January 26, 1970; Warren Weaver Jr., "Narcotics Raids Without Warning Voted by Senate," *New York Times*, January 28, 1970; Spencer Rich, "'No-Knock' Drug Raids Are Approved by Senate," *Washington Post*, January 28, 1970; and Warren Weaver Jr., "Drug Bill Clause Divides Senators," *New York Times*, January 25, 1970.

13. Clancy, *Just a Country Lawyer*, p. 222.

14. Paul Delaney, "Concern Voiced over Crime Bill," *New York Times*, May 24, 1970.

15. "Appropriate Action" (editorial), *Washington Post*, May 14, 1970; "Shipley Blasts Eaton, Phillips on No-knock," *Washington Afro-American*, May 19, 1970.

16. Lesley Oelsner, "A Look at 'No-Knock' Clause in DC Crime Bill," *New York Times*, July 26, 1970.

17. James K. Batten, "Crime in Washington," *New York Times*, March 22, 1970.

18. Quoted in Michael Flamm, "Politics and Pragmatism: The Nixon Administration and Crime Control," in *White House Studies Compendium*,

vol. 6, ed. Anthony J. Eksterowicz (Hauppauge, NY: Nova Publishers, 2007), p. 131.

19. Tom Wicker, "A Danger to All," *New York Times,* January 30, 1970; Art Buchwald, "A Knock at the Door" (syndicated) *Fredericksburg Free Lance-Star,* November 24, 1970.

20. "Appropriate Action," *Washington Post,* May 14, 1970.

21. William F. Buckley Jr., "Evils Must Be Weighed in No-Knock Raid Law" (syndicated), *Milwaukee Sentinel,* February 3, 1970.

22. Oelsner, "A Look at 'No-Knock' Clause in DC Crime Bill."

23. DC Superior Court chief judge Harold H. Greene, quoted in Robert M. Smith, "Detention Power and No-Knock Warrants Used Little in Capital in First 7 Months," *New York Times,* September 27, 1971.

24. Clancy, *Just a Country Lawyer,* pp. 222–223.

25. "Nixon Signs No-Knock Bill, Hits Anti-Crime Inaction," Associated Press, July 30, 1970.

26. Ervin, *Preserving the Constitution,* p. 289.

27. Donald Santarelli, interview with the author, August 2012; see also Baum, *Smoke and Mirrors,* p. 65.

28. "Detroit: Heroin Shooting War," *Time,* June 21, 1971. Also quoted in Baum, *Smoke and Mirrors,* pp. 58–59.

29. Leonard Curry, "DC Police Chief Cuts Crime Rate by Working with People," *Washington Afro-American,* March 6, 1971.

30. Ibid.

31. Ibid.

32. "The Law: What the Police Can—and Cannot—Do About Crime," *Time,* July 13, 1970.

33. Ibid.

34. Wilson, interviews with the author, August 2012.

35. 5 Crime data from the FBI's Uniform Crime Reports table-making website application, available at: http://www.ucrdatatool.gov/Search /Crime/State/StateCrime.cfm (accessed October 10, 2012).

36. Wilson, interviews with the author, August 2012.

37. Other sources for the Wilson narrative include Robert M. Smith, "Detention Power and No-Knock Warrants Use Little in Capital in First Seven Months," *New York Times,* September 27, 1970; and Metropolitan Police Department of the District of Columbia, "Biography: Jerry V. Wilson," available at: http://mpdc.dc.gov/node/226552 (accessed October 8, 2012).

38. As quoted in Baum, *Smoke and Mirrors.*

39. John W. Dean, *The Rehnquist Choice: The Untold Story of the Nixon Appointment That Redefined the Supreme Court* (New York: Simon & Schuster, 2002), p. 84.

40. "Floor Vote on Rehnquist Nomination," *Congressional Record,* December 10, 1971, available at: http://www.loc.gov/law/find/nominations /rehnquist-aj/vote.pdf (accessed September 30, 2012).

41. Richard Nixon, "Special Message to the Congress on Drug Abuse Prevention and Control," June 17, 1991.

42. Quoted in Flamm, "Politics and Pragmatism," p. 132.

43. Edward Jay Epstein, *Agency of Fear: Opiates and Political Power in America* (London: Verso, 1990), ch. 24.

44. Ibid., p. 71.

45. Baum, *Smoke and Mirrors,* pp. 59–60.

46. Epstein, *Agency of Fear,* p. 140.

47. Ibid., p. 136.

48. Richard Nixon, "Remarks About an Intensified Program for Drug Abuse Prevention and Control," June 17, 1971, available at: http://www .presidency.ucsb.edu/ws/index.php?pid=3047 (accessed October 5, 2012).

49. Haldeman's diary, pp. 327–328, quoted in Baum, *Smoke and Mirrors,* p. 62.

50. Epstein, *Agency of Fear,* pp. 193–202.

51. Baum, *Smoke and Mirrors,* p. 67.

52. Michael J. Sniffen, "Knock at Door Strikes Terror into These Families," Associated Press, June 26, 1973.

53. Epstein, *Agency of Fear,* pp. 193–202.

54. Unless otherwise indicated, the primary source for the Dirk Dickenson narrative, from which I have borrowed heavily, is Joe Ezsterhas, "Death in the Wilderness," *Rolling Stone,* May 24, 1973. See also "Suit Impugns Integrity of Judge on Freeing Drug Agent in Death," *New York Times,* February 4, 1975; "Narcotics Agent Clear in Slaying," *New York Times,* September 29, 1974; "Murder Prosecution of Agent Clifton Upheld," *Eureka Times-Standard,* March 22, 1973; Richard Harris, "Probe into Dirk Dickenson Shooting Still Continuing," *Eureka Times-Standard,* June 29, 1972; "Humboldt Named Target of $6,050,000 Claim," *Eureka Times-Standard,* July 7, 1972; and United States v. Zagari, 419 F.Supp. 494 (1976).

55. The Berti narrative is from Wally Lee, "Secrecy Shrouds Sunday Killing," *Eureka Times-Standard,* October 5, 1970; "Justice Has Berti Probe," *Eureka Times-Standard,* November 20, 1970; and Ezsterhas, "Death in the Wilderness."

56. Quoted in Ezsterhas, "Death in the Wilderness."

57. Ibid.

58. Ibid.

59. Richard Harris, "Agent Arraigned Here for Murder," *Eureka Times-Standard*, January 17, 1973.

60. Richard Harris, "Narcotics Agent's Case Opens Here Monday," *Eureka Times-Standard*, February 4, 1973.

61. James R. McKittrick, letter to the editor, *Eureka Times-Standard*, February 12, 1973.

62. Clifton v. Cox 549 F.2d 722 (1977).

63. The raid narratives and quotes are from Andrew H. Malcolm, "Drug Raids Terrorize 2 Families—by Mistake," *New York Times*, April 29, 1973; and Epstein, *Agency of Fear*, "Prologue."

64. Epstein, *Agency of Fear*, pp. 221–224.

65. Interview with Egil "Bud" Krogh Jr., from *Drug Wars*, PBS *Frontline*, 2000, transcript available at: http://www.pbs.org/wgbh/pages/frontline/shows/drugs/interviews/krogh.html (accessed October 10, 2012).

66. "Agents Suspended After Erroneous Raid in Illinois," Associated Press, May 2, 1973.

67. "No-Knock Law Backfires in Illinois Drug Raids," *Baltimore Afro-American*, May 18, 1973.

68. Epstein, "Prologue," pp. 17–22; "Third Mistaken Drug Raid Suit Filed," Associated Press, July 12, 1973.

69. "Agents Indicted for No-Knock Raids," Associated Press, August 25, 1973.

70. Andrew H. Malcolm, "Violent Drug Raids Against the Innocent Found Widespread," *New York Times*, June 25, 1973.

71. Michael J. Sniffen, "Knock at Door Strikes Terror into These Families," Associated Press, June 26, 1973.

72. Ibid.

73. Malcolm, "Violent Drug Raids."

74. "Drug Aide Chary on Curbing Raids," *New York Times*, July 6, 1973.

75. US Drug Enforcement Administration, "In Depth History: 1970–1975," available at: http://www.justice.gov/dea/about/history.shtml (accessed October 15, 2012).

76. Linda Charlton, "'No-Knock' Drug Raids Curbed Under New Federal Chief," *New York Times*, July 17, 1973; "DEA Stiffens Regulations on No-Knock Drug Raids," Associated Press, July 17, 1973.

77. Quoted in Andrew H. Malcolm, "Drug Law Change Sought by Percy," *New York Times,* November 4, 1973.

78. "Senate Votes to Repeal No-Knock Drug Rule," United Press International, July 12, 1974.

79. "Ford Signs Repeal of 'No-Knock' Law," United Press International, October 29, 1974.

80. Interview with Krogh, *Drug Wars,* PBS *Frontline.*

81. Donald Santarelli, interview with the author, August 2012.

82. The narrative of the SLA shoot-out is taken from Chris McNab, *Deadly Force: Firearms and American Law Enforcement* (Westminster, MD: Osprey Publishing, 2009), pp. 122–126; Jon Nordheimer, "Los Angeles Will Pay for Damage in Its Raid on SLA," *New York Times,* May 23, 1974; "Shootout Report Quotes Death Threat," Associated Press, July 20, 1974; Jon Nordheimer, "Coroner Reconstructs Terrorists' Deaths," *New York Times,* May 24, 1974; and Gates, *Chief,* pp. 150–159.

83. Ibid., pp. 154–155 (emphasis added).

84. McNab, *Deadly Force,* p. 126.

85. Gates, *Chief,* p. 159.

86. Jon Nordheimer, "Tough Elite Police Units Useful but Controversial, *New York Times,* July 14, 1975.

87. Ibid.

88. Russell Jones, interview with the author, August 2012. See also Jones's book, *Honorable Intentions* (self-published, 2012), available at: http://www.honorable-intentions.com.

89. Ervin, *Preserving the Constitution,* p. 291.

90. Baum, *Smoke and Mirrors,* pp. 69–71; Jon Nordheimer, "Tough Elite Police Unites Useful but Controversial, *The New York Times,* July 14, 1975; "DEA History in Depth, 1975–1980," Drug Enforcement Administration, available at: http://www.justice.gov/dea/about/history/1975 –1980.pdf; "Summary of Findings from the 1998 National Household Survey on Drug Abuse," Substance Abuse and Mental Health Services Administration, Office of Applied Studies, DHHS Publication No. SMA 99–3328, 1999; Andrew Malcolm, "Violent Drug Raids Against the Innocent Found Widespread," *The New York Times,* June 25, 1973.

## Chapter 6: The 1980s—Us and Them

1. Drug Policy Foundation, "Policy Briefs: Asset Forfeiture," 1999, p. 3, available at: http://www.drugpolicy.org/docUploads/Asset_Forfeiture _Briefing.pdf.

2. Dan Baum, *Smoke and Mirrors: The War on Drugs and the Politics of Failure* (Boston: Little, Brown, 1996), p. 38.

3. Ronald Reagan, "Remarks Announcing Federal Initiatives Against Drug Trafficking and Organized Crime," October 14, 1982, available at: http://www.presidency.ucsb.edu/ws/index.php?pid=43127 (accessed October 20, 2012).

4. Ibid.

5. Baum, *Smoke and Mirrors*, pp. 171–173.

6. Reagan, "Remarks Announcing Federal Initiatives Against Drug Trafficking and Organized Crime."

7. Trebach, *The Great Drug War*, p.157.

8. Baum, *Smoke and Mirrors*, p. 175.

9. Philip Hager, "US Launches 50-State Drive on Marijuana," *Los Angeles Times*, August 6, 1985; "Raid on Pot Fields/Eradication Program Called Biggest Ever in US," Associated Press, August 5, 1985; "Officials Raid Marijuana Crops on US Land," United Press International, August 6, 1985.

10. Illinois v. Gates, 462 US 213 (1983).

11. United States v. Leon, 468 US 897 (1984).

12. Massachusetts v. Sheppard, 468 US 981 (1984).

13. Segura v. United States, 468 US 796 (1984).

14. Nix v. William, 467 US 431 (1984).

15. Ray Raphael, *Cash Crop: An American Dream* (Caspar, CA: Ridge Times Press, 1985), p. 105.

16. Daryl Gates, with Diane K. Shah, *Chief: My Life in the LAPD* (New York: Bantam, 1993), p. 322.

17. Ibid., p. 323.

18. Unless otherwise indicated, the Tommie DuBose narrative is from the author's interviews with Norm Stamper, October 2012; Richard Serrano, "Police Ponder Changes in Tactics in Response to DuBose Slaying," *Los Angeles Times*, June 22, 1988; Richard Serrano, "DuBose Killing Justifiable, DA Inquiry Finds," *Los Angeles Times*, June 21, 1988; Alan Abrahamson, "Southeast SD Man Was Slain by Police: City, Widow Reach Tentative Pact in DuBose Killing," *Los Angeles Times*, July 27, 1989; and Richard Serrano, "Shooting by San Diego Police Officer His 3rd in 10 Years on Force," *Los Angeles Times*, March 22, 1988.

19. "7 Arrested in Raid Marred by Wrong Entry," Associated Press, March 9, 1987; Marcos Breton, "Drug Raid at Wrong House Under Investigation by Police," *Los Angeles Times*, March 10, 1987; John Dentinger,

"Narc, Narc: Diary of Police Drug Raids on the Wrong Houses," *Playboy* (April 1990).

20. H. G. Reza, "Was Warrant Warranted? Raid Yields No Drugs, Leaves Family Fearful and Upset," *Los Angeles Times,* September 8, 1989.

21. Amy Wallace, "Drug Raiders Broke in Wrong Home, Police Say," *Los Angeles Times,* February 13, 1990.

22. Tony Perry, "Keeping Lid On in San Diego: Police: Department Reforms and a Resourceful Crisis Management Plan Are Credited with Maintaining Relative Calm After Verdicts in King Case," *Los Angeles Times,* April 2, 1993.

23. Ibid.

24. Kristina Davis, "San Diego Boasts One of Nation's Lowest Violent Crime Rates," *San Diego Union-Tribune,* May 25, 2010.

25. "San Diego Historical Crime Actuals, 1950–2011," available at: http://www.sandiego.gov/police/pdf/crimeactuals.pdf (accessed October 22, 2012); see also Keegan Kyle, "How Crime's Changed in San Diego: 12 Graphics," Voice of San Diego, October 4, 2012, available at: http://www.voiceofsandiego.org/community/article_869cf294-0e6d-11e2-9072-0019bb2963f4.html (accessed October 22, 2012).

26. See US Department of Justice, Federal Bureau of Investigation, "Table 302: Crimes and Crime Rates by Type of Offense: 1980 to 2008," available at: http://www.census.gov/compendia/statab/2011/tables/11s0302.pdf (accessed October 20, 2012).

27. "Gravely Ill, Atwater Offers Apology," Associated Press, January 13, 1991.

28. William Bennett, "Should Drugs Be Legalized?" *Reader's Digest* (March 1990).

29. The Bennett narrative is from Baum, *Smoke and Mirrors,* pp. 260–266.

30. Ibid., p. 266. The Bennett quote also appears in his books *Body Count: Moral Poverty . . . And How to Win America's War Against Crime and Drugs* (New York: Simon & Schuster, 1996), and *The De-Valuing of America: The Fight for Our Culture and Our Children* (New York: Simon & Schuster, 1994).

31. William Bennett, "The Top Drug Warrior Talks Tough," *Fortune,* March 12, 1990.

32. *Larry King Live,* CNN, June 15, 1989.

33. Baum, *Smoke and Mirrors,* p. 280.

34. Richard Morin, "Many in Poll Say Bush Plan Is Not Stringent Enough," *Washington Post,* September 8, 1989.

35. For a roundup of stories of DARE kids turning in their parents, see James Bovard, "DARE Scare: Turning Children into Informants?" *Washington Post*, January 29, 1994.

36. Eric Slater and Sue Fox, "Ex-LAPD Chief Gates' Son Arrested," *Los Angeles Times*, October 11, 2004.

37. "Edward Byrne Memorial State and Local Law Enforcement Assistance Program," Program Brief, Bureau of Justice Assistance, August 2002. (Available at: http://www.abtassociates.com/reports/byrne-formula.pdf). The grants are named for Edward Byrne, a New York City police officer slain by drug dealers. The grants grew out of a similar program established under the expansion of LEAA in 1968. The grants also fund a number of criminal justice programs other than drug policing and task forces.

38. Joint Chiefs of Staff, *Joint Counterdrug Operations*, Joint Publication 3-07.4 (2007).

39 "President's Anti-Drug Plan Already Embroiled in Dispute," Associated Press, September 5, 1989.

40. Robert Wagman, "Anti-Drug Plan Under Fire by Many" (syndicated column), December 6, 1989.

41. Lynn Norment, "Charles Rangel: The Front-Line General in the War on Drugs," *Ebony* (March 1989). The article also includes an amazing ad encouraging *Ebony*'s mostly black readership to apply for jobs as DEA agents. The ad features a short profile of DEA special agent Michele Leonhart, who would go on to head the agency under Presidents Bush and Obama.

42. Tony Mauro, "The War on Drugs: Are Our Rights on the Line?" *USA Today*, November 15, 1989.

43. Milton Friedman, "An Open Letter to Bill Bennett," *Wall Street Journal*, September 7, 1989.

44. Dentinger, "Narc, Narc: Diary of Police Drug Raids on the Wrong Houses."

45. Doris Sue Wong," Judge Assails Policy on Gangs; Calls Police Searches Unconstitutional," *Boston Globe*, September 20, 1989. See also: Peter S. Canellos, "Youths Decry Search Tactics," *Boston Globe*, January 14, 1990.

46. Mike Kataoka, "County settles with man in mistaken drug raid," *Riverside Press Enterprise*, February 11, 1994.

47. Lorine Harris v. Milton Grimes, 104 Cal. App. 4th 180 (2002). "News from Southern California," Associated Press, June 1, 2004.

48. Jeffrey Yorke, "Show of Force," *Washington Post*, May 18, 1988.

49. "Police Officer Shot to Death in Drug Raid," Associated Press, September 1, 1988; Jeffrey Yorke, "A Show of Force; Pr. George's Unit

Strives to Dent Drug Traffic," *The Washington Post*, May 19, 1988; "Drug Suspect WoundedBy Pr. George's Police," *The Washington Post*, October 28, 1982; James Rupert and Carlos Sanchez, "Pr. George's Officer Shot in Drug Raid," *The Washington Post*, September 1, 1988.

50. Joseph F. Sullivan, "Police Gun's Blast Kills Officer on a Drug Raid," *The New York Times*, August 4, 1989.

51. "Man Innocent of Police Murder During Drug Raid," United Press International, August 17, 1989; Lynne Bumpus-Hooper, "DiGristine Sues Titusville Over Drug Raid," *Orlando Sentinel*, February 15, 1990; Laurin Sellers, "Chase, No-Knock Rules for Police," *Orlando Sentinel*, January 2, 1990.

52. Francis P. Garland, "2 counties sued over Ripon truck stop slaying," *Modesto Bee*, July 3, 1990; Stuart Gordon, "Shooting victim's kin sues; Damages sought from owners of truck stop," *Modesto Bee*, October 20, 1990; Frankie Garland, "Lawsuit Likely in Fatal Raid," *Modesto Bee*, October 25, 1989; Michael Winters, "Raid's Shock Still Felt," *Modesto Bee*, February 15, 1994.

53. Florida v. Riley, 488 US 445 (1989).

54. George Orwell, *1984* (1949; reprint, New York: Penguin/Signet Classic, 1961), p. 2.

55. The forfeiture figures are from Terrance G. Reed, "American Forfeiture Law: Property Owners Meet the Prosecutor," Cato Policy Analysis 179 (Washington, DC: Cato Institute, September 29, 1992); the figures on SWAT teams are from Peter Kraska and Victor Kappeler, "Militarizing American Police: The Rise and Normalization of Paramilitary Units," *Social Problems* 44 (1, February 1997); the figures on SWAT teams in smaller cities are from Peter Kraska and Louis Cubellis, "Militarizing Mayberry and Beyond: Making Sense of Paramilitary Policing," *Justice Quarterly* 14 (4, December 1997).

## Chapter 7: The 1990s—It's All About the Numbers

1. James Bovard, "Flash. Bang. You're Dead," *Playboy* (March 1, 2000): 201.

2. Tom Hundley, "US Drafts Military in Drug Battle," *Chicago Tribune*, February 11, 1990.

3. Brad Knickerbocker, "Military Drafted in Effort to Find, Eradicate American 'Pot' Growers," *Christian Science Monitor*, August 27, 1990.

4. Figures are from Herb Robinson, "Disturbing Duty for National Guard," *Seattle Times*, August 6, 1990; and "Tackling Illegal Drugs," *The*

*ONGuard* (newspaper of the Army and Air National Guard) 22 (11, September 1993).

5. John Painter Sr., "Police Launch Massive Drug Raid," *The Oregonian,* July 22, 1989.

6. Ann Everest, "Putting Dealers Out of Business," *The ONGuard* 22 (11, September 1993).

7. Michael Isikioff, "Interest in Grateful Dead Was Not Musical," *Washington Post,* August 14, 1990.

8. Jerry Harkavy, "BIDE Tactics Help Drive Marijuana Legalization Effort," Associated Press, April 8, 1992.

9. Ed Vaughn, "National Guard Involvement in the Drug War," *Justica* (December 1992), quoted in Bovard, "Flash. Bang. You're Dead," p. 201.

10. Bovard, "Flash. Bang. You're Dead," p. 201.

11. The Donald Carlson narrative is taken from Carlson's prepared testimony before the House Legislation and National Security Committee hearing, "Review of Federal Asset Forfeiture Program," June 22, 1993; Bill Moushey, "The Damage of Lies," *Pittsburgh Post-Gazette,* November 29, 1998; Phillip J. LaVelle, "Excesses Blamed in 'Bad' Raids," *San Diego Union-Tribune,* December 13, 1992; and Valerie Alvord, "Drug Agents Say Informants Are an Essential Weapon in the War on Drugs," *San Diego Union-Tribune,* May 29, 1995.

12. Myron Orfield Jr., "The Exclusionary Rule in Chicago," *Search and Seizure Law Report* 19 (December 1992): 9.

13. Russell Jones, interview with the author, August 2012.

14. Richard Van Duizend et al., "The Search Warrant Process: Preconceptions, Perceptions, Practices" (Williamsburg, VA: National Center for State Courts, 1985), quoted in David E. Steinberg, "Zealous Officers and Neutral Magistrates: The Rhetoric of the Fourth Amendment," *Creighton Law Review* 43 (June 2010): 1019.

15. David Migoya, "Judges Rubber-Stamp No-Knocks; Easy Approval Among Flaws in Process, Records Show," *Denver Post,* February 27, 2000.

16. "Report of the Independent Commission on the Los Angeles Police Department," Warren Christopher, chairman (1991), available at: http://www.parc.info/client_files/Special%20Reports/1%20-%20Chistopher%20Commision.pdf (accessed October 10, 2012).

17. The Gallup Organization, Inc., reprinted at Sourcebook of Criminal Justice Statistics Online, "Respondents' Perceptions of Police Brutality in Their Area" (table), available at: http://www.albany.edu/sourcebook/pdf/t200012005.pdf (accessed October 10, 2012).

18. Norm Stamper, *Breaking Rank: A Top Cop's Exposé of the Dark Side*

*of American Policing* (New York: Nation Books, 2005), p. 162 (emphasis in original).

19. The narrative of Norm Stamper's demilitarization proposal in San Diego is from the author's phone interviews with Stamper, September 2012, and from Stamper's book, *Breaking Rank*, pp. 162–165.

20. Tom Gabor, "Rethinking SWAT—Police Special Weapons and Tactical Units," *FBI Law Enforcement Bulletin* (April 1993).

21. Quoted in Steven Elbow, "Hooked on SWAT; Fueled with Drug Enforcement Money, Military-Style Police Teams Are Exploding in the Backwoods of Wisconsin," *Madison Capital Times,* August 18, 2001.

22. Timothy Egan, "Soldiers of the Drug War Remain on Duty," *New York Times,* March 1, 1999.

23. Christian Parenti, "SWAT Nation," *The Nation,* May 31, 1999.

24. New Haven Department of Police Service, "Crime Trends: 1990–2000: A Ten-Year Snapshot." For a comparison with Connecticut crime rates, see US Department of Justice, Bureau of Justice Statistics, "Reported Crime in Connecticut."

25. Kit Miniclier, "Critics Say 'No-Knocks' Dangerous, Unnecessary," *Denver Post,* January 27, 1995.

26. Egan, "Soldiers of the Drug War Remain on Duty."

27. US Department of Justice, National Institute of Justice, "Department of Justice and Department of Defense Joint Technology Program: Second Anniversary Report" (February 1997).

28. Michelle Alexander, *The New Jim Crow: Mass Incarceration in the Age of Colorblindness* (New York: New Press, 2012), pp. 141–145.

29. The ABC *World News Tonight* episode, which aired March 28, 1996, is summarized in Peter Kraska and Victor Kappeler, "Militarizing American Police: The Rise and Normalization of Paramilitary Units," *Social Problems* 44 (1, February 1997).

30. 18 USC § 3109.

31. Wilson v. Arkansas, 514 US 927 (1995).

32. Richards v. Wisconsin, 520 US 385 (1997).

33. United States v. Ramirez, 523 US 65 (1998).

34. G. Gordon Liddy, *The G. Gordon Liddy Show* (syndicated radio program), August 26, 1994.

35. Ibid.

36. The Ruby Ridge narrative is from Alan W. Bock, *Ambush at Ruby Ridge* (New York: Berkley, 1996); and US Department of Justice, "Department of Justice Report Regarding Internal Investigation of Shootings at Ruby Ridge, Idaho During Arrest of Randy Weaver" (1996), redacted

version available at: http://www.byington.org/carl/ruby/ruby1.htm (accessed October 30, 2012).

37. The Waco narrative is from Tim Lynch, "No Confidence: An Unofficial Account of the Waco Incident," Cato Policy Analysis 395 (Washington, DC: Cato Institute, April 9, 2001); Bovard, "Flash. Bang. You're Dead"; and David B. Kopel and Paul H. Blackman, *No More Wacos: What's Wrong with Federal Law Enforcement and How to Fix It* (Amherst, NY: Prometheus Books, 1997).

38. In their book *No More Wacos,* Dave Kopel and Paul Blackman document numerous other incidents of botched raids, excessive force, and abuse of citizens at the hands of the ATF.

39. The Elián González narrative is from Ed Vulliamy, "Elián González and the Cuban Crisis: Fallout from a Big Row over a Little Boy," *The Guardian,* February 20, 2010; "The Elian Gonzalez Case," PBS *Newshour* Online, articles and commentary available at: http://www.pbs.org/newshour/bb/law/elian (accessed November 10, 2012).

40. Clarence Page, "Abuse by Immigration Agents Did Not Begin with Elian Case," *Chicago Tribune,* May 16, 2000.

41. Quoted in Will Saletan, "The Elian Pictures," *Slate,* April 25, 2000.

42. Ibid.

43. Unless otherwise noted, the Peter Kraska narrative and the SWAT figures are from Peter Kraska and Louis Cubellis, "Militarizing Mayberry and Beyond: Making Sense of American Paramilitary Policing," *Justice Quarterly* 14 (4, December 1997); Peter Kraska and Victor Kappeler, "Militarizing American Police: The Rise and Normalization of Paramilitary Units," *Social Problems* 44 (1, February 1997); Peter Kraska, "The Military-Criminal Justice Blur: An Introduction," and "Playing War: Masculinity, Militarism, and Their Real-World Consequences," both in *Militarizing the American Justice System: The Changing Roles of the Armed Forces and the Police,* ed. Peter Kraska (Evanston, IL: Northwestern University Press, 2001); Peter Kraska, "Questioning the Militarization of US Police: Critical Versus Advocacy Scholarship," *Policing and Society* 9 (1999): 141–155; and author conversations with Kraska.

44. 4 *Logan Herald-Journal,* April 23, 2006.

45. Peter B. Kraska and V. E. Kappeler, "Militarizing American Police: The Rise and Normalization of Paramilitary Units," *Social Problems* 13 (1997): 1–18.

46. Kraska and Cubellis, "Militarizing Mayberry and Beyond," pp. 661–662.

47. Kraska, *Militarizing the American Justice System,* p. 12.

48. Megan Twohey, "SWATs Under Fire," *National Journal,* January 1, 2000.

49. Neill Franklin, interview with the author, August 2012.

50. Stephen Downing, interview with the author, September 2012.

51. Ed Sanow, "Does SWAT Need to Be Explained?" *Tactical Edge* (September 2011).

52. Twohey, "SWATs Under Fire."

53. Peter Kraska, "Playing War: Masculinity, Militarism, and Their Real-World Consequences," in *Militarizing the American Justice System: The Changing Roles of the Armed Forces and the Police,* ed. Peter Kraska (Evanston, IL: Northwestern University Press, 2001).

54. Author interviews with Franklin, Downing, and Haase, all conducted in August 2012.

55. Federal News Service, White House briefing news conference, December 30, 1996.

56. Peter McWilliams, "The DEA Wishes Me a Nice Day" (self-published), available at: http://uts.cc.utexas.edu/~wbova/fn/earth/2000_6_03.htm.

57. The McWilliams narrative is from R. W. Bradford, "The Life and Death of Peter McWilliams," *Liberty* (August 2000); "Los Angeles Drug Case Bars Medical Marijuana Defense," *New York Times,* November 7, 1999.

58. Paul Richmond, "True Stories from the Front Line," *PDXS,* October 22, 1995.

59. Kraska and Kappeler, "Militarizing American Police," p. 13.

60. Steven Elbow, "Military Muscle Comes to Mayberry; U.S. Donates Gear, Grenade Launchers," *Madison Capital Times,* August 18, 2001.

61. John L. Worrall and Tomislav V. Kovandzic, "Cops Grants and Crime Revisited," *Criminology* 45 (1, February 2007).

62. The McNamara narrative is taken from Julie Lew, "What's Doing in San Jose?" *New York Times,* April 7, 1991; Peggy Y. Lee, "Violent Crime Up; Homicide Looms," *Los Angeles Times,* August 8, 1991; Kathleen O'Toole, "Panelists Play Themselves in Fictitious Drug Raid," *Stanford Report,* November 12, 1997; Joseph McNamara, "Changing Police Attitudes in the War on Drugs," paper presented at the 37th International Congress on Alcohol and Drug Dependence, August 1995; various materials from the conference "Pragmatic Solutions to Urban Drug Problems," Hoover Institution, November 6–7, 1997; and Joseph McNamara, interview with the author, August 2012.

63. The North Hollywood narrative is from Rick Orlov, "North Hollywood Shootout, 15 Years Later," LA Daily News, February 27, 2012; 44 Minutes: The North Hollywood Shoot-Out, directed by Yves Simoneau (2003); Peter Prengaman, "10th Anniversary of Infamous LA Shootout That Changed Policing," Associated Press, February 28, 2007.

64. The Columbine narrative is from David Kopel, "Police Stood Idle," *New York Post,* April 20, 2000; Bovard, "Flash. Bang. You're Dead"; "What Really Happened at Columbine?" CBS News, *60 Minutes,* April 29, 2009.

65. J. R. Clairborne, "Members Start Training, Learn New Jobs, Cross Train," *Ithaca Journal,* March 15, 2000.

66. Scott Andron, "SWAT: Coming to a Town Near You? Academics Decry 'Military' Mind-set," *Miami Herald,* May 20, 2002.

67. Seth Koenig, "Portland Police Get New Military Grade Armored Vehicle," *Bangor Daily News,* June 7, 2012.

68. Leslie A. Maxwell, "School Shootings in Policy Spotlight," *Education Week,* October 11, 2006.

69. Lauren Dunn, "UNC Charlotte SWAT Team—An Asset We Hope to Never Use," *NinerOnline,* October 23, 2011.

70. Norm Stamper, interview with the author, August 2012.

71. Kopel and Blackman, *No More Wacos;* Kraska and Kappeler, "Militarizing American Police"; 2001 estimate from author interview with Kraska, March 2006; Kraska and Kappeler, "Militarizing American Police"; 2001 estimate from author interview with Kraska, March 2006; Edward Ericson Jr., "Commando Cops," *Orlando Weekly,* May 7, 1998; Richmond, "True Stories from the Front Line"; Kraska and Cubellis, "Militarizing Mayberry and Beyond."

## Chapter 8: The 2000s—A Whole New War

1. Betty Taylor, interview with the author, September 2012.

2. William Rhodes, Christina Dyous, Meg Chapman, Michael Shively, Dana Hunt, Kristen Wheeler, "Evaluation of the Multijurisdictional Task Forces (MJTFs), Phase II: MJTF Performance Monitoring Guide, National Institute for Justice, February 2009.

3. For a thorough, well-reported account of the Tulia scandal, see Nate Blakeslee, *Tulia: Race, Cocaine, and Corruption in a Small Texas Town* (New York: Public Affairs, 2006).

4. The Hearne narrative is from the author's interviews with Regina Kelly and ACLU personnel who handled her case; Jay Jorden, "Seventeen Drug Cases Dismissed," Associated Press, April 4, 2001; American Civil

Liberties Union, "In Wake of ACLU Civil Rights Lawsuit Settlement, African Americans Affected by Texas Drug Task Force Scandal Call for Reconciliation at Town Meeting" (press release), June 2, 2005; Nathan Levy, "Bringing Justice to Hearne," *Texas Observer,* April 29, 2005.

5. "As the Well Runs Dry, Texas Drug Task Forces Ride Off into the Sunset," *Drug War Chronicle,* April 7, 2006.

6. Radley Balko, "Wrong Priorities," FoxNews.com, April 7, 2008.

7. US Department of Justice, "Overview of the American Recovery and Reinvestment Act of 2009," available at: http://www.ojp.usdoj.gov /recovery.

8. The Sepulveda narrative is from Rebecca Trounson, "Deaths Raise Questions About SWAT Teams," *Los Angeles Times,* November 1, 2000; Ty Phillips and Michael G. Mooney, "How Did the Gun Go Off? Police Report Fails to Answer Question in SWAT Shooting of Alberto Sepulveda," *Modesto Bee,* January 11, 2001; Michael G. Mooney, "Boy's Death Costs Modesto $2.55M," *Modesto Bee,* June 20, 2002; Rebecca Trounson, "Suit Could Put Limit on Use of SWAT Teams," *Los Angeles Times,* January 16, 2001; and California Attorney General's Commission on Special Weapons and Tactics (SWAT), "Final Report," September 10, 2002.

9. The drug war–terrorism narrative is culled from Radley Balko, "The Drug War: Throwing Good Money at a Bad Idea," FoxNews.com, February 28, 2002; "Thailand's Drug War: Back on the Offensive," *The Economist,* January 24, 2008; Ted Galen Carpenter, "How Washington Funded the Taliban," Cato Institute, August 2, 2002; Dan Kovalik, "The US War for Drugs and of Terror in Columbia," *Huffington Post,* February 16, 2012.

10. See Heidi Lypps, "Bush's Crackdown on Medical Marijuana," *Counterpunch,* September 17, 2002.

11. Mitch Albom, "A Serious Look at Wacky Weed and Suffering," *Detroit Free Press,* September 22, 2002.

12. Louise Witt, "Bush's Reefer Madness," *Salon,* November 5, 2002.

13. Quoted in Lypps, "Bush's Crackdown on Medical Marijuana."

14. See Ronald T. Libby, "Treating Doctors as Drug Dealers: The DEA's War on Prescription Painkillers," Cato Policy Analysis 545 (Washington, DC: Cato Institute, June 6, 2005).

15. For examples of such raids, see Frank Owen, "The DEA's War on Pain Doctors," *Village Voice,* November 5–11, 2003; and Eric Fleischauer, "Physicians Casualties in the War on Drugs," *Decatur Daily News,* October 27, 2003.

16. Keene-DHS narrative from author interviews and reporting and Andrew Becker and G.W. Schulz, "Local Police Stockpile High-Tech, Combat-Ready Gear," Center for Investigative Reporting, December 21, 2011.

17. Rob Golub, "City, Police Go on Trial for Response at 2002 Rave Party," *Racine Journal Times,* January 10, 2005; "Stories from the Racine 'Rave Raid,'" ACLU, January 17, 2003.

18. Glenn Reynolds, "Raving Lunacy," FoxNews.com, July 25, 2002; Will Doig, "Chemical Warfare: The RAVE Act," *MetroWeekly,* October 7, 2002.

19. Rashae Ophus Johnson, "Witnesses Say Undue Force Used at Rave," *Daily Herald,* August 23, 2005; Michael N. Westley, "Police Raid Rave Party in Spanish Fork Canyon," *Salt Lake Tribune,* December 14, 2005.

20. "Drug Raid at SC High School," CBSNews.com, November 7, 2003; "Principal at Drug Raid School Resigns," CNN.com, January 5, 2004; Tony Bartelme, "Raid Settlement Gets Initial OK," *Charleston Post and Courier,* April 5, 2006.

21. "Profile of Le'Quan Simpson," ACLU, December 15, 2003.

22. John Stevenson, "All Cheek Road Drug Raid Charges Dropped," *Durham Herald-Sun,* July 13, 2002.

23. Maki Becker, "How Effective Is the Drug War?" *Buffalo News,* May 24, 2006; Vanessa Thomas and T. J. Pignataro, "Three Days of Secret Police Drug Raids Bring 78 Arrests Throughout City," *Buffalo News,* April 21, 2006; "Giambra Suggests Discussion on Legalizing Drugs," *WBEN News,* April 19, 2006.

24. United States v. Banks, 540 US 31 (2003).

25. Hudson v. Michigan, 547 US 586 (2006).

26. Samuel Walker, *Taming the System: The Control of Discretion in Criminal Justice, 1950–1990* (New York: Oxford University Press, 1993), p. 51.

27. Samuel Walker, "Thanks for Nothing, Nino," *Los Angeles Times,* June 25, 2006.

28. Commonwealth v. King, 302 S. W. 3d 649, 653 (2010).

29. Kentucky v. King, 131 S.Ct. 1849 (2011).

30. Ibid., Ginsberg dissent.

31. "Brooklyn Couple Haunted by More Than 50 False NYPD Raids Want Answers," *New York Daily News,* April 18, 2010.

32. Jim Dwyer, "Police Raid Gone Awry: A Muddled Path to the Wrong Door," *New York Times,* June 29, 2003.

33. Rivka Gewirtz Little, "More NYPD No-Knocks; New Yorkers Tell Their Tales of Botched Raids," *Village Voice,* June 18–24, 2003.

34. Rivka Gewirtz Little, "More NYPD No-Knocks; New Yorkers Tell Their Tales of Botched Raids," *Village Voice,* June 18–24, 2003.

35. The Martins narrative is from John Lauinger, "Brooklyn Couple Haunted by More Than 50 False NYPD Raids Want Answers," *New York Daily News,* April 18, 2010; Kate Nocera and John Lauinger, "Computer Snafu Is Behind at Least 50 'Raids' on Brooklyn Couple's Home," *New York Daily News,* March 19, 2010.

36. See Radley Balko and Joel Berger, "Wrong Door," *Wall Street Journal,* September 2, 2006.

37. Robert F. Moore, "Cops Smash Wrong Door—$2G Missing," *New York Daily News,* May 20, 2007.

38. The Spruill narrative is from Austin Fenner, Maki Becker, and Michelle McPhee, "Cops' Tragic Grenade Raid; Storm Wrong Apt., Woman Dies," *New York Daily News,* May 17, 2003; William K. Rashbaum, "Report by Police Outlines Mistakes in Ill-Fated Raid," *New York Times,* May 31, 2003; Fernanda Santos and Patrice O'Shaughnessy, "Snitch Had Shaky Rep," *New York Daily News,* May 18, 2003; Leonard Levitt, "Focus on Kelly, Race After Raid," *Newsday,* May 19, 2003; Graham Rayman, "Tracking Errors; Board Asked to Focus on Wrong-Door Raids," *Newsday,* June 12, 2003; Karen Freifeld, "Warrant Policy Under Scrutiny; Spruill Raid Prompts Record-Keeping Review," *Newsday,* June 4, 2003; "Judge Keeps Documents Sealed in Fatal Police-Raid Case," Associated Press, June 11, 2003; Karen Freifeld, "Media Denied Spruill Info," *Newsday,* June 11, 2003; Al Guart, "'Spruill Effect' on Drug Busts," *New York Post,* January 25, 2005; Graham Rayman, "Cops in the Clear: Board Policy Absolves Police in Bad Raids," *Newsday,* June 9, 2003; Barbara Ross, "Judges to Be Tutored on Drug Warrants," *New York Daily News,* August 6, 2003; Larry Celona, "NYPD Brass Back to School," *New York Post,* October 13, 2003; Florence L. Fincle, executive director, New York City Civilian Complaint Review Board, "Police Recommendations Memorandum: Recommendations That the New York City Police Department Develop a Database to Track Search Warrant Executions," New York City, January 2003; C. Virginia Fields, "Report and Recommendations on the Execution of No-Knock Warrants: In the Aftermath of the Death of Alberta Spruill," Office of Manhattan Borough, June 2003; and Andrew Case, director of communications, New York City Civilian Complaint Review Board, interview with the author, December 2005.

39. Christopher Koper, "An Updated Assessment of the Federal Assault Weapons Ban: Impacts on Gun Markets and Gun Violence, 1994–2003,"

Report to the National Institute of Justice (Washington, DC: US Department of Justice, 2004).

40. Bureau of Justice Statistics, "Selected Findings," in US Department of Justice, "Guns Used in Crime" (Washington, DC: US Department of Justice, July 1995).

41. Edie Gross, "SWAT: 'Be Safe, Be Strong, Be Mean!'" *Palm Beach Post,* June 8, 1997.

42. Edward Ericson Jr., "Commando Cops," *Orlando Weekly,* May 7, 1998.

43. David Doddridge, interview with the author, August 2007.

44. Eric Morgan and David Kopel, "The Assault Weapon Panic: 'Political Correctness' Takes Aim at the Constitution," Paper 1291 (Denver, CO: Independence Institute, October 10, 1991).

45. Joseph McNamara, "50 Shots," *Wall Street Journal,* November 29, 2006.

46. Fox Butterfield, "When the Police Shoot, Who's Counting," *New York Times,* April 29, 2001.

47. Ibid.

48. Alan Maimon, "National Data on Shootings by Police Not Collected," *Las Vegas Review-Journal,* November 28, 2011.

49. Abbie Boudreau and Scott Zamost, "FBI Agents Speak Out on Injuries from Faulty Grenades," CNN.com, November 17, 2008.

50. "NC SWAT Officer Killed at Home by Flash Bang," WSOC-TV, February 26, 2011.

51. Lou Michel, "FBI Agent Remains Hospitalized," *Buffalo News,* December 7, 2001.

52. Clay Conrad, interview with the author, February 2010.

53. Carol Comegno, "Judge: 'Flash Bang' Grenade Unnecessary," *Courier-Post,* August 28, 2008.

54. Zach Benoit, "Grenade Burns Sleeping Girl as SWAT Team Raids Billings Home," October 12, 2012.

55. Mara H. Gottfried, "St. Paul to Pay Record-Tying $400K in Police Violence Case," *St. Paul Pioneer-Press,* November 6, 2012.

56. Donald E. Wilkes, "Explosive Dynamic Entry," *Flagpole,* July 30, 2003.

57. Lenora Menai, "Rap Group Denounces Police Raid," *St. Petersburg Times,* June 14, 2001.

58. Ric Kahn and Zachary R. Dowdy, "'Iron Fist' of Police; SWAT Team Use Questioned," *Boston Globe,* May 11, 1998.

59. Joseph McNamara, interview with the author, August 2012.

60. Spradley v. State, 933 So.2d 51 (Fla. Dist. Ct. App. 2d Dist. 2006).

61. For a list of such cases, see the page maintained by University of Georgia law professor Donald E. Wilkes Jr., "Explosive Dynamic Entry," available at: http://www.law.uga.edu/dwilkes_more/46explosive.html.

62. Boyd v. Benton County, 374 F.3d 773 (2004).

63. The Culosi narrative is from author interviews, research of court documents and materials, and reporting.

64. Tim McGlone, "Beach SWAT Team Cleared in Shooting; Family Spokesman Cites Guard's Dying Words, Says Report Contradictory," *Virginian-Pilot*, November 13, 1998.

65. Justin Fenton, "Baltimore Co. Police Bust Illegal Poker Game in Edgemere," *Baltimore Sun*, February 16, 2011.

66. Meg Kinnard, "Is It Skill or Gambling? Poker Players Watch as SC Judge Considers Legality of Texas Hold 'Em," Associated Press, January 29, 2009.

67. "Texas Close 'Em," Reason.tv, December 3, 2007.

68. Gene Smith, "Oh No! It's a Raid!" *Fayetteville Observer*, April 7, 2007.

69. Radley Balko, "Poker Game Turns into Gunfight," Reason.com, November 5, 2010; "73-Year-Old Sentenced for Poker Raid Shootout," WYFF.com, October 25, 2011.

70. Jeff Weiner, "Criminal Barbering? Raids at Orange County Shops Lead to Arrests, Raise Questions," *Orlando Sentinel*, January 4, 2013.

71. Thomas MacMillan, "DeStefano: We Shouldn't Have Sent SWAT Team," *New Haven Independent*, October 8, 2010.

72. Dayna Bagby, "Atlanta City Council Settles Third Eagle Lawsuit for $330,000," *GA Voice*, March 19, 2012.

73 Club Retro LLC v. Hilton (5th Cir. 2009).

74. Swint v. Wadley, 51 F.3d 988 (1994).

75. The Ruttenberg narrative is from author interviews and reporting. See also Ruttenberg v. Jones (4th Cir. 2010) (unpublished).

76. Bellotte v. Edwards, 629 F.3d 415, No. 10-1115 (4th Cir. 2011).

77. See Mike Masnick, "SWAT Team Raids Home Because Guy Had an Open Wireless Router," TechDirt, April 25, 2011; and Nate Anderson, "SWAT Team Throws Flashbangs, Raids Wrong Home Due to Open WiFi Network," Ars Technica, June 28, 2012.

78. Sean Gregory, "10 Questions for Shaquille O'Neal," *Time*, October 30, 2006.

79. Tim Kenneally, "Steven Seagal Lawsuit: Don't Bring a Tank to a Cockfight," TheWrap.com, March 8, 2012.

80. See Steve Silberman, "Don't Try This at Home," *Wired*, June 2006.

81. See Naureen Khan, "Man whose home was searched cries foul in koi case," Austin-American Statesman online, July 16, 2010, available at: http://www.statesman.com/blogs/content/sharedgen/blogs/austin /blotter/entries/2010/07/16/man_cries_foul_in_koi_fish_cas.html.

82. Radley Balko, "Dogs Caught in a Deadly Crossfire," *The Daily Beast*, July 19, 2009.

83. Joseph Pentangelo, interview with the author, July 2009.

84. Norm Stamper, interview with the author, August 2012.

85. Russ Jones, interview with the author, August 2012.

86. Mackenzie Carpenter, "The Reluctant Poster Boy," *Pittsburgh Post-Gazette*, October 4, 2009.

87. Radley Balko, "Scenes from a Crackdown," *Reason*, October 5, 2009.

88. Pat Pheifer, "Few Arrested at RNC Face Charges," *Minneapolis Star-Tribune*, February 20, 2009.

89. Felisa Cardona, "Undercover Cops Were Among the Unruly at DNC," *Denver Post*, November 6, 2008.

90. Ernest Luning, "Denver Police 'Beat the Crowds' T-shirt No Laughing Matter, Protesters Charge," *Colorado Independent*, September 25, 2008.

91. "Scott Olsen, Iraq War Veteran Hurt in Occupy Oakland Protests, Leaves Hospital," Associated Press, November 13, 2011.

92. Colin Moynihan, "Three Sue over Pepper-Spraying by Police at Fall Occupy Wall St. Protest," *New York Times*, July 31, 2012.

93. Steven Greenhut, "Conservatives Side with Pepper-Spraying Thugs," LewRockwell.com, November 23, 2011.

94. Jesse Walker, "Report: When Obama Became President, Right-Wing Violence Fell," Reason.com, January 22, 2013; Spencer Ackerman, "Report: US Muslim Terrorism Was Practically Nil in 2012," *Wired*, February 1, 2013.

95. Bill Morlin, "Ruby Ridge Carved Niche in History," *Idaho Spokesman-Review*, August 19, 2012.

96. Craig Barrett, "From the Program Manager," *All Points Bulletin* 3 (1, October 2011), published by the Law Enforcement Support Office.

97. G. W. Schulz and Andrew Becker, "Free Military Surplus Gear a Boon to Local Calif. Law Enforcement," California Watch, March 29, 2012.

98. Charles Earl Barnett, interview with the author, August 2008.

99. Scarlet Sims, "The Case of the .50 Caliber Rifle," *Log Cabin Democrat*, September 26, 2012.

100. Donovan Slack, "Even Small Localities Got Big Guns," *Boston Globe,* June 15, 2009.

101. Avina v. US, 681 F.3d 1127, No. 11-55004 (9th Cir. 2012). See also Mike Riggs, "Here's How the Obama Administration Defended DEA Agents Who Put a Gun to a Little Girl's Head," Reason.com, June 19, 2012.

102. David Frum, *How We Got Here: The 70s: The Decade That Brought You Modern Life—For Better or Worse* (New York: Basic Books, 2000).

103. Ed Burns, interview with the author.

104. Jim Stewart, "Use of SWAT Teams Up Greatly Across the Country," *CBS This Morning,* December 9, 1997.

105. Michael Cooper, "As Number of Police Raids Increase, So Do Questions," *New York Times,* May 26, 1998; Al Guart, "'Spruill Effect' on Drug Busts," *New York Post,* January 25, 2004; Brian A. Reaves, "Federal Law Enforcement Officers, 1996"; Brian A. Reaves, "Federal Law Enforcement Officers, 2008," US Department of Justice, Bureau of Justice Statistics; "Johnston Police Use Military Surplus Assault Rifles, Humvees to Train, Equip SWAT Team," *Providence Journal,* December 5, 2012.

## Chapter 9: Reform

1. The Calvo raid narrative is from multiple author interviews with Cheye Calvo, other reporting by the author, and April Witt, "Deadly Force," *Washington Post Magazine,* February 1, 2009; Cheye Calvo, "Berwyn Heights Mayor Cheye Calvo Recounts Errant SWAT Raid," *Washington Post,* September 20, 2009; Cheye Calvo, "Should No-Knock Police Raids Be Rare or Routine?" partial transcript of his speech at a Cato Institute Policy forum, published in *Cato Policy Report* (November-December 2008); Cheye Calvo, "Live Chat with Mayor Cheye Calvo," TheAgitator.com, February 26, 2009; "Deadly Force" (live chat with Cheye Calvo and April Witt), WashingtonPost.com, February 2, 2009.

2. See Maryland House Bill 577, signed into law May 26, 2005, available at: http://mgaleg.maryland.gov/2010rs/bills/hb/hb0577f.pdf.

3. Rosalind S. Helderman, "Pr. George's Officers Lacked 'No-Knock' Warrant in Raid," *Washington Post,* August 6, 2008.

4. Daniel Valentine, "Prince George's Council Confirms Magaw as Police Chief," Gazette.net, July 6, 2011.

5. Ruben Castanada, "Lawyers Find Fault with Pr. George's Drug Arrests," *Washington Post,* October 14, 2008.

6. Marc Fisher, "No Police Work in This Botched Action," *Washington Post,* September 14, 2008.

7. Rosalind S. Helderman and Aaron C. Davis, "Pr. George's Police Arrest 2 in Marijuana-Shipping Plot," *Washington Post,* August 7, 2008.

8. "Deadly Force" (live chat with Cheye Calvo and April Witt), WashingtonPost.com.

9. Michelle Gielan, "Mayor's Dogs Killed in Drug Raid," *CBS Early Show,* August 8, 2008.

10. Daniel Valentine, "Johnson: County on Good Path," Gazette.net, October 23, 2008.

11. Rosalind S. Helderman and Aaron C. Davis, "Killing of Mayor's 2 Dogs Justified, Pr. George's Finds," *Washington Post,* September 5, 2008.

12. CNN *American Morning,* August 8, 2008.

13. "Deputies Raid Wrong Address, Kill Couple's Dog," WJLA-7, Washington, DC, November 19, 2007.

14. Rosalind S. Helderman and Aaron C. Davis, "FBI to Review Raid That Killed Mayor's Dogs," *Washington Post,* August 8, 2008.

15. Brendan Kearney, "Family Sues Howard County over Dog Shooting," *The Daily Record,* July 28, 2009.

16. Mike Santa Rita, "Two County Residents Detail Police Raids," *Columbia Flier,* March 3, 2009.

17. Don Markus, "Questionable Force," *Baltimore Sun,* March 1, 2009.

18. Cheye Calvo, "Statement of Berwyn Heights Mayor Cheye Calvo on Passage of SWAT Team Reporting Legislation" (press release), April 9, 2009.

19. Peter Hermann, "Numbers Paint Portrait of SWAT Team Use," *Baltimore Sun,* February 24, 2010.

20. Ruben Castaneda, "Settlement in Md. Town Mayor's Lawsuit," *Washington Post,* January 24, 2011.

21. Donald Santarelli, interview with the author, August 2012.

22. See "Monks Arrested In SWAT Team Action," KETV Omaha, February 24, 2006, available at: http://www.ketv.com/Monks-Arrested-In-SWAT-Team-Action/-/9675214/10073774/-/13mbrtfz/-/index.html.

23. Stephen Downing, interview with the author, August 2012.

24. Neill Franklin, interview with the author, August 2012.

25. Norm Stamper, interview with the author, August 2012.

26. Ibid.

27. Neill Franklin, interview with the author, August 2012.

28. Carolyn Carlson, "Email Reveals Shocked Sheriff," *Albuquerque Journal,* December 21, 2006.

29. Russell Jones, interview with the author, August 2012.

# INDEX

ABC News, 195, 209

Abolitionists, 20

Accountability, 34, 39, 125, 242, 261, 268–269, 280, 297, 304, 319, 328–331, 334, 335

ACLU, 156, 163, 247, 257, 295

Adams, John, xi, 1, 10, 15

Adams, Sam, 15

Administrative searches, 284–285

Afghanistan, 251

*Ain't Nobody's Business if You Do* (McWilliams), 217

Albom, Mitch, 252

Alcohol, 30, 32, 164, 284, 285–286, 289, 322

Aleutian Islanders, 12

Alito, Samuel, 263

Alpert, Geoffrey, 274

Al Qaeda, 251

Ambrose, Miles, 81, 105, 108, 119, 121, 122

American Recovery and Reinvestment Act, 248

American Revolution, 10, 14, 16, 22, 45, 196. *See also* Colonial period

Ames, Mel, 106, 107

Amsterdam, Anthony, 174

Antiwar movement, 41, 67, 69, 71, 99

Armored vehicles, xii, 63, 64, 96, 136, 154–157, 233, 239, 253–255, 256–257, 288, 302, 332

Army Rangers, 208

Arnold, Judy, 107, 110, 111, 112, 114

Arpaio, Joe, 288, 302

Arson, 52, 106

Arthur Murrah Federal Building in Oklahoma City, 203

Articles of Federation, 17

Ashcroft, John, 253

Askew, Don and Virginia, 118, 120

Assassinations, 2, 67, 68

Assault weapons, 192, 224, 252, 255, 256, 258, 269–271, 273, 303

Assets forfeiture, 14, 140, 146, 152–154, 157, 175, 219, 240, 244, 249, 321

ATF. *See* Bureau of Alcohol, Tobacco, and Firearms

Augustus (Emperor), 2, 3

*Avina v. US*, 303

Awtry, Aaron, 283

Badway, James, 330
Bail system, 66, 67, 84, 144
Bain, Donald, 275
Barnett, Charles Earl, 302
Barrett, Craig, 301
Barry, Marion, 91, 98
Bartels, John, Jr., 123
Bartlett, Richard, 50
Basile, Richard, 233
Batten, James, 91–92
Battering rams, 155–157, 279, 283
Baucum, David, 280–281
Baum, Dan, 67, 149, 255
Bell, Sean, 273
Bennett, William, 163–166, 169, 170, 177, 250
Bernhardt, Edwina and Catherine, 333
Berti, Patrick, 106
Biden, Joe, 140, 146, 167–168, 218, 219, 247, 257
Big government, 144, 300
Black markets, 32–33, 97, 250
Black Panthers, 66, 76–80, 129
Blacks, 10, 23, 24, 25, 35, 40, 66, 67, 69, 71, 87, 95, 98, 169, 187, 212, 245. *See also* Slavery; Watts riots
Blair, David, 33
Blakey, Robert, 140
Blass, Arnold, 117–118
Bloomberg, Michael, 333
Bollman, Bob, 107, 108, 111, 112–113
Bologna, Anthony, 296
Bonus March, 37, 41
Boston, ix, xi, 9, 12, 17, 19–22, 30, 170
Boston Massacre, 14, 21–22
*Boston Globe*, 169, 209
Bowdoin, James, 17

Bradley, Tom, 186
*Brady v. Maryland*, 54
Brandeis, Louis, 6
Braudis, Robert, 192
*Breaking Rank* (Stamper), 56, 189–190, 234
Brennan, William, 44, 45–47, 49, 76, 139, 174, 196
Brockman, Timothy, 264–265
Brooks, Pierce, 189
Brown, John, 22
Browning, James L., 113, 114
Browning, Richard III (Col.), 180
*Brown v. Board of Education*, 40, 41, 82
Brunkle, Archie, 107
Buchwald, Art, 92
Buckley, William F. 55, 92, 217
Buffalo, New York, 259–260
Bulger, Whitey, 326
Bullock, Deval (Det.), 281
Bureau of Alcohol, Tobacco, and Firearms (ATF), 108, 134, 199–204, 220
Bureau of Narcotics and Dangerous Drugs (BNDD), 68, 72, 73, 103, 104, 107–108, 114, 119, 123, 237, 280, 282, 290
Burgreen, Bob, 160, 189, 190
Burns, Anthony, 20, 21
Burns, Ed, 304
Burns, Eric, 33
Bush, George H. W., 163, 167, 180–181, 244
Bush, George W., 205, 208, 247, 250, 252, 253, 301
Butman, Asa O., 20
Byrne grants, 167, 221, 243–244, 245, 247, 248, 255, 301, 321

California, 215–216, 248, 252, 301–302. *See also* Humboldt

County, California; Los
Angeles/Los Angeles Police
Department; *individual cities*
Calling Forth Act, 17–18
Calvo, Cheye, 309–320
Campaign Against Marijuana
Production (CAMP), 147–149,
152
Carlson, Donald, 181–183
Carswell, G. Harrold, 101
Carter, Jimmy, 129, 135, 136
Castle Doctrine, 6–8, 9, 10, 12, 45,
46, 48, 83, 88, 94, 136, 196,
198, 199, 260, 261, 320
Cato Institute, vii, viii, 247, 289,
310, 315, 316, 336
Center for Investigative Reporting
(CIR), 254, 255–256
Charleston, South Carolina, 28, 282
Chavez, Cesar, 59
Cheney, Dick, 167, 178
Children, 240, 241, 246, 248,
249–250, 264, 267, 289–290,
303
child pornography, 286–287
Christopher Commission, 186, 188
Churchill, Winston, 43
Cicero, 1, 6
Civil liberties, 2, 4, 29, 31, 39, 86,
150–151, 174, 216, 218
Civil Rights Act (1964), 82, 87
Civil rights issues, 24, 40, 41, 66, 68,
115, 121, 236, 285, 286
Civil War, 12
Clark, Mike, 254
Clark, Ramsey, 66
Clark, Tom, 45, 47, 48, 49, 92
Clifton, Lloyd, 108–109, 110–111,
113, 114, 115
Clinton, Bill, 129, 193, 194–195,
200, 203, 204, 215, 218, 219,
247, 252, 297, 300

Cocaine/crack, 136, 141, 155–157,
171, 179, 223, 260–261, 262,
263
Coleman, Tom, 245
Colombia, 251
Colonial period, x–xi, 3, 6, 8–9, 12,
13–14, 27–29, 140
Columbine High School in Littleton,
Colorado, 230–233
Common law, 4–5, 6, 45, 46, 88,
140, 196, 199, 261
Communism, 37, 38, 40, 178,
204
Computers. 98, 221, 268, 287,
324. *See also* Internet
Connecticut, 191–192, 218
Conrad, Clay, 276–277
Constables, x, 5, 28
Constantine (Emperor), 3
Constitution, ix–x, 16, 168, 236
Bill of Rights, xiv, 10, 13, 15
Commerce Clause, 87
Constitutional Convention, 17
Second/Tenth Amendments, 15
Third Amendment, 11–13, 15, 16,
39 (*see also* Symbolic Third
Amendment)
Fourth Amendment, 10, 45,
47–48, 54, 55, 114, 125, 139,
145, 150–151, 156, 157, 174,
184, 186, 196, 226, 236, 259,
263, 266, 277, 279, 284, 285,
286, 289, 303, 320, 325
Fifth Amendment, 54
Eighth Amendment, 54
Thirteenth/Fifteenth
Amendments, 23
Fourteenth Amendment, 10, 23,
25, 48, 54, 153
Eighteenth Amendment, 32, 33
Consumer Products Safety
Commission (CPSC), 289

Controlled Substances Act, 88
COPS program, 218, 221–222, 223, 255, 301
Coral, Valerie and Michael, 252
Cornell, Dewey, 233
Corruption, 5, 31, 32, 34, 141, 247
Costales, Sam, 329–330
Coulter, Ann, 205
Counterculture, 40, 41, 67, 68, 71, 76, 86, 106, 133, 152, 193
Craig, Malin (general), 39
Crime, 2, 4, 5, 8, 23, 26, 27, 28, 31, 32, 34, 50, 52, 64, 102, 198, 209, 225, 323
    crime bills/policy, 65, 66–67, 68, 70, 71, 72, 73, 83–96, 100, 151–152, 167, 178
    drugs and violent crime, 68, 103
    organized crime, 140, 146
    statistics concerning, 144, 163, 270, 272
    victims of, x–xi, 3
    *See also* Washington, D.C.: crimes in
Crime Control Act (1994), 274
Culosi, Sal, 280–281
Culture wars, 142, 143
Curtis, Richard,
Cushing Doctrine, 22, 24, 208

Daley, Richard, 68
Damon, Matt, 288
Davis, Ed, 62, 78
Death penalty, 80, 163, 166, 178
Declaration of Independence, 10
Defense Department/Pentagon, 36, 78–79, 145, 158, 167, 178, 191, 193–194, 209–210, 230, 254, 296, 303, 308, 321
DeGuerin, Dick, 280
Delano Grape Strike, 59
Dellinger, Walter, 205
Democracy, 39

Denver, Colorado, 185–186, 192, 288, 296
Detroit, Michigan, 96–97, 306
Dickenson, Dirk, 106–107, 108, 109–112, 116
DiGristine, Charles, 171–172
Dillinger, John, 132
Dodd, Thomas J., 86–87, 88–89, 90, 95
Doddridge, David, 270
Dogs, xiii, 117, 200, 241, 288, 290–293, 307, 309, 311, 316, 317, 332
Dorsen, Norman, 92
Douglass, Frederick, 20
Downing, Stephen, 211, 214, 325
*Dragnet*, 34
Drones, 256
Drudge, Matt, 294
Drug Abuse Resistance Education (DARE) program, 165–166
Drug Enforcement Administration (DEA), 65, 122–123, 135, 148, 154, 184, 202, 215, 216, 248, 252, 253, 303
    vs. Customs, 181–182
Drugs/drug war, xii, xiv, 7, 32, 35, 42, 65, 66, 69–70, 71–74, 76, 80, 97, 119, 125, 133, 134, 135, 137, 139, 149, 151, 163–169, 174, 192, 194, 197, 202, 220, 226–227, 233, 240, 247, 307, 324, 333
    antidrug programs/bills, 72–73, 86–87, 87–88, 102–105, 165–166
    calling police on drug-using relative, 165–166
    drug users as supporting terrorists, 250–251
    and national security, 157
    reforms concerning, 321–322

use of military concerning, 141,
    145, 154, 157, 158, 175,
    177–180, 206 (*see also* Police:
    militarization of)
  *See also* Cocaine/crack; Ecstasy
    drug; Evidence, destruction of;
    Heroin; Marijuana; Rockefeller
    drug laws
DuBose, Tommie, 159
Due process, 165
Dukakis, Michael, 163
Duncan, Stephen, 178
DuPont, Robert, 73, 136
Duran, Robert, 130
Dyer, Heyward, 74–75, 76

Ecstasy drug, 257
Ehrlichman, John, 70, 71, 72, 92
Eisenhower, Dwight, 37, 40–41, 53
Elsass, Richard, 172–173
Emerson, Ralph Waldo, 20
England, 3, 4–5, 6–7, 13, 26, 27. *See
    also* Colonial period; London
Enlightenment era, 1, 6, 10
Enright, John, 123
Epstein, Edward Jay, 103, 104
Equitable sharing law, 154
Ervin, Sam, 81–83, 83–84, 85, 88,
    89, 94–96, 102, 123–124,
    135–136
Evidence, destruction of, 45, 46, 47,
    49, 75, 85, 89–90, 93, 99–100,
    155, 161, 186, 192, 196–197,
    260–261, 325
Exclusionary Rule, 56, 141, 144, 145,
    150, 151, 184, 261, 262, 263
Ezsterhas, Joe, 110

Faubus, Orval, 40
FBI, 126, 134, 141, 166, 190, 201,
    248, 271, 276, 308, 326
*Law Enforcement Bulletin* of, 191

Federalists/antifederalists, 15, 16, 36
Federal military, 22–23, 24, 36,
    37–38, 40, 41, 206
  US Army *Basic Field Manual*, 39
"Federal Troops in Domestic
    Disturbances" (Patton), 37–38
Ferroggiaro, William, 113–114, 115
Fields, Virginia, 267
Finlator, John, 105
Flash-bang grenades, 156, 170, 172,
    192, 194, 264, 269, 275–280,
    307, 324
  fires/deaths caused by, 275, 276,
    277–278
Fleischer, Matthew, 77, 78
Florence, 4
*Florida v. Riley*, 174
Flynn, Ed, 334
Force Acts, 23
Forced-entry raids, 46, 123, 159,
    183, 197, 259, 322, 323, 331.
    *See also* No-knock raids
Ford, Henry, 33
Fortner, Ken, 161–162
Fox News, xiii
Franklin, Neill, 210–211, 214,
    325–326, 328
French, William, 139
French and Indian War, 13
*French Connection, The* (movie),
    304–305
Friedman, Milton, 168–169, 224
Frum, David, 304
Frye, Marquette, Ronald and Rena,
    51
Fugitive Slave Acts, 19, 21, 22
Fulcher, Tommy, 225, 226
Fullmer, Rick, 191

Gabor, Tom(Lt.), 191
Galvin, Jerry, 193
Gambling, 280–283, 322

Garner, Robert, 225, 226
Garrison, William Lloyd, 20
Gates, Daryl, 35, 53, 60, 61–64, 76, 78, 80, 126–130, 154–156, 165, 166, 188, 189
General Accounting Office (GAO), 140, 141
Gerry, Elbridge, 15
*Gideon v. Wainwright*, 54
Giglotto, Herbert and Evelyn, 116–117, 120
Ginsburg, Ruth Bader, 263
Giuliani, Rudy, 139–140
Glaspy, Will, 252
Glasser, Ira, 225, 226
González, Elián, 200, 204–205, 297
Goodman, Amy, 295
Gore, Larry, 161, 162
Graham, Katharine, 72
Grand juries, x–xi, 105, 114
Grants, 96, 104, 180, 210, 218, 299, 240, 253, 254, 255, 300, 321, 336. *See also* Byrne grants; COPS program
*Great Drug War, The* (Trebach), 149
Greene, J. L., 291
Greenhut, Steven, 297–298
Griffin, Robert, 89, 90
Guerrilla warfare, 53, 60
Gun control, 65, 199, 202, 273, 298

Haase, Jamie, 214
Habeas corpus, 38, 165
Haldeman, H. R., 101
Hale, Matthew, 7
Hallinan, Terence, 225, 226
Hamilton, Alexander, 1, 15
Hammer, Susan, 225–226
Hampton, Fred, 77
Harlan, John II, 48, 101
Harrelson, Hondo, 130–131, 132

Harris, Kevin, 200
Hasenei, Mike and Phyllis, 317–318
Hawkins, William, 6–7
Hawn, David, 248
Hayes, Rutherford B., 24, 25
Haynsworth, Clement, 101
Heal, Sid (Lt.), 58
Healy, Fran, 333
Hearst, Patty, 126, 128, 131
Heatly, Dr. Maurice Dean, 56–57
Heckler and Koch company, xii
Helicopters, xii, 63, 78, 108, 110, 112, 116, 136, 147, 148, 149, 173–174, 178, 179, 180, 210, 246, 282, 301
Henderson, Kevin and Lisa, 317
Henry, Patrick, 15
Heroin, 67, 68, 97, 103, 119, 136–137, 141, 157, 251, 331
High, Melvin, 314
Hill, Victor, 333
Hobson, Julius, 91
Homeland Security, Department of (DHS), 253–254, 255, 256–257, 296, 298, 299, 336
Hoover, Herbert, 37
Hoover, J. Edgar, 76, 141
Horton, Willie, 163
Hoxsie, Jack Ray, 60
Hruska, Roman, 70–71, 124
Hudson, Orlando, 259
*Hudson v. Michigan*, 261–262
Huffman, Josh (Lt.), 233–234
Humboldt County, California, 105–116, 136, 147–148
Humphrey, Hubert, 69, 146
Hutchison, Asa, 253

*Illinois v. Gates*, 150
Immigrants, xi, 31, 204, 228, 286, 288, 297, 301

Immigration and Naturalization
Service (INS), 204, 205
Informants, xiii, 45, 77, 107, 121,
123, 150, 171, 182, 200, 202,
246, 249, 262, 264, 267, 322,
324, 325, 331
Ingersoll, John, 103, 104, 105
Insurrection Act, 18, 41
Internet, xiii, xiv, 243, 287, 296,
297, 307

Jackson, Michael, 314
James, Amber, 317
Jay, John, 1
Jefferson, Thomas, 15
Johnson, Amir, 312
Johnson, Daryl, 298–300
Johnson, Jack, 315
Johnson, Lyndon, 61, 64, 65, 98
Jones, Russ, 133–135, 184, 330
Julius Caesar, 2, 3
Justice Department, 71, 73, 82, 86,
87, 88, 122, 136, 141, 152,
193–194, 204, 244, 270
Community Oriented Policing
Services (COPS) program, 218,
221–222, 223, 255, 301
Equitable Sharing Program,
219–220, 321
forfeiture fund of, 175
Justice Assistance Grants (JAG)
program, 167
Office of Legal Counsel, 102,
177

Kane, Richard, 333
Katzenbach, Nicholas, 64
*Katz v. United States*, 55
Keene, N.H., 253–255, 256–257
Kelly, Raymond W., 265, 266
Kelly, Regina, 245–246
Kennedy, John F., 71

Kennedy, Robert, 68
Kerlikowske, Gil, 321
*Ker v. California*, 44–48, 49, 75, 92
Kilpatrick, James, 55
King, Martin Luther, Jr., 67
King, Rodney, 162–163, 186, 188
Kleindienst, Richard, 114, 115
Knock-and-announce raids, 45, 46,
47, 48, 67, 121, 123, 134, 135,
159, 160, 172, 183, 185,
195–196, 197, 260, 261, 279,
283, 324. *See also* No-knock
raids
Knott, J. Proctor, 24, 25
Kopel, David, 271
Kraemer, Donn, 231
Kraska, Peter, 206–214, 220,
296–297
Krogh, Egil, 70–71, 92, 103, 119,
125

Lane, Kendall, 253
Latinos, 35, 40
Law and order issues, 70, 71, 84, 94,
101, 102, 135, 330
Law Enforcement Assistance
Administration (LEAA), 65, 72,
96, 104, 119
Law Enforcement Support Program,
209, 301
Lawmaster, John, 202–203
Lema, Larry, 106
Liddy, G. Gordon, 74, 104, 199,
203
Littleton, James G., 63
Llovera, Jesus, 288
Lockwood, Randal, 290
Lockyer, Bill, 248, 249, 252
Logan, Utah, 207–208
London, 5, 29–30, 31
Loring, Charles, 19
Loring, Edward G., 21

Los Angeles/Los Angeles Police
Department (LAPD), 34–35,
40, 51–53, 59–60, 63, 73, 75,
76–80, 126–130, 131, 154–157,
165–166, 211, 216, 229, 230,
232, 301
LAPD's use of excessive force,
186–189
Tactical Operations Planning unit
in LAPD, 61
*Los Angeles Times*, 161, 162, 248, 262
Lott, Leon, 239, 302
Lynch, Tim, 289–290, 336

MacArthur, Douglas (Gen.), 37, 38,
39, 41
McCaffrey, Barry, 215
McCormick, Todd, 216–217
McGovern, George, 68, 136
McKinley, Patrick, 77, 79
McKittrick, James, 114–115
McMillan, John, 84, 85
McNab, Chris, 130
McNamara, Joseph, 212, 218,
224–228, 273–274, 279
McVeigh, Timothy, 203, 298
McWilliams, Peter, 216–217
"Mad Dog Brown," 223–224, 227
Maddow, Rachel, 298, 299
Madison, James, ix, xi, 1, 15
*Madison Capital Times*, 221
Magaw, Mark (Maj.), 312–313
Magna Carta, 9
*Mallory v. United States*, 82
Mansfield, Mike, 86, 89
*Mapp v. Ohio*, 54
Maricopa County, Arizona, 288,
302, 307
Marijuana (pot), xiii, 68, 74, 86,
105–116, 136, 141, 142,
147–150, 157, 164, 173, 178,
193, 195, 234, 247, 251, 259,
263, 313, 314, 317, 331, 332

legalization of, 215, 306
medical marijuana, 205, 206,
215–216, 252, 301, 322
Marines, 11, 21, 33, 60, 78, 97, 188
Marshals, x, 20, 22, 24, 25, 200,
201, 208
Martial law, 21, 22, 169, 170
Martin, Walter and Rose, 268
Martini, David (Det. Sgt.), 312
Mason, George, 15
*Massachusetts v. Sheppard*, 151
Massery, Jim, 255, 256–257
Massett, Eric and Rebecca Sue, 149
Mastrogiovanni, Roberta, 254
Matasareanu, Emil, 228–229
Mathers, Cortland, 169
Media, 91, 92, 93, 94, 101, 103,
104, 107, 108, 194, 203, 228,
243, 268, 269, 272, 273, 290.
*See also* Social media; Television
Meese, Ed, 149, 190, 224
Mehan, Florence, Susan, and Linda,
74
Meiners, John, 120
Mena, Ismael, 185, 288
Mencken, H. L., 27
Methadone programs, 73, 92, 100,
143, 168, 224
Methamphetamine, 133, 135, 202,
247, 277
Mexico, 250, 251
Middle Ages, 4, 5
Militarism, 3, 15, 16, 133, 193, 200,
207, 214, 249. *See also* Police:
militarization of
Military Cooperation with Law
Enforcement Act, 145
Militias, 15, 18, 20, 203
*Miller v. District of Columbia*, 44, 48
*Miranda* decision, 54–55, 56, 66,
94, 141, 144
Mission creep, 242, 281, 283,
322–323

Mistaken/botched raids, xiii, 121,
122, 123, 172, 181–183, 185,
198, 199, 203, 242, 243, 249,
265–266, 268, 269, 276, 287,
303, 307, 311, 317–318, 319,
324, 331, 335
Mitchell, John, 71, 83, 93, 94,
100–101, 102
Moore, Mack Charles, 170–171
Morality, 145, 164, 165, 168
Morgan, Eric, 271
Morley, James J., 277
Morton, Ted, 76–77
Mueller, Ron, 59–60
Murder/homicide, 7, 27, 32, 56–59,
67, 68, 79, 91, 97, 106, 113,
114, 157, 233, 270, 271
Murphy, Patrick, 312
Myers, Frank and Pam, 316

National Defense Authorization
Security Act of 1997, 209
National Guard, xii, 36, 40–41, 52,
68, 136, 147, 158, 178,
179–180, 188, 189, 202, 220,
235, 282
National Institute for Justice (NIJ),
269–270, 324
National Institute on Drug Abuse
(NIDA), 143
National Journal, 209, 210
National Rifle Association (NRA),
203
Navy Seals, 208
Nelson, John (Sgt.), 60
New Jersey State Police, 63
*Newsday*, 266–267
*Newsweek*, 69
Newton, Huey, 76
Newton, Juanita Bing, 267
Newtown, Connecticut, 298
New York City, 30–31, 32, 50, 139,
224, 263–269, 296, 307, 333

Civilian Complaint Review Board
(CCRB) in, 265–266, 267
*New York Times*, 49, 50, 64, 88, 91,
92, 118, 121, 122, 132, 192,
209, 264, 265, 274
Nichols, John, 97
Nixon, Richard, 50, 53, 66, 68, 69,
70, 71–74, 82, 84, 86, 94, 95,
100, 101, 104–105, 140–141,
143
*Nix v. William*, 151
No-knock raids, 71, 73, 75, 83, 84,
85, 88–96, 99–100, 100–101,
102, 105, 113, 116–117, 119,
121, 122, 123, 126, 135, 137,
151, 171, 183, 192, 195,
197–198, 226, 248, 261, 262,
263–264, 266, 288, 312, 313,
320, 322, 324
repeal of no-knock law, 124–125
requests for warrants for, 185–186
*See also* Forced-entry raids;
Knock-and-announce raids
Noriega, Manuel, 177
Norman Conquest, 5, 13
North Carolina, University of,
233–234
Nuckols, A. J., 287, 288

Obama, Barack, 223, 247–248, 255,
300, 303, 321
Occupy protesters at UC Davis, 237
O'Connor, Sandra Day, 173
Office of Drug Abuse Law
Enforcement (ODALE), 105,
107–108, 119, 120, 121, 122,
137, 147, 199, 305
Office of National Drug Control
Policy (ONDCP), 164, 250
Olmstead, Stephen (Lt. Gen.), 11
Olson, Scott, 296
Omnibus Crime Control Act, 83
O'Neal, Shaquille, 287–288

*Onion, The*, 11
Open fields doctrine, 173
Operation Alliance, 182
Operation Byrne Blitz, 247
Operation Clean Sweep, 178
Operation Delta-9, 149–150
Operation Intercept, 73–74, 105
Operation Shock and Awe, 259–260
Operation TAPS, 259
Orfield, Myron, 184
Otis, James, Jr., 9–10, 45
*Overkill: The Rise of Paramilitary
   Police Raids in America* (Balko),
   315–316
Ozark National Forrest, 149–150

Packer, Herbert, 83
Page, Clarence, 205
Page, Wade Michael, 299
Painkillers, 253, 322
Palmer, A. Mitchell, 38
Parker, William, 34–35, 52, 61
Parks, Bernard, 225, 227
Paschall, John, 246
Pastore, Nick, 191–192, 218
Patrick, Deval, 303
Patronage, 31, 32, 34
Patterson, Robert, 186
Patton, George S. (Maj.), 37–38, 39
*Paxton's Case*, 9
Peel, Sir Robert, 29–30, 31
Pentangelo, Joseph, 291
Percy, Charles, 123–124, 136
Perjury, 184, 245
Perry, Rick, 245, 247
Pfeil, Suzanne, 252
Philadelphia, 30, 179
*Philadelphia Inquirer*, 55
Phillips, Channing, 91
Phillips, Larry Jr., 228–229
Pierce, Franklin, 21
Pike, John (Lt.), 296
Podell, Bertram, 91

Police
   community policing, 34, 100, 162,
      189, 190, 193, 218, 220–223,
      224, 325
   and control issues, 292, 327, 328
   deaths of, 171–172, 269,
      271–272, 273, 276
   first police forces, 1–2, 29, 30
   local vs. centralized policing, 4
   as lying, 184, 334
   militarization of, 35–42, 157, 163,
      167, 171, 175, 188, 189–190,
      191, 193, 202, 204, 205–206,
      208, 209, 210, 215, 219, 224,
      225, 228, 229, 230, 234, 242,
      243, 255, 272, 292, 293, 296,
      297, 299, 300, 334, 335, 336
      (*see also* Drugs/drug war: use of
      military concerning; Militarism)
   military gear of, 209–210, 213, 221,
      242, 254, 294, 301, 308, 321
   misconduct/excessive force of,
      187–189, 225, 243, 247, 267,
      286, 297, 298, 323, 332
   physical fitness of, 328
   police culture, 273, 292, 325–328
   police unions, 329, 330
   private police for hire, 29, 31
   public's opinion of, 169–170
   raids by, xii, xiii, 7, 8, 72, 83, 84,
      115, 120, 121, 159–163,
      170–171, 175, 179–180, 214,
      215, 237, 240–241, 258–259,
      269, 285, 307–308 (*see also*
      Castle Doctrine; Forced-entry
      raids; Mistaken/botched raids;
      No-knock raids)
   recruitment of, 98, 300, 306, 326
   titles used by, 189–191
   training, 291, 292, 327 (*see also*
      SWAT teams: training)
   "troops to cops" program,
      194–195, 219

uniforms of, xi, 29, 30, 134, 135, 189, 195, 255, 318, 329–330
Police state, 335
Policy issues, xv, 25, 50–51, 53, 125, 142, 143, 158, 167–168, 205, 289, 293, 315, 336. *See also* Crime: crime bills/policy; Reforms
Political machines, 31, 32
Polls, 64, 69, 104, 156, 165, 189, 272
Pop culture, 304, 307
*Popular Justice* (Walker), x
Pornography, 54. *See also* Children: child pornography
Porter, Georgia, 309, 310, 311
Portland, Oregon, 219–220, 237–238
Posse Comitatus Act, 24, 25, 139, 177, 180, 208
Postal workers, 291–292
Potter, John, 19
Poverty, 4, 31, 65
Powell, Louis, 101
Praetorian Guard, 2, 3
President's Commission on Law Enforcement and Administration of Justice, 64–65
Preventive detention, 66, 67, 71, 73, 83, 84, 85, 90, 91, 100, 102, 105
Prince George's County, Maryland, 171, 309–320
Prisons, 147, 166
Privacy, xiv, 6, 55, 320
Professionalism, 32, 34, 35, 262
Progressive movement/progressives, 31, 32, 298, 300
Protests, 36–37, 40, 59, 61, 68, 99, 133, 143, 242
    at Democratic/Republican National Conventions, 68, 80, 295–296
    at G-20 Summit (2009), 293–295

Occupy protests of 2011, 296–298
World Trade Organization (WTO) protests in 1999, 234–237, 293
Public housing, 195, 220, 224

Quartering in homes, 11–12, 13, 14, 15
Quota systems, 325

Racial issues, 64, 68, 115. *See also* Blacks
Rape, 27, 91, 157
RAVE Act, 257
Ray, James Earl, 67
Ray, Richard, 166
Reagan, Ronald, 125, 136, 139, 142, 143–147, 149, 157, 167, 244
Reconstruction, 23, 24–25
Reddin, Thomas, 61
Red Scare, 37, 38
Reed, Edward C., 281
Reforms, 31–32, 34, 162, 242, 269, 309–332
Regulatory laws, 284, 285, 289, 322, 332
Rehnquist, William, 101–102
Renner, Ross (Lt.), 256
Reno, Janet, 193, 200, 202, 204
Republicans, 66, 70, 247, 295, 330
Reynolds, Glenn, 331
Ribicoff, Abraham, 68
*Richards v. Wisconsin*, 196–197, 198
Richmond, Paul, 219, 220
*Richmond Times-Dispatch*, 55
RICO law, 140–141
Rights, 4–5, 9, 10, 15, 18, 23, 25, 29, 31, 95, 124, 143, 152, 161, 165, 166, 251, 262, 267, 268, 326, 331, 333, 335
    of police officers accused of crimes, 328–330

Riots, 2, 3, 18, 25, 28, 35, 40, 51–53, 63, 64, 66, 67, 68, 80, 188–189
  riot squads, 234–237
Robberies/burglaries, 27, 61, 68, 71, 91, 136, 137, 157
  bank robberies, 65, 126, 168, 228–229, 230
Robbins, Gary (Sgt.), 278
Roberts, John, 56
Robinson, Herb, 179
*Robinson v. California*, 54
Rockefeller drug laws, 48–51, 67
Rogan, Joe, 306
Rogers, Jeff, 60
Roker, Al, 306
Rome (ancient), 1–4, 5
Roots, Roger, ix–x
Rose, Ron, 111
Ruby Ridge, Idaho, 200–201, 297, 298, 299
Russell, Orlando, 265
Ruttenberg, David, 285–286
Ruzzamenti, William, 148, 152

Saletan, Will, 205
Sanders, David, 232
San Diego, California, 159–163, 175, 181–183, 189–190, 218
San Jose, California, 133–135, 218, 224–228, 293
Santa Cruz, California, 252
Santarelli, Donald, 66, 67, 71, 93, 96, 100, 125, 320
Scalia, Antonin, 56, 261–262
Scarlata, Shawn (Det.), 313, 315
Schell, Paul, 235
Schumer, Charles, 280
Scott, Hugh, 89
Seagal, Steven, 288
Seale, Bobby, 76
Search warrants, 44, 48, 49, 55, 72, 74, 77, 84, 107, 120, 137, 150,
  169, 180, 183, 184–185, 198, 208, 214, 217, 233, 258, 265, 267, 269, 279, 284, 285, 320, 322, 324
Sears, Richard and Sandra, 170
Seattle, Washington, 163, 175, 234–237, 293, 285
Security issues, 2, 10, 15
*Segura v. United States*, 151
Self-defense, 79, 123
*Semayne's Case*, 6
Sepulveda, Moises, 248, 249–250
*Seton Hall Constitutional Law Journal*, ix
Sex, 32, 239, 240, 284, 289, 306, 307
Shays Rebellion, 16–17, 18
Sheriffs, x, 4, 5, 7, 28
Siegel, Norman, 263
Sikh Temple in Oak Creed, Wisconsin, 299
Silent Majority, 53, 68, 69
Simpson, Le'Quan, 258
Sims, Thomas, 19
Slavery, 18, 19–20, 28
Smith, J.V.C., 20–21
*Smoke and Mirrors* (Baum), 67
Smuggling, 8, 140, 145
Snipers, 60, 80, 130, 188, 194, 201, 213
Social media, 242, 297, 332
Soloff, Brenda, 267
Souter, David, 260–261
Spanish-American War, 36
Speck, Richard, 59
*Spirits of America, The* (Burns), 33
Spruill, Alberta, 264, 268, 269, 280
Squad cars, 32, 34, 130, 229, 230, 305
Stamp Act, 13
Stamper, Norm, 56, 158–160, 162, 189–191, 218, 234–237, 292, 293, 326, 327–328

Standing armies, xi, 3, 12–13, 15, 16, 17, 29, 220, 335. *See also* Federal military

*State, The* (newspaper), 55

Stevens, John Paul, 197

"Stop and frisk," 55–56, 169, 170

Stop Snitch'n movements, 334

Street, Jim, 130

Supreme Court, 7, 12, 40, 44, 53–56, 64, 75, 80, 82, 86, 87, 101–102, 150–151, 173–174, 195–196, 198–199, 260–263, 288

*SWAT* magazine, xii

SWAT teams, xi, xii–xiii, xv, 53, 59, 60, 61–64, 125, 126–130, 130–131, 132–133, 154, 155–157, 168, 172, 177, 188, 190, 191–193, 204, 206–214, 225, 241, 244–246, 248–249, 252, 270, 278, 281–283, 296, 310–320, 331

at Columbine High School, 230–232

and community policing, 220–221

first raid by, 76–80

INS SWAT teams, 205

numbers of teams/deployments, 137, 175, 207, 209, 212, 237, 238, 308, 319–320

in small towns, 210–211, 221, 240

and sports/movie stars, 287–288

training, xii, 208, 211, 212 (*see also* Police: training)

and Whitman shootings at University of Texas, 58

*SWAT* TV shows, 131–132, 305–306

Sweeney, Frank (Det. Sgt.), 74, 74

Sweet, Robert, 225, 226

Symbionese Liberation Army (SLA), 126–129, 131

Symbolic Third Amendment, 13, 18, 22, 23, 25, 41, 62–63, 139, 193

*Tactical Edge, The* (magazine), 58, 211

Tanks, 256, 288, 332

Tanner, Emily, 294

Task forces, 108, 135, 147, 167, 199, 202, 208, 220, 244, 245, 248, 285, 321–322

Taxes, 2, 8, 18, 86

Taylor, Betty, 239–242

Taylor, John and George, 161

Tear-gas, 235, 236, 294, 296

Television, 69, 130, 162, 202, 250, 288, 304–307. *See also* SWAT TV shows

1033 program, 301–303

Terrorism, 42, 194, 254, 256, 297, 299, 317

attacks of September 11, 2001, 242, 250, 251, 297

*Terry v. Ohio*, 55–56, 169

Texas, 57, 63, 244–245, 247, 256, 277, 282–283, 290, 292. *See also* Waco, Texas

Thailand, 251

Thomas, Clarence, 56, 196

Thomas, Karen, 317

Thoreau, Henry David, 20

Thornton, Fred, 276

Thurmond, Strom, 145–146

Tomsic, Trinity, 309, 311, 313

Trebach, Arnold, 149

Turner, Carlton, 141–142, 143, 147

Tydings, Joe, 84–85, 90, 94, 95

Tyler, Peter, 23

Tythings, 4, 5

Unemployment, 69

*United States v. Banks*, 260, 261

*United States v. Ramirez*, 198–199
Unser, Al, Sr., 329
Urbanization, 5, 26, 28, 30
Urine testing, 84, 85
US Coast Guard/Navy, 206
*US v. Leon*, 150
U-2 spy planes, 147–148

Venice, 4
Vietnam War, 53, 82
Vigilantes, 29
Vigiles, 2
*Village Voice*, 265, 267
Violence, 7, 14, 16, 23, 24, 25, 40,
    52, 67, 99, 129–130, 133, 187,
    198, 203, 207, 214, 218, 230,
    253, 254, 324, 332. *See also*
    Murder/homicide
Vollmer, August, 32
Volstead Act, 32–33, 34

Waco, Texas, 200, 201–202, 203,
    204, 280, 289–290, 297, 298
Wagner, Dean, 276
Walczak, Vic, 295
Walker, Larry, 192
Walker, Samuel, x, 27, 32, 192–193,
    262
*Wall Street Journal*, 168–169, 273
Walters, John, 250, 253
War of 1812, 12
Warrants, 8. *See also* Search warrants;
    Writs of assistance
Warren, Earl, 53–56, 82, 87, 89, 95
Washington, D.C., 70–71, 72, 73,
    84, 85–86, 88–95, 97–101,
    124, 165, 179, 271

crimes in, 91, 92, 94, 163
Washington, George, xi, 18
*Washington Post*, 92, 169, 171, 209
Watchmen, 5
Watergate, 83, 122, 125
Watts riots, 35, 51–53, 188–189
Weapons, xii, 33, 57, 63, 64, 76,
    78–79, 96, 112, 123, 127, 132,
    148, 158, 185, 192, 201, 207,
    213, 221, 224, 230, 256, 259,
    301, 308, 328
  firing .50 caliber rounds, 302–303
  *See also* Assault weapons
Weaver, Randy, Sammy and Vicki,
    200, 201, 298. *See also* Ruby
    Ridge, Idaho
*Weeks v. United States*, 54
Weinberger, Caspar, 167
Whiskey Rebellion, 18
Whitman, Charles, 56–59
Whitworth, Jonathan, xii–xiii
*Wickard v. Filburn*, 87
Wicker, Tom, 92
William (King), 13
Wilson, Clarence True, 33
Wilson, Jerry, 97–101, 124, 234
*Wilson v. Arkansas*, 196
Wiretapping, 55, 66, 72, 73, 83, 84,
    102, 105, 136, 146
Wisconsin, 221
Wolfgang, Marvin, 132
World Wars I/II, 12, 37, 40, 54, 81
Writs of assistance, 8–9, 10, 14, 45,
    72

Yorty, Sam, 78
YouTube, xiii, 306

**RADLEY BALKO** is an award-winning investigative journalist who writes about civil liberties, police, prosecutors, and the broader criminal justice system. He is currently a senior writer and investigative reporter for the *Huffington Post*. Previously, he was a senior editor for *Reason* magazine and a policy analyst for the Cato Institute. In 2011, the Los Angeles Press Club named him "Journalist of the Year."